✕

Rutgers: A Bicentennial History

✕

For Leland G. Merrill, Jr.
who is advancing a fine heritage!

Respectfully,
RWM Carmichael

By RICHARD P. McCORMICK

Rutgers:
A
Bicentennial
History

Rutgers University Press
New Brunswick   *New Jersey*

Foreword

It is especially fitting that as Rutgers celebrates the bicentennial of its founding the observance should be marked by the publication of this comprehensive and discerning account of the evolution of Queen's College to its present position as Rutgers, The State University. Unique among American educational institutions in that it combines the traditions of the Colonial college, the land-grant college, and the state university, Rutgers exemplifies the major influences that have shaped our colleges and universities over the span of two centuries.

Of the many themes that recur throughout this narrative, two in particular seem most impressive. One is the extraordinary dedication of those charged with guiding the destiny of the institution as they sought constantly, usually in the face of adverse circumstances, to sustain it and to enhance its usefulness to the students and to the larger community beyond the campus. The achievements recorded here, and they are not inconsiderable, are a tribute to those hosts of devoted individuals and an inspiration to their successors. Also striking is the facility with which the institution adapted itself continually to new roles and assumed new functions in response to changing conditions within the American society. Yet, as a constant factor, concern with intellectual integrity and humane values provided a sure sense of direction to guide the University through all the stages of its growth and development.

The general reader will find Professor McCormick's compact account of interest for the insights that it offers into the history of American higher education as reflected in the career of a single long-lived and vital university. For those with a closer relationship to Rutgers—members of the governing boards, administrative officials, faculty, students, alumni, and citizens of New Jersey—this volume should greatly enhance their understanding of Rutgers, past and present, and strengthen their sense of pride in its progress toward preeminence.

On January 4, 1966, Professor McCormick addressed the opening convocation of the bicentennial year and said in part:

"Excellent though it was in its fine standards, Rutgers still remained small, and its identity—partly private, partly public—remained uncertain. It had yet to encounter its true destiny.

"But now, within the past two decades, that destiny has at last become manifest, and the most wondrous era in the history of Rutgers glows with unprecedented achievements. Rutgers has found its mission as the State University of New Jersey, and the state at last has confidently conferred that role on Rutgers."

This volume tells brilliantly how these events came to pass.

MASON W. GROSS
President
Rutgers, The State University

Preface

The history of a university, and especially of one that has developed over two centuries to assume the multi-dimensional complexity of the modern Rutgers, might properly be assigned to the category of universal history, for the boundaries of the subject are virtually limitless. A university is a constantly changing combination of intellectual disciplines, a specialized type of social community, a variegated administrative entity, a sprawling conglomeration of physical facilities. It serves, and looks for support to, numerous constituencies. Although it generates within itself innovative forces, it is highly responsive to external influences from many sources. Viewed in the large, it is a formidable institution, but it is as well an aggregation of individuals, each of whom has a distinct role to play.

Because no single-volume history of Rutgers could approach definitiveness, I have been obliged to be selective in my treatment of the subject. In the main, I have focused attention on those developments that seemed to me to be of largest significance in determining the character of the institution at any particular time and in shaping its course to the present. I have been especially concerned to delineate the crucial relationships of Rutgers to the Reformed Church and later to the State of New Jersey, for these relationships account for much of what is distinctive in the University's heritage. I have sought to trace the evolution of the curriculum and the complementary sphere of the extracurricular; to describe the varying roles of the trustees, the faculty, the student body, the alumni, and the administration in the affairs of the institution; and to account for the emergence of new divisions, schools and colleges and for the expansion of physical plant and the acquisition of new resources. In all too restricted a manner, I have endeavored to relate developments at Rutgers to the world beyond the campus, among other reasons in order to escape the pitfalls of parochialism and filiopietism.

In attempting to deal with the University as an entity, especially in the past few decades, I have had to slight the internal history of the several colleges and departments while consoling myself with the hope that each may eventually have its own historian. My self-imposed limitations also made it impossible for me to accord proper recognition to hundreds of individuals, whose services to the University merited acknowledgment; to the hosts of notable alumni, who brought distinction to their alma mater; and to the scores of valiant athletic teams and other student groups that have represented the University honorably and successfully. Neither have I attempted to evaluate the tangible contributions of Rutgers to New Jersey and to the nation, for beyond those that are conspicuous, or even obvious, are those that are embodied in the careers of hundreds of faculty members and tens of thousands of alumni.

My primary consideration has been to make the University intelligible to those most directly concerned with its welfare. Because Rutgers has followed an unusual and at times tortuous course in arriving at its present status and because the University today exhibits so many aspects that are of quite recent origin, the influence of the past is not always apparent. But it is my conviction that Rutgers, like other long-lived institutions, can be understood best within an historical context.

This study has been based almost entirely on the voluminous source materials that have been gathered together to form the University Archives. Including the minutes and papers of the Board of Trustees and the Board of Governors, the minutes and reports of the several faculties, the correspondence of Presidents Demarest, Thomas, Clothier, and Jones, the records of countless student organizations and administrative offices, and hundreds of individual files on trustees, alumni, and faculty members, as well as several series of printed publications—ranging from the annual *Catalogues* and president's reports to the *Alumni Monthly* and such student organs as the *Targum* and the *Scarlet Letter*—the archives are overwhelming in their sheer bulk and provide abundant documentation for every facet of the University's history.

With affection as well as gratitude, I express my indebtedness to William H. S. Demarest's *History of Rutgers College*, published in 1924, which made my path less blind than it might have been. And I should like to pay my tribute to Frederick Rudolph's *The American College and University: A History* (New York: Alfred A. Knopf, 1962) and to George P. Schmidt's *The Liberal Arts College* (New Brunswick, N.J.: Rutgers University Press, 1957), both of which were exceedingly useful in orienting me to the general history of American higher education. I have also profited from the unpublished studies by Stephen DeWitt Stephens of the history of the Newark Colleges and by Henry E. Vittum of the development of the Rutgers College curriculum as well as from Carl R. Woodward and Ingrid Nelson Waller's *New Jersey's Agricultural Experiment Station, 1880–1930* (New Brunswick, 1932).

I welcome the opportunity to record my appreciation of the inestimable assistance given to me by members of the staff of the Rutgers University Library, in particular Mr. Donald A. Sinclair, head of the Department of Special Collections, Mr. William G. Miller, University Archivist, and their associates, Mr. Anthony S. Nicolosi, Miss Irene K. Lionikis, Miss Ruth M. Kohlstadt, and Mrs. Anthony Coppola. Mr. Jeffrey Barist and Mr. Joseph Biesinger, who assisted me in my research on parts of two chapters, and Miss Paris Legrow and Miss Arlene Szabatin, who transformed my handwritten scrawl into neatly typed pages, also earned my gratitude. For their constant encouragement and for their willingness to read critically major portions of the manuscript, I am most grateful to Dr. Donald F. Cameron, Dr. William H. Cole, Dr. Mason W. Gross, Dr. Albert E. Meder, Dr. Roy F. Nichols, and Dr. Carl R. Woodward, although they are not chargeable with any errors that may have escaped their scrutiny, as well as mine. My thanks are due also to my colleagues in the Department of History for their charitable patience with me during the past three years while I have neglected other concerns to bring this study to completion.

Finally, it might be well to observe that although this is in a sense an "official history," I have enjoyed complete freedom in my research and in my writing, and I alone am accountable for any opinions or judgments expressed.

RICHARD P. McCORMICK

August 25, 1966

Contents

List of Illustrations

Rutgers: A Bicentennial History

Chapter One

Child of Controversy

The solemn group of ministers and elders who convened in New York City late in May 1755 were intensely aware that the Dutch Church in America confronted its greatest crisis. The issue at stake was the autonomy and purity of their denomination. They knew that after years of heated controversy King's College had received its charter and that now there was the imminent prospect that Dominie Johannes Ritzema and his faction would not only support the new college but succeed in having a Dutch theological professorship established in that predominantly Anglican institution. They had been called together by the Reverend Theodore Frelinghuysen of Albany, who had ridden forth in January to travel for ten weeks among the churches, inveighing against the union with King's. Zealous, fiery, and determinedly persuasive, Frelinghuysen called for a college wholly under Dutch sponsorship as well as for an American classis to govern the affairs of the Church. His ardor infused the conference. Although several churches were not represented and some had declared their hostility, those present made the fateful decision to adopt Frelinghuysen's plan and commissioned him to go to Holland to seek approval and financial assistance for the projected school of the prophets. By their actions they brought about the complete disruption of the Church and gave the first impetus to the founding of Queen's College.

Queen's College owed its existence to the zeal of members of the Dutch Church; it owed many of its early tribulations to the sad fact that it had been sponsored by one faction of that church in a period when partisan feelings were intense. The controversy had many dimensions, but the central issue involved the degree of autonomy that should be enjoyed by the Church in America, both with regard to general matters of ecclesiastical government and to the special matter of training and ordaining ministers. Underlying these issues was the concern felt by many that an "Americanized" Church would mean the end of the Dutch Bible, Dutch preaching, and, indeed, a total loss of the deeply revered Dutch culture.

1

The churches in America were all under the jurisdiction of the Classis of Amsterdam, which in turn was part of the Particular Synod of North Holland. Local Church consistories in the colonies had recourse to the Amsterdam Classis for the settlement of disputes and to that classis they looked for a supply of Dutch-trained clergy. There was no semblance of Church organization in America above the consistory; neither was there any provision for training or ordaining ministers.

By the 1730's many Dutch Church ministers and elders had become convinced that an American church organization was essential. There were at the time sixty-five congregations, served by only nineteen ministers. Of the sixty ministers who had labored in the colonies since 1628, all but seven had come from Europe. Now the supply seemed to be inadequate to the demands of the multiplying churches. The Great Awakening, in which Theodorus Jacobus Frelinghuysen at his churches in the Raritan Valley played a prominent role, had rekindled religious fervor and served to stimulate a wide concern within the Dutch Church about its future. Accordingly, at a meeting of ministers and elders in New York City on September 5, 1736, it was determined to seek approval from the Amsterdam Classis for the formation of a coetus.* Although not of classical status, such an assembly might exercise limited powers of supervision over the several churches. It was also intended that it should have the authority to examine and license candidates for the ministry.

The Classis withheld its full approval from these proposals for several years. Finally, in 1747, some progress was made. Amsterdam agreed to grant highly restricted authority for the examination and ordination of ministers, and on these conditions the Coetus was organized. The restrictive conditions produced frustration and discontent on the part of many who feared that unless ministers could be trained and ordained in America the Church was doomed. Too few ministers were coming directly from the Netherlands, and it was both expensive and hazardous to send young men from the colonies abroad for their education and ordination. Accordingly, a meeting of the Coetus on September 19, 1754, decided to seek the full status of a classis.

To this point discussions within the Church had not been productive of serious discord, but now an issue arose that created a deep cleavage that was to have long-lasting consequences. Some years earlier the New York legislature had authorized the holding of lotteries to provide funds for the founding of a college. By 1751 these funds had been vested in trustees, most of them Anglicans, who were to serve until a site had been

---

* The term "coetus" was occasionally used to designate church bodies that lacked full classical authority and were subordinate to the Classis of Amsterdam. Java, Surinam, and Cape Colony each had a coetus.

selected and a charter had been secured. Then a violent controversy developed, with opponents of the proposed college, led by William Livingston, insisting that it must be completely nonsectarian and not, as they correctly feared it would be, closely connected with the Anglican Church. At first the ministers and other leaders of the Dutch Church in New York City sided with Livingston. But then a sudden shift occurred. On October 1, 1754, the New York City church not only declared its support for the college but also took the occasion to declare its opposition to the plan for an American classis, which had been adopted by the Coetus less than two weeks earlier.

It soon appeared that a deal had been made to unite the Anglican and Dutch interests in New York City. When King's College received its charter on October 31, 1754, twenty-five of its forty-one original trustees were Anglicans and eight were of the Dutch Church. Furthermore, plans were already under way to secure the appointment of a professor of divinity at the College who should be a minister of the Dutch Church. The leader of the pro-King's group was the Reverend Johannes Ritzema, who was a Trustee of the College and who entertained some hopes that he might secure the Professorship of Divinity. At his urging, the original charter was amended in June 1755 to make provision for such a professorship.

The surprising actions of the New York City church in casting its support to King's, proposing to have a divinity professor connected with that institution, and withdrawing its support from the movement for an American classis created consternation throughout the denomination and produced prompt and even violent reactions. It was this crisis that inspired the Reverend Theodore Frelinghuysen, son of Theodorus Jacobus, to undertake his mission of rousing the ministers and their consistories and rallying them behind his call for a Dutch college. At his urging numerous ministers and elders met in New York City on May 27, 1755, in an "extra" convening of the Coetus. Ominously, no representatives of the city churches were present.

It was at this conference that definite form was first given to the idea of founding a Dutch college. Frelinghuysen and his colleagues resolved "to plant a university or seminary for young men destined for study in the learned languages and in the liberal arts, and who are to be instructed in the philosophical sciences; also that it may be a school of the prophets in which young Levites and Nazarites of God may be prepared to enter upon the sacred ministerial office in the Church of God." Frelinghuysen was commissioned to journey to the Netherlands, where it was confidently expected he could secure support for the projected college. Of the eleven ministers who signed Frelinghuysen's commission, six were subsequently to become Trustees of Queen's, and, of those six, five had been trained and ordained in America. In addition to laying plans for a college, the

Coetus also decided to assume the full powers of a classis, without awaiting approval from Amsterdam, and to examine and license candidates for the ministry.

Ritzema, and those who sided with him, at once denounced the actions of the Coetus as illegal and appealed both to Amsterdam and to the American churches. Conservatives who feared that the plans of the Coetus would lead to the weakening of ties with the Fatherland and to a deterioration in the quality of the clergy then mobilized. Several churches, especially those in New York City and those with ministers who were natives of the Netherlands, broke with the Coetus and subsequently organized under the name of Conferentie. Bitter quarrels developed within individual consistories, and the entire denomination was rent with discord. The Classis of Amsterdam, to which both factions appealed, would not concede classical authority to the Coetus and ridiculed the proposal that a Dutch college should be established. Nevertheless, leaders of the Coetus adhered to their plans.

Theodore Frelinghuysen, who was having difficulties with his own church in Albany, was unable to sail for Holland until 1759. Although he spent two years there, his mission was fruitless, and on his return, as his ship neared New York, he perished, presumably drowned at sea. Other ministers assumed leadership of the college's cause, notably Samuel Verbryck of Tappan, John Henry Goetschius of Hackensack, John Leydt of New Brunswick, and David Marinus of Acquackanonck (Passaic). In time they were joined by the youthful Reverend Jacob Rutsen Hardenbergh, destined to play the largest role of all in the history of Queen's College. The descendant of a family long prominent in the area of Kingston, New York, Hardenbergh had been prepared for the ministry by John Frelinghuysen, brother of Theodore, at Raritan. When his mentor died, Hardenbergh married his widow. He was ordained by the Coetus in 1758 and was called to the Raritan parish, serving several churches in the area. He quickly became one of the leaders of the Coetus faction and was to serve in important civic and political offices as well.

Because New Jersey ministers had come to the fore in the Coetus, it was to the governor of that colony that they turned for a college charter. Beginning in 1761, petitions were addressed to successive governors, without success. We can only surmise the reasons for these early rebuffs, but undoubtedly the dissension within the denomination over the college question was a contributing factor. Again, no encouragement was forthcoming from the Netherlands. While visiting there on domestic matters, Hardenbergh found that the Amsterdam Classis was still adamantly opposed to an American classis in 1763 and that there was little prospect that funds for the proposed college could be raised there by subscriptions. Despite these setbacks, and the unrelenting opposition of the Conferentie faction, the efforts were continued until at last they bore fruit.

On November 10, 1766, Governor William Franklin granted a charter for Queen's College, so named in honor of Charlotte, the Queen Consort. No copy of this charter is known to be in existence, but there are numerous contemporary references to it, and meetings of the Board of Trustees appointed by the charter were held at intervals over the ensuing four years. The Trustees, forty-one in number, included the Governor, president of the Council, the Chief Justice, and the Attorney General of New Jersey ex officio, five ministers and sixteen laymen from the Province of New York, six ministers and eight laymen from the Province of New Jersey, and two ministers from Pennsylvania. All of the ministers were of the Dutch Church, as were all but a few of the laymen. Despite the preponderance of New Yorkers, subsequent developments were to make it clear that responsibility for the college was in fact to rest largely on the New Jersey members. The coveted charter had at last been obtained, but ahead lay grave problems, many of them common to all the early American colleges.

The American college, as it evolved from the earliest experiments at Harvard (1636), William and Mary (1693), Yale (1701), and their later counterparts—the College of Philadelphia (1740), the College of New Jersey (1746), King's College (1754), the College of Rhode Island (1764), Queen's College (1766), and Dartmouth College (1769)—was a novel creation. In common with the European model, it owed its existence largely to denominational sponsorship and derived much of its curriculum from the Renaissance tradition of scholarship, but these resemblances were more superficial than real. European institutions of higher education could not be transplanted to the distinctive new environment of Colonial America. European universities for the most part originated as self-governing associations of highly learned clerics, favored with the ample patronage of established churches or wealthy nobles, and were usually composed of several faculties that offered graduate and professional training as well as undergraduate studies. Entirely different conditions obtained in America.

In those colonies where a denomination enjoyed an established or favored position, the Church organization might be weak and it was surely lacking in large financial resources. Throughout the colonies generally, religious heterogeneity prevailed, and as each denomination sought to found and maintain a college of its own, and ultimately several colleges in different localities, the meagre resources available were dissipated in such a manner as to enfeeble all. In some instances aid was forthcoming from the provincial governments, but this source of support was often rendered unreliable, because, among other reasons, it gave rise to competition and dissension among rival denominations. Even where strong denominational bodies had been formed, they did not accept responsibility for the management or operation of colleges, although they would commend them to their constituencies, insist upon standards of orthodoxy, dominate governing boards, and look to the colleges as the sources of a learned ministry. Substantial private benefactions were hardly to be hoped for in a society where there were few men of great wealth. It was exceedingly rare for a Colonial college to receive large individual donations and even more rare for one to be the beneficiary of a bequest.

In addition to these considerations, the would-be founders of American colleges had to contend with the fact that there was no profession of college teachers upon which they could draw for the creation of a faculty. Throughout the Colonial period, and indeed well into the nineteenth century, there were available few men of learning comparable to those who graced the faculties of European universities. Of necessity, then, the colleges had to rely very largely on youthful tutors, whose ultimate careers might be in the ministry or the law, to assist the president in imparting instruction to the students.

It must also be recognized that the American colleges faced special problems in recruiting students, a problem that was to persist late into the nineteenth century. In Europe a baccalaureate degree was highly desirable, if not essential, for those who contemplated a career in the civil service or in the professions of theology, law, or medicine. Such careers, moreover, were attractive and conferred high status as well as material rewards. In America, abundant opportunities existed for young men in agriculture or business, for which no special educational attainments were required, and easy access to government positions and the so-called learned professions was available to those who lacked a college degree.

Deprived of the patronage, the professional competence, and the attendance available in Europe, and confronted as well with educational demands peculiar to a new society, the American college assumed distinctive form by the middle of the eighteenth century. It was governed not by an academic fellowship but by a lay board of trustees, in part because of the lack of mature academicians who might constitute a fellowship and in part because of the particular financial conditions that it faced. Funds came chiefly in small amounts from individual subscriptions, from fund-raising expeditions in Great Britain, from grants made by the communities in which the institutions were located, and in occasional instances from lotteries and from the provincial governments. In general, heaviest reliance, especially in the early years, had to be placed upon the generosity of a local constituency. Academic personnel, and especially the versatile men-of-all-work who served as presidents of the colleges were recruited largely from the clerical profession. As for the students, they were lured by glowing reports of the many excellences of the institution, never omitting its healthful location and low tuition rates. Or they were put forward by interested ministers, eager to swell not only the thin ranks of the clergy but also the small body of students in attendance at their favorite institution.

The curriculum, too, had a decidedly American flavor. It incorporated the classical studies traditional in the older universities. By the middle of the eighteenth century, however, it had borrowed heavily from the dissenting academies of Great Britain and had added liberal amounts of mathematics and natural philosophy. It had become established that the colleges were not to be exclusively concerned with training ministers; neither were they to have associated with them graduate or professional faculties. Within the restricted intellectual concepts of the time, they were to serve the general purposes of instilling piety, training the several faculties of the mind, affording a reasonably broad diet of what was accepted as ornamental and useful knowledge, and preparing young men to assume positions in a variety of professions and callings. The president pro tem of Queen's stated the aims of higher education succinctly in his address at the College's first commencement: "The Improvement of the human mind, for the proper discharge of our Several Duties towards God, ourselves and our Neighbours."

Adapting the forms of higher education to the conditions inherent in the American environment created severe challenges for all the Colonial colleges. In addition to the problems it shared with its sister institutions, Queen's had to contend against special difficulties. The members of the Dutch Church clung with extraordinary tenacity to their distinctiveness, adhering to the customs and language of their fatherland for generations. More than a century after his ancestors had emigrated to America, the first president of Queen's, Jacob Rutsen Hardenbergh, still regarded Dutch as his mother tongue and apologized in public for his lack of familiarity with English. Closely related to a "foreign" church, Queen's was debarred from seeking financial support in Great Britain, as did other Colonial colleges with varying degrees of success. It could, of course, look to the Netherlands for aid, but this source proved to be quite unproductive. As the "Dutch College," Queen's could appeal for funds and for students to a relatively small and restricted constituency. Moreover, it shared this constituency with the College of New Jersey, with King's College, and, after 1795, with Union College. Strongly determined to maintain their distinctiveness as a minority national group, the Dutch sustained the hope of a college of their own, but factors associated with their distinctiveness were to create obstacles to the attainment of that hope.

The cause of the College was impaired by the continuing discord within the Dutch Church. Indeed, the securing of the charter by the Coetus party exacerbated the controversy. Ritzema and his Conferentie brethren heaped scorn on the project and wrote fully and frequently to Amsterdam in opposition to it. The Amsterdam Classis, inspired in part by discussions with the Reverend Dr. John Witherspoon, president of the College of New Jersey, who visited Holland in 1768, proposed most earnestly that the Dutch in America should unite in support of the Presbyterian college at Princeton. This suggestion was acceptable to neither the Coetus nor the Conferentie.

Difficulties also arose because of certain objectionable features in the charter. The exact nature of the problem is obscure, because of our ignorance of the terms of the first charter. But the Trustees, in petitioning almost at once for an amendment to the charter, explained that they felt unable to raise money in New York because of some distinctions that were made in the charter between residents and nonresidents of New Jersey. After repeated petitions, Governor Franklin at last yielded to this request. Instead of granting an amendment to the original charter, however, he presented them with a new one, dated March 20, 1770.

The new charter presumably followed closely the terms of the original one. Like its predecessor it named forty-one Trustees, including with few exceptions the same individuals who had been appointed in 1766. The preamble of the charter recited that members of the Reformed Dutch Church believed it necessary that an institution should be established to supply the churches with an able and learned ministry because of the inconvenience and expense involved in sending young men abroad for their education. Accordingly, the Trustees were empowered to erect a college "for the education of youth in the learned languages, liberal and useful arts and sciences, and especially in divinity; preparing them for the ministry, and other good offices." The Trustees, not more than one-third of whom might be ministers, were incorporated and were empowered to receive and hold property producing an annual income of not more than £3,000 sterling. The Governor, or, in his absence, the other ex officio Trustees in turn were to preside at meetings of the Board, or if none were present the Board might elect a presiding officer from among those attending.

The Trustees were to appoint a president of the College, who must be a member of the Dutch Church as well as a professor of divinity. They were also to appoint professors and tutors to assist the president in the education and government of the students. Doubtless in recognition of the Dutch character of the College, the charter required that there should always be residing at or near the College at least one professor or teacher whose function it would be "grammatically to instruct the students . . . in the knowledge of the English language." The Trustees

were vested with full power to make laws for the wholesome government of the College; the authority of the president and faculty was
limited to executing such laws.

Although the charters of the early colleges conformed to no very rigid
pattern, the Queen's charter contained features that were common to
most. Like all others, except those of Harvard and William and Mary,
it definitely lodged responsibility for governing the College in a board
of trustees, rather than in the faculty. The inclusion on the board of
governmental officials was common to all charters except those of Yale,
Pennsylvania, and Brown. There was a religious test for the president
also at King's and Brown. The Queen's charter was unique in limiting
clerical representation to one-third of the Board membership, but the
Board as originally constituted was more heavily made up of one denomination than were most others. The numerous denominational references were not at all extraordinary, since, except for the College of
Philadelphia, all of the Colonial colleges owed their very existence to
sectarian sponsorship. However, it is no less significant to observe that,
like the other colleges, Queen's was not founded by a denominational
body nor did its charter contain any form of religious test for students
or professors.

Equipped at last with an adequate charter, the Trustees could now
proceed to the next step in the founding of the College. The first question
to be determined was its location. New Brunswick and Hackensack, representing respectively the centers of strength of the Raritan Valley
Dutch and the Bergen Dutch, were rivals for the honor. The Reverend
John H. Goetschius of Hackensack, an ardent early advocate and original
Trustee of the College, had started an academy there in order, no
doubt, to strengthen the claims of that town. The Reverend John Leydt
of New Brunswick, with like motives in mind, had joined with other
community leaders to launch a similar school in 1768. New Brunswick
may have been especially zealous for the choice because in 1753 the
town had been outbid by Princeton when it aspired to become the site
of the College of New Jersey. At a meeting of the Trustees in Raritan
in October 1770, it was agreed that each town should be invited to
secure subscriptions, with the implied promise that whichever one made
the better offer would be selected at the next meeting.

The Trustees convened in Hackensack on May 7, 1771, at which time
the subscriptions received from each town "were laid on the table and
the reasons in favour of said place offered." The question was then put,
and New Brunswick was selected by a vote of ten to seven. The vote
was largely along geographical lines, with the strong Raritan Valley contingent prevailing, but it is probable that New Brunswick had the advantage of superior financial inducements as well. Fortunately, this issue of

location was not productive of lasting animosities, although there were to be occasions in the future when Hackensack would reassert its pretensions. The selection of New Brunswick represented a decision of crucial importance, for circumstances were to decree that it was to the local community that the College would have to look for leadership and sustenance, at least through its first half century.

First settled in the 1680's near the head of navigation on the Raritan River and on the main route between New York and Philadelphia, New Brunswick was familiar to early travellers as Inian's Ferry. By 1730, when it received a city charter, it had begun to attain prominence as the market town for the prosperous farming region through which the Raritan flowed and it served as a shipping point for produce destined for New York. Its mingled population—Dutch, English, and Scotch-Irish—erected churches to serve the Reformed Dutch, Anglican, and Presbyterian congregations. At the time of the founding of the College, the city contained some 150 houses, which made it the most considerable place between Elizabeth and Philadelphia. The town had acquired prominence in the 1740's as a center of "New Light" enthusiasm within the Presbyterian church and had also responded to the evangelical preaching of Theodorus Jacobus Frelinghuysen among the Dutch brethren. It had acquired sufficient standing by the 1770's to support numerous men of modest wealth, several members of the various learned professions, two or three schools, three able ministers, a substantial military barracks, and, in the opinion of one discriminating traveller, the handsomest women in America.

It was in New Brunswick, with Governor Franklin presiding, that the Trustees met on October 5, 1771, to arrange for the start of college work. There was unanimous agreement on the choice of a tutor. Frederick Frelinghuysen, grandson of Theodorus Jacobus, son of John, and stepson of Jacob Rutsen Hardenbergh, was chosen. A graduate of the class of 1770 at Princeton, only eighteen years old at the time of his appointment, young Frelinghuysen was "to instruct the students who shall offer themselves, in the learned Languages, liberal Arts and Sciences" and was also expected "to teach the English Language grammatically." A committee of three Trustees was appointed which, together with the tutor, was to perform the function of a faculty, "to take upon them the Government and direction" of the College.

To provide quarters for the College, as well as for the Grammar School that had been started a few years earlier, the Trustees acquired a former tavern, the "Sign of the Red Lion," located on the northeast corner of Albany and Neilson Streets. The building housed the tutor and some of the students and provided adequate classroom space as well. What resources the College possessed at this time is not known precisely, although by 1773 it was reported that £4,000—proclamation money, $10,000—had been raised. New Brunswick had doubtless contributed a sizeable portion of this amount, although small sums were probably obtained elsewhere by subscriptions.

A tutor and a building had been secured with ease; the most urgent problem was that of obtaining a president. Great importance attached to this matter, for in the early colleges everything depended on the ability of the president. He must raise funds, direct the young tutors, give instruction to the upper classes, provide religious guidance, and inspire the Trustees to give their attention to the needs of the institution. Queen's in its infancy suffered greatly from the lack of such an officer, but the selection of a president was necessarily delayed because of complications resulting from the difficulties within the Dutch Church.

In the same year that the College was getting ready to open, peace was restored to the Church. Largely through the efforts of John Henry Livingston, who after graduating from Yale in 1762 had gone to the University of Utrecht for theological study, the Coetus and Conferentie were induced to agree upon certain Articles of Union. The basic elements of the agreement had been brought back from Holland by Livingston when he returned to assume a pastorate in New York City in 1770. On his initiative, representatives of both factions met in New York in October 1771, and from this convention there emerged a comprehensive American organization for the reunited Church. A General Assembly, later known as the General Synod, was created, which was all but independent of the Classis of Amsterdam. Thus the long breach between Coetus and Conferentie was ended and autonomy for the American Church was secured. But the Coetus, and Queen's College, had to pay a price for reconciliation. The Articles provided that funds should be raised to support one or more professors of theology "with the provision, that such professors shall not stand in any connection with English academies, but shall give lectures in their own dwellings. . . ." Because Queen's College had been started by the Coetus faction, it remained a sore point with the Conferentie. Therefore, it could not be brought into connection with the Church through the establishment there of a Church-supported professorship of divinity.

The Trustees had contemplated that the man to be selected as president would also hold the Professorship of Divinity; the charter had made specific provision for such an arrangement. Now the road to making such a joint appointment in cooperation with the General Assembly, with all that such action might promise in terms of denominational support, seemed to be blocked. The Trustees then turned directly to Holland, asking the Classis of Amsterdam, in consultation with the faculty at Utrecht, to recommend a suitable candidate for the combined offices.

Because of the recent discord in the Church, the Classis sought the opinion of the General Assembly on the matter. Somewhat surprisingly, that worthy body, at its session in October 1773, heartily endorsed the Trustees' plan. More than that, it resolved that if the Trustees would agree to call no one to the post except on the recommendation of Amsterdam and with the approval of the General Assembly, they would endeavor to raise funds for the College.

Matters now seemed to be advancing well for Queen's. The action of the General Assembly was transmitted to Amsterdam, where, despite the continuing coolness to the whole plan for a Dutch college, consideration was given to the choice of an individual who could meet the specifications of the Trustees. Eventually the recommendation was forthcoming; the man best qualified was the Reverend Dr. John H. Livingston. This word was not received until April 1775. Plans were made to act on this recommendation at a meeting of the General Assembly in October 1775. But because of the unsettled times, this meeting was not held. Not until 1784 was there to be another full meeting of the Church's governing body. Because of this unfortunate and complicated chain of events, Queen's College was to go through its first critical decade without a president.

Out of the travail and discord within the Dutch Church had come the founding of a college. From the day in 1755 when an aroused Dominie Frelinghuysen had set out from Albany to denounce Dominie Ritzema's plan to connect the Dutch Church with King's College and to call instead for a separate Dutch college, the course had been more productive of discord than of united support. Nevertheless, a small band of Coetus leaders had procured an adequate charter, modest funds, and humble quarters for their college. The foundation had been laid, but its strength and durability remained to be tested.

Chapter Two

Old Queen's College

If the Queen's Trustees felt any misgivings about the venture they were about to launch, they did not reveal those feelings in the announcement they published in the newspapers in October 1771. Stating that the College would open on the second Tuesday in November, they proudly called attention to the "singular Genius" of the lone tutor and intimated that a "well qualified" president would soon be procured. Mundane appeals were not neglected. "The Public may depend upon finding good and sufficient Board at private Houses . . . as cheap (if not cheaper) than at any other Places where colleges are erected." Assurances were given that "Students may expect to be treated with becoming Candour, without any Discrimination with Respect to their Religious Sentiments." Prospective applicants were advised that they would be "admitted into such of the Classes as they shall be qualified for."

The initial response to this inviting prospectus was not encouraging. When tutor Frelinghuysen assembled his students on the first day, he found a single candidate of Sophomore standing and a handful of Freshmen. Sharing the facilities of the former "Sign of the Red Lion" were the more numerous students of the Grammar School. Prospects brightened in the succeeding two years, however, and by 1774, when the first commencement was held, there were about twenty students enrolled. Frelinghuysen soon received assistance from John Taylor, also of the Princeton class of 1770, whose initial responsibility was the Grammar School. When Frelinghuysen left his teaching duties to study law, probably by 1773, Taylor succeeded him as tutor, a post that he was to retain with some interruptions down to 1790. In actuality, Taylor was the mainstay of the College during most of its first two decades of life. A man of considerable ability, he served as a colonel in the militia during the Revolution, seeing action at Trenton and in numerous other engagements, and occupied prominent positions in the city government and in the local Presbyterian church.

13

Because of the background of the tutors, the course of studies was in general patterned after that of the College of New Jersey, with such considerable modifications as were necessitated by the smallness of the staff and the student body. The two lower classes were largely engaged in the study of Latin and Greek, with some attention to arithmetic and geometry. The upper classes were introduced to geography, natural philosophy, mathematics, logic, and grammar. Instruction was based almost entirely on textbooks. Tuition fees were modest; twenty shillings on admission and four pounds a year, together with small assessments for firewood. Those students who did not board with the tutor found accommodations in town.

If the prescribed curriculum held little attraction for the students and seemed remote from their interests and needs, they found a stimulating alternative in their "literary society." By 1773, at the instigation of Taylor, who had been a member of the Cliosophic Society at Princeton, the Athenian Society had been organized. "It is Learning which irradiates the Soul and dispels those Clouds of Ignorance which continually surround the Minds of the Illiterate," declaimed the preamble to the Society's constitution. "From these Considerations we . . . are induced to form ourselves into a Society . . . in order to polish our Minds, and beautify our Manners." The Athenians were to meet weekly in the rooms of the College to listen to an oration by the president pro tem, read selections from approved works, deliver original compositions, and recite passages from favorite authors. Every member performed at each meeting and was free "to make his Remarks upon the performance of each Member, provided it is with Candour. . . ." Funds derived from an entrance fee of twenty shillings, from annual dues of one dollar, and from fines were all used to acquire books for the Society's library.

The Society was a remarkably vigorous institution, in which the tutor, the students, and in time distinguished townsmen indulged their forensic and literary interests. In addition to reading original compositions on such standard subjects as "Happiness," "Matrimony," and "Love," the young men recognized the temper of the times with discourses on "Liberty," on the "Horrors of War," and on "The Rising Glory of America." The books from which readings were selected evidenced a wide acquaintance with the best of English literature and included Addison and Steele, Milton, Pope, Shakespeare, and Sterne as well as Johnson, Richardson, Fielding, Robertson, Thompson, and Hume. Assuredly it was in the extracurricular environment of the Athenian Society, no less than in the classroom, that the students of Queen's College acquired their education.*

---

* There are references to the existence of a "Polemical Society," which may have been organized contemporaneously with the Athenian, but no records have been found and it had surely ended its career by 1777.

It was a proud day for the fledgling institution when with appropriate public ceremonies it held its first commencement on October 12, 1774. In the presence of the Trustees, students, tutors, and a large assemblage of the public, the Reverend Jacob Rutsen Hardenbergh, selected by the Trustees to preside, delivered a memorable address. His stated theme was "The Advantages of Education," and his aim was to demonstrate "that men of Learning are of absolute necessity and extensive advantages to Society." In proof of this proposition, he expatiated on the manner in which the community benefited by having men well educated in the learned languages and the liberal arts and sciences in positions of civil authority and in the professions of law, medicine, and theology. "And if this be true," he continued, "how reasonable and necessary is it, that the Community should promote and Incourage the Seats of Learning. . . ." This could be accomplished by providing adequate funds, by enrolling gifted children, regardless of means, and by "smileing on the honoust & earnest endeavors of those who are engaged in that Business."

After appropriate words of encouragement to the Trustees and of appreciation to the tutors, the good Dominie next addressed cautionary advice to the single graduate and then exhorted the other students to renew their application to their studies. He did not neglect the public audience, thanking those who had contributed funds and urging others to send their children to the College. In his peroration he gave voice to his ardent patriotism: "O! may America never want Sons of consumate Wisdom, intrep'd Resolution and true Piety to defend her civil and Religious liberties, and promote the public weal of the present and rising Generation!" His final duty was to introduce the graduate, but before doing so he considerately provided "opportunity for relaxation of thought and renewed attention, by the singing of a Psalm."

The object of all this public attention was Matthew Leydt, whose father was a devoted Trustee and minister of the local Dutch Church. He had been the only member of his class to enter the College in November 1771. In evidence of his achievements, he proceeded to deliver orations in Latin, Dutch, and English. He was followed by five members of the new Senior class who "spoke with gracefulness and propriety on various subjects." The occasion was further enlivened by vocal selections, provided by ladies and gentlemen of the town, and it was rendered promising by the announcement that six students from the Grammar School had been admitted to the Freshman class.

Despite its obvious deficiencies, Queen's had passed a significant milestone. Those who had labored for nearly twenty years to bring the institution to its present condition doubtless gave thanks for their achievement. But at this juncture an unforeseen contingency arose; the developing crisis in relations between the colonies and England steadily worsened.

Before another commencement was held, the War for Independence was under way. Soon New Jersey became a major battleground of that conflict, and the College became a casualty of the war.

> General Howe with the British Fleet ariving at Sandy Hook, all the Members of the Athenian Society who were able to bear Arms immediately marched to oppose the Enemy. Matters being thus in Confusion, July the 27th the College was suspended to the 21st of October.

This terse but moving entry in the minutes of the Athenian Society records the first interruption of the routine of the College. After the immediate crisis passed, the students returned and for a brief period the Society met according to custom. But soon another journal entry recorded a second disaster:

> The British Army under the command of General How having invaded the State of New Jersey, and penetrating as far as the City of New Brunswick on the first day of December in the year 1776— The Members of the Athenian Society, still inspired by Patriotism, and zealous to promote the interests of America, leaving their peacable abodes, again assisted their Countrymen to repel an Enemy endeavouring to establish a system of Tyranny and Oppression.

The British Army remained in New Brunswick, which became the principal enemy stronghold in the state, until late in June 1777. With the city thus occupied, with many students serving in the army, and with much of the state in turmoil, the College was again suspended, this time for nearly a year.

All members of the small College community were caught up in the Revolutionary struggle. Dominie Hardenbergh, foremost Trustee and most active member of the small committee that constituted the "faculty," devoted his patriotic energies to service in the Provincial Congress and in the state legislature. The reliable tutor, John Taylor, entered military service as a captain and soon rose to colonel. In between leading his troops on numerous battlegrounds from Trenton to Springfield, he found intervals when he could resume his teaching duties. Frederick Frelinghuysen, erstwhile tutor, sat in the Provincial Congress, served with Taylor in the field, and represented the state in the Continental Congress. Among recent graduates who played conspicuous roles were Simeon DeWitt, 1776, who soon became Geographer General under Washington, and James Schureman, 1775, prominent in both the state

legislature and the Continental Congress. Others won distinction in civil
and military offices.

It seems almost incredible that in spite of the turmoil of war the
College was soon reestablished. Late in 1777 John Taylor and a half-
dozen students came together at a small hamlet then known as "North
Branch," situated at the juncture of the north and south branches of
the Raritan River, nearly midway between Readington and Raritan. Using
as a classroom a long-abandoned church and boarding with farmers in
the vicinity, the students resumed their studies and even revived their
cherished Athenian Society. In time they were joined by others, until
there were ten students in all. In July 1779, Taylor was again called
to active service, but his place was filled by John Bogart, who had
received his degree a year earlier and who had been conducting the
Grammar School at Raritan. As Taylor hurriedly prepared to take the
field, he wrote to Bogart, giving him directions for supervising the work
of the students.

Mr. [Simeon] V[an] arsdalen will return I expect sometime in
August when you will set him at natural Philosophy. . . . The sophe-
more Class are reading Euclid. I would advise that they read the
Three first Books before vacation and the third book of Xenophon.
I think it will be best to set them at Xenophon half the Day.
Let their lessons be short, and particular attention paid to grammar.
I judge it will be best to construe their lessons. Messrs. [Timothy]
Blauvelt, [Jeremiah] Smith, & [John] Bray should study whole num-
bers in arithmetic, and [Daniel] V[an] Wyck Logic. I will leave a
Compend of arithmetic with V[an] Wyck. I have spoke to Mr.
[Robert] Eastburn in Brunswick to procure for me three Blank books
for them to write Arithmetic, which you will send for if you please.
Bray is behind in Euclid, I would therefore advise that he be kept
at it the whole time while the others read Xenophon. He has read
the third book of Xenophon. I have spoken to Mr. Brinson to make
a blackboard, and have procured lampblack. You will hurry him on
and get Col. D. Vroom to paint it, and keep an account of the
expence.

Mr. [Henry] Remsen is reading Geography; I think it best for him
to go thro it and then review it, and study the Introduction, which
he omitted when he began Geography. After he has done with that
let him study English Grammar; you will find a Compend[ium]
in the old Chest, or in the closet. You will make any other additions
to it you shall see fit. For assistance I would recommend to you
Johnston's Dictionary & South's Grammar. Messrs. Courtlandt [Pierre

Van Cortlandt] & [William] Crooke are reading Virgil & Greek
Grammar. I did not intend they should read above 3 Eniads before
they began to review the Eclogues & Cicero. V Harlegen [John Van
Harlingen] & [William] Stewart are reading Greek Grammar. I
would advise to keep them at it untill they have got it, and then
let the four begin Greek, and review Latin together. Be pleased to
hurry them on in Greek.

At the end of the summer campaign Taylor rejoined his small band
of students at North Branch. There were plans to return to New Brunswick in October 1779, but they did not materialize, and in the spring
of 1780, the tutor and his charges moved instead to Millstone, about
eight miles west of New Brunswick. After more than a year in that
community, they at last returned to New Brunswick in May 1781. The
long delay in reestablishing the school in its original quarters may have
been due to the severe damages inflicted on the city during the several
months of British occupation. Or the stays at North Branch and Millstone may have been dictated by the consideration that such locations
were less subject to enemy activity than New Brunswick, which lay on
the main route across the state. Having survived the crisis of the war,
the College had again to confront problems that it had failed to solve
earlier.

The prospects were anything but encouraging. The modest College
funds, amounting to $7,600 invested in Continental Loan Office Certifi-
cates and a few hundred pounds in personal bonds or mortgages, produced
little income. The redoubtable Dominie Hardenbergh, long a mainstay of
the College, had left New Jersey in response to a call from the churches
in the area of Kingston, New York. Other Trustees who had worked
valiantly for the establishment of Queen's had died or moved elsewhere,
and their places remained unfilled. Most serious of all, the College still
lacked a president, and the Dutch Church, to which the Trustees might
have turned for aid, was utterly disorganized as the result of the war.
The Trustees had been unable during the war to do much more than
afford encouragement and some support to John Taylor. Beyond that,
they had secured an amendment to the charter eliminating the requirement that not more than one-third of the Board might be ministers and
making other minor changes.

Despite the ominous circumstances, Taylor doggedly kept the College
going, and in October 1782 he was able to report that there were eighteen
students, twelve of them Freshmen, in attendance. He was determined,
he confided to a friend, to "make one great exertion to raise *Queen's
College* from its present obscurity, to grandeur and usefulness." His exertions were unavailing. By 1784, discouraged because his salary had

fallen considerably in arrears and resentful of Trustee criticism of his efforts, he left the College. The few remaining students dispersed, some of them entering other institutions. As a stopgap measure the Trustees announced the appointment of Frederick Frelinghuysen "to take the superintendence of such students as shall offer themselves for any of the classes in the College." Whether any appeared is doubtful; in any event there were no graduates in 1784, 1785, or 1786. The Grammar School continued in operation under a succession of youthful teachers.

With affairs at this low ebb, the Trustees resumed their search for a president. Uniting with the local churches at New Brunswick and Six Mile Run, they issued a call to the Reverend Dirck Romeyn, then minister at Hackensack. Romeyn was to serve as pastor of the churches in addition to his presidential duties. Only through such an arrangement could he be assured an adequate salary. After deliberating for eight months, Romeyn declined in October 1784. The Trustees then communicated with the recently revived General Synod, proposing that the Reverend Dr. John H. Livingston be called on the basis of the plan that had been formulated in 1773. That is, he would serve both as president and as professor of divinity. The Synod, however, had already named Livingston as the Church's Professor of Theology, with the provision that he remain in New York City. The Synod also made it plain that it was not disposed to undertake any general subscription for the benefit of the College.

Following these severe rebuffs, the College turned to the Reverend Dr. Hardenbergh. He was called to the presidency of the College and to the pastorate of the New Brunswick church. Devoted as ever, he accepted, and returned to the city in February 1786 to undertake the immense challenge of restoring life to the moribund institution.

The next few years witnessed unusual activity. The Trustees came to terms with John Taylor respecting his arrears of salary and offered him £150 a year to resume his duties as tutor. The energetic president, aided by several ministers in the vicinity, launched a campaign for subscriptions among the churches to meet current expenses. Students enrolled in surprising numbers; the graduating class in 1789 included ten members. The Trustees were sufficiently heartened by Hardenbergh's leadership and the evident signs of growth to formulate a comprehensive set of rules and regulations for the government of the College.

The president was given general powers to execute the Trustees' regulations, but broad authority was vested in the faculty, which was composed of the president, two Trustees, and the tutors. The faculty was to settle disputes among students, maintain discipline and inflict penalties, determine qualifications of candidates for admission, and conduct quarterly examinations. For breaches of discipline students might be admonished, suspended, or expelled, depending on the severity of the offense. However, every student was guaranteed the right to appeal to the faculty against any of the penalties and might present his case to the Trustees if he were sentenced to suspension or expulsion. The deportment of students was minutely regulated. They were required to take off their hats when they met the president or the tutors. They were "strictly forbidden" to frequent taverns, keep cards, dice, or game-fowls, or liquor in their lodgings, or engage in fighting or riots. The president and tutors were given the right to enter students' rooms, and if they were refused admittance, they might break open the door. Repairs to such broken doors were to be paid for by the students. Hours of study were prescribed, as was attendance at morning and evening prayers and Sunday services. Because "distinguishing habits of dress" had been found useful in other colleges, the students were required to procure black gowns, with distinctive badges for each class, to be worn at all College exercises. Tuition was fixed at six pounds a year, with reduced rates for those entering from the Grammar School. Additional charges met the expenses of ringing the College bell and providing firewood for the classrooms.

Candidates for admission to the Freshman class were required to be able "to render into English Caesar's Commentaries, the Eclogues of Virgil, or one or more of the Aeniads; at least one of the Gospels from the Greek." The curriculum was set forth with equal simplicity:

> In the progress through the four different classes of the College they shall read in Latin, the principal Orations of Cicero, Virgil, and Horace; in the Greek Language, they shall read such parts of the Greek Testament as the President and Tutors shall direct; Xenophon's Cyropaedia, Homer and Longinus; they shall also read Kennet's Antiquities, Logick, Geography, Rhetoric, Arithmetic, Algebra, Euclid's Elements of Geometry, Trigonometry, Navigation and Surveying, Natural and Moral Philosophy, and English Grammar, and composition to be attended to in the respective classes.

Here, in brief outline, was the complete specification for the typical classical college in all its limited dimensions. It was an outline that at Queen's and at dozens of comparable institutions that were soon to arise underwent little alteration until the next century was well advanced.

As was to happen on more than one occasion in the future, the Trustees in an excess of optimism forged ahead with their plans for the College without due regard for the means at their disposal. In 1787 they decided to erect a new college hall. The old house that had served since 1771 was inadequate; moreover, the title to it was not clear. The new building, a simple two-story frame structure, was erected on a lot owned by the College across what was then the south end of George Street, near the present Monument Square. President Hardenbergh undertook another subscription campaign to pay for the building, which was ready for full occupancy in 1791. Meanwhile, expenses continued to run considerably beyond income. By 1790 the president's salary was £330 in arrears and funds to pay the tutors in the College and the Grammar School were lacking. By October 1790, conditions had become desperate. An anguished appeal was made to the Synod by President Hardenbergh, and that body responded by requesting the consistories of all the churches to aid the College.

Before this promise of aid could become effective, the College suffered two blows that ultimately brought it again to the brink of extinction. Dominie Hardenbergh, who since 1771 had been the leading champion and promoter of Queen's College, died on October 30, 1790, three weeks after making his fervent appeal to the Synod. His loss was all but irreparable. At about the same time John Taylor, who almost single-handedly had constituted the teaching staff of the College from its earliest days, left to assume charge of an academy in Elizabeth. After three years there, he journeyed on to Schenectady, where he taught in the Academy and subsequently in Union College. For the next few years the Trustees employed a succession of young tutors, chief among whom was Charles Smith, a Princeton graduate of 1786, who was engaged in studying medicine with a local physician, Dr. Moses Scott.

The Trustees embarked once more on a futile search for a president, again issuing calls to John H. Livingston and Dirck Romeyn, both of whom declined. As in the past, they called upon the General Synod to implement the plan that had been devised in 1773. The Synod agreed, provided the necessary funds could be raised, and subscriptions were actually undertaken for the purpose. But the Trustees, having previously been disappointed in their reliance on the denomination, turned to another alternative.

In June 1793, they appointed a committee to confer with a comparable committee of the Princeton trustees to consider a union of the two colleges. The joint committee met in September and devised a plan for a consolidated board of trustees, which, under a new charter, would maintain a preparatory school at New Brunswick and a college at Princeton. The plan was considered by the Queen's Trustees in October, and, after what must have been a tense debate, was rejected by the narrow vote of nine to eight. Rejected also was another plan under which the Queen's Trustees would have operated an academy and a theological seminary, both maintaining close affiliation with the college at Princeton. Desperate though the prospects might appear, a majority of the Queen's Trustees were determined to try to sustain their institution.

The chief consequence of the negotiations with Princeton was a worsening of relations with the General Synod. When the Synod learned of the merger plan, it immediately ordered that none of the funds being raised by subscriptions should be turned over to the College. Subsequently, in June 1794, when it became apparent that the merger would not be effected, the restriction was removed. But at the same time another issue was raised. Many in the Church had long felt that New Brunswick was a poor location for the College because it was too remote from major centers of Dutch population in New York and northern New Jersey. Hackensack had not relinquished its aspirations and in 1783 and 1788 had attempted to secure from the legislature a charter for a college. Schenectady, where Dirck Romeyn had established an academy that would become Union College in 1795, also had its champions. Responsive to pressures from anti-New Brunswick elements, the Synod proposed that Queen's College should be moved to Bergen (Jersey City) or some place still further north; if this were done, the Synod would unite its theological professor with the College and attempt to provide adequate support.

A special meeting of the Queen's Trustees deliberated on this alarming proposition in August. With their resources exhausted, unable to secure a president, and sorely divided as a result of the recent controversy over the proposed merger with Princeton, they now had to deal with another in a long series of bewildering shifts in attitude by the General Synod. Acceptance of the Synod's plan would mean the end of the College in New Brunswick. Rejection would leave the Trustees with no apparent alternative means of sustaining the institution. After a careful review of relations with the Synod since 1773 the Board, dominated by members from New Brunswick and vicinity, resolved

> that no reasonable expectations can be entertained from the exertions of Rev. Synod for the better support of this College in any other place that it has hitherto experienced, and therefore
>
> *Resolved,* that this Board cannot comply with the request of Synod to remove this Colledge to Bergen or elsewhere.

If the College must perish, let it expire in New Brunswick.

Having faced this issue squarely, the Trustees then accepted the consequences of their action by resolving "that the Collegiate Exercises in the Colledge be suspended after the next [1795] commencement." In the meantime the instruction was to continue under the Reverend Ira Condict, who had recently assumed the pastorate of the local Dutch church. Condict had graduated from Princeton in 1784, and soon after his arrival was elected to the Board of Trustees of Queen's and appointed to the faculty. Now, in August 1794, he was chosen president pro tem, a position he was to retain for the next thirteen years. He presided at the 1794 commencement, when degrees were conferred on five graduates, and again in 1795, when the number had declined to two. The Trustees' edict then became effective, and College work ceased. Arrangements had been made to continue the Grammar School, which operated with relative success under the Reverend Benjamin Lindsay until 1801 and the Reverend John Croes thereafter until the revival of the College. The Trustees did not meet again until 1800, and they held a total of only five sessions between 1795 and 1807, chiefly for the purpose of transacting routine financial business.

After twenty-four years of tenuous existence, the College had expired. Born out of the controversy that had rent the Dutch Church, distracted almost at the outset by the impact of the Revolution, deprived of a president through all but four years of its existence, and frustrated in its efforts to secure consistent denominational support, the wonder is not that the College collapsed but rather that it survived as long as it did. Its difficulties were not unique. King's College had been suspended early in the war, to be revived in 1784 as Columbia. The College of Philadelphia had but a shadowy existence for a decade after 1779, when it fell victim to political attacks. Princeton also experienced its time of trial in the war years. Queen's, lacking the state support, aggressive leadership, or the broad denominational constituency on which other colleges were to rely, was unable to weather its trials.

Such interest and support as the College enjoyed came almost entirely from the New Brunswick area. Although the Board of Trustees as originally constituted numbered forty-one members drawn almost equally from New York and New Jersey, few of the New Yorkers played an active role, especially after 1776. Of the fifty Trustees who qualified between 1770 and 1795, thirty-two were from Middlesex and Somerset counties. Attendance at Board meetings was generally poor. Rarely were as many as fifteen present, and of those the majority were local men. Ministers had been most active in the founding of the College, but by the 1780's laymen predominated at the meetings. The denominational complexion of the Board was altered as local Presbyterians and Episcopalians were admitted to membership. By the 1790's Queen's had become, in actuality, the responsibility of the community rather than of the Church, and the community lacked the means to support a college.

During its brief and uncertain existence, the College had sustained the proposition advanced by Dominie Hardenbergh in his 1774 commencement address—that men of learning were an asset to society. Of the approximately eighty-five students who attended down to 1795, fifteen entered the ministry of the Reformed Dutch Church and ten were ordained by other denominations. An equal number entered the professions of law, medicine, and teaching. A large proportion attained positions of distinction. James Schureman held high political office, serving in the Continental Congress, the first Federal Congress, and the United States Senate. Simeon DeWitt was for fifty years Surveyor General of New York State following his wartime career as Chief Geographer of the Army. Jeremiah Smith returned to his native New Hampshire to become successively Governor and Chief Justice of that state. Isaac Stoutenberg, state senator in New York, Pierre Van Courtlandt, lawyer and member of Congress, Samuel Kenneday Jennings, president of Washington College; Albert Oblensis, principal of Erasmus Hall Academy, and John Schureman, professor and vice-president of Queen's College, were others who made notable achievements. The varied callings of these graduates make it evident that Queen's, like other Colonial colleges, was considerably more than a seminary for prospective ministers; the vast majority of the alumni entered secular vocations.

After twelve years of almost complete somnolence, the Queen's Trustees suddenly roused themselves to action in 1807. Within the next few years the College was revived, an imposing building was erected, substantial funds were raised, and a new plan of cooperation with the Reformed Dutch Church was tested. Momentarily this great burst of energy promised success, but then it became apparent that in many respects the Trustees had misjudged the situation, and another collapse followed.

The Trustees met in special session on March 25, 1807, at the request of some members who obviously had been contemplating the revival of the College. Andrew Kirkpatrick, former teacher in the Grammar School and now Chief Justice of New Jersey offered the resolution that got the movement under way. Urging that conditions were propitious for reviving the College, he proposed that funds should be sought for the erection of a proper building. On his motion the Board resolved to seek $12,000 to "complete the necessary buildings, re-establish the College and its courses of instruction, and raise it to that pitch of publick utility which the present view of things seems to encourage, and which the present situation of our country, and the church with which this institution is particularly connected seems to call for."

This effort to revive the College originated entirely with leaders of the local community, and at the outset no formal cooperation with the Dutch Church or its General Synod was sought. All nineteen men present at the Board meeting were from the New Brunswick area. Eight were alumni of the College and three others had taught in the institution.

Seven were Dutch Church ministers, serving congregations in Middlesex and Somerset counties. Virtually all were to involve themselves actively in the revival effort, but the leading part was taken by the Reverend Ira Condict. He customarily presided at Board meetings, assumed the largest responsibility for fund raising, and took charge of instruction when classes were resumed. Kirkpatrick was the foremost personage on the Board and lent his vast influence to the cause, although subsequently he became alienated when the Trustees ignored his caution to keep the cost of the proposed College building within bounds. Another major figure was Abraham Blauvelt, an alumnus, a local publisher and bookseller, who headed the committee charged with the large task of supervising the erection of the new building. The Board elected some additional members in the succeeding years, but it remained essentially an assemblage of local notables.

Taking stock of their resources, the Trustees found that their total assets consisted of $4,902.67 in old funds, together with the College building and lot. They had decided that a new location must be sought because the old site was near the center of the city and was threatened by the impending extension of streets. Their first problem was to devise a plan to raise the $12,000 required for a proper building. No thought, apparently, was given to ways and means of financing instruction, nor was any consideration given to the selection of a president. It was determined to send agents through New York and New Jersey, appealing especially to the Dutch Church members. Before putting this plan into effect, however, it was deemed prudent to seek the "approbation and concurrence" of the Particular Synods of New York and Albany and of the General Synod as well.

It was at this juncture that the whole movement assumed an unexpected complexion. In 1806 the General Synod had undertaken, very belatedly, to raise funds for the support of its theological professor. This post had been filled since 1784 by Dr. John H. Livingston, who had labored at the task without any compensation other than that derived from his salary as minister of the Dutch Church in New York City. With the Synod's effort in mind, the Particular Synod of New York responded to the Trustees' request with the counterproposal that all monies raised by the Trustees' agents in New York should constitute a fund for "the education of young men for the ministry and the establishment of a Theological School upon such conditions, and under such stipulations, as shall be proposed by the General Synod and mutually agreed upon between the Synod and Trustees." This response was a blow to the Trustees, but after postponing its consideration for a few weeks, they felt obliged to accept it. Without the support of the denomination, any fund raising would be all but impossible. The terms were onerous, and eventually their acceptance proved to be ill-advised. They forecast the fact that while the denomination might be induced to support a theological seminary, it had little real interest in Queen's College.

Formal articles of agreement were adopted at an extraordinary meeting of the General Synod in September. The essential features were that all funds raised in New York by the Queen's Trustees were to constitute a fund for the support of a theological professorship in the College and that as soon as the fund was adequate the Trustees were to call to that post the person nominated by the General Synod. In a final article the General Synod agreed to contribute a proportionate share of the cost of erecting the building, which would be jointly occupied by undergraduates and theological students. The Trustees, having originally had in mind the raising of funds for a building, now found themselves committed to raising an additional fund for a professor who would serve not the College but the Theological Seminary. They accepted the agreement and immediately appointed agents to canvass for subscriptions. Money secured in New York would go to what became known as the "professoral fund." Subscriptions secured in New Jersey would be donated to the building fund.

At the same meeting at which the Trustees accepted the articles of agreement—on September 17, 1807—they made arrangements for the immediate reopening of the College. The devoted Ira Condict agreed to teach the Junior class, the sole class admitted, for compensation not to exceed £100. The following year he undertook to instruct the two upper classes. The Freshmen and Sophomores remained in the Grammar School until the fall of 1809, when Condict's son, Harrison, was appointed College tutor in charge of the two lower classes. Students appeared in modest numbers. Five men graduated in 1809, and by the following year there were twenty-one students enrolled.

Meanwhile, the building committee under Abraham Blauvelt was extremely busy selecting a site, having plans drawn, and supervising construction. After considering various locations, the Trustees, in November 1807, accepted an offer from the heirs of James Parker, a distinguished citizen of Perth Amboy, of a five-acre site, soon augmented by the purchase of slightly more than an acre. Bounded by Somerset and George Streets, this tract became the present Queen's Campus. Once the site had been chosen, preliminary building plans, prepared by the noted New York architect, John McComb, were studied. After undergoing several alterations dictated by the need for economy, the final plans were approved in June 1808, and the cornerstone of the building was laid with appropriate ceremonies on April 27, 1809.

The building was designed to accommodate the academic work of the Grammar School, the College, and the Theological Seminary. In addition, provision was made in the two wings for apartments for two faculty members. Oddly enough, in view of the general practice at the time, there were no living quarters for students, although it was foreseen that an extension might sometime be constructed for that purpose. The first and second floors were divided into large classrooms while the third floor remained for some years unfinished. Handsomely proportioned and built of brown stone, the building was almost entirely lacking in ornamentation except for four pilasters on the front, extending from the top of the first-story windows to the roof. McComb, its designer, was the architect of several New York City churches and had also collaborated on the design of the City Hall there. Respected today for its fine architectural qualities and revered as "Old Queen's," the building, with its varied uses through the decades, epitomizes much of the history of Rutgers.

Construction was carried forward rapidly by the several contractors engaged by the building committee. By the fall of 1811, the fabric of the structure had been completed and the interiors of the two wings and the first floor of the central portion were ready for occupancy. At that point it was necessary to suspend further work because of a shortage of funds. By that date, nearly $20,000 had been expended, an amount far in excess of the $12,000 originally contemplated.

With classes under way and plans for the new building well advanced, the Trustees turned to the problem of securing a president. Not unexpectedly, they thought first of John H. Livingston and in August 1808 called him both to the office of president and to the professorship of theology. After some correspondence relating to the terms and conditions of his service, he declined. The presidency was then offered to Ira Condict, who was in large measure performing the functions of that office. He declined the honor and would not accept the vice-presidency either, although he expressed his willingness to continue his general superintendence of the College. Again the Trustees renewed their calls to Livingston. Because of his refusal to undertake any active role in the College, the call now specified that he was merely "to preside at commencement and authenticate diplomatic documents and take general superintendence of the institution as far as . . . [his] time and health [would] admit." Under these conditions, with a promised salary of $200 as president and $750, soon raised to $1,400, as professor of theology, Livingston accepted in April 1810. Now sixty-four years old, the respected patriarch of the Church moved to New Brunswick in the fall. There he carried on the instruction of theological students until his death in 1825. This was the work to which he was dedicated, and his services as president were, in accordance with his call, minimal.

The most time-consuming and difficult task confronting the Board in these years was fund raising. The mechanics of the operation were relatively simple. Having secured the promise of cooperation from the General Synod, the Trustees appointed more than a score of agents, most of them ministers, who travelled from church to church soliciting pledges and donations. The agents received for their services two dollars a day and expenses. The subscription accounts disclose that contributions of more than five dollars were rare—most were three dollars or less—and that pledges were difficult to collect. New York and New Jersey were, of course, the chief fields in which the agents labored, but some carried the campaign into Pennsylvania and one team journeyed as far south as Georgia and South Carolina.

Most of the funds for the new building had to be raised in New Jersey, and as the costs of construction mounted the cause became increasingly desperate. At the time the cornerstone was laid, only $6,389.72 was in hand, most of it having been subscribed locally. When construction was suspended late in 1811, the total receipts had risen to $11,942.58, but this was some $8,000 less than had already been expended. The subscription campaign having failed to produce the required funds, the Trustees turned to another expedient, a lottery. Lotteries were resorted to by many colleges, as well as churches and charitable agencies, in the Colonial period and later. Permission to conduct a lottery was sought from the legislature, and, after some initial rebuffs, was obtained in January 1812. It was hoped this device would yield $20,000. The Trustees undertook to manage the complicated venture through a committee, rather than turn their privilege over to a professional lottery agent. The consequences were disastrous. Many difficulties arose, with the result that the net proceeds, if any, fell far short of the goal.

Difficulties of other kinds were encountered in trying to secure the "professoral fund." The effort was launched first in New York City in September 1807, with very heartening results; nearly $10,000 was subscribed within a few months. Ominously, however, no contributions were forthcoming from the churches outside the city. Then Jefferson's Embargo produced a period of economic stagnation, and the agents suspended their efforts. In 1809, by which time conditions had improved, the Trustees called upon the General Synod to remind the consistories to lend assistance to the fund campaign, and the agents returned to the field. After three more years of canvassing, the fund amounted to only $16,440.47.

The Trustees had made an earnest effort; they were commended by the General Synod for their "watchfulness, zeal and engagedness," but again they had failed. The theological professor had been promised a salary of $1,400, plus $300 for house rent, but the "professoral fund" did not yield nearly that amount. For many years the professor received no more than half his promised stipend; ultimately the Board resorted to borrowing to meet their obligation to him. The pledge made by the General Synod to contribute to the cost of the new College building by having annual collections taken up in the churches was totally unproductive. The Trustees therefore felt justified in borrowing approximately $2,000 from the "professoral fund," an action that later produced recriminations and threats of lawsuits, until the amount was finally restored.

Many reasons could be advanced to explain the indifferent support given to the Trustees' appeals. Of first importance was the widespread feeling in New York that New Brunswick was not a proper location for the Theological Seminary. This opposition had been manifested earlier and was to come to a head later. Even those whose zealousness for the theological work overcame their objections to New Brunswick hesitated to give liberally because they feared that the Trustees might somehow use the money for the College. Its prospects were blighted, too, by the fact that during the years after 1795, when the College was dormant, Union College had come into existence and had commended itself strongly to the Dutch Church people of the Albany-Schenectady region. Queen's had been founded by a faction of the Church and had not been able to extend the geographical base of its ardent supporters beyond the Raritan Valley.

The College, so hopefully revived in 1807, was sustained for nine years by the increasingly harassed Trustees. For the first two years the burden was carried by Ira Condict. In the fall of 1809 his son took charge of the two lower classes. As the numbers of students increased, the Trustees sought a professor of mathematics and natural philosophy, and eventually they secured Robert Adrain, who began teaching in December 1809. Born in Ireland, though of French ancestry, Adrain had taught in several academies and through his publications had acquired a fine reputation as a mathematician. In addition to his fields of specialization, he was at once called upon to give instruction to the two upper classes in all subjects except moral philosophy and composition, which Condict retained.

Affairs were proceeding well until Condict died in June 1811, followed in August by his son. With Condict's death, the College lost its real leader, for he, rather than Livingston, was performing the duties of president. After a lapse of a year and a half he was succeeded by the Reverend John Schureman, who had graduated from the College in 1795. Schureman for a brief time divided his efforts between the pastorate of the local Reformed Dutch church and his College appointment as Vice-president and Professor of Languages, but finding this dual assignment too demanding, he relinquished his pastorate and gave his full time to the College as Professor of Moral Philosophy and Belles Lettres. Other changes followed; Adrain was lured away to Columbia in 1813, and his place was filled by Henry Vethake, a Columbia graduate, who, after his brief service at Queen's, acquired considerable distinction at Princeton and the University of Pennsylvania. While these men directed the work of the upper classes, a succession of tutors supervised the Freshmen and Sophomores.

The academic life of the College during these uncertain years hardly realized the high aspirations that were held by the Trustees in 1807. The number of students in attendance never exceeded thirty at one time, and the curriculum was limited by the smallness of the staff and the inadequacy of facilities. Entrance requirements remained much as they had been when the College first opened, except that in addition to some mastery of Latin and Greek the students were supposed to be able to "perform any ordinary exercise in vulgar arithmetick, at least as far as the rule of proportion." The Freshmen and Sophomores were confined to their classroom six hours daily under the supervision of their tutor; the two upper classes were obliged to attend only two recitations or lectures a day. Dr. Condict lectured on Witherspoon's *Moral Philosophy*, Blair's *Rhetoric*, a manual of logic, and the Bible. Adrain, in addition to drilling his students on Hutton's *Mathematics*, taught them trigonometry, surveying, and nautical astronomy through lectures. The lower classes concentrated on the classics and Morse's *Geography*. At afternoon prayers each day, one or two upperclassmen were required to deliver set speeches; the lowerclassmen had a similar weekly exercise in oratory.

As in earlier times, the students found stimulation and good fellowship in their literary society—Calleopean—which soon accumulated a library of more than two hundred volumes. Their leisure-time activities were severely restricted by the stringent rules laid down by the Trustees, but because they resided in various boarding houses around the town it is doubtful that they adhered strictly to all the injunctions laid upon them. They were readily identifiable in the small community, for when attending church services and on other public occasions they wore their black gowns with distinguishing tassels—two on each sleeve for a Freshman, four for a Sophomore, six for a Junior, and nine for a Senior.

The Trustees did all that was within their power to sustain work of satisfactory quality. In 1810 they published a new set of College laws, running to twenty-five printed pages, that carefully defined the responsibilities of faculty and students and provided elaborate specifications for a regimen that emphasized piety and abstemiousness. Despite their limited means they had a second-floor room fitted up for use as a library in 1812 and appointed agents to solicit donations of books and money. A year later the faculty drafted rules to govern the use of the library and appointed a librarian. In response to the request of Professor Adrain, a modest investment was made in "philosophical apparatus," including two globes, a quadrant, surveying equipment, magnets, and a prism.

Insights into the attitudes of the students of that era are rare, but one incident is especially revealing. On the eve of commencement in 1813, three of the four members of the Senior class addressed a respectful petition to the Trustees in behalf of a classmate who had not been recommended by the faculty for his degree. The young man, they conceded, was often giddy and inattentive and had justifiably incurred the wrath of his teachers. But they pointed to the fact that in such a small class his absence at graduation would be so conspicuous as to be mortifying to the unfortunate candidate. Moreover, they contended, never in the history of the College had a Senior failed to receive his degree. They explained why his performance on his examination, conducted publicly by the faculty on the entire four-years' work, was so poor. He had done part of his work at another institution, from which he had transferred to Queen's.

Now, young men are apt to study the particular authors which are put into their hands, and not the *subjects* on which those authors treat. So that, to have studied any branch of science in *one College*, is of little advantage to the student who is examined in *another*, upon the same subject, indeed, but not upon the same book.

The Trustees, no doubt impressed by the cogency and earnestness of this appeal, voted that the degree should be conferred "for special reasons."

Altogether 52 students attended the College in this period, of whom 46 received degrees. Three quarters of them came from the Raritan Valley. Again, the values of a college education would seem to be abundantly evidenced by the subsequent careers of these men. Thirteen became ministers, 8 as Reformed Dutch Church pastors; 10 entered the legal profession and 9 became physicians; 10 became farmers or businessmen, including 3 bank presidents. In the field of education, Jacob Green achieved distinction as a professor of chemistry and natural history at Princeton and at Jefferson Medical College, and William W. Blauvelt taught at Hampden Sydney. Among those who subsequently had notable public careers were Charles C. Stratton, Congressman and Governor of New Jersey, James S. Nevius, Justice of the State Supreme Court, Edward Mundy, Lieutenant Governor of Michigan, and Samuel Judah, legislator and leading Jacksonian politician in Indiana. Surely, Dominie

Hardenbergh would have contended that the services of these men to society justified the efforts of those in the community who made their education possible.

During these years, in addition to the Grammar School and the Theological Seminary, there was also associated with Queen's College a medical faculty. The association was a tenuous one, but it was not without interest. During the first period of the College's existence, in 1792, a loose agreement had been made between the Trustees and a group of physicians in New York City who had organized a medical school. The leading figure in this enterprise was Dr. Nicholas Romayne, whose efforts to secure a charter for his school from the Regents of the University of the State of New York had been successfully opposed by Columbia College. Romayne and his associates proposed that Queen's should grant medical degrees to their graduates, and in 1792 and 1793 several such degrees were in fact conferred. Then the relationship lapsed, and Romayne turned to other ventures. In 1811, however, having lead a group of medical professors in a secession from the College of Physicians and Surgeons, Romayne organized the "Medical Institution of the State of New York" and again sought a connection with Queen's. In January 1812, the Trustees approved fourteen "articles of agreement" whereby Romayne and his colleagues were constituted the medical faculty of Queen's College and were vested with full autonomy to conduct medical training in New York City. Under this arrangement, which imposed no financial obligations on the Trustees and produced no revenue, twenty-one medical degrees were awarded between 1812 and 1816. When the College suspended in the latter year, the connection with the medical faculty was severed. A comparable arrangement was made in 1826 with another medical faculty, again a seceding group from the College of Physicians and Surgeons, this time under Dr. Daniel Hosack. The Trustees created the Rutgers Medical College and appointed a six-man faculty, which displayed its gratitude by presenting a gift of $1,000 to the College. In 1827, twenty-seven medical degrees were conferred, but the New York legislature in the same year enacted legislation that effectively discouraged the granting of medical degrees by out-of-state institutions for studies pursued in New York. This action ended the third venture by the Trustees into the area of medical education.

The Trustees of Queen's College had made a valiant effort to place the institution on a firm foundation, but it was becoming evident by 1814 that their exertions had not met with success. The fund-raising campaigns in behalf of the new building and the theological professorship had fallen short of their goals, the lottery had proved to be disappointing; and local banks were pressing for payment of accumulated debts. Understandably, the Board was becoming wearied under the burden of its responsibilities. It had held twenty-eight meetings during the three years after the decision was made to revive the College, but it no longer possessed the energy to contend against mounting difficulties.

The increasingly desperate plight of the institution was brought to the attention of the General Synod, which responded in 1815 with a plan to transform Queen's into a "Theological College." There were to be three professors of theology appointed by the Synod and one professor of mathematics and natural philosophy appointed by the Trustees. The Trustees were to pay the full salary of their professor and half the salaries of the professors appointed by the Synod. In addition to giving instruction in theology, the Synod's professors would devote a portion of their time to teaching in the undergraduate department, which would be regarded as an appendage to the theological school. The Trustees evidenced willingness to accept this plan in principle, but problems arose over matters of detail, and no agreement resulted.

The time had now arrived to confront an inescapable decision. In April 1816, the Board heard a detailed financial report, which showed that over the three preceding years the College had operated at a loss of nearly $4,000 and that other debts, largely incurred in connection with the new building, amounted to over $7,000. No means were in sight to eliminate these deficits. The Board therefore concluded that instruction in the College should be suspended and that the College building should be turned over to the General Synod for the use of the theological school. One room would be reserved for the Grammar School as well as one wing to serve as a residence for the headmaster of the School. Final action on this plan was deferred for a month and was then taken by a vote of eleven to four. The proposal was next communicated to the General Synod, which expressed mild regret at the closing of the College, declared its inability to afford any assistance, and accepted the Trustees' offer with respect to the use of the College building. When the Trustees assembled in September 1816, they heard the response of the Synod to their proposal and resolved "that the exercises of the College be suspended on the rising of this Board." Queen's College then held its final commencement.

At the very time that the College was passing out of existence, the theological school was gaining new strength. In 1814 the Trustees received by deed of gift from the Reverend Elias Van Bunschooten a sum that ultimately amounted to $17,000, for the specific purpose of aiding students preparing for the ministry. Although the Trustees were the actual custodians of the fund, its disposition was to be directed by the General Synod. A year later a fund of $2,000 was received from Rebecca Knox for similar purposes. Presumably these gifts were directed to the Trustees of Queen's because at the time the General Synod was not an incorporated body and doubt existed respecting its ability to hold funds. In a related area, a second professor was added to the theological staff when two churches agreed to underwrite his salary for a period of six years. Possessed of free accommodations, fortified with ample funds for assisting needy students, and with an augmented faculty, the Seminary was enabled to survive while the College languished.

The suspension of the College did not release the Queen's Trustees from all their problems. On the contrary, for the next several years they were engaged in a long-drawn-out controversy with the General Synod that was ultimately to have a crucial effect on the future history of the institution. The basis for the discord lay in the fact that the Trustees remained in full control of the "professoral fund," the Van Bunschooten fund, and the Knox fund, the proceeds of which were to be applied to the work of the Theological Seminary, over which the General Synod had jurisdiction. Obviously, such a situation was bound to be productive of discord.

A crisis developed almost immediately when, in 1817, the General Synod proposed that the Seminary should be moved to New York City. The wealthy churches there had for several years declined to contribute to the support of the New Brunswick institution, but now they pledged $6,000 annually if the school were relocated. The Queen's Trustees argued the superior advantages of New Brunswick, remote as it was from the evil influences of the metropolis, and also contended that the articles of agreement entered into in 1807 would be infringed if the school were moved. But their most effective point was that they could not apply the funds under their control "to the support of the [Theological] School except in connection with Queen's College."

Clearly rebuffed in this exchange, the Synod then launched a series of efforts to wrest from the Trustees the funds in question. Charges were made that the Trustees had not exercised due care in handling the funds, and there were repeated conferences between committees appointed by both parties. Finally, in 1820, the Trustees made a shrewd counterproposal; they would turn the "professoral fund" over to the General Synod if that body would agree to keep the Seminary in New Brunswick. As was anticipated, this proposal was not accepted because the General Synod wanted to move the Seminary. The Trustees then made a candid statement of their position:

> If the Genl. Synod shall be of opinion that it is the best to remove the Theological Seminary to some other place—we have not a word to say—the Synod are the Watchmen and we submit in silence, but in such case, the funds raised and given for a Theological Seminary

at New Brunswick will remain as they are, in the hands of the Board of Trustees; and if there should be no professor of Theology here to claim the interest arising therefrom, it will be suffered to accumulate and may perhaps be very useful to some generation after us.

Thus the two parties remained deadlocked; by the very nature of their involved financial relationship they were tied together in an inharmonious partnership.

The wrangling continued. The Church body proposed that the issues in dispute should be submitted for decision to the Chancellors of New Jersey and New York, but the Trustees—having nothing to gain from such a verdict—repulsed this suggestion. Time, however, was running against the Trustees. Their large debts remained unpaid, and they were constantly pressed by their bankers to discharge their obligations. There were those high in the councils of the General Synod who sensed this situation and were disposed to force the Trustees to accept their terms. This opportunity was apparently close at hand when in 1823 the Trustees felt obliged to offer to sell the College building to the General Synod in order to pay a $4,000 bank debt and repay $2,212 that had been borrowed from the "professoral fund." Fortunately, the prevailing disposition in the General Synod was undergoing a change. The sentiment now was for peace and compromise. Instead of pressing its advantage to the full, which might well have meant the complete extinction of Queen's College, the General Synod sought a constructive solution for the problem. The Trustees responded in kind, and a new round of negotiations began that was to lead to the revival of the College on a permanent basis.

Chapter Three

Rutgers College:
Child of the Covenant

Queen's College presented a forlorn, even desolate appearance in 1823. A student in the Grammar School at the time described the scene. "The College," he recalled, "unadorned by cupola or dome, stood lonely and bare, upon its bleak little eminence, exposed to the scorching rays of sun in summer, without a tree to shade us as we approached it, or to break for us in winter the chilling blasts of the whistling north wind." Here and there a few stunted trees struggled for their existence, but they did not relieve the drabness of the landscape and left ample areas for the boys to play their games of corner ball. "The grounds were surrounded and divided into three parts by a rough board fence, except in front, where the enclosure and the intersecting lines were drawn by a white washed paling, not always in good repair; for sometimes the cow could stray out of pasture in the east or west end; or a stray pig could wander in, threatening serious damage to the vegetable or corn patch planted in a portion of either lot for the benefit of the President or Rector's commissariat of subsistence."

Much of the interior of the building remained unfinished and the entire structure was in need of repair. The east wing was occupied by a theological professor; in the west wing resided the rector of the Grammar School. Only one classroom, or hall, was in use—the west front room on the ground floor—and there the school students assembled for their daily recitations. The large rooms on the second floor, later the library and chapel, had not yet been plastered, and the third floor was in even more primitive condition. The remnants of the College library consisted of a few old books in Dutch; of the "philosophical apparatus" all that remained was a large spy glass, or telescope. When Professor Philip Milledoler and his family took possession of the east wing in 1825 the place was so depressing that his wife, who seldom gave vent to her emotions, "burst into a flood of tears."

Bleak though the prospect appeared, there continued to be those who clung to the hope that the dormant college might somehow be revived. A half-century of discouragement and frustration, broken only now and then by a glimpse of success, had not extinguished that hope. Foremost among those who refused to concede defeat and who provided leadership in the movement to revive the College was Jacob Rutsen Hardenbergh, Jr. Son of the old Dominie who had served with such devotion as the first president of Queen's, Hardenbergh had graduated from the College in 1788, entered the legal profession, and became president of the Bank of New Brunswick. Elected to the Board of Trustees in 1792, he was to serve in that office for nearly fifty years. Between 1822 and 1825 he was the key figure in the intricate negotiations that gave to the College a new and lasting existence.

Many circumstances combined to create conditions favorable to the College. First in point of time was the successful effort on the part of the General Synod to procure an endowment for the so-called second theological professorship. Ever since 1815 this professorship had been financed from year to year by certain consistories, but in June 1822 the Synod appointed a committee, of which Hardenbergh was the most active member, to raise for the chair $25,000 by general subscriptions in the Particular Synod of New York. Within a year the amount had been oversubscribed. The success of the effort may have been due in part to the fact that the Synod was now in a position to hold and administer its own funds, having been granted corporate powers by the New York legislature in 1819. It was largely because the Synod had previously lacked such powers that the old "professoral fund" as well as the Van Bunschooten and Knox funds had been vested in the Trustees of the College, thereby producing mutual suspicions and difficulties and inhibiting fund-raising efforts on the part of the Synod. From this point on, the Synod was in command of its own funds, and this circumstance profoundly affected its relations to the College Trustees.

While the campaign to endow the second theological professorship was under way, the Trustees were stimulated to action by the prospect of large resources from an unexpected quarter. The New York firm of McIntyre and Yates, specialists in the management of lotteries, brought to the Trustees' attention the fact that the College still retained some rights from the old lottery of 1812, which they proposed to purchase. By August 1822, an agreement had been reached whereby, contingent upon the approval of the state, McIntyre and Yates would conduct the lottery and guarantee a return of $20,000 to the College. After some initial resistance, the legislature sanctioned the arrangement, with the provision that the money obtained was to be invested as an endowment for a professorship of mathematics. Drawings began early in 1824 and continued over the course of a year, when the state intervened and enjoined any further proceedings. Despite this action, which led to involved negotiations both with the state and the lottery firm, McIntyre and Yates honored their commitment and turned over to the Trustees in annual installments the total amount stipulated. Thus by 1825 the College had a fund in hand to pay the major portion of a professor's salary.

The next step was to liquidate the debts that were owed to the local bank and the Synod. The solution to this problem was to sell the College building and lot to the Synod. An agreement was reached in July 1823 whereby the Synod agreed to pay the debt owed to the bank, approximately $4,000, plus interest, and forgive the debt of $2,212 incurred by the Trustees when they had "borrowed" that amount from the "professoral fund" in order to meet building expenses. Various complications developed in working out the proper legal arrangements, and ultimately the Synod had to secure an act of the New Jersey legislature to enable it to own property in that state, but the title finally passed in 1827. Meanwhile, however, a committee of the Synod took charge of the building and spent about $2,300 finishing all the rooms except those on the third floor, repairing the roof, erecting new fences, and planting trees in front of the building. The sale of the College property to the Synod afforded relief from pressing financial difficulties, but it was not without unfortunate consequences, and the Trustees came to regret their action.

Free from debt and provided with funds from the lottery, the Trustees began to formulate a plan to revive the College. In its essentials, it bore many resemblances to the proposal for a "Theological College" that had been considered in 1815. That is, it was contemplated that the theological professors, in addition to instructing the Seminary students, should devote a portion of their time to teaching undergraduates. The feasibility of this arrangement became clear when the venerable Livingston, nominal president and senior theological professor, died in January 1825. He was succeeded in the Seminary by the Reverend Dr. Philip Milledoler, who, unlike his honored predecessor, was in a position to undertake the additional burden of teaching in the College. As the plan matured, the conclusion was reached that it would be desirable, if not essential, to create a third theological professorship, and in May 1825 the Trustees were ready to approach the General Synod with concrete proposals.

The revival of the College was to be a cooperative enterprise of the Trustees and the Synod and was to involve as well a close relationship between the College and the Seminary. Despite the record of contention, disappointment, and even rivalry that had clouded the previous relations between the Trustees and the Synod, both parties obviously shared common interests, and with past differences adjusted there was now a willingness on both sides to undertake the joint enterprise. At the urging of the Trustees, the Synod in June 1825 appointed committees to secure the endowment for the third professorship. While the fund was being raised, chiefly in the Particular Synod of Albany, the New York City churches agreed to underwrite the professor's salary. At the same session, the Synod appointed a committee to prepare a detailed plan for the resumption of College work, in consultation with the Queen's Trustees. By September, when the Synod met in special session in New Brunswick, coincident with a meeting of the Board of Trustees, the subscriptions for the third professorship had been obtained and a plan, known as the Covenant of 1825, awaited the approval of the two bodies.

The Covenant made possible the resumption of College work, but it effectively limited the authority of the Trustees and all but placed the College under the complete control of the Synod. The Synod agreed to allow the Trustees to use such parts of the College building as might be required and to assign to the theological professors such duties in the College as it deemed appropriate. The Trustees were to appoint one of the theological professors as president, and they were required to name as their treasurer the treasurer of the General Synod. As their major contribution to the joint enterprise, the Trustees assumed responsibility for naming a professor of mathematics and a professor of languages and paying their salaries, but no additional professors could be appointed, nor could salaries be altered, without the concurrence of the Synod. If the College was unable to pay the salaries of the two professors, the Synod might be called upon to make up the deficiency. However, the Synod reserved the right to dissolve the connection with the College if it could not be sustained without impairing the funds devoted to the Theological Seminary. Finally, the course of studies, and all regulations relating to government and discipline, were to be determined jointly by the faculty and a Board of Superintendents, made up of three trustees and three Synod appointees.

At the time, many who were involved in devising the arangement viewed it as a temporary expedient. The expectation was that when the Trustees developed their financial resources to the point where they could support a full corps of professors, as well as a president, they might assume the autonomous status defined in their charter. But because they were so inextricably connected with the Synod, the Trustees were to find it all but impossible to move toward the desired goal. Moreover, even if the Synod and the Trustees had approached their joint task with the best possible understanding and good will, which unfortunately was not the case, the relationship was bound to produce difficulties.

In accordance with the principles laid down in the Covenant, specific duties were assigned to the theological professors. The Professor of

Didactic Theology was to teach moral philosophy and evidences of Christianity, the Professor of Biblical Literature was assigned logic, belles lettres, and elements of criticism, and the Professor of Church History gave instruction in metaphysics and the philosophy of the human mind. In turn, the College's Professor of Languages was to instruct Seminary students in Hebrew and Greek.

There was strong agreement that piety should be given high place in the College's program:

> The General Synod and the board of trustees, deeply sensible of the importance of instilling the principles of Christianity into the minds of the rising generation and to this end render the institution under their care most beneficial to the community, for promoting the interests of morals and religion, as well as the progress of science, mutually determine that, besides the literary exercises during the week . . . [there should be] a regular attendance morning and evening upon prayers by the students in both departments.

In addition to the twice-daily prayers, the students were required to attend a recitation on the Bible each Sunday, conducted by the president, and a discourse "on the Fundamental doctrines and principles of the Christian religion, maintained and received by our reformed Churches." The remainder of each Lord's day was to be spent in attending services at any church in town. Taken together with the decidedly religious orientation of much of the regular instruction, this regimen was well calculated to produce informed, if not inspired, Christians.

In the process of being reborn, the College appropriately acquired a new name. Dr. Milledoler, who had been installed as the Professor of Didactic Theology in May 1825, and who was also a member of the Board of Trustees and an influential figure in the General Synod, described how the change was made.

> Having previously conversed with Mr. Jacob R. Hardenbergh on the expediency of Changing the Name from Queens to Rutgers College, and he having heartily approved thereof, I proposed that change and Name to a large Company of Members of the Synod who dined with me during the Session [September 14–16, 1825], when it was agreed to use their influence to obtain a Unanimous Vote, which was done accordingly and Measures taken to obtain the Sanction of the Legislature of this State.

The legislature responded by making the necessary amendments to the charter in 1825, and the name of Queen's passed swiftly, and seemingly without regret, into oblivion.

Colonel Henry Rutgers, the recipient of the signal honor, was among the most prominent laymen in the Dutch Church, president of its Board of Corporation, and an elder in the church that Dr. Milledoler had served in New York City. Descended from an old New York Dutch family, he possessed valuable land holdings in the city. Rutgers had graduated from King's College, served in the Revolution, and held various posts of civic importance in New York. A bachelor, he devoted a large part of his means to philanthropic objectives, especially schools and churches.

In honoring Rutgers, the Synod and the Trustees were paying their respects to a man highly esteemed for his Christian qualities. They may also have had some expectation that the good Colonel would use his vast influence within the denomination, to say nothing of his considerable means, for the benefit of the College. He did, in fact, deposit his bond for $5,000 with the Synod, with the stipulation that the interest was to be paid annually to the College. In addition, he purchased the bell that was to peal forth from the new cupola erected on the College building through the generosity of Stephen Van Rensselaer. Perhaps of greatest significance, the adoption of the new name symbolized the addition of a new constituency in support of the College. Queen's had been sustained almost entirely by local men. Now an influential group from New York City, including Milledoler, Abraham Van Nest, the Reverend John Knox, the Reverend Isaac Ferris, and others, assumed positions of prominence on the Board of Trustees and brought modest additional resources to the institution.

At the same momentous meeting at which the Covenant was adopted and the change of name was agreed upon, Philip Milledoler was elected president. A Dutch Church minister in New York City since 1813, he had previously held pastorates in both German Reformed and Presbyterian churches. Now in his fiftieth year, he was to undertake the dual responsibility of guiding the renascent College and serving as professor in the Seminary. Genuinely devoted to the College, he soon became embroiled in controversies that severely limited his effectiveness. Many of his difficulties stemmed from his inordinate sensitivity and his intense suspicion of his colleagues. Some were the result of his identification with the "ultras" within the denomination, who sought to hold fast to the old doctrines and traditions in the face of attacks by the "liberals." Students, especially those in the Seminary, condemned his teaching methods, which emphasized rote memorization of prescribed texts. Altogether, his position was not to be a happy one, and ultimately it became completely untenable.

All of the basic preparations for the College having been made by mid-September, the Trustees decided, despite the lateness of the season, to begin work at the earliest opportunity. Robert Adrain was lured away from Columbia by the promise of a salary of $1,750, to become the Professor of Mathematics, and the Reverend William C. Brownlee, who, like Adrain, had taught for a brief period at Queen's, left his academy at Basking Ridge for the post of Professor of Languages. With this small but able staff, augmented by the three theological professors, the College was reactivated with thirty students in attendance on November 14, 1825.

The "literary institution," as it was commonly referred to in order to distinguish it from the closely allied Seminary, adhered closely in curriculum and organization to the pattern that had become traditional in the previous century. If any change was discernible, it was the increased emphasis placed upon piety and the enhanced role of clergymen, both in the faculty and on the Board of Trustees. If the Age of Jackson into which the College was reborn was anti-authoritarian, secular, and dynamic, such influences had little observable effect within the bounds of the campus. There the views were toward the ancient past and an eternal future. Conservatism was the watchword, intellectual discipline was the immediate desideratum, and salvation was the ultimate goal.

The basic routine of the College was defined in statutes formulated by the Board of Superintendents in collaboration with the faculty. The president, professors, and tutors were entrusted with responsibility for conducting the institution in accordance with the statutes; no longer were designated Trustees to serve as members of the faculty. Faculty meetings, over which the president presided, were held monthly. The College year was comprised of three terms, extending from September 15 to December 21, January 7 to April 7, and May 1 to the third Wednesday in July, on which day the annual commencement was held. Each class was examined as a unit at the end of a term in the presence of the entire faculty; a student's rank was determined "in proportion to his moral behavior, his diligence and attainments in the several branches of science passed through, and his talents." Seniors were examined four weeks before commencement on all the studies they had pursued over the four-year course. Proper moral and religious behavior was enjoined upon the students by the requirements governing attendance at prayers and church services as well as by stringent penalties for a lengthy list of proscribed offenses. Tuition was set at forty dollars a year, plus fees of five dollars upon entrance and five dollars when the diploma was granted. Admission requirements remained much the same as a half-century earlier—knowledge of Latin and Greek and proficiency in arithmetic as far as the rule of proportion. As in the past, most students entered with Sophomore standing.

The curriculum was heavily concentrated on the classics, mathematics, and the several branches of philosophy. Latin and Greek were studied throughout all four years. In addition to the ancient authors, the Freshmen mastered Hassler's *Arithmetic,* Bonnycastle's *Algebra,* and Woodbridge's *Geography.* In the Sophomore year, the students proceeded to Legendre's *Geometry* and, for trigonometry and navigation, Day's *Mathematics,* as well as Blair's *Lectures on Rhetoric.* The Junior year featured Campbell's *Philosophy of Rhetoric* and Young's *Analytical Geometry* and *Differential Calculus.* With this solid, if somewhat stultifying background, the Seniors were introduced to a wide variety of studies, some of which were pursued for but one term. Included in the intellectual bill of fare were natural philosophy, Christian ethics, philosophy of the mind, history and chronology, evidences of Revelation, and political economy, utilizing at various times such standard texts as Cavallo's *Natural Philosphy,* Butler's *Analogy,* Hedge's *Logic,* Kames' *Elements of Criticism,* and Story's *Commentaries on the Constitution of the United States.*

The burdens on the two professors who devoted all of their efforts to the "literary institution" were, by modern standards, considerable. Professor Theodore Strong, who succeeded Adrain in 1827 and served until 1861, not only taught all of the mathematics but instructed the Freshmen in geography and the Seniors in natural philosophy. A mathematician of high reputation, he was a frequent contributor to mathematical journals and an active member of several learned societies. The Professor of Languages, a post held from 1832 to 1840 by the Reverend David Ogilby, a graduate of Columbia and an Episcopal clergyman, taught the four-year sequence of courses in the classics, including ancient geography. The remaining courses, chiefly those in the Junior and Senior years, were conducted by the three theological professors, of whom the most colorful and beloved was the Reverend James Spencer Cannon. A gentleman of the old school, largely self-educated, he clung until his death in 1852 to the dress and manners of the Federal era—knee breeches, silk stockings, silver buckles, and stiff, broad brimmed hat. Dignified but kindly in manner, and a fervent Democrat in politics, he won the affection of the students for his warm interest in their affairs and for his able teaching of metaphysics and the philosophy of the human mind. President Milledoler gave courses in Christian ethics, moral philosophy, and political economy and Professor John DeWitt was responsible for logic and belles lettres.

The prescribed curriculum underwent little change for fifteen years, with one notable exception. Science had had a modest place in the College since the beginning under the rubric of natural philosophy, taught by the Professor of Mathematics. Although the content of the instruction varied, it dealt essentially with elementary principles of physics and astronomy. That the Trustees attached considerable importance to this branch of study is evident from the fact that they appropriated nearly

$2,000 from their meagre funds for "philosophical apparatus," including $750 for a telescope. Certain members of the Board, with an amateur dedication to experimental science, were interested in expanding instruction in the field, and in 1826, they made it possible for John Finch, an itinerant Englishman who had some competence as a geologist, to use one of the rooms in the College to deliver a course of fifteen lectures on chemistry. These lectures, open to students as well as townspeople, were repeated in subsequent years, and a local Society of Natural History, which collected cabinets of minerals and acquired a small scientific library, was established. No doubt encouraged by the favorable response to these extracurricular offerings, the Trustees were soon considering the addition of a regular course of lectures on geology, mineralogy, and chemistry, and in October 1830 they appointed Dr. Lewis Caleb Beck as Professor of Chemistry and Natural History.

Beck had graduated from Union College in 1817, studied medicine at the College of Physicians and Surgeons, and practiced briefly in St. Louis and Albany. Diverted from medicine to the study of natural history, he had published extensively in such diverse fields as botany, mineralogy, and chemistry and worked on the early geological survey in New York. He was to remain on the Rutgers faculty, with some interruptions, until his death in 1853, meanwhile retaining connections with other institutions—notably the Albany Medical College—because his College appointment did not require his full services.

Beck's role in the College was an extremely limited one during the first decade of his appointment. Lacking any endowment for the chair, the Trustees were able to offer a stipend of but $200, which had to be raised annually by subscriptions. In return for this meagre remuneration, Beck lectured on chemistry and botany for five weeks in the spring term of 1831. Essentially the same arrangement obtained during the two following years. In 1833, at the urging of the faculty, Beck's salary was doubled, and he devoted the whole of the first term to lecturing to both the Junior and Senior classes.

After five years of such partial and ill-paid services, Professor Beck submitted a lengthy statement to the Trustees requesting them to decide "whether the Chemical Department in this Institution shall be abolished or permanently established." Observing that chemistry was regularly taught "in every respectable collegiate Institution in our country & even in many of our Academies," he expressed the opinion that to exclude this branch of study would have an injurious effect on the College. The Trustees evidenced their good intentions and their woeful lack of means by resolving to secure an endowment of $20,000 for the chair, having received assurances that the recently organized alumni of the College would raise $5,000 and that the Synod had commended the cause to its constituency. After a year, however, the effort was abandoned, and at this point Beck, understandably discouraged, accepted an appointment at New York University. A year later, however, he returned to New Brunswick and lectured for one term each year to the Juniors on "Elements of Chemistry" and to the Seniors on "Chemistry Applied to the Arts." After 1840 his tenure was extended to two terms at a salary of $1,000, and he was then able to add courses in mineralogy, physiology, and botany to his schedule. Professor Strong, meanwhile, continued to teach physics and astronomy, based upon Cavallo's *Natural Philosophy*.

As Beck correctly noted, Rutgers was following the trend toward increased emphasis on science that was evident in all colleges. In 1795 John MacLean had pioneered in lecturing on chemistry at Princeton. Benjamin Silliman, the towering scientific figure of his age, had been appointed professor of chemistry and natural history at Yale in 1802, and in 1824 Amos Eaton began his extraordinarily fruitful teaching at the new Rensselaer Institute. By the 1830's experimental science had won a secure place in American colleges. Its practical applications were appreciated and respected and, as taught by religiously oriented professors, its findings with respect to God's creations involved no conflict with piety.

From time to time the Trustees considered the establishment of additional professorships, but they were constantly frustrated by their lack of adequate funds. In 1830, at the same time that Beck was appointed, they studied the expediency of naming a professor of law and a professor of anatomy and physiology, but no action resulted. Five years later, stimulated by the prospect of a legacy restricted to such a purpose, they hastened to appoint a professor of law—Cornelius L. Hardenbergh—who actually delivered his inaugural lecture in January 1836. Unfortunately, the bequest did not materialize, and Hardenbergh's tenure, which was "without pecuniary compensation," lapsed.

The formal education of the students was carried on very largely through the thorough study of assigned textbooks, which were rarely changed, but modest use was also made of the library that jointly served both the College and the Seminary. As soon as the College reopened, small sums were spent by the Synod and by the Trustees to supplement the few volumes, many of them in Dutch, that constituted the old library. The library was open for one hour a week, on Friday mornings, with one of the Senior theological students in charge. From the ledgers that he maintained, listing the books borrowed by each student, it is evident that general works of literature and theological treatises were most in demand. The insignificant holdings were multiplied several times over when, in 1832, the Synod purchased for some $2,000 the excellent library of the late Professor DeWitt. Although theology predominated, every branch of knowledge then taught at the College was well represented, and the authorities took pride in publishing a printed catalogue of the entire library, which amounted to 2,254 volumes.

The conditions under which the library operated left much to be desired. A new set of rules adopted in 1835 provided for the appointment of a faculty member as librarian, and it was his obligation to arrange the books in proper order, maintain registers of loans and acquisitions, and serve borrowers while the library was open, now only a half hour a week. Members of the faculty had virtually unlimited privileges, but students could not withdraw at one time more than one folio, two quartos, and two octavos or smaller volumes at one time. Folios might be kept for five weeks; octavos for but three weeks. Each student paid one dollar semi-annually "for the use and increase of the library." When the new incumbent, Professor Alexander McClelland, took charge, he found the books in complete disorder—"Owen on Communion with God was found with Tristram Shandy on the one side and Woodbridge's Geography on the other"—and a substantial number were missing. Methodically, he arranged all the volumes into ten classes, each of which occupied a separate portion of the shelves, and with the assistance of a theologue endeavored with moderate success to enforce system and order. Housekeeping, rather than building, was the chief preoccupation of the librarian, with the result that as late as 1845 the total collection numbered no more than 5,000 volumes.

The formal educational program prescribed by the Trustees and the faculty, intended as it was to strengthen the mental faculties and provide the students with a highly ornamental store of knowledge, allowed little scope for genuine intellectual inquiry nor did it afford adequate opportunities for creative self-expression. The heavy diet of classics, mathematics, and theologically-oriented philosophy, didactically presented by teachers of limited pedagogical skills, was scarcely intended to excite interest or arouse curiosity; neither did it appear to have much relevance to everyday concerns. Occasionally, in the colleges of that era, a daring president or an inspired group within a faculty sought to introduce innovations in the standard curriculum, but the heavy weight of authority and collegiate inertia usually brought defeat to such efforts; and the old tradition remained. Because they made so little in the way of concessions to the new society that was emerging in America after 1815, the colleges, although they multiplied in numbers, continued to find remarkably little demand for their services. In New Jersey, Princeton rarely had as many as 250 students prior to 1850, while Rutgers' enrollment never rose above 85.

The College scene, however, embraced more than the regime of classicism and piety embodied in the formal curriculum. In part because those in authority took such a restricted view of the role of the College, the students proceeded to create their own institutions to meet the intellectual and social needs that the College ignored. Because Rutgers, unlike most colleges, lacked dormitories and dining halls, the students were unusually free to devise their own way of life. Collegiate life, in a broad sense, embraced two distinct spheres. One—controlled by the faculty and Trustees—was tradition-bound, sterile, and even irrelevant. The other—created by the undergraduates—was lively, innovative, and meaningful. The relative contributions of the two spheres to the educational process is not precisely determinable, but certainly the extracurricular cannot be slighted.

Much of the intellectual and social life of the students was concentrated in the two literary societies, Peithessophian and Philoclean, both of which were organized within a week or two of the reopening of the College. They conformed to the general pattern that prevailed in virtually every college during that era, offering their members training in declamation, composition, and debate as well as the satisfactions to be derived from membership in closely knit social groups. Within a year after they were organized, both societies had developed a range of activities that varied little over the seventy-year period in which they flourished.

The societies were secret, but they were not exclusive, and in time nearly every undergraduate was elected to one or the other. Members of the faculty were instrumental in bringing the societies into existence and were elected to membership, although only the president might join both societies. Honorary members, usually men of some literary or political prominence, were elected in great numbers and to them, as well as to graduates, the societies looked for financial aid in building their libraries and furnishing their rooms. Each society had its distinctive badge and ribbon—pink for Peitho and blue for Philo—as well as elaborate rituals and intricately contrived constitutions.

Meetings were held weekly, customarily for an entire evening. At first these were held in rooms in the College, but in 1830, when a new building was erected for the Grammar School, two rooms on the second floor were assigned to the societies, and there they installed their libraries and conducted their affairs. Each meeting featured performances by several students in declamation and composition, and a debate on a topic announced in advance. Matters were so arranged that every member would be called on to participate at least once each month. Committees of criticism evaluated the performances, and the debate was judged by both the audience and the president. The high point of each term was the election of officers, which produced a good deal of horseplay and excitement.

Both societies were zealous in building their respective libraries, which before many years outstripped the College library in size. Featuring current works of literature, biography, history, and travel, as well as the leading periodicals, they provided a basis for a very different kind of intellectual experience from that offered by the curriculum. Through them the students enhanced their knowledge of literature and contemporary affairs and acquired tastes and values not derivable from their formal studies.

In addition to the activities carried on within the precincts of their well-appointed meeting rooms, the societies arranged two public occasions that were among the high points of the College year. The Junior Exhibition, held the evening before commencement, featured four Junior orators selected by each society. First arranged on a trial basis in 1826, it became a fixed part of the College program in 1827 and endured, with some vicissitudes, down to 1923. The Exhibition was traditionally held in a local church and attracted a capacity audience of friends, townspeople, and derisive underclassmen, who often marred the dignity of the occasion by their heckling and their pranks. Nevertheless, in the era before intercollegiate athletics, no event excited more interest, or engendered more intense rivalry, than the Junior Exhibition. Also during commencement week, the societies alternated in securing an outstanding personality to deliver an address under their joint sponsorship. Especially memorable was the oration by William Wirt in 1830.

The societies played a large, even an indispensable role in the College, for they engaged the interest of the undergraduates in intellectual activities, successfully met an obvious social need, provided opportunities for leadership, and even helped to bridge the chasm that separated the faculty from the students in their formal relationship. They constituted a strong cohesive force within the College and stimulated lasting feelings of loyalty among their graduates. Indeed, to returning alumni, the halls of Peitho and Philo, rather than the professorial classrooms, seem to have evoked the warmest memories of their college years. Recognizing that the societies were an essential feature of the College, the faculty and the Trustees gave them every encouragement, even to providing them with rooms. Relations between them and the authorities were usually harmonious, although when they felt that their autonomy was unduly threatened, the societies were capable of taking a firm position, secure in the knowledge that they could count on considerable sympathy from their graduates and honorary members. No doubt the very absorption of the students in their societies served to divert them from an outright rebellion against the curriculum and, in this sense, to inhibit academic reform.

So strong was the hold of the literary societies on the small student body that other organizations were of minor importance. The Bible

Society and the Temperance Society, both organized in 1829, reflected prevailing concerns with piety and reform. In a different area, the Philosophical Society was formed in 1833, with the encouragement of Professor Beck, to further interest in the collecting of specimens of natural history. But the full flowering of the extracurricular did not occur until after the Civil War.

The students who were drawn to the College were a remarkably homogeneous group. The overwhelming majority of them came from New Jersey and New York; they were predominantly from Dutch Church backgrounds and characteristically bore such names as Frelinghuysen, Blauvelt, Terhune, DeWitt, or Van Liew. Prepared in local private academies, or by their ministers, they were often no more than fourteen years old when they entered, although many were as old as twenty. Whatever their career objectives might have been when they embarked upon their studies, the vast majority of them ultimately became lawyers or physicians, with clergymen forming the next largest category; relatively few of them entered upon business careers.

Arriving in New Brunswick, the prospective students were examined orally by the professors of mathematics and languages to determine whether they were properly qualified and what class they should enter. Their next important step was to select a boarding house, where they might obtain their room and meals for two dollars a week or a trifle more. Many houses, it would seem, included eligible young ladies as members of the family; the experience of dining *en famille* in such pleasantly mixed company was thought to exert a civilizing effect on the young men.

From time to time consideration was given to erecting dormitories, but not until near the end of the century was such a plan effectuated. Reliance on the boarding houses was partly a matter of financial necessity, but there was opposition to dormitories on other grounds. A Trustees' committee that dealt with the matter in 1835 raised the question: "What System is on the whole best calculated to secure industry in study and sound morals and to prevent idleness, immorality and irregularity of conduct?" The committee recognized that there were valid objections "to the collecting of a large body of Students in one edifice on the ground that such an arrangement is unfriendly to domestic feelings and habits and to the polish of manners which intercourse with the ladies of a family is calculated to give." At the same time they argued that "During Study hours the Young Men should be in their rooms and attending to their studies and have no business to be loitering with ladies. . . ." Moreover, the faculty was expected to stand in the relation of parents to the students, a responsibility they could scarcely fulfill if the students were dispersed throughout the town. Without reflecting on either the faculty or the students, the committee voiced fears for the moral welfare of the students under the existing system. "Will they be found especially during evenings in their rooms, or owing to the want of inspection and restraint, will they not be strongly tempted to be frequently out of their rooms, and is there not danger but they may be out at improper hours of the night and that they may visit places where they will be exposed to strong temptations to vice?" The solution proposed was to have the students reside and study in a dormitory but take their meals at boarding houses in town. "A stronger restraint will be thrown in the way of forming irregular and vicious habits," their report concluded, "and thus both the intellectual and moral improvement of the Students will be promoted; while by permitting them to board in private families all the advantages which result from the present System will be secured." As was to happen frequently in the future, these proposals were tabled and came to naught.

Whether the boarding-house system was productive of the evils that the committee feared, or of the virtues claimed by its defenders, is far from clear. That the students did go abroad at night and that they did indeed visit places where they were subject to temptation are evident. But nocturnal adventures were not unknown in colleges possessed of dormitories. The students gave no indication that they were discontented with their housing arrangements, and serious breaches of propriety arising out of such informal living arrangements are remarkably rare in the records of the faculty. For better or for worse, the students formed an integral part of the society of New Brunswick, developing close friendships with townspeople, attending local churches, being entertained frequently by mothers with eligible daughters, and engaging in such diversions as the city offered.

Despite the strong religious emphasis within the College and the continual injunctions against frivolity and vice, the young men were as high-spirited as those of any generation. Confronted with a professor whom they disliked, they could devise such wicked torments as throwing noxious substances in his stove, or discharging pistols outside his room, or even setting fire to his privy. Among themselves they enjoyed rollicking evenings at Stelle's tavern, moonlight sleigh rides to Bound Brook in company with local belles, and elaborate pranks, such as the famous mock duel between Reynolds and Vredenburgh. Periodically the pursuit of worldly pleasures would give way to the experience of conversion. The most notable revival occurred in 1837. President Milledoler noted in his diary: "At the Assembling of the Students on the 1st of May, I observed an uncommon seriousness and solemnity among the students of the College. . . . The flame has now broken out and appears to be spreading rapidly. The students have frequent meetings for Prayers, and such as are pious and impressed are much engaged in seeking the Salvation of their fellows." The revival, initiated by the fervent preaching of two students from the Baptist Theological School, spread through the local churches and soon pervaded the campus. Obviously affected by the experience, twelve of the twenty-one graduates of the Class of 1837 entered the ministry.

Profound changes in the local scene influenced the College and its members in these years. Given its location, New Brunswick felt the full impact of the transportation revolution in the decade of the 1830's. The Delaware and Raritan Canal, completed in 1834, passed within a stone's throw of the campus and emptied into the river below the town. Within a few years, the New Jersey Railroad and the Camden and Amboy Railroad linked the city to New York and Philadelphia, running so close to the campus that the noise of the trains reverberated through the classrooms. Now the character of the town began to alter, as industry developed rapidly and new immigrant stocks entered the community. In contrast to the stability and isolation of the academic curriculum, the city was being transformed and was becoming ever more closely tied to an expanding New York metropolis. Immured though they were in the study of ancient civilizations and in the contemplation of enduring verities, the students could scarcely be unaware of the fact that a new and dynamic society was in the process of being created beyond the confines of the campus.

During the first few years after its revival, the College seemed destined to surmount the difficulties that had blighted its first half century. Staffed with an able faculty, assured of adequate physical facilities, guided by new leaders, and sustained by a carefully matured agreement with the General Synod, it seemingly faced a promising future. Students appeared in adequate, if not overwhelming, numbers, and jointly with the faculty, they succeeded in creating a lively and relatively elaborate collegiate environment. Meanwhile, within the Board of Trustees and the Synod, vigorous interest in the welfare of the institution persisted for a time and produced modest achievements.

Finances remained a problem, for aside from the endowment that had been secured by the lottery for the mathematics professorship, the Trustees had no income-yielding funds. The old "professoral fund" that had been raised for Dr. John H. Livingston's professorship had dwindled to less than $10,000, and in 1828 it was transferred to the Synod on the condition that it be applied to the salary of a professor of theology in the College. The so-called "Old Fund," which dated back to the founding of the College, had a nominal value of $2,720, but the security for the fund became worthless and it was cleared from the books in 1830. In order to pay the professor of languages and meet other operational expenses the Trustees were compelled to resort to the practice of sending agents abroad to solicit subscriptions among the congregations. Year after year the solicitations continued, with Jacob R. Hardenbergh and Abraham Van Nest bearing, with Christian fortitude and perseverance, the heaviest responsibility for these necessary efforts. Although such endeavors kept the College going, they did not produce funds sufficient to add to the endowment.

In 1829 a special campaign was undertaken to raise money to construct a separate building for the Grammar School. With the College and the Seminary now in a flourishing condition, all of the available space in what is now called Old Queen's was required for their use; moreover, it was desirable to separate the young boys from the older students. Several committees were appointed to conduct solicitations, but ultimately the Trustees had to tap their slim capital resources and also borrow money to complete the building in 1830. Because the Synod held title to all the campus property, a lot was purchased nearby, at the corner of College Avenue and Somerset Street, on which the simple two-story brick building was erected. The school occupied the first floor, and in the two rooms above the literary societies were comfortably installed. The Grammar School, which had maintained an unbroken existence since 1768, continued to serve as a feeder for the College, operating under general regulations set forth in some detail by the Trustees in 1832. It offered both classical and English courses to a student body that rarely rose above sixty students and experienced many vicissitudes as the result of frequent changes in the rectorship.

A new and important source of aid for the College seemed to come into prospect with the organization in 1831 * of the Alumni Association. Although there were scarcely two hundred alumni at the time, the enthusiastic young graduates of the years since 1825 were fired with lofty ambitions. The Association sought not only the perpetuation of College friendships and the promotion of the interests of Rutgers but also the general advancement of the cause of education. Accordingly, at a meeting in 1834, several committees were appointed to inquire into the state of education everywhere in the world, not excluding New Jersey, and to explore the possibility of uniting with the alumni of other colleges to form an association "for the more equal diffusion of knowledge, and for raising the standard of public instruction throughout the Union." One committee interested itself in the cause of public schools in New Jersey, hoping to effect some reform, but "it was discovered to be impracticable from the state of public feeling on the subject, the condition of the

---

* The Association organized and adopted a constitution July 19, 1831, but this constitution was lost and a new one was adopted in 1833.

public treasury, and the limited amount of funds provided for the purpose." Narrowing their views to the immediate needs of the College, the Association in 1834 resolved to raise $5,000 toward endowing a chair for Professor Beck. Here again, their goal exceeded their capacity, and after several years they had to report that only $120 had actually been secured. In actuality the Association could do little more than hold an annual meeting at commencement, featuring an oration by one of its members. This pleasant custom did serve to maintain alumni interest in the institution, which in time was to yield results.

The years from 1825 to 1832 were full of achievement, but then the course of affairs altered abruptly, and for nearly a decade the College was embroiled in controversies that racked the Dutch Church, and the College had to struggle to maintain its very existence. Many influences combined to produce an environment of discord, but the essence of the problem was that the College became inextricably involved in deep-seated personal, factional, and sectional conflicts within the Church. Because of the captive position that it occupied under the Covenant of 1825, it could hardly avoid such entanglements, but the difficulties were compounded by the fact that President Milledoler himself was one of the principal sources of dissension.

The Church at this time, like other Protestant denominations, was divided into two factions usually referred to as the "liberals" and the "ultras." At issue were broad matters of policy regarding the liberalization of Church doctrine, cooperation with other denominations, the management of mission activities, and even the nature of the instruction to be offered in Sunday schools. The "ultra" forces had their greatest strength in New York City and numbered Milledoler as one of their staunchest figures while the "liberal" stronghold was in the Albany region, where John Ludlow exerted leadership. The "liberals" were hostile to Milledoler because of what they contended was his excessively rigid teaching as Professor of Didactic Theology and for his consistent support of the "ultra" faction. He was told that the College was "a Stink in the North." The cleavage was further exacerbated by the long-standing personal rivalry between Milledoler and Ludlow and by the strong connection that existed between the "liberals" and Union College, which in the previous two decades had supplied more ministers to the Church than had Rutgers. The conflict manifested itself even within the faculty of the College, where Milledoler became embroiled in feuds with certain of his colleagues—notably DeWitt and McClelland—whom he believed to be in league with his enemies.

Much of the criticism of the College, then, was motivated by a determination to bring about the downfall of Milledoler and the forces that he represented. But the specific charges levelled by the opposition often obscured this basic consideration. The chief complaint was that the College constituted a drag on the Theological Seminary because of the extra teaching burden that was imposed on the Seminary professors. Other contentions were that board was so high in New Brunswick that students were discouraged from attending the College, that the College sent too few graduates to the Seminary, that the alumni were indifferent to the welfare of the institution, and that the finances were improperly managed. While the controversy raged the harassed Trustees were obliged to devote most of their energies to defending the College on the floor of the Synod and in numerous joint committee sessions and to maintaining some semblance of harmony within the institution. Meanwhile, until the issues could be adjusted, they could anticipate little success in raising funds within the denomination.

The first of a series of crises erupted in 1832, when the Synod decreed that Professor McClelland was under no obligation to teach in the College and then appointed a special committee to examine whether it would be desirable to alter or abolish the connection that existed between the College and the Seminary. A heated controversy ensued, both within the committee and on the floor of the Synod in 1833, where a resolution to leave the Covenant unaltered passed by the narrow margin of thirty-two to twenty-eight. The Trustees succeeded in fending off the attack, which was led by Ludlow and his allies, by agreeing to appoint an additional professor, the Reverend Jacob J. Janeway. Janeway, who had recently retired from a long pastorate in Philadelphia, was to offer instruction in evidences of Christianity, in belles lettres, rhetoric, and political economy and was also to serve as vice-president of the College, all for a nominal salary. The objective was clearly to relieve Milledoler as well as McClelland of some of their teaching duties and to entrust the routine management of College affairs to Janeway.

The critics renewed their attack in 1836, insisting that the theological professors were overburdened by their services to the College. In the negotiations that followed, the Trustees proposed a plan whereby the Queen's building would be reconveyed to them, the services rendered by the theological professors would be reduced, and, as soon as funds permitted, a new president—not selected from among the theological professors—would be elected. The Synod committee that dealt with the matter in 1837 acknowledged after due investigation that the professors were not overworked and were, in fact, "far from complaining or even being sensible of any burden in their additional labors." In sanctioning the existing arrangement, however, they did express the conviction that, when ample funds became available, the College should appoint additional professors and have its own, separate president. Referring to the Panic of 1837, they found the times unpropitious for fund raising but urged all in the denomination to close ranks in support of their College and Seminary. At the same meeting of the Trustees at which this heartening report was read, the resignation of the Reverend Dr. Ludlow from the Board was accepted. Another crisis passed, but the basic issues still remained unresolved.

The controversy exploded with unusual ferocity at the meeting of the General Synod in June 1839. Numerous speeches critical of the College were made from the floor, many of them in the nature of veiled attacks on Milledoler, and specific proposals were advanced to loosen the connection between the College and the Seminary. Recognizing at last the untenability of his position, Dr. Milledoler presented his resignation to the Trustees on July 2. Two weeks later, with the Synod holding an adjourned session in New Brunswick, coincident with a meeting of the Trustees, an agreement was hammered out. The essential terms were that the Trustees were to elect a new president, subject to Synod approval, whose salary was to be paid from a special fund of $40,000 to be raised by the Synod; that the Trustees were to be assured by a written guarantee of adequate space in the College building; and that thereafter tuition fees would be paid by those students who attended the College as beneficiaries of the Van Bunschooten and Knox funds. Having accepted these terms, the Trustees proceeded by a narrow margin to elect the Reverend Dr. John Ludlow as president, contingent upon the attainment of the promised fund. Although the new conditions were in many respects highly favorable to the College, the means by which they had been imposed engendered much bitterness. Milledoler and his friends saw the whole affair as a plot by Ludlow and his faction to take over the College and charged that the Synod session had been packed and that there had been much unseemly intrigue.

In part because of the confusion and discord that resulted from the Synod's actions, the attempt to secure subscriptions toward the president's salary was a total failure. Consequently the entire plan agreed upon in 1839 had to be reconsidered. When the General Synod met in June 1840, the faction that had prevailed the year before was quiescent, and the committee to whom the matter of the College was referred succeeded in identifying the cause of past difficulties and pointing the way toward a solution.

> It cannot be concealed [the committee reported], that a difference of opinion exists throughout the church, both as to the nature of the relation of Rutgers College to the General Synod, and also as to the advantages which the church has derived from that relation. In regard to the relation itself, it is contended by some, that the Board of Trustees of the College is a mere instrument, in the hands

of the Synod, having no will of its own. On the other hand, it is claimed, that the trustees are an independent body, chartered for specific objects, and organized with suitable powers to carry out the intention of those who first originated the plan of the college and secured its accomplishment by legislative enactment.

After reciting the tangled background of the Church-College relationship, the committee concluded that the Trustees, under their charter, were legally quite independent of the Synod and argued that it would be wholly inexpedient to modify this status so as to bring the Trustees under the control of the Synod.

To modify it so as to subject it to the regulations of General Synod would not answer the purpose of the church. The conflicting opinions, the oftentimes hurried deliberations of such a body, would never suit the objects of an institution, whose prosperity mainly depends upon the stability of its plans and operations.

Accordingly, the committee recommended that the autonomy of the Trustees be explicitly recognized and the Synod resolved:

That . . . the efficiency of the college depends mainly upon the wise and energetic administration of its affairs, by the Board of Trustees, and to the said board the Synod refers its whole administration, embracing the appointment of professors and instructors, providing and disbursing the funds of the college, and controlling and directing its concerns generally; and that the Synod repeals, on its part, all former action on this subject, which may or can interfere with the tenor of this resolution.

The net effect of the various actions taken in 1839 and 1840 was to increase the authority and responsibility of the Board of Trustees. They were now free to elect a president without any restraints by the Synod, and to manage the internal affairs of the College. They received a written guarantee of their privilege to use the Queen's building and were assured of tuition fees from students who were supported by the beneficiary funds. At the same time, the Synod requested the theological professors to give such instructional assistance as they could to the College. Although the new arrangement marked a substantial step forward in establishing the independence of the College from the Church, it did not constitute a final solution. So long as the College property was owned by the Synod and the theological professors taught in the College, the Trustees would, in fact, continue to be under obvious restraints. These matters were to be sources of misunderstanding and disagreement in the future. Moreover, with the passage of time, it became evident that the precise nature of the Church-College relationship was subject to varying interpretations, with the result that another twenty years passed before a reasonably clear understanding was achieved. In the meantime, however, the College enjoyed some respite from the constant wranglings and sudden shifts in policy that had featured successive sessions of the General Synod and was able to devote attention to matters of internal development.

Chapter Four

The College Achieves Maturity

After fifteen years of captivity under the Covenant of 1825, the College was partially released from the most onerous of the limitations that had been set upon it. A heavy—but necessary—price had been paid in order that the institution might be revived. In spite of the difficulties that had marred and even retarded the forward movement, a backward look from the vantage point of 1840 would have revealed that in every dimension the College had indeed approximated the hopes of those who had devoted so much of their energy and their prayers to its welfare. Now cast largely upon its own slim resources, it faced an uncertain future. For those who anticipated a sudden acceleration of tempo and the manifestation of new resources, the years ahead were to be disappointing and even, at times, disheartening. But for those who were disposed to labor with dogged persistence for each small gain, content with the assurance that the institution would survive and send forth its small host of graduates into the learned professions, the public service, and the world of business as "educated men," there was a continued sense of achievement. The next two decades, then, were not to be characterized by large undertakings or abrupt developments but rather by the same halting progress in the face of adversity that had become a part of the heritage of the College.

Armed with new authority, the Trustees confronted a host of problems as they sought to reconstruct the College in accordance with the principles agreed upon in 1840. Their most immediate task was to secure a president. Dr. Milledoler had continued in office pending a choice of a successor, but was eager to be relieved of his responsibilities. The Synod having failed to meet its pledge to endow the salary of the office, Ludlow declined the post, and in July 1840 the Board elected Dr. Jacob Janeway. He was in many respects an obvious choice, for he had served as professor and vice-president and had been more active than anyone on the Board in directing the strategy of the College in its long conflict with

58

the Synod. But Janeway refused the office, and in August the Trustees elected A. Bruyn Hasbrouck, who promptly accepted.

A native of Kingston, New York, and a member of a family long prominent in that area, Hasbrouck had graduated from Yale in 1810, studied law at the famous school in Litchfield, Connecticut, attained some distinction at the bar, and served briefly in Congress. Although he had become a member of the Board of Trustees in 1837, he had attended few meetings and had not played a significant role in the recent controversies. He was a man of cultivated tastes, widely read in classical and English literature and possessed of considerable elegance of manner and discourse. Handsome and urbane, with a wife who was equally amiable, he was an ornament to the College and the community, but he was neither a forceful educational leader nor an effective fund raiser. He was to be remembered chiefly for his able lectures in constitutional and international law and for his graciousness as a host on numerous social occasions. As the first layman to occupy the presidency of the College, he reflected the willingness of the Trustees to strike out in a new direction, away from clerical control and close involvement with Church politics.

"It is manifest that the present is a crisis in the history of the College," a Trustees' committee reported at the time of Hasbrouck's election, but they hopefully added that "with the favour of Providence and a wise course of action on the part of the Trustees there is much more in the existing crisis to inspirit our hopes than to beget despondency." The financial situation, as always, was desperate. Invested funds yielded an income of only $1,800; total annual expenditures would amount to at least $5,400, including a salary of $1,600 for the president. The budget might be balanced if there were ninety tuition-paying students, but the enrollment at the time was barely seventy, and during the ensuing decade it rarely exceeded that figure. Because of the financial stringency it was necessary to reduce the salaries of the professors of mathematics and languages. A determined effort had to be made to secure funds by subscriptions, and the ever-devoted Abraham Van Nest pursued this objective with renewed zeal and encouraging success. By 1843 he was able to report that nearly $30,000 had been secured in cash and pledges. In their extremity the Board even turned to the state for assistance, petitioning in 1842 for annual donations of $3,000 over a period of five years, without success. Operating on a year-to-year basis and devoting much of the money that was raised by subscriptions to current purposes, the Trustees somehow managed to remain solvent and even make modest additions to the College's plant and academic program.

During the final years of Dr. Milledoler's administration, great difficulties had been experienced in maintaining the prescribed courses of study. As the theological professors reduced their services to the College, an impossible burden was placed upon the professors of languages and mathematics, and when Dr. Janeway resigned from his teaching post in 1839, conditions became critical. From time to time tutors had been employed to assist in language instruction and on occasion Dr. McClelland volunteered his aid, but these expedients hardly sufficed. Additional staff was required, and by 1841 suitable arrangements had been devised.

As a first step, Professor Beck's salary was doubled and thereafter he was to teach two full terms, adding courses in geology, mineralogy, botany, and physiology to the course that he had previously given in chemistry. Instruction in the classical languages was vastly improved when the Reverend John W. Proudfit replaced Professor Ogilby in 1840 and was joined a year later by William H. Crosby, who bore the title of adjunct professor. After a few years Proudfit, an able scholar who had previously taught at New York University, devoted all of his time to Greek, and Crosby, a lawyer by training, had charge of Latin. President Hasbrouck contributed substantially to the teaching program, meeting the Juniors for instruction in rhetoric and the Seniors for lectures on constitutional law and political economy. He also presided over the weekly forensic exercises of the Seniors. Courses in moral philosophy, in evidences of Christianity, logic, and mental philosophy continued to be given by the three members of the theological staff. The three full-time professors, reenforced by the five part-time men, gave the College a faculty that was fully adequate to the needs of the small student body and the restricted curriculum.

Although in its general outlines the curriculum was not substantially altered by these developments, the availability of a larger teaching corps did result in some enrichment of the offerings. The scientific instruction was doubled after 1840 and embraced additional fields. Hasbrouck's teaching in the areas of constitutional law and political economy may be viewed as establishing the place of those disciplines in the curriculum, even though Milledoler and Janeway had given some attention to them previously. The appointment of Proudfit and Crosby in the field of the classics resulted in a reorganization of those studies. In addition to the traditional concern with disciplined mastery of the languages, the professors emphasized ancient history and geography, requiring the students to "draw maps representing the march of armies and other historical events, and illustrative of allusions in the authors which they read." Portions of the ancient authors were assigned to be learned and declaimed, "this practice being found exceedingly to improve the compass and modulation of the voice, without the same tendency to monotony which is observed in our own language." The students also wrote essays on classical subjects as well as biographical sketches of classical authors and historical personages.

Most interesting of all was the statement in the College catalogue of 1842 describing the educational philosophy that underlay instruction in the classics:

> And as the knowledge of the past is principally valuable from its relations with the present, those relations are constantly pointed out; all the studies are as far as possible *comparative*, the geography, history, literature, ethics and politics of the ancient world, exhibited in connection with those of the modern, and the inestimable instruction and discipline of classical studies, rendered to the utmost of our power, a direct and actual preparation for the professional and social life of an American citizen.

Here, quite obviously, was something more than a restatement of the revered faculty psychology, with its preoccupation with the "training of the mind." Knowledge was to have some relevance to the needs of the student and to the world in which he would function.

There were other signs of reform in the curriculum, the most significant of which was the introduction of the study of modern languages. In a very few colleges instruction in French had been offered late in the previous century, and by the 1820's, when in numerous institutions attempts were made to break away from the rigid classical pattern, modern languages gained wide acceptance. These earlier stirrings had had no discernible repercussions at Rutgers, but now, in the 1840's, innovations appeared.

In April 1841, without any apparent previous discussion within either the faculty or the Board of Trustees, Peter J. G. Hodenpyl was appointed Professor of German Languages and the Reverend Thomas L'Hombral was named Professor of the French Language. Neither professor was to receive any compensation nor were they to be members of the faculty. L'Hombral passed almost immediately from the scene, but Hodenpyl, a native of Holland, who also held an appointment in the Grammar School, sought to make the best of his tenuous status. For the next three years he taught not only German but also French, Spanish, and Low Dutch to any students who were able to afford his modest tuition fees. But almost at once he besought the College authorities to regularize his position. "Justice to the Institution of which You are the Guardians . . ." he urged, "would seem to demand that the Professorship of Modern Languages be placed upon the same basis as the other Professorships in the Institution, as it will otherwise never be regarded as constituting an essential part of the Institution, and never receive the respect due to it as such." Responding to this plea, the Trustees in July 1842 appointed Hodenpyl Professor of Modern Languages and stipulated that each student studying with him should pay five dollars annually, the proceeds to be paid to the professor up to a maximum of $300.

That Hodenpyl succeeded in generating some interest among the undergraduates is evidenced by the fact that in 1843 the Junior Exhibition featured orations in French and German. He also acquired the support of the faculty, which petitioned the Trustees in 1844 to make modern languages a regular part of the course of instruction. "The importance of these languages, and especially the French and German, none will hesitate to admit," they stated, "and indeed some acquaintaince with them by the educated men of our country appears to be almost absolutely necessary." Experience had proved, however, that voluntary election was unsatisfactory, and the time had come to make the subject a requirement. The professor's salary could be financed by raising the tuition fees of all students by five dollars to a total of forty-five dollars for the year. These proposals were promptly adopted, and in October 1844 Hodenpyl took his place as a full-fledged member of the faculty. He regularly offered instruction in French for two hours each week to the Freshmen, three hours to the Sophomores, and during the first term two hours to the Juniors. Occasionally, by special arrangement, he taught German to individual students. When he was replaced in 1846 by Charles R. von Romondt, who had the title of Professor of French and German Languages and Literature, the same schedule was maintained. Modest as these provisions were, they did add a new dimension to the old curriculum and brought the College into harmony with prevailing practices.

Of comparable significance was the effort to accommodate special students in what was commonly known as the "Scientific Course." As early as 1796 Princeton had accepted special scientific students, who were awarded a certificate—rather than a degree—upon the completion of their studies, but the experiment had been abandoned after a decade. In 1802, Union College adopted a similar policy with marked success, and in the decade of the 1820's, several colleges experimented with "parallel courses" that enabled students to bypass the classics. The movement did not achieve general popularity at the time, and, strongly influenced by the famous Yale report of 1828, which admitted of no compromise with curricular innovations, most colleges adhered to the classical pattern. Those that did continue to offer alternative, non-degree programs, with the notable exception of Union, found that few students were interested.

Influenced, perhaps, by an awareness of the experiments at Princeton and Union, Queen's had made provision for special students as early as 1810. The statutes adopted in that year permitted such students "to study and recite such parts of science as they shall choose," and if they sustained a satisfactory examination they would "receive a testimonial from the faculty of their character and progress in science." There is no evidence that any applicants availed themselves of this option, and subsequent revisions of the statutes in 1825 and later made no reference to it. In 1841, however, the College catalogue somewhat surprisingly announced:

> There is a Scientific or Commercial Course which permits the student to select such studies as have a direct bearing on his intended pursuits in life. Those who take this course receive a certificate according to the branches of study which they pursue. Where the student is a minor, the consent of his parent or guardian is necessary to his entering upon this course.

The same statement reappeared in subsequent catalogues down to 1864, when the Rutgers Scientific School was established.

Over the next two decades, perhaps a score or more students were admitted to the Scientific Course; on occasion there were as many as five in the College at the same time. Their programs of study were exceedingly varied, depending upon their previous education and their particular objectives, but all omitted work in Latin and Greek. Although the Scientific Course attracted relatively few students, it suggests that the College was not immune to the feeble viruses of reform that were abroad in the land, and in a remote way it was a forerunner of the courses that were to be established when Rutgers became a land-grant college.

While the curriculum was exhibiting some symptoms of change, the general features of the academic routine altered little from those that had been fixed in 1825. Admission requirements remained the same, although prospective candidates were now advised to supplement their preparation in the ancient languages with other reading. "The historical books of Scripture, with Rollin, Plutarch's Lives, and Goldsmith's histories of Greece and Rome, will furnish him with a general knowledge of ancient history, which would greatly relieve and animate the toil of classical study; and they might be very profitably followed by Russell's Modern Europe (or some other approved compend) and Marshall's or Spark's Life of Washington, for the history of our own country." Also recommended were Butler's *Ancient Geography* and Lempriere's *Classical Dictionary*. The College day began with prayers in the chapel each morning at nine, followed at nine-thirty by the first of three classes. The students were then free the remainder of the time for relaxation or study, except on Sundays, when, as formerly, they were obliged to spend most of the day in attendance at religious services. The faculty, meeting now without the theological professors, assembled weekly to attend to minor disciplinary matters.

The campus, in the opinion of critical observers, presented a barren and even disorderly appearance, still with its lone building, intersecting fences, professorial gardens, and unsightly outhouses. The erection in 1841–42 of a spacious residence for the president to the east of Queen's building, on a plot leased from the Synod, added a new and distinguished element to the scene. Hasbrouck enhanced the attractiveness of the landscape by planting numerous trees. Across College Avenue the Grammar School presented a forlorn appearance, for attendance had declined to a mere twenty-six students. Soon, under a vigorous new rector, it enrolled triple that number and threatened to outgrow its meagre facilities.

The most remarkable aspect of the life of the College in this era was the vitality of its tiny student body, especially in the extracurricular area. The literary societies and other student organizations that had been formed soon after the revival of the College continued to be vigorous, and new enterprises were undertaken. In 1842 the first student literary publication made its appearance—prematurely, as it developed—and endured through twelve monthly issues. Titled the *Rutgers Literary Miscellany,* it resulted entirely from the efforts of Benjamin F. Romaine, 1842. Romaine had first sought to enlist faculty patronage for his brainchild, but when aid was not forthcoming from that source, he undertook to edit, publish, and distribute the magazine himself. Made up largely of original pieces, many of them contributed by faculty members and contemporary authors of some reputation, the *Miscellany* was highly dignified, moral, and serious. Only occasionally did the editor utilize his prerogative to comment on College affairs, but he did observe that because the entire curriculum was designed to train the memory, rather than the creative powers, a College periodical offered a valuable opportunity to the students to develop their gifts of expression. He tried without success to establish an association that would ensure the continuance of the publication. "All are ready to write articles," he lamented, "but none are ready to assume responsibility." He was especially chagrined at this failure, for many respectable colleges of the time had flourishing journals.

Rather than a literary journal, the students turned to quite a different type of publication. With the encouragement of the faculty they undertook the issuance of the annual catalogue, beginning in 1844. The success of this venture may have been attributable to the fact that in addition to giving the courses of study, the schedule of classes, and general information regarding admission and similar matters, the catalogue listed the names of all the students by classes, together with their home addresses and local places of residence. The catalogue continued to be published annually by the students until 1866, adding over the years data on various organizations, prize awards, and major events in the College calendar. It was, in fact, the forerunner of both the *Targum* (1867) and the *Scarlet Letter* (1870). The cultural interests of the undergraduates even extended to the field of music. A chapel choir was formed, for which the Senior class apparently was expected to provide leadership, and in 1847 members of that class received permission to hold a "musical and oratorical exhibition" following the semiannual examinations.

These stirrings of student activity, significant as they were, took place within a familiar context; they represented no departure from accepted patterns. But now the College was suddenly thrown into confusion by the appearance of a radically different type of organization that threatened its unity, inspired competing loyalties, and in time formulated a new set of student values. These were the "Secret Societies," or fraternities. They had made their earliest appearance at Union and Hamilton in the late 1820's and early 1830's, and from there had spread to other colleges. Exclusive, secret, and completely outside the collegiate way, as it was then conceived, they obviously met a student need for establishing new group identities and for institutionalizing social customs and modes of competition that were not fulfilled by the old literary societies.

The first such society at Rutgers was Delta Phi, organized surreptitiously in February 1845 by a group of twelve students with the encouragement of the chapter at New York University. Within a year the membership had increased to nineteen, or a quarter of the student body. Almost at once the fraternity was brought under attack. Trouble first came to a head within the literary societies, where factional conflict developed when it appeared that the secret society was exerting undue control. The Philoclean, especially, was entirely disrupted by controversies that resulted in the resignation of six members of Delta Phi and at one point provoked a serious riot. By July 1846, the campus was seething over the issue, and a determined campaign was launched to drive the fraternity from the campus.

The matter was debated at the meeting of the Alumni Association, all of whose members were deeply attached to the literary societies, and they called upon the Trustees to "devise measures which will result in restoring harmony among the Students and promoting the prosperity of the College." Their major concern, quite simply, was that the rise of secret societies would spell the doom of their highly cherished Philoclean and Peithessophian societies. While the problem was under study by a committee, the Trustees instructed the faculty to inform the students that it would be "unwise and indiscreet" of them to join secret societies. The members of Delta Phi, meanwhile, sought to explain and justify their fraternity both to the Trustees and the faculty. After wrestling with the novel situation for several months, the Trustees finally concluded that "no Secret Societies should be permitted to exist in connection with the College" and left it to the faculty to take such measures "as they in their wisdom and discretion may think proper."

The faculty, it developed, contained a majority favorable to the fraternity. A committee reported that Delta Phi, as a voluntary association for the promotion of "friendship, literature, and morality," included some of the most estimable young men in the College and that it posed no threat to the literary societies. It was anticipated that when the secret societies ceased to be a novelty they would disappear, for the faculty found "no principle of vitality which can give them permanent existence." The proper course, then, was to leave them alone rather than to irritate them by attempts at dissolution. Accordingly, they solemnly resolved that it was "unnecessary and inexpedient to take any action in reference to secret societies," with President Hasbrouck alone in the negative. This mild tactic did not suit the alumni, who formally resolved in July 1847 that secret societies were "prejudicial to the best interests of the College" and should be "discountenanced and discontinued." The Trustees were of similar persuasion, and they ruled that no secret society could exist at the College and that students belonging to such societies should be disciplined.

Placed under this rigid ban, Delta Phi continued a clandestine existence. Late in 1848 a second secret society, Zeta Psi, was organized, again by way of the chapter at New York University, and they shared the persecution. In 1850, the faculty ruled that no Senior would be recommended for his degree if he belonged to a secret society, but when every member of the class, on being queried, denied such affiliation, it became apparent that this tactic would not be effective. Two years later, every entering student was required to sign a pledge that he would not join a secret society. For more than a decade the attempts at repression continued. "It is in vain for us to expect to exist in peace," one harassed brother wrote in 1853, "until our worthy Prex is in Heaven or our Trustees are brought to a more rational state of mind on the subject of secret societies." Meeting at first in one another's rooms, then in hotels or rented halls in town, the two fraternities survived every assault, developing in the process a fervent devotion to their societies and increased respect from their peers. In time, Delta Upsilon (1858), a distinctively "anti-secret society," and Delta Kappa Epsilon (1861) made their appearance, indicating that the societies had won acceptance among the students and had succeeded in defying attempts at repression by constituted authority. By 1864 they had achieved secure status, even to gaining a place in the College catalogue.

The fraternities were to have a profound influence on undergraduate life for a century. Intensely competitive, they sought initially to claim for their members such posts of honor as the Junior Orators or the first places at commencement or offices in the literary societies. Later, when literary and athletic activities came into vogue, they aspired to leadership in those realms. Increasingly they were oriented toward the extracurricular, toward nonacademic goals and values. Indeed, the exceedingly rapid expansion in the extracurricular area coincided with the full recognition of the fraternities in the College. With the flowering of the fraternities the distinction between the College of the faculty and the College of the undergraduates increased and the old collegiate way was transformed.

The older literary societies managed to survive both internal strains and external competition resulting from the rise of the secret societies, in part because admirable, new facilities were provided for them. The initiative came originally from the faculty, which proposed in 1843 that a new building should be erected for the societies as well as for a museum, a chemical laboratory, and a library. The building, they decided, should be named in honor of Abraham Van Nest, in recognition of his years of extraordinary devotion to the College. Pledging in their own behalf $500, they undertook—with the approval of the Trustees—to raise the necessary funds. They met with little success until the alumni, concerned as they were about the societies, agreed to raise $2,000. Although this goal was not achieved, plans for the building proceeded, and the cornerstone was laid with elaborate ceremonies on April 21, 1847. A year later Van Nest Hall, standing west of Queen's, had been completed. Two large and well appointed halls on the first floor were given over to the literary societies—Peitho to the right and Philo to the left of the entrance—and the remainder of the plain two-story brick structure housed the museum and the chemical laboratory of Professor Beck.

Gratified though they were with the splendor and magnitude of their new halls, the societies rebelled against the Trustees' edict that henceforth their meetings must be held in the afternoon, instead of in the evenings as heretofore. In this stand they were stoutly defended by the alumni, and the Trustees relented. For decades to come, the halls shared with the fraternity lodges the loyalties of the undergraduates. So long as they furnished the Junior Orators and managed the Junior Exhibition they maintained their vitality and combined respect for academic attainment with exuberant sociability.

Despite the new outlets for their energies, the students became more rambunctious with each passing decade. Scarcely a month passed without serious breaches of discipline. The faculty had constantly to deal with "gross insults," assaults on the janitor, indignities to females, drunkenness, card playing, the firing of guns and pistols, and like barbarities. The annual trials for the selection of Junior Orators were inevitably followed by a hilarious celebration at Benny Stelle's hospitable barroom, where brandy punch, crackers and cheese, and "seegars" fortified the assemblage for songs, speeches, and recitations. At commencement times "burlesques" would appear mysteriously. Patterned on the commencement program, they offered scandalous insults to students and faculty alike. Denounced by the faculty as indecent and libellous and gravely injurious to the College, they nevertheless persisted as a source of great merriment.

Intellectually and socially gratifying though student life may have been in the easy days of President Hasbrouck, the College was not flourishing. Enrollments, instead of rising to the hoped-for figure of ninety, actually reached a low of sixty-five in 1850. The Trustees were puzzled as to why the Dutch Church could not supply more students and urged members of the faculty—during their vacations—to visit among the churches in quest of candidates. Because of the inadequate receipts from tuition fees, committees were constantly at work soliciting funds. In 1845 the Synod directed that collections be taken up throughout the denomination for the benefit of the College, but only thirty-seven of the 274 churches responded to the appeal. Members of the faculty attributed the low attendance to various causes—the high price of board, the lack of proper library and laboratory facilities, and the unattractive state of the campus. Considerable effort was directed toward beautifying the campus and enclosing it with a picket fence in 1849. If the lithograph made at the time is a faithful one, the results were admirable. But other problems remained unsolved. The Alumni Association declared in 1849, "That whatever may be the causes which have operated to retard the growth and prosperity of the College for the last 9 years . . . such causes have been beyond the control of the President." Possibly they were correct. Many "causes" might be cited, but foremost was the fact that there were too many colleges in the land, and they were offering a commodity for which there was little demand. To this general assessment it could be added that Rutgers continued to experience peculiar difficulties in its relations with the Dutch Church.

For several years after 1840, relations with the Synod were relatively tranquil; the Church confined its attention largely to the affairs of the Seminary and left to the Trustees the management of the College. A new round of difficulties began, however, in 1847, when a Synod committee, on the basis of what was soon acknowledged to be erroneous information, intimated that the Trustees had made improper use of the Van Bunschooten Fund. When the Synod then appointed a special committee to confer with the Trustees, the Board—after an exhaustive review of the past history of the Covenant relationships—decided to press for the reconveyance of the College building and campus. The Synod committee agreed to this proposal, but, when it was presented to the General Synod in September 1848, a heated discussion ensued, revealing the persistence of old animosities, and no action was taken. Greatly disturbed by this development, which they viewed "as calculated to disturb if not to interrupt the harmony and good feeling which ought to exist between the General Synod and this Board" the Trustees sought further conferences with the Synod. To their dismay, the committee that was appointed to negotiate with them was headed by J. L. Schermerhorn, an old adversary, and it took the astonishing view that no legal alterations had ever been made in the Covenant of 1825. This position was totally unacceptable to the Trustees and they declined to have any further discussions with Schermerhorn's committee.

The Synod in September 1849 entrusted the whole matter to a new committee, which, after several meetings with a Trustees' committee, brought about a satisfactory adjustment. The Trustees abandoned their effort to regain ownership of the College property, and it was jointly agreed that the alterations that had been made to the Covenant in 1839 and 1840 were valid and remained in force. The Synod was assured by its committee that the Trustees had not been guilty of any irregularity in the handling of funds. The net effect of the furore, therefore, was to leave matters essentially as they had been since 1840. But the whole incident revealed the persistence of some hostility toward the College within the Synod and the survival of suspicions that damaged the institution within the Church. Many members of the Board of Trustees felt that the only ultimate solution would be a complete separation of the College from all connection with the Synod and deeply regretted that this objective could not be attained at once. Looking back on the tangled history of the Covenant relationship, the astute Dr. Janeway aptly observed: "It might furnish a useful lesson of the utter vanity of any attempt to bind into complete harmony and in perfect unity of purpose two coordinate and independent bodies without first completely extinguishing the rivalries and the jealousies and the ambition of our common nature."

With the College under attack and in anything but a prosperous condition, President Hasbrouck in July 1849 presented his resignation. It was accepted in September, at which time the Board elected Theodore

Frelinghuysen as his successor. After repeated refusals, Frelinghuysen was prevailed upon to accept the office in April 1850 and was inaugurated on Commencement Day, July 24, 1850.

The new president bore a name long distinguished in the annals of the College and a high reputation as a statesman and an outstanding Christian layman. The great-grandson of Theodorus Jacobus Frelinghuysen, he was the son of Frederick, the College's first tutor. Born in Millstone, he had been educated at Princeton and had entered upon a legal career that brought him into political life. He had served in the state legislature and as Attorney General before going to the United States Senate in 1829. As the vice-presidential candidate on the Whig ticket headed by Henry Clay in 1844, he had achieved national prominence. In 1839 he had become the second Chancellor of New York University, serving there until he was called to Rutgers. His administration at New York University had not been entirely successful. Severe financial difficulties and violent internal dissensions had brought that institution by 1850 to the verge of ruin and bankruptcy. Although Frelinghuysen had endeared himself to the faculty by his kindliness, his humility, and his remarkable Christian qualities, he had not been a commanding or forceful figure and he was unable to resolve the host of problems that afflicted the University. Sixty-three years of age when he came to New Brunswick, he was held in reverent esteem by those who knew him, and it was anticipated that the lustre of his name would bring strength and renown to the College.

During the dozen years that Frelinghuysen presided over the College, it remained faithful to the old classical tradition, yielding only in minor ways to feeble currents of change. His educational philosophy was founded on conservative principles. "The mind must be subdued to self control—and instructed in the knowledge of its powers—its capacities and its infirmities," he declared in his inaugural address. "It should pass through the healthful discipline of mental and moral culture—and regular, systematic and severe study." He recognized that a proper education should include knowledge of the nation's history and government, of one's God, and of mathematics and science, but he took his strongest stand in defense of the study of the ancient languages. These views were very largely shared by members of his faculty and by the Trustees, if not by the students and those who—but for the nature of the curriculum—might well have become students.

The major effort of the administration was directed toward increasing the funds of the College to the point where recurring annual deficits might be eliminated. The total endowment, exclusive of beneficiary funds, amounted to about $40,000 in 1850, but substantial sums had been "borrowed" from the principal to erect the President's House and Van Nest

Hall. The grand objective was to increase the endowment to $100,000, and after weighing various alternatives it was decided that the goal might best be reached through the sale of perpetual scholarships. Any individual, group of individuals, or congregation subscribing $500 would thereafter enjoy the privilege of having one student in the College free of all tuition charges. Dozens of colleges had adopted this technique, which seemed to promise not only large capital funds but also that equally scarce commodity—students. In an era when philanthropic giving had not yet begun to flow toward higher education, the sale of scholarships offered the benevolent donor something for his money, but in the final analysis the results to the College were meagre, and in time the scholarships were to become a source of acute embarrassment.

Committees were appointed, the support of the Alumni Association was enlisted, and momentarily the prospects seemed bright. Then the effort bogged down, and in 1853 the Trustees retained the services of an agent, the Reverend James Scott of Newark, to conduct the solicitation. He met with an indifferent response, and for a few years the campaign lapsed, having produced in all about $28,000. In 1858 an energetic clergyman, the Reverend Dr. B. C. Taylor of Jersey City, joined the Board of Trustees and took the lead in a new effort to reach the goal. The plan was to concentrate first on obtaining individual subscriptions for scholarships; when that source had been exhausted the solicitors would offer scholarships to congregations. When it again became apparent that volunteer committees would not carry out their assignments, an agent, the Reverend Charles Parker, was sent into the field. Still the goal could not be achieved. By 1862 the total amount secured approximated $35,000. The College still faced an annual deficiency of more than a $1,000 out of a total budget of about $10,000.

Many circumstances, not the least of which was the business recession that began in 1857, were cited as responsible for the poor response to the financial appeal. But a Trustees' committee in 1861 put the blame on the College itself. "Moreover," they pointedly observed, "there is found a great apathy if not actual opposition to Rutgers College on the part of a large number who should be its patrons and friends, and even on the part of some of its own alumni, resulting from the deplorably low condition into which the discipline and instruction of the College had fallen." The deficiencies were alarming. "Students have realized this when they entered upon the duties of professions for which their training had imperfectly fitted them. Parents and guardians felt it, and the disastrous consequences it will require time and a manifest elevation of the College effectually to remove."

The Trustees had long been sensitive to complaints about the deficiencies of the College. There had been rumblings of criticism at meetings of the alumni, culminating in 1854 in a determined effort to have a committee of enquiry appointed to look into the internal condition of the College; but after a heated debate and some devious parliamentary maneuvers the movement was smothered, and it was made known that the Trustees themselves had the problem under study. One cause of dissatisfaction was that Professor Strong, now well advanced in years, had long neglected the teaching of geography, and he was summarily ordered to resume instruction in that field. More serious was the situation in classical languages. Professor Crosby had departed in 1849, and the whole burden of classical instruction had fallen on Professor Proudfit, assisted by a tutor. Proudfit was not pleased with the additional load, and when pressed by the Trustees he declined to undertake all that they sought to require of him. William Irvin, a recent graduate who had served as tutor, was then made Professor of Latin. The Trustees also wanted to improve instruction in modern languages and increase the amount of time devoted to English grammar, composition, history, and chronology, but they lacked the means to implement these proposals.

The modest efforts that were made in 1854 to improve conditions did not suffice, and five years later the Trustees undertook drastic measures to meet mounting criticism. Professors Strong and Proudfit were informed that, although the Board acknowledged their high scholarly attainments, "yet circumstances have compelled us painfully to feel that a change that shall bring more youthful energies to the service of the Institution has become imperatively necessary." Proudfit was relieved of all his duties, while Strong was permitted to remain another two years at reduced salary to teach only the Seniors. Strong was succeeded by Marshall Henshaw, an Amherst graduate who had been principal of Dummer Academy. Irvin departed with Proudfit, and the chairs of Latin and Greek were soon filled by DeWitt T. B. Reilly and Howard Crosby. The Professor of Modern Languages, Charles R. von Romondt, had also incurred displeasure, and he, too, was dismissed. His replacement, Gustavus Fischer, was appointed "without compensation," and for a period of five years modern languages disappeared from the required curriculum, in part for financial reasons but also to provide more time for the classics. Of the faculty as it had existed a year earlier, only George H. Cook remained. A man of remarkable abilities, who had been trained by Amos Eaton at Rensselaer and who had taught in that institution and later at Albany Academy, Cook had joined the faculty in 1853 following the death of Lewis Caleb Beck. In addition to being Professor of Chemistry and the Natural Sciences, he was Assistant State Geologist.

The wholesale shakeup of the faculty was unprecedented, but it had become apparent that reform was needed and that it would not come from within the faculty itself. By 1860 the Trustees felt that conditions had been vastly improved. "A new zest seems to have been given to the operations of each department," they reported. "The course of instruction is excellent in character and thorough in its inculcation. The discipline of the college is firm but affectionate and the students in general are attentive and studious."

The plan of reform was completed in 1860 with the creation of a new professorship, that of English Language and Literature. Heretofore rhetoric and belles lettres had been taught by members of the theological faculty—most recently by the Reverend Dr. William H. Campbell—or by the president. Now the field was to be given greater recognition and emphasis. The new incumbent, the Reverend John Forsyth, a graduate of the College in 1829, had taught Hebrew, archaeology, and church history at the Reformed Theological Seminary and had been Professor of Latin at Princeton. Obviously a man of broad interests, his assignment at Rutgers involved teaching Parker's *Aid to English Composition* to the Freshmen, Blair's *Rhetoric* to the Sophomores, Day's *Rhetoric* to the Juniors, and English literature to the Seniors. In addition, he instructed all the students in composition and declamation. Formerly, exercises in declamation had followed the daily religious services in the chapel. Now the entire student body was to assemble at four o'clock each Wednesday, at which time they would be subjected to speeches by two Seniors, two Juniors, three Sophomores, and three Freshmen. The Juniors and Seniors delivered original speeches, the texts of which had been scrutinized by Professor Forsyth, while the Freshmen and Sophomores recited approved selections. Extensive as were his responsibilities, Forsyth received but a partial salary and was at the College only three days a week. He resigned in December 1862 upon the faculty's request that he meet his classes every day. In the meantime, however, he had succeeded in making substantial additions to the library holdings in his field. With the departure of Forsyth, the Professorship of English Language and Literature remained unfilled until 1880, although instruction in rhetoric was continued by other professors.

Concern for the quality of the educational program was not confined to revisions of the curriculum and shakeups in the faculty. There was an awareness that somehow the lagging interest of the undergraduates must be revived and stimulated; some new spur to their motivation was required. It was hoped that the solution lay in offering prizes for outstanding achievement. There had always been the places of honor at graduation to inspire the vainglorious, and the posts of Junior Orators had long been the objects of competition, but these awards apparently did not suffice. Accordingly, in 1853, James Suydam, a wealthy member of the Board of Trustees, established two prize funds, both for Seniors. The prize in composition was offered for the best essay on an assigned subject, and a comparable award was given to the student having the best record in natural science. A year later another Trustee, John Romeyn Brodhead, established jointly with his father a prize for the best Senior classical student, the award to be determined by an examination and an essay. Proficiency in mathematics was recognized after 1864 when Joseph P. Bradley founded a prize for Seniors in that discipline. A year later the Myron W. Smith prizes were instituted to honor the best orators in the Sophomore class. Whether the prizes had the desired effect is questionable, but they did represent an attempt to encourage academic excellence at a time when other values and interests were coming into vogue among the undergraduates.

Despite the harsh judgments that were rendered on the College, even by those most concerned with its welfare, enrollments increased remarkably during the decade. From the low point of 65 in 1849–50, the numbers in attendance rose steadily, reaching 124 in 1860–61 when 52 new students were admitted. Precisely half of the students came from New Jersey, including 14 from New Brunswick. Forty-six were from New York, and the remaining 16 came from Connecticut, Vermont, Iowa, Michigan, Kentucky, Alabama, Georgia, Texas, and Japan. Several factors contributed to the increase, including the sale of scholarships, the national renown of President Frelinghuysen, and improved boarding facilities after the opening of Hertzog Hall in 1856. Whether the complaints about the poor preparation received by the students while at College was valid seems dubious in light of their subsequent careers. Of the 31 graduates of the class of 1859, for example, 14 entered the ministry. Those following other callings included George William Hill, one of the most brilliant mathematicians of the age and the recipient of international honors; Henry W. Bookstaver, Justice of the New York Supreme Court; Jonathan Dixon, Justice of the Supreme Court of New Jersey; William H. Vredenburgh, member of the New Jersey Court of Errors and Appeals; Theodore S. Doolittle, longtime professor and vice-president of the College; and Gideon Lee Stout, president of the Merchants Insurance Company, as well as assorted lawyers, physicians, bankers, and manufacturers.

If the College, in the eyes of its sponsors, left much to be desired, the undergraduates were blissfully unaware of the fact. Although they were duly critical of their professors and apathetic toward the intellectual bill of fare, they continued to build for themselves a way of life that was agreeable, exciting, and even stimulating. What with the literary societies, the new fraternities, the Natural History Society, and the Bible Society, there were frequent meetings to attend. The Junior Exhibition held its secure place in the College calendar, although fraternity politics created so much discord in the choice of the Junior Orators that in 1856 the societies turned the selection over to the faculty. When formal activities seemed dull, there was opportunity for improvisation. The first recorded instance of that classic college stunt—stealing the clapper from the College bell—occurred in 1851, when four daring young men succeeded in accomplishing the feat. More common as an outlet for youthful exuberance was the "Calliathumpian Serenade," or "Calithump," which acquired popularity in this era and persisted for thirty years. Bands of students would make the night hideous with noise as they prowled the campus and its environs, arousing wrathful professors from their slumbers, tearing down fences, and generally engaging in mischief. When rumors of a Calithump were heard, the president prudently alerted the local police force and stationed a professor or two in safe, but strategic, locations in order to secure the names of the offenders. Another word to enter the College vocabulary in this era was "slope," which designated the increasingly common practice among students of absenting themselves en masse from the class of a professor at whose hands they had suffered some affront, or merely excessive boredom.

Student energies were also turned to constructive purposes. It was a notable achievement when the two literary societies cooperated to produce a highly respectable monthly—*The Rutgers College Quarterly*—which made its first appearance in April 1858 and expired three years later, when the outbreak of the Civil War disrupted the College. Featuring poems, stories, essays, and orations, the magazine assiduously avoided controversial topics and rarely commented on College affairs. One story, however, that lampooned an unpopular professor earned for its author, Stephen Fiske, later a highly successful journalist and dramatist, the ultimate plaudit of expulsion from the College.

Along with other less virile amusements, there were signs of growing interest in athletics. In 1858 the editor of the *Quarterly* launched a campaign for a gymnasium, thirty-five years in advance of the event. "Ball playing became quite the rage last fall," is a tantalizing item in January 1861. "Two well contested matches were played between the Junior and Sophomore clubs, the Junior at both games bearing off the palm. The want of a good gymnasium is very much felt at Rutgers," continued the editorial campaign, "and as ball playing in part supplies the want, it should be encouraged." Foot racing was reportedly very popular at the time. Physical prowess, it would appear, was emerging as one of the admired attributes of the College man.

Dwarfing all other developments in the internal life of the College was the physical separation of the Seminary from the College. Increasing enrollments in both institutions strained the meagre facilities. One hot

July day in 1854, as Dr. William H. Campbell prepared to teach his Seminary class in an oven-like room on the third floor of Queen's, he decided that the intolerable conditions must end. Launching into a vehement speech, he exhorted the students to protest against their lot and demand a new building. Soon students and faculty alike in the Seminary were bombarding Church authorities with their pleas, until, providentially, Mrs. Anna Hertzog of Philadelphia was induced to provide the funds for a building. A site was obtained a block north of the College campus, and by 1856 a spacious hall, adequate to house the seminarians and their classroom and library facilities, was ready for occupancy. All of the Seminary work, which had been carried on in Queen's since its erection, was now transferred to the Theological Hall, ending the long era of intimate association between the two institutions. Now that the physical separation had been accomplished, the College Trustees sounded out the Synod on the long-cherished plan to have Queen's reconveyed to them, but after preliminary inquiries it was deemed inexpedient to press the issue. Within a few years, however, the time would be propitious, and the College would at last be the master of its own house.

Although it was scarcely apparent at the time, old Rutgers College— the College of the Covenants—was approaching the end of a long era. The event that most decisively marked the transition to a new age was the Civil War. The impact of the war itself on the College was considerable, but during the course of the conflict fundamental changes took place that were only indirectly, if at all, the consequence of the tragic strife that divided the nation. Nevertheless, in the history of the College, as in the larger life of the nation, it was the Civil War that signalled a great transformation.

On April 12, 1861, the day of the bombardment of Fort Sumter, all was quiet at the Colleges; classes had been suspended for the spring recess, not to be resumed until May 1. Then, as the students returned to the campus, they were caught up in the excitement of the times. Already New Brunswick had been the scene of fervent activity as patriotic assemblages were held to express loyalty to the Union. The conflict became real when troops from Massachusetts and New York passed through the city on their way to Washington. A recruiting office had been opened in Greer's Hall and the local militia company, the "National Rifles," had been ordered into service.

The normal academic routine was temporarily disrupted by heated political discussions and talk of enlistment. The two Texans in the College, J. Greenville McNeel, 1862, and his brother, Pleasant D. McNeel, 1864, were made to feel so uncomfortable that they quickly departed to enter the Confederate service, joining their older brother, George W. McNeel, 1860. All three subsequently gave their lives for the "Lost

Cause." Andrew B. S. Moseley, 1861, departed before commencement to enlist in an Alabama regiment, but according to tradition he was given a special examination and was awarded his diploma at the railroad depot. When President Lincoln on May 3 called for troops to serve for three years, several undergraduates joined with local townsmen to organize the "Olden Guards" and devoted most of their days to drilling and recruiting.

Patriotic enthusiasm reached its climax on the campus on May 13, when faculty, students, and hundreds of local citizens gathered in front of Queen's to witness the presentation to the College of a large flag made by the ladies of New Brunswick. A huge pole, extending forty feet above the front of the building, had been set in place, and a large platform had been erected to accommodate the distinguished guests and those who were to address the assemblage. President Frelinghuysen stirred the crowd with a vigorous denunciation of secession and was followed in like vein by members of the faculty and civic leaders. Several days later, on May 22, there was a second flag presentation ceremony. The Olden Guards had been accepted for service as Company G, 1st Regiment, 1st Brigade, New Jersey Volunteers, and 2,000 citizens gathered to see the company receive its flag. On the following day the eager troops boarded the train for Trenton, and, to the cheers of multitudes who lined the tracks, rode away to war.

Among those hurrying to the front were eight Rutgers undergraduates: Robert A. Johnson, 1861; Francis S. Keese, Nicholas W. Meserole, George Seibert, and N. Hixon Van Arsdale, all 1862; William Henry Pohlman, 1863; and John Dooly and John S. Bliss, both 1864. They arrived in Virginia in time to participate in the disaster of the First Battle of Bull Run. Most of them fought throughout the war; Pohlman died of wounds received while leading his regiment at Gettysburg. Other students soon responded to the President's call. William H. H. Ayars, 1862, and Thomas L. Stringer, 1864, joined the 5th Kentucky Volunteers and the Navy respectively. Ernest L. Kinney, 1861, waited until he had received his degree before accepting a commission in a New York regiment. Altogether, by July 1861, eleven Rutgers men had gone from the campus into the Union forces; three others were fighting for the Confederacy.

By the time the College reopened late in September 1861, the intense excitement had subsided and the campus seemed remote from the terrible holocaust. Although enrollments fell sharply—from 124 in 1861 to 105 a year later and then in succeeding years to 77 and 64—the decline was caused less by enlistments than by a reduction in the number of those entering and by a heavy drop-out rate. Only 8 undergraduates left the College to enter the army during the remainder of the war; with them went 1 graduate from each of the classes of 1863, 1864, and 1865. Of those who interrupted their studies to fight for the Union, only 1 subsequently returned to complete the work for his degree.

Twenty-five young men from the classes of the war years had gone off to battle. Joining them in uniform were 58 alumni, drawn from the classes as far back as 1829. Collectively, they participated in nearly every engagement of the fratricidal war. Sixteen of them, including three who fought under the Stars and Bars, died. A few served humbly in the ranks; most became company or field-grade officers; one—George Henry Sharpe, 1847—attained the rank of major general and served on Grant's staff.

For the dwindling numbers of students who remained in the College, life continued much as usual. The two literary societies met regularly to debate such remote subjects as: "Which is most effective, vocal or instrumental music?" The minutes of the faculty offer little reflection of the war. The even course of affairs continued until April 17, 1865, when a committee of students waited on the president and advised him "that on account of their feelings occassionid by the Assasination of the President of the United States & by the attempt upon the life of Secretary Seward they were not in a mood to attend properly to their studies, & therefore asked that they be released from College exercises until after the funeral of President Lincoln on Wednesday April 19th." The faculty assented, provided the students presented themselves at the usual chapel services and observed due solemnity and decorum. A few days later, on April 24, a large body of students journeyed to New York "in order to witness the Celebration of the Obsequiees of Mr. Lincoln." With this tragic occasion, the war at last seemed to end.

Early in the war, on April 12, 1862, President Frelinghuysen's twelve-year administration ended with his death at the age of seventy-five. A man of noble qualities, whose entire life was governed by a deep religious sensibility, he symbolized in his passing the end of a distinctive era in the history of the College. Reared in a family tradition that was closely intertwined with that of the College, embodying in his own person the respect for classical learning and piety that inhered in the old college ideal, much of the past died with him. Under his vigorous successor, shaped by new influences of the times, Rutgers would embark upon a new course.

In retrospect the College had come a long way in the nearly four decades since its revival. To Rush Van Dyke, who had recalled the College "unadorned by cupola or dome . . . lonely and bare upon its bleak little eminence," the scene was very different when he returned for his thirtieth reunion in 1860. Queen's building, now complete with cupola and bell and with its interior long since finished, was flanked on the east by the President's House and on the west by Van Nest Hall, while across College Avenue was the Grammar School building. Splendid trees, nurtured through the years by Dr. DeWitt and President Hasbrouck, softened the appearance of the campus, which was enclosed by a handsome iron fence. Initially shared with both the Grammar School and the Seminary, and then with the Seminary alone, Queen's was now wholly at the service of the College, except for the two apartments that for a brief time continued to be occupied by Seminary professors.

The faculty, too, had changed. Instead of the two professors of mathematics and languages, aided by the three Seminary professors, there were now five instructors, in addition to the president and the two Seminary professors who continued to teach mental philosophy and evidences of Christianity. Except for George H. Cook, all of the professors were clergymen, but in the period before the rise of graduate schools this was the common situation. The expansion of the faculty was in part the result of the slow transformation that had taken place in the curriculum. Science, which had been barely represented in 1825, received added recognition with the appointment of Dr. Beck in 1830 and developed gradually until it required the full services of Dr. Cook and part of the time of Professor Henshaw. Modern languages had next made their appearance on a tentative basis in 1841, ultimately to gain acceptance in the curriculum. Under Hasbrouck and Frelinghuysen, both able lawyers and public figures, political economy and constitutional law had become established subjects, and Professor Forsyth had given new stature to the study of the English language. Despite the addition of new subjects, the classics retreated only slightly from their former preeminence, as is evidenced by the presence on the faculty of two men in that field. The added subjects were accommodated partly by increasing the number of actual class hours and partly by reducing the number of hours devoted to the classics and to the various branches of philosophy and rhetoric.

The student body, considerably expanded in size, still reflected the predominantly Dutch character of the College. Drawn almost equally from Dutch Church strongholds in New Jersey and New York, with small but increasing numbers from other states and foreign countries, they were a homogeneous group. As in the past, some graduated at the early ages of eighteen or nineteen, but late in the era the age level rose markedly. Of the 31 graduates in 1859, 12 were over the age of twenty-two and one was twenty-nine. Many had obviously interrupted their education for long periods of time in order to acquire the money to pay their college expenses. Their career objectives remained much the same. Nearly 1,000 students attended the College between 1825 and 1862, of whom 726 graduated. In all, 234 entered the Dutch Reformed ministry and 97 were ordained by other denominations. The law claimed 248, while 97 became physicians. Business careers were the primary occupation of 93. Only 30 entered the teaching profession, although many of the clergymen added teaching to their calling. Of the remaining 200, data is lacking for most, but many followed such varied pursuits as farming, journalism, engineering, military service, or architecture. Most of the graduates filled creditable positions in the learned professions and a remarkable number acquired eminence.

The College had indeed progressed over the four decades, and the chief credit for the gains that were made must go to the Board of Trustees, or to specific individuals of the Board. The three presidents were neither forceful leaders nor educational statesmen; they were not of the stature of Eliphalet Knott of Union, or Francis Wayland of Brown, or Mark Hopkins of Williams. The faculty confined their attention to instructing their students and maintaining discipline; only rarely—as when they proposed the erection of Van Nest Hall—did they attempt to formulate large plans or institute major reforms. It fell to the Trustees to manage relations with the Synod, raise funds, establish new courses of study, appoint professors, settle disputes between students and faculty, and generally to chart the course the College was to follow. Although the Board treated the faculty with great respect, rarely intervening in those areas that were by statute entrusted to the president and the professors, it frequently supplied the initiative for innovation. Within the Board certain men were outstanding for their wisdom, fidelity, and achievements, men like J. R. Hardenbergh, Jr., Cornelius L. Hardenbergh, Abraham Van Nest, Jacob J. Janeway, Peter D. Vroom, Peter Labagh, Littleton Kirkpatrick, and Benjamin C. Taylor.

The composition of the Board of Trustees underwent significant changes over the years. In 1822, when the movement for the revival of the College began, there were 35 Trustees, exclusive of the ex officio members of the Board. A distinct majority—20—were clergymen, 9 were businessmen, and 6 were lawyers or physicians; 15 were residents of New Brunswick and vicinity; the remainder, except for 8 New Yorkers, came from other New Jersey towns. Twelve were alumni of the College. Especially noteworthy is the heavy clerical dominance and the essentially local character of the Board. Between 1823 and 1849, 45 new members were elected, of whom only 18 were clergymen; 21 were from New York and 24 resided in New Jersey, all but 8 of them in the New Brunswick area. Only 4 were alumni. During President Frelinghuysen's administration the makeup of the Board continued to change. Of 31 new members, 11 were clergymen, 11 were lawyers or doctors, and 9 were businessmen. In sharp contrast with the previous period, 14 were alumni. Sixteen of those elected were New Yorkers as against 15 from

New Jersey, of whom only 7 were local residents. Over the forty-year period, then, clerical representation was reduced, New Yorkers approached a position of equality with residents of New Jersey, local influence declined, and alumni representation was on the rise.

Finally, in surveying how the College altered, the matter of the relationship to the Dutch Church—and more particularly to the General Synod—must be considered. Under the Covenant of 1825 the College was placed in a position of heavy dependence upon the Synod, which came close to adopting the view that the Trustees were their agents in conducting an institution that would serve as a feeder for the Seminary. The Trustees, however, never waived the autonomy with which they were vested by the charter, and in a long series of struggles with the Synod they moved toward a position of independence. By 1860 they had nearly complete responsibility for the College, except that they were tenants of a building owned by the Synod and utilized the part-time services of two theological professors.

It was unfortunate that the relationship between the College and the Church was the source of so much dissension, for the Church genuinely needed the College, and from the Church the College derived most of its funds and students. In so many respects the history of the troubled relationship between the College and the Church is strikingly similar to the history of the subsequent relationship between the College and the State of New Jersey.

Rutgers College in the era of the covenants, then, was a struggling, church-related institution, serving a small constituency and preparing a limited number of students for the older learned professions by means of a curriculum that rested heavily on the classics and that sought to develop discipline, inculcate piety, and inspire reverence for traditional values. In the years ahead, the long-stifled demands that the American college should broaden its function, enlarge its constituency, strengthen its intellectual qualities, and place itself more directly at the service of society could no longer be ignored, and as Rutgers moved conservatively to heed these demands, the institution was to be transformed.

Chapter Five

The Transformation of the College

In the decade after 1862 Rutgers College experienced such a burst of vitality as it had never exhibited before and would rarely exceed in the next century. Within that brief span of time the assets of the College increased fivefold, relations with the Dutch Church were all but severed, the Rutgers Scientific School was established and was designated the land-grant college for New Jersey, impressive new buildings were erected, a group of remarkably vigorous professors joined the faculty, the curriculum underwent profound changes, and undergraduate life suddenly took on new dimensions. Although the impetus did not carry forward to succeeding decades, the foundations were laid for a new Rutgers.

There was little hint of the radical changes that lay ahead in the inaugural address of the new president, the Reverend Dr. William H. Campbell. Declaring his faith in an education that would stress thoroughness in the mastery of assigned subjects and that would emphasize Christian values, his one proposal in the way of curricular reform was that more time should be allotted to the study of the Bible and Hebrew. The College should "afford to the youth who frequent its halls that Biblical education which befits the sons of Christian parents." This goal was to be achieved "not so much by the study of books of evidences and learned apologies" but rather "from a diligent study and an accurate understanding of the Bible itself." Campbell's objectives were entirely traditional, and even conservative, but in his concluding remarks he forecast the new role of aggressive leadership that he would bring to the College. "The people," he declared, "should be kept under a constant pressure of importunity, which should result in the education of all their sons. Then, in a simultaneous, accordant step with this advance, there must be sought the founding of new professorships, the enlargement of libraries, and the increase of the apparatus of our institution, so that the means of doing good may be indefinitely enlarged." Here spoke the authentic voice of President Campbell.

In Dr. Campbell the College found its first effective head. Vigorous, indefatigable, enthusiastic—and on occasion tempestuous—he combined the qualities of teacher, preacher, administrator, and leader. Behind him lay a career that had included principalships of Erasmus Hall and Albany Academy, pastorates in New York City and upstate New York, and a professorship in the Theological Seminary for a dozen years. A graduate of Dickinson College, he was of Scottish and English ancestry and had begun life as a Presbyterian before entering the Dutch Church. In his religious beliefs he was conservative, founding his faith on the plain words of the Scriptures. But in his actions he was dynamic, even explosive, as he sought to accomplish swiftly whatever task he undertook. He was a man among men, enjoying close friendships with a host of his contemporaries, with whom he corresponded on a wide range of topics. Long addicted to the use of tobacco, he struggled against the habit for many years and finally conquered it, but he confessed that ever after he would follow in the streets a man smoking a pipe in order to obtain a whiff of the delightful aroma. Plain in appearance, with a rugged, homely face dominated by a large nose and tired, kindly eyes, he infused his associates with his own fiery zeal until in the final decade of his presidency, afflicted with almost complete blindness, his steps faltered and his effectiveness diminished.

Campbell was unquestionably a strong, positive force in the affairs of the College, but others joined with him to produce the forward movement. He was greatly aided by a strong group of Trustees, among whom were Joseph P. Bradley, James Suydam, Maurice E. Viele, Peter D. Vroom, Peter S. Duryee, David Bishop, Henry L. Janeway, Johnson Letson, Jacob R. Wortendyke, and James A. Williamson. Businessmen and men of affairs, they brought unusual dedication and ability to their responsibilities. New men within the faculty, most notably David Murray, DeWitt T. B. Reilly, Theodore S. Doolittle, Jacob Cooper, Francis C. Van Dyck, Isaac E. Hasbrouck, Edward A. Bowser, and George W. Atherton brought unprecedented strength to the teaching program and exhibited a willingness to embrace new ideas. Some of them had been trained as clergymen, but unlike many of their predecessors their primary and lasting commitment was to the academic sphere.

The new movement also owed much to the temper of the times. In the two decades following the Civil War, higher education in the United States was transformed. Colleges, and now universities as well, adapted their curricula to what seemed to be the needs of society, placing increased emphasis on science and on "practical" subjects. At the same time, they turned their energies toward the discovery of new knowledge; no longer were they restricted to transmitting what had been learned in earlier centuries. Provision was at last made for differing interests within the student population, through the introduction of the elective system and by the multiplication of the several courses of study that might be pursued. Not only were the objectives of higher education being redefined, the very institutional structure was being revolutionized as well. The land-grant college, with its commitment to "agriculture and the mechanic arts" and its public subsidy, came into existence. The state university, generally a feeble institution in most states prior to 1860, now advanced to preeminence, especially in the Middle West. Of equal significance was the emergence of the graduate school, turning out its doctorates in increasing numbers and providing trained academicians to replace the clergymen of previous generations.

The transformation extended to the student-body. No longer exclusively oriented toward the learned professions—and most particularly toward the ministry—the colleges offered enticing opportunities to youths of widely diverse backgrounds and aspirations. As public support for land-grant colleges and state universities mounted and as admission requirements were altered or reduced, higher education became a possibility for those to whom it had previously been denied. The rapid increase in the number of public high schools, supplementing and in time almost replacing the private academies, greatly multiplied the number of those eligible for college. The process of expansion was facilitated when it became apparent that there were places of profit and prestige for those who possessed a college degree, even in the business life of the nation. Finally, higher education ceased to be the exclusive privilege of males and was extended to women as well, both in separate colleges for women and in coeducational institutions.

As piety and classicism gave way to secularism and science, the colleges turned to new sources of financial support. Reliance on the meagre bounty of a denominational body declined. America had by now produced a host of millionaires, to whose philanthropic instincts a new breed of college presidents appealed with notable success. In many regions, though not in the East, taxpayers contributed generously to the development of their state universities. The Federal Government, too, played an influential role, initially through the land-grant subsidy of the Morrill Act and subsequently through such legislation as the Hatch Act and the second Morrill Act.

Rutgers felt the influence of the currents of change that were agitating and reshaping the whole structure of higher education, but for a variety of reasons it responded conservatively to them. Because it continued to identify itself strongly with the Dutch Church, both its resources and its student-body remained limited. Unquestionably, too, the persistence of the religious orientation operated to inhibit radical departures from traditional ways. The land-grant designation, important as it was, did not mean a complete break with the past, for while the College took on an additional function, it did not abandon its commitment to classical education. Furthermore, the State of New Jersey manifested almost no interest in higher education; nearly forty years were to pass before it made its first appropriation to the College. Also relevant is the fact that New Jersey lagged in the development of its school system. New Jersey was the last state—in 1871—to eliminate tuition charges in the public schools. Public high schools had scarcely come into the picture. Before 1870 they existed in but four communities, although in the succeeding decade sixteen secondary schools of varying quality were established. Operating, then, within the generally conservative environment of the Dutch Church and the State of New Jersey, Rutgers could follow, but not lead, the movement of reform that transformed higher education in the post-Civil War decades.

The first need of the College as it looked to the future was for what Dr. Campbell termed the "sinews of war"—money. Elected to the presidency in July 1862, with the understanding that he could continue to teach in the Seminary through the following academic year, he lost little time in setting the fund-raising machinery in operation. In February the Trustees appointed a committee to seek $100,000, the income of which was to be devoted exclusively to professorial salaries. Headed by Campbell and made up in almost equal numbers of clergymen and laymen, the committee met monthly in the rooms of the General Synod in New York City to manage the campaign. They began by drafting a strong appeal to all within the bounds of the Dutch Church, setting forth the desperate plight of Rutgers and warning that "the day is not far distant when the doors of the College must close. Friends of Education and religion, members of the Dutch Church, baptized children of our Zion," the exhortation continued, "are you prepared for such disaster and disgrace?"

The Church was divided into eleven districts, and committees were appointed to solicit within each area, offering to every donor of $100 a full scholarship for his son. In June, Dr. Campbell made a moving personal appeal to the General Synod and received in return a fervent endorsement of the campaign. Campbell and the dozens of other ministers of the several subcommittees preached in the churches and solicited relentlessly. Within a year from the day the drive began, the goal had been attained, and when the final results were announced in June 1864—with rejoicing and thanks to God—the so-called New Endowment Fund exceeded $137,000. Although there were a few gifts in excess of $1,000, most of the money had come in sums of $100 or less, and nearly all of it had come from members of the Dutch Church. It was a magnificent achievement and provided a heartening contrast to the disappointing results of earlier efforts. For the next few years, at least, income would exceed expenditures.

Now assured of a secure financial position, the Trustees next directed their efforts toward separating the College from its relationship to the Synod. With remarkable dispatch and mutual good feeling, the two parties readily came to terms. The General Synod at its session in June 1864 agreed to reconvey Queen's building and the campus property to the Trustees for $12,000, which roughly represented the amount that the Synod had paid in 1823, plus certain sums that had subsequently been spent on improvements. The reconveyance, however, was to be "subject . . . to such conditions as shall secure the paramount influence of the Reformed Dutch Church over the management of the institution." With the agreement of the Trustees the deed of reconveyance contained the provision, therefore, "that the President of the College, and three-fourths of the members of its Board of Trustees shall always be members in full communion of the Reformed Dutch Church of North America."

The denominational requirement respecting the president was, of course, contained in the charter of the College, but previously there had been no requirements affecting Board members, although more than three-fourths of them had been communicants of the Dutch Church.

Other adjustments swiftly followed. With the money obtained from the Trustees, the Synod built two houses for Seminary professors, and Dr. Berg and Dr. Woodbridge soon vacated their apartments in Queen's, which then became available for classrooms. The last vestige of teaching in the College by Seminary professors was also brought to an end. After 1862 only the Professor of Didactic Theology, who, under the terms of the old Covenant of 1807, held the appointment of Professor of Theology in the College, continued to teach. But in 1867 the Synod and the Trustees agreed to abrogate that Covenant. Because the College charter required a "professor of divinity," the Trustees appointed Dr. Campbell to that nominal office. Meanwhile, the Seminary professors had asked to be relieved of any responsibility for preaching in the College chapel on Sundays, and their request was granted. "[It] . . . certainly is a subject of congratulation," stated the College faculty "that these two institutions, which in their early history like two ships had to be lashed together for mutual safety and could command only the divided labor of the same crew, have been so enlarged and strengthened as to move on independently and to demand individual labors."

Fortified with an adequate endowment and in full command of the College at last, Dr. Campbell and the Trustees looked forward to building on the old foundations. Then—from quite an unexpected source—an unanticipated opportunity presented itself. Within a year the College had plunged into an entirely new venture and assumed responsibilities that brought it into a relationship with the State of New Jersey. It had become a land-grant college.

The movement had its origins within the faculty. Late in 1863 Professor Cook and Professor David Murray—who had joined the staff as professor of mathematics in July after having served as principal of Albany Academy—proposed that a "Scientific Department" should be established and that funds for its support might be obtained under the Morrill Act. Cook and Murray were designated by the faculty to present the matter to the Trustees and, if such action was indicated, before the legislature. When the Trustees met in January 1864, they had before them a persuasive report, drafted by Murray, explaining that Congress in July 1862 had offered to each state 30,000 acres of public lands, or land scrip, for each member of Congress, the proceeds of which were to be invested as an endowment for the support of a college

> where the leading object shall be, without excluding other scientific and classical studies, and including military tactics, to teach such branches of learning as are related to agriculture and the mechanic arts, in such manner as the Legislatures of the States may respectively prescribe, in order to promote the liberal and practical education of the industrial classes in the several pursuits and professions in life.

The report pointed out that the New Jersey legislature had accepted the land grant in March 1863 and was now expected to apply the proceeds—which it was estimated might amount to $160,000—either to an existing college or to a new institution. Because none of the money could be used to erect buildings, it seemed unlikely that a new institution would be founded at state expense. Cook and Murray accordingly urged the Trustees to seek the land-grant designation, which otherwise might go to a less worthy school. "Will Rutgers College be the almoner of this government munificence," they queried, "or will she stand back and see it put into less safe and less capable hands?" They argued that the College was bound to expand its offerings and facilities in the various fields of science. "Surely then it would be a want of foresight to fail to seize an opportunity which will enable the trustees . . . to do on a liberal scale what will require to be done in any event before many years shall lapse." Insisting that the regular collegiate curriculum would not be interfered with by the establishment of a scientific department and that no additional expense would be involved and emphasizing "the educational advantages and enlarged usefulness which would result to the College," the two earnest advocates presented a most persuasive case.

The response of the Trustees was immediate and unequivocal. Adverting to the phrase in the College charter that had included not only "learned languages" but also "other branches of useful knowledge" as proper subjects of instruction, they resolved that the "Scientific Course of Study," which had been authorized in 1810, should be organized and established as a department of the College under the name of the Rutgers Scientific School. At the same time they decided to petition for the land-grant designation and appointed a committee of politically experienced Trustees to present the matter to the legislature.

The Rutgers forces then embarked on an intensive campaign to secure the benefits of the land grant. Most active of all was George H. Cook, who sought out legislators, and men who might influence legislators, with unrelenting zeal. For some years he had been carrying on the work of State Geologist under the sponsorship of the New Jersey Agricultural Society and was engaged in a successful quest for funds from the legislature for that project. He was therefore widely known throughout the state and was not unfamiliar with the ways of Trenton. Peter D. Vroom, Trustee and former Governor, also worked valiantly. Initially the chief competitor was the State Normal School at Trenton, but its claims were not strong and Princeton soon emerged as the most formidable adversary. Princeton professors and trustees were observed lobbying in the State House, and two pamphlets setting forth the superior advantages of their institution were distributed. Rutgers in turn produced a circular, which evidenced Cook's intimate acquaintance with the agricultural and industrial resources of the state and argued that New Brunswick offered unexcelled opportunities for prospective students to visit farms, factories, and public works.

The campaign reached its climax on the evening of February 23 when the rival institutions presented their cases at a legislative hearing. The Normal School, Princeton, and Rutgers were all represented by able advocates. President John McLean pleaded Princeton's cause, aided by two professors, while President Campbell, Governor Vroom, and Professor Cook spoke in behalf of Rutgers. Their eloquence, abetted no doubt by the behind-the-scenes efforts to round up votes, prevailed, and the legislative committee reported in favor of Rutgers. A last-minute threat arose when the Methodist Conference urged the legislature not to award the grant to a denominational institution, but this contention was put aside, and by the end of March the bill had passed both houses of the legislature and was signed by the Governor on April 4, 1864.

The state, as was ultimately discovered, drove a hard bargain. The

College was to receive the income from the fund derived from the sale of the land scrip, which for some years amounted to approximately $6,900.* In return for this bounty the Trustees were obliged to maintain in the Rutgers Scientific School such courses of instruction as were called for by the Morrill Act. They also pledged themselves to furnish, at no expense to the state, such additional buildings as might be necessary and "a suitable tract of land conveniently located for an experimental farm." Moreover, they were to provide free scholarships, equal in amount to one-half of the land-grant income, to students in the Scientific School. This meant approximately forty scholarships. Finally, a ten-member Board of Visitors, appointed by the Governor, was given "general powers of supervision and control" over the School, which it was to visit twice each year and on whose condition it was to make an annual report to the legislature. Within a very few years it became apparent that the obligations assumed by the Trustees involved expenditures far in excess of the modest income derived from the land-grant fund.

The Morrill Act had permitted the states considerable latitude in determining how land-grant colleges should be established, and many arrangements were tried. In some states, existing state universities received the land-grant designation, in others new "A and M" colleges were founded, in still others new state universities with "A and M" divisions were established. New Jersey's decision to award the designation to a private institution was not unique; six states did likewise. Yale, Brown, and Dartmouth, for example, were selected by their respective states, although all of them subsequently divested themselves of the designation.

The land-grant colleges, however they were organized, represented the culmination of years of effort by educational reformers to establish institutions that would offer technical and scientific training, especially in the broad fields of agriculture and engineering. Practical farmers and businessmen had played little role in the movement, whose chief spokesman in Congress was Justin Morrill of Vermont. By the 1850's the Sheffield Scientific School at Yale and the Lawrence Scientific School at Harvard had become well established, and in several states institutions devoted to "practical" education were being launched. It was still far from clear, however, how technical knowledge, especially in relation to agriculture, should be organized for instructional purposes at the college level, how long the course of studies should be, what admission standards

* New Jersey was allotted scrip for 210,000 acres, or 1,312 quarter sections. Commissioners sold the scrip to New York brokers, receiving $.70 an acre for 2,259 quarter sections and $.50 an acre for 1,087 quarter sections, with a total of $112,160. This sum was invested by the state in securities whose yield varied over the years. The average return received by all the states for land scrip, or land, was $1.65 an acre.

should be set, and where instructors in the new departments would come from. The land-grant college idea, vague though it was, represented a wholly new concept of the role of higher education, and many years of trial-and-error experimentation ensued before a common pattern emerged. The end result was to be a distinctively American alternative to the old classical college and a general transformation of American higher education.

Planning for the new Rutgers Scientific School began in earnest in April 1864, when the Trustees accepted the obligation placed upon them by the legislature, established committees to carry out the provisions of the recent act, and named George H. Cook as vice-president of the College at a modest increase in salary. Cook, in close association with Murray and on the basis of his own experience at Rensselaer and extensive correspondence with people in other schools who were grappling with similar problems, worked for several months devising suitable arrangements. It was his philosophy that the Scientific School should stress rigorous intellectual activity in the basic scientific disciplines rather than vocationally oriented courses combined with on-the-job training. Education for farmers, he explained on a later occasion, "must be like that for other men, mainly, it must train their minds, teach them to acquire knowledge, and by opening to them the stores of knowledge treasured in the earth which is given to them to subdue, show them in a somewhat enlarged measure where their special knowledge is to be found."

The plan as ultimately formulated called for two courses of study, one in civil engineering and mechanics and the other in chemistry and agriculture, each extending through three years. Students in both courses would study the same subjects during the first year, but in the second and third years they would follow different patterns. Candidates for admission to the Scientific School would have to be sixteen years of age and pass entrance examinations in arithmetic, algebra through quadratics, English grammar, and geography. It was assumed that thirty students would enter in September 1865 and that they would have their own classes, separate from the classical students. Tuition was set at seventy-five dollars, plus certain fees, although it was expected that a substantial proportion of those admitted would hold free scholarships.

Before these plans could be implemented, additions had to be made to the staff and the facilities. The faculty had proposed the erection of a new building, but when, as a result of the removal of the theological professors, the east and west wings of Queen's became available, classrooms and laboratories were installed there, adding to the facilities already available in Van Nest. To provide for additional instruction, Luther H. Tucker, a Yale graduate and editor of the *Country Gentleman*, was appointed Professor of the Theory and Practice of Agriculture and John

C. Smock, a recent graduate, was made tutor in chemistry and agriculture. On the engineering side, the appointment of a tutor was contemplated, but after a protracted search Captain Josiah H. Kellogg, a West Point graduate, was installed as Professor of Civil Engineering and Superintendent of Military Instruction, effective September 1866. Meanwhile, a badly run-down farm of about 100 acres on the south side of the city had been purchased for $15,000, as required by the legislature, and a handsome, well-equipped observatory—largely the gift of Daniel S. Schanck—had been erected on the east end of the campus.

The arrangements for the new school had been contrived with considerable care, and the Trustees had spared no effort or expense in carrying through the recommendations of the faculty. But at the very outset the sponsors were disappointed in their expectations, and within a few years extensive changes had to be made in the original plan. Only seven students—rather than the thirty that had been anticipated—entered the Scientific School in September 1865. The Boards of Chosen Freeholders in the counties, who were supposed to appoint scholarship students, had been negligent; only two had been appointed. Those who did matriculate were interested in engineering rather than in agriculture. The financial picture was also discouraging. Because of delays in disposing of the land scrip, the College received only $1,200 the first year, which did not begin to meet the additional expenses that had been incurred. The experimental farm alone was operating at an annual deficit of $3,000, despite the fact that much of its equipment and stock had been donated. Conditions improved only slightly in the succeeding two years; fourteen students entered in 1866 and seventeen in 1867. In that year the selection of scholarship students was entrusted to the county school superintendents, but many counties still failed to produce candidates. By this time it was becoming clear that enrollments would not be large and that the agricultural course would not attract students.

Because of the smallness of the classes, the contemplated courses of study could not be undertaken. For several years all students in the Scientific School pursued a single curriculum, which included French, German, rhetoric, history, mathematics, chemistry, physics, physiology, and geology, together with specialized courses in mechanics, engineering, and military drill. Many of the courses were taken together with the classical students. Professor Tucker delivered a few lectures on agriculture and then submitted his resignation. A year later the Trustees named Cook as his successor, with the title of Professor of Chemistry and of the Theory and Practice of Agriculture, but with his manifold duties as State Geologist, director of the College Farm, and instructor in chemistry, geology, and physiology, his teaching in the field of agriculture was negligible. More time-consuming were the agricultural lectures that he was obliged to give annually in every county of the state until he was relieved of that onerous responsibility by the legislature in 1873.

The small band of students, quickly dubbed "Scientifs" by the classical students, initially found themselves in an awkward position, not knowing quite what their status was. Within a few years, however, they had become accepted, were invited to join the literary societies and even the fraternities, and took part generally in College affairs. When the first class had completed its studies in July 1868, the members were deeply offended because separate graduation exercises, at which they received the degree of Bachelor of Science, were held for them. But a year later the "Scientifs" participated in the regular commencement, and in 1873 the faculty decided that scientific and classical students should have identical status with respect to prizes, honors, and all other positions within the College.

After these disheartening early years of experimentation, the program of the Scientific School was extensively revised in 1871. In order to increase the thoroughness of the instruction, especially in the sciences, and make the entire program comparable to that of the classical curriculum, it was lengthened from three years to four. There were still to be two courses, one oriented toward engineering and the other toward chemistry, but students did not elect their field of specialization until the Junior year. Effectively this meant that in their final two years the engineers worked with Professor E. A. Bowser, who succeeded Kellogg in 1871, and the chemists studied with Professor Francis C. Van Dyck, a graduate of the College, who had spent a year of study in Europe before taking up his appointment as Professor of Analytical Chemistry in 1871. For those who could not undertake the full program, there were two-year special courses in chemistry and in agriculture, which enjoyed little popularity, and so-called "partial students" were admitted to take such subjects as they felt qualified to pursue. Admission requirements were raised to include plane geometry, history of the United States, and physical geography, in addition to grammar, spelling, geography, arithmetic, and algebra. This basic format obtained for nearly twenty years. A total of 159 students attended the Scientific School during the first fifteen years of its existence, of whom 99 graduated. Of the graduates, 41 made engineering their careers, 24 became businessmen or manufacturers, 25 entered the professions of law, medicine, or teaching, 3 became architects; only 6 followed the occupation of farming.

President Campbell and the Trustees were understandably disappointed by the course of events. "The expenses attending an undertaking of this public character have been found much greater than would be at first supposed," reported Dr. Campbell in 1868, "and it is a burden on the funds of the Institution. Its usefulness, however, is undoubted," he added, "and we think it will make itself appreciated by the State." It was indeed appreciated by the Board of Visitors, who year after year were unstinting in their praise of the Scientific School and who repeatedly commended the Trustees for the sincere efforts they were making to honor unreservedly the commitments they had assumed. The Board of Visitors were especially impressed by the willingness of the College to pour money into the model farm. "It is to be regretted," they stated in 1871, "that the Legislature has not made ample provision for the even more rapid improvement of this property, instead of throwing, as they have, all the expense of its development on the College." But for another thirty years the legislature declined to afford any financial assistance to its "State College for Agriculture and the Mechanic Arts," as it was styled in official reports.

By 1876 the Visitors were thoroughly persuaded that students would not go to college to study agriculture. The College, they concluded, could most directly benefit the farmers of New Jersey by operating the Farm as an agricultural experiment station. Dr. Cook had long been conducting experiments, especially with fertilizers, and the results had been acclaimed by progressive farmers. It was therefore recommended that the state appropriate funds annually to the Trustees to finance experiments at the farm. With the strong support of the State Board of Agriculture and the constant guidance of Cook, they succeeded after several years of effort in securing an act of the legislature in 1880 establishing the State Experiment Station, the third such station in the country. The Station, although located in New Brunswick, was independent of the College and the Trustees and under the management of its own Board of Directors. Dr. Cook was appointed its director, with a small staff, and the College provided two rooms in Van Nest for his operations and also allowed the farm to be used for experimental purposes. For several years it was through the work of Dr. Cook at the State Experiment Station, rather than through courses of instruction, that Rutgers made indirect but very substantial contributions to New Jersey agriculture.

The Rutgers experience was not at all unique. Everywhere the new land-grant institutions had to deal with unfamiliar problems, and they adopted widely varying approaches before arriving at satisfactory solutions. Many moved from three- to four-year courses; nearly all found it next to impossible to attract students into their agricultural programs. In the case of most land-grant institutions, however, the state offered financial assistance, supplementing the small income from land-grant funds. No such aid was forthcoming for Rutgers. Although the Rutgers Scientific School was unquestionably a worthwhile enterprise, providing as it did a much-needed type of education, it strained the resources of the Trustees and may well have retarded the overall development of the institution for several decades.

The establishment of the Rutgers Scientific School was the major innovation of President Campbell. Less spectacular, but of comparable significance, were the changes that took place in the faculty in the same period. Not only did it double in size, but it altered in character and in the role that it played in the affairs of the College. No longer clergymen who had exchanged the pulpit for the desk and not yet the highly trained specialists of later decades, the professor of that period was nevertheless a professional academician who identified himself closely with the welfare of the College and its students.

In 1864 the faculty was made up of two professors of ancient languages, one in mathematics and natural philosophy, one in science, one in rhetoric and philosophy, and two part-time instructors in modern languages and history. By the end of Dr. Campbell's administration in 1882 there were two professors in the classics, one in modern languages, one in rhetoric and philosophy, one in history, three in the sciences, three in mathematics and engineering, one in English language and literature, and an instructor in military science. Several of the newer men had pursued advanced studies in their fields. Jacob Cooper, who joined the faculty in 1866 as professor of Greek and who remained until his death in 1904, was a Yale graduate who had obtained a doctorate at Berlin in 1854. Charles G. Rockwood, professor of mathematics from 1873 to 1877, was a Yale Ph.D., and Peter T. Austen, professor of analytical chemistry from 1877 to 1890, held a doctorate from Zurich. Francis Cuyler Van Dyck and Isaac E. Hasbrouck had each spent a year in advanced study in Europe to prepare themselves for their teaching assignments. These men and their colleagues were seriously interested in their fields of knowledge, sought to keep abreast of the latest developments, and in several instances engaged in scholarly publication. Edward A. Bowser in particular, who graduated with the first class from the Scientific School, was a prolific author of textbooks in mathematics, David Murray wrote an able history of education in New Jersey, and Jacob Cooper achieved high reputation for his classical scholarship. Unlike many of their early predecessors, they brought a scholarly, disciplined approach to their teaching duties.

As the faculty grew in size and strength, it assumed more and more responsibility for the development of the College. The initiative displayed, especially by Cook and Murray, in establishing the Scientific School and securing the land-grant designation is a notable example. But through the years the faculty was aggressive in proposing building programs, urging the establishment of additional professorships, and calling for new fund-raising efforts, as well as in dealing with matters of curricular reform and student discipline. As a consequence of this energy and assertiveness, they, rather than the president or the Board of Trustees became the major force in guiding College affairs.

With growth, both in the faculty and the student body, came the necessity for organization. Aside from the president, there were no administrative personnel in this period, but gradually certain administrative responsibilities were assigned to specific faculty members or committees. Ever since 1832 a professor had occupied the post of librarian, and this arrangement was to continue until 1884. In 1864 President Campbell proposed some division of labor among the faculty, and his suggestion that several standing committees be created was adopted. Professor David Cole was to furnish information to teachers and students regarding admissions and serve as a placement agency for prospective teachers; Professor Reilly, the librarian, was to devise ways and means of increasing the library; Professor Murray was to have similar responsibility for augmenting facilities for instruction in science; and Cook and Murray were assigned to prepare a building program for presentation to the Trustees. Following the adoption of a new and extremely elaborate system of numerical grading in 1864, faculty registrars were appointed for the Scientific School and the classical students. It was their onerous function to maintain records of grades furnished them by other faculty members. In order to relieve the president of the tedious chore of excusing individual students for absences, "division officers" were appointed after 1873 from the faculty for each of the four classes; student monitors maintained records of chapel attendance. Because minor disciplinary matters took up most of the time of faculty meetings, the president and Professor Reilly were appointed a permanent committee to consider all such cases and report to the faculty. There was even a modest arrangement for handling public relations. When a friend of the College proposed in 1876 that if the faculty would supply him with items of interest he would secure their publication in the daily newspapers, the president appointed a committee headed by Professor Reilly to prepare such materials. From these simple arrangements there was ultimately to emerge the elaborate structure known as "the Administration."

The economic situation of the faculty underwent considerable improvement. Between 1825 and 1860, the salaries of professors had ranged between $1,500 and $1,750. The inflation produced by the war occasioned distress. "The salaries at present are not more than were needed for a respectable support before the war," Professor Cook complained to the Trustees in 1865. "Since that time the cost of living has about doubled and the salaries have been and and are now quite inadequate to meet the expenses which must be incurred." Over the preceding three years, he pointed out, his own expenses had exceeded his income by $2,000.

Moved by this appeal, and with funds now available from the New Endowment, the Trustees authorized general increases, raising Cook's salary to $2,800 and those of the other professors to $2,000. Other increases followed until by 1871 the president received $4,000, Cook $3,000, and the other full professors $2,700. At a time when the salary of the College janitor was $300 and when skilled workmen rarely earned as much as $800, these salaries were relatively munificent and enabled the faculty to build fine residences and keep pace with the economic and social elite of the community. The salaries remained near the same level through World War I, by which time, of course, they had become sadly inadequate.

Growth in the size of the faculty was accompanied by major revisions in the curriculum. New fields of knowledge were introduced, the actual content matter of traditional subjects was greatly altered, the place of the classics was weakened, the elective principle was adopted on a very conservative basis, and modest steps were taken to provide for postgraduate studies. All of these developments were in harmony with the general transformation that was taking place in American higher education, but although Rutgers was receptive to the new influences in the 1870's, the pace of reform soon slackened, in part because of financial difficulties.

The most notable feature of the revised curriculum was the emphasis that was given to science. By 1882 half of the members of the faculty were in the fields of science and mathematics. This proportion is explainable in part by the establishment of the Scientific School, but there was also an increase in scientific instruction for the classical students. The physical sciences—especially physics, chemistry, and astronomy—were most strongly represented. The natural sciences—botany, physiology, and zoology—were confined to the Freshman year and were not taught by a specialist. The method of instruction involved extensive work in the laboratories, field trips, and lectures by the professors, in contrast to the earlier preoccupation with the study of textbooks.

There was also some strengthening of the work in the areas of the social studies and the humanities. History was recognized as a distinctive discipline in 1864, when a Professorship of Ancient and Modern History was instituted. The first incumbent, the Reverend Cornelius E. Crispell, was appointed on a part-time basis, and—to judge from the adverse reaction of his students—he was not a success; he soon resigned. In 1867 the College received a bequest from Abraham Voorhees to endow a professorship, and the Trustees decided to appoint a professor of history, political economy, and constitutional law. George W. Atherton, a Yale graduate who had taught at St. John's College, Maryland, and at what was to become the University of Illinois, was selected for the post and took up his duties in 1869. A Civil War veteran, he served also as military instructor. His normal program included a two-term course in general history, and one-term courses in English constitutional history, European history, American constitutional history, political economy, and international law. For the next forty years only slight additions were made to the fields of study now embodied in the disciplines of history, political science, and economics.

With the appointment in 1864 of the Reverend T. Sanford Doolittle to the newly established Collegiate Church Professorship of Rhetoric, Logic, and Mental Philosophy, a modern basis was laid for courses in the fields of psychology, philosophy, and logic. A man of wide-ranging intellectual interests, Doolittle introduced his students to the most recent literature in what was still called "mental philosophy," and in his course on "moral philosophy" he dealt with the major philosophers, ancient and modern, including Coleridge, Mill, Spencer, Kant, Fichte, and Hegel. Although Doolittle devoted a portion of his time to rhetoric, this field remained relatively weak until 1880, when the Reverend Charles E. Hart was appointed Professor of English Language and Literature, reviving the title that had lapsed in 1863 with the departure of Professor Forsyth. Under Hart a series of courses in English entered the curriculum, including work in the history of the language, readings in the major authors, and essays in literary criticism. The teaching of modern languages, which had been dropped from the prescribed curriculum in 1859, was resumed in 1864, and courses in French and German were offered to both the scientific and the classical students.

Throughout the two decades after 1862 the faculty was frequently engaged in revising the courses of study, not only to include new subject matter, but also to incorporate other innovations, the most notable of which was the elective principle. Prior to 1860 a few colleges, among them Virginia, Brown, and Harvard, had permitted students limited choices among subjects, and within the next decade several of the most vigorous and progressive institutions, led by Harvard, vastly increased the number of "electives" that were permitted. This drastic attack on the traditional concept that a college education involved the mastery of a relatively fixed body of knowledge provoked a great debate that lasted till the end of the century. But as new subjects claimed their rightful places in higher learning, the only alternatives were the multiplication of distinct courses of study or the acceptance of the elective principle.

The solution adopted at Rutgers in 1868 was a conservative one. In explaining the departure from a rigidly prescribed curriculum, the faculty stated:

The general theory of the arrangement is that up to the close of
the Sophomore Year, all the studies should be obligatory, and of
such a character as would be equally desirable whatever subsequent
profession or career was chosen; and that during the Junior and
Senior years, there should be certain subjects required of all students,
while in regard to others there should be an election depending
upon the future intentions of the students.

Accordingly, Latin and Greek were no longer required after the Sophomore year, and in each of the last two years a student might select
one course from among several offered—Latin, Greek, astronomy, analytical chemistry, or German. This significant step having been taken,
evidently with a minimum of controversy, there was no substantial extension of the elective system until 1891.

Instead of increasing the number of electives, the faculty in 1881 proposed the establishment of a so-called "Third Course" to meet the needs
of those who found the program of the Scientific School to be too specialized but who at the same time did not wish to devote so much time
to the classics and mathematics as was required in the classical course.
By requiring only two years of Latin and two years of mathematics,
the Third Course permitted more work in modern languages, the social
sciences, and philosophy. It was believed that such a course would "meet
the rapidly growing demand for what may be called a liberal but not a
technical education, and at the same time . . . [would] enable the College to retain the patronage of friends who might otherwise be compelled to seek the advantages of such a course elsewhere." At the same
time, the faculty took the radical step of proposing that "young women,
of proper age and fitness" be admitted into the College to pursue the
new course. Pointing out that in the numerous institutions that had
recently accepted coeducation, the experience indicated an elevation of
standards of scholarship and deportment, they concluded: "Nor ought
it to be overlooked that there is everywhere among thoughtful people a
growing conviction of the importance of providing for young women,
equally with young men, largely increased facilities for acquiring the
Higher Education."

The Trustees rejected the proposal for coeducation, without any explanation, but they did give approval to the Third Course, with the
provision that the degree to be awarded should be Bachelor of Philosophy,
rather than Bachelor of Arts. A Trustee committee was appointed to
work out with the faculty the necessary detailed arrangements, and at
this point the Third Course abruptly vanished. Twenty years later, in
1901, it reappeared under the name of the Latin-Scientific course. Why
the course was dropped is not apparent, but a change in administration,

accompanied by new faculty appointments, may have had some relevance.

The progressive temper of the faculty was also evidenced by their interest in establishing postgraduate work. There had been premature attempts in some American universities to offer formal programs leading to advanced degrees in the 1850's, but even after Yale awarded the first American Ph.D.'s in 1861, the movement acquired little momentum until the founding of Johns Hopkins in 1876. At Rutgers, arrangements were made for Francis C. Van Dyck to spend a year of postgraduate study in chemistry in 1865–66, and in 1873 a faculty committee first considered the formal establishment of graduate courses. By 1876, after extended discussion that reflected internal differences of opinion on the problem, the faculty was prepared to recommend that they be authorized to offer postgraduate courses. Obviously with some misgivings, the Trustees gave their approval, with the important condition that such work should not "interfere in any degree with the efficiency of the undergraduate courses of study. . . ." Up to this point no proposals had been made involving the conferring of advanced degrees, but in 1882 the Trustees approved a comprehensive set of faculty recommendations on this matter.

Advanced students who spent a year in residence taking approved courses, passing a comprehensive examination, and presenting a satisfactory thesis could receive the degree of Master of Arts or Master of Science. A two-year course of study embracing subjects in two related disciplines, together with an examination and a thesis, could lead to the degree of Doctor of Philosophy or Doctor of Science. Although a few students enrolled each year for postgraduate studies, few of them actually earned their degrees. One Ph.D. was awarded in 1884 and a second in 1912, by which date there had been only one Master of Science and no Master of Arts.

The attempt to establish earned advanced degrees coincided with the termination of the practice of awarding the master's degree routinely to all graduates three years after they had received the bachelor's degree. This practice, common in nearly all American colleges, ended in 1881. However, alumni who graduated from professional schools of theology, law, or medicine, or who presented other acceptable evidence of intellectual progress could apply for the appropriate master's degree three years after graduating. Practicing engineers who presented a description of some work accomplished might receive the advanced degree of Civil Engineer. A very high proportion of graduates who were eligible applied for and were awarded such degrees through the next four decades. The fact that master's degrees could be obtained in this manner no doubt inhibited formal graduate study. More important, however, was the fact that Rutgers in the 1880's lacked the resources to establish a graduate school and assume the full status of a university.

Among other considerations, the College library was woefully inadequate. It had been maintained over the years by occasional gifts of money or books; there were no regular annual appropriations for new acquisitions. Despite the efforts of the faculty member who served as librarian, an alarming number of books were "lost" each year. A new librarian who surveyed the holdings in 1866—after the Seminary had removed its portion of the collection—found that they amounted to some three thousand volumes, plus about eight hundred Congressional documents. Very few of the books were of recent vintage; in the field of chemistry not one new work had been added in twenty years, and even in the classics the critical editions were all those of a past generation. "In short," he concluded, "the Library is without the apparatus to make and keep men scholars." Over the next decade, the faculty frequently urged the need for additional library resources, and from time to time the Trustees made small sums available. After 1874, when the library was moved to new quarters in Kirkpatrick Chapel, conditions for the use of its modest resources were improved. By 1877 arrangements had been made to hire a student assistant in order that the library might be open every weekday for two and one half hours and two hours on Saturdays in order "to increase the culture and usefulness of the institution."

The faculty also grappled with the problem of admissions procedures, seeking both to maintain the same standards as other institutions and to find some alternative to examining each candidate individually. Over the years the requirements were steadily increased, until by 1881 plane geometry, ancient and modern geography, English grammar and spelling, and American history were included, along with substantial achievements in Latin and Greek. In 1876 it was decided to admit without examination students who held the appropriate certificates from the Regents of the State of New York. Meanwhile, a small number of colleges had begun the practice of admitting students from specified schools on the basis of certificates from their teachers or headmasters. A faculty committee in 1879, after a careful study of this procedure, recommended that it be followed at Rutgers. When the Trustees refused to sanction this innovation, the faculty responded with a telling argument: "We may mention that not a single classical student has been received this year from any of the schools in the Hudson Valley, one of our greatest sources of patronage, those colleges which admit on certificate having drawn away all the pupils we should naturally get in this quarter." Confronted with this alarming fact, the Trustees capitulated, and in 1881 the faculty announced a list of thirteen approved schools—all of them private academies—from which students would be received on certificate. Subsequently the list was greatly extended. The certificate procedure relieved the faculty of the burden of examining each candidate. More important, it was greatly to encourage public high schools to maintain approved academic courses of study in order that their students might be eligible for the certificate privilege.

While the faculty sought to keep the College abreast of contemporary movements in higher education, it continued to be the lot of the president and the Trustees to find the necessary funds to sustain the institution. Despite the spectacular success of the campaign for the New Endowment Fund, the unanticipated costs of maintaining the Scientific School, and especially the College farm, together with generous expenditures from capital funds on an addition to the Grammar School and improvements to Queen's building, had sorely depleted invested funds. Happily, it seemed, an ideal occasion presented itself as the basis of a new appeal for money. Unaware that the College had received its first charter in 1766, the alumni and Trustees arranged to celebrate the centennial of the College in 1870, the anniversary of the second charter. The observance was planned not only "To recount the goodness of God in His care of the College and to return thanks for the same," but also "To further in some marked way and degree the interests of the College."

Under the energetic direction of President Campbell and with the wholehearted cooperation of the Alumni Association, a successful one-year campaign brought in over $121,000. Again, as a special enticement, donors of $1,000 received perpetual scholarships and those who subscribed $500 were granted scholarships tenable for their lives. When the alumni, students, and friends of the College gathered in unprecedented numbers at commencement on June 21, 1870, to commemorate the Centennial and listen to an address on the history of the College by Supreme Court Justice Joseph P. Bradley, they had reason to feel confidence in the future as well as pride in the past.

With the money in hand, the Trustees debated the uses to which it should be put. One horrifying proposal was that $25,000 should be expended "for the purpose of adorning and enlarging . . . [Queen's building] by adding a stone portico in front extending to what is now the second story; by putting on a mansard roof with an additional story" to contain a library and chapel. Fortunately, wiser counsels prevailed, and the ultimate decision was to use about half of the newly raised money to build a geological hall between Queen's and Van Nest. Designed by Henry Janeway Hardenbergh and completed in 1872, the brownstone structure contained an armory in the basement, facilities for physical sciences on the first floor, and a large museum on the second floor.

Even before work had begun on Geological Hall, the good news was received that Mrs. Sophia Astley Kirkpatrick of New Brunswick had left her residuary estate, amounting ultimately to some $65,000, to the College. The Trustees, with the hearty concurrence of the faculty, decided to use this unexpected benefaction to erect a combined chapel and library, named in honor of the donor. Hardenbergh was again called upon for plans, and he produced an eminently satisfactory building, in modified Gothic style, which was dedicated in December 1873. The front portion contained a chapel, and in the rear the library was installed on the second floor and classrooms and offices on the first floor. With the removal of the library and chapel from Queen's and the shifting of certain functions from Van Nest to Geological Hall, there was a very considerable rearrangement of physical accommodations. More than thirty years passed before the College was able to build additional instructional facilities.

Because such a large proportion of the new funds was expended on buildings, the Trustees were soon confronted with annual deficits, and in 1874 President Campbell announced a plan to raise $184,000, much of which was to be used for faculty salaries. Despite his best efforts, and those of a financial agent, the campaign was totally unsuccessful. By 1880, when the budget of $31,350 showed a deficit of nearly $4,000, the Trustees were endeavoring to raise $2,000 annually by subscriptions among themselves. During Dr. Campbell's presidency nearly $430,000 had come to the College through gifts and bequests, but expenditures for needed buildings and for an expanded faculty ran ahead of income.

The enlargement of College affairs and the rise to prominence in the Board of Trustees of men accustomed to the ways of business brought about a more formal structure of organization for that body. New rules adopted in 1869 decreed that the president of the College, in the absence of the Governor, should be the permanent president of the Board. In place of the various special committees that had previously been created to deal with particular matters, five standing committees, appointed by the president, were established: finance, instruction and discipline, agricultural college, grammar school, and properties. The growing strength and interest of the alumni led to demands that they be represented on the Board, and in 1882 a plan was adopted whereby the Alumni Association was to nominate candidates who would be seated for limited terms. As the president and the faculty assumed more and more initiative, the Trustees played less of a role than formerly in shaping the College, although they did not abdicate their responsibility for passing upon every proposal that affected policy or operations.

Despite the increase in staff and facilities, the new programs of studies in the Scientific School, the availability of forty land-grant scholarships, and other favoring factors, enrollments remained at a discouragingly low level. There were rarely more than 170 undergraduates in the College, and by the last year of Dr. Campbell's administration there were only 113. Usually the classical students outnumbered the scientific about two-to-one. There was a steady decline in the proportion of students from New York State; by 1881 two-thirds of the undergraduates were from New Jersey and the remainder, except for a handful from other states, came from New York. Because about half of the students were recipients of scholarships, income from this source usually accounted for only about one-seventh of the annual income, despite the fact that tuition for all students was increased to seventy-five dollars in 1871.

A distinctive group within the undergraduate body consisted of several Japanese students, the first of whom enrolled in 1868. Their presence was due very largely to the influence of several Rutgers graduates who went to Japan in this period as Dutch Reformed clergymen and teachers. Thirteen Japanese youths, most of them destined to fill positions of the highest importance in their native land, attended the College over the course of a decade, and four received their degrees. A far larger number studied at the Grammar School. The connection between the College and Japan was further strengthened when Professor David Murray accepted the post of educational advisor to the Japanese government in 1873 and devoted six years to reorganizing the entire educational system of the country. Another major figure was William Elliot Griffis, 1868, who returned from his teaching post in Japan to write voluminously about the little known land. From all accounts the exotic visitors were well received in the College and the town, and many of them formed enduring friendships during their residence.

If the students were few in numbers, they were not lacking in vitality and imagination. In no other era in the history of the College did they display more inventiveness in developing their extracurricular life than in the decade after the Civil War. Many of their creations were intended to provide outlets for intellectual, esthetic, or spiritual expression. More of them, however, reflected a strong revolt against traditional precepts respecting frivolity, idleness, and sociability, and the full-blown emergence of new concepts of what truly constituted manliness in the male undergraduate. In a special sense the undergraduates now became "organization men," throwing themselves enthusiastically into the activities of fraternities, classes, clubs, teams, and editorial staffs. Such terms as leadership, loyalty, spirit, courage, and competition acquired new meaning and recognized a new set of virtues. And because such virtues were highly relevant to the "real" world of affairs beyond the campus, they came to be glorified as representing among the best fruits of the collegiate way of life.

No development better exemplified the new orientation of collegiate mores than the enthusiasm for organized athletic competition. Previously, students had engaged in such casual physical activities as walking, fishing, boating, skating, or informal games of ball, and their competitive instincts had found expression chiefly in oratorical contests. But in the post-Civil War decade team competition in baseball, rowing, and football suddenly came into vogue, offering new outlets for energy, recognition for new types of accomplishments, and inspiration for new expressions of group loyalties. It is needless to add that the exciting discovery of sports further diluted the students' involvement in the curriculum.

Rowing and baseball were the first sports to arouse student interest. The organization of a local rowing club offered the inspiration for the undergraduates to organize a crew, which in 1865 won a victory over the townsmen's Raritan Club. By 1867 a student boating association had been organized, and within the next two years a six-oared gig, christened the "Henry Rutgers," had been purchased, and a boathouse had been built. Because the Trustees took the position that no College funds could be appropriated to support athletic activities, the Boating Association had continual financial difficulties, dependent as it was on the dues and contributions of members. It sponsored interclass competition, arranged a program of races with town crews during commencement week, and on rare occasions met other colleges on the Raritan, including the champion Harvard crew in 1870, Stevens in 1877, and Princeton in 1882. A disastrous flood in the last year wrecked the boathouse and boats, and although there were intermittent revivals of the sport, fifty years were to pass before it became firmly established.

Baseball soon competed with crew for student interest and financial support. A casually chosen Rutgers team ventured to Princeton in May 1866 to engage the nine of Old Nassau, losing by the horrendous score of 40–42. For the next few years the sport continued on an informal basis, but, following another severe trouncing by Princeton in October 1870, the need for organization and discipline was recognized, and the Rutgers Base Ball Club was promptly formed. Perceiving the serious issues at stake, the College newspaper exhorted the team to practice faithfully, obey the instructions of their captain, and not permit society or fraternity rivalries to impair their dedication to the common cause. Now attired in what were described as "very pretty suits," the team was soon winning its share of victories—often by such scores as 37–17—and became a permanent part of the athletic scene.

For many years the students had engaged in a loosely defined game that bore a vague resemblance to soccer, except that there were no limitations on the number of participants, that the ball might be batted with the hands as well as kicked, and that considerable physical contact was allowed. At Princeton a similar game was popular. Early in the autumn of 1869, the men of Rutgers organized a team of twenty-five players, chose a Sophomore, William J. Leggett, as captain, and with much formality invited the men of Princeton to meet them in a series of three contests. The challenge was accepted, and on the afternoon of November 2, 1869, after some preliminary negotiations to clarify the rules of the simple game, the two teams met in New Brunswick on an unused field—now the site of the gymnasium—to engage in the first intercollegiate football game. The story of that historic encounter has been told and retold until it has become part of the American legend. Suffice it to say that Rutgers, behind in the early stages of the contest, rallied in the closing minutes to win by a score of 6–4. In a second match, played at Princeton in accordance with local rules, Rutgers met with the first of a series of defeats that was not to end until 1938. But the American game of football had been launched, and it soon exceeded all other collegiate sports in popularity. Rutgers continued its rivalry with Princeton and added Columbia to its schedule in 1870, Yale in 1873, Stevens Institute in 1874, and in due course other Eastern colleges. The original game was transformed after 1876 into something resembling the modern version, chiefly because Harvard insisted on incorporating many of the features of English Rugby. In spite of the small size of its student body, Rutgers each year fielded teams that were highly praised for their spirit and that courageously went down before the Yale juggernauts of the 1880's by scores too embarrassing to record.

In striking contrast with the situation today, intercollegiate athletics in that early era was wholly a student enterprise. The Trustees gave no funds or facilities, provided no coaches, counted no gate receipts. The faculty did its best to remain officially ignorant of the fact that athletic organizations existed, although individual members vouchsafed encouragement and support. The undergraduates organized the Rutgers Athletic Association in 1876–77 by merging the earlier baseball and football clubs. Supported by student dues and meagre returns from ticket sales, the Association maintained playing fields, purchased uniforms, arranged schedules, and—in a later era—hired coaches. When the Association was incorporated in 1879 a nine-man board of trustees composed largely of resident alumni and one or two faculty members exercised remote supervisory powers, but alumni influence did not become significant until after 1910.

While the more robust students were displaying their prowess on the gridiron, the diamond, and the river, others were organizing cultural activities. In 1867 a new publication, the *Targum*, made its appearance. Originally devoted largely to publicizing the fraternities and societies, it was issued only once a year. In January 1869, it was transformed into a monthly paper and not only concerned itself with presenting student "literary contributions" and College news but also sought "to awaken the interest of the Alumni in their Alma Mater and to bring the College before the public." One of its first successful campaigns resulted in the adoption of scarlet as the College color by the students in May 1869; a decision that was formally ratified by action of the Trustees in 1900. The idea of an annual, featuring College organizations, was carried on in the *Scarlet Letter,* the first volume of which was published in 1871. It continued to appear under the auspices of the fraternities until 1913, when the Junior class took it over. Those with musical talents formed a glee club in 1873, which gave concerts in neighboring towns, for one of which the song "On the Banks" was hastily composed by Howard N. Fuller and set to the tune of "On the Banks of the Old Dundee." Religious interest found expression in the Rutgers Christian Association, formed in 1876 at the instigation of Dr. Campbell. Setting itself "the purpose of promoting Christian growth and zeal in the College," it held noontime prayer meetings and weekly sessions for the discussion of serious subjects.

Contrary to the early predictions of the faculty, the zeal for exclusive fellowship continued unabated. When the Trustees at last relented in 1864 and agreed to recognize the existence of fraternities, new chapters were founded—Chi Phi in 1867, Beta Theta Pi in 1871, and Chi Psi in 1879—bringing the total to seven. Each had an average membership of around fifteen, which meant that considerably more than half of the undergraduates were Greeks. None of the chapters as yet possessed houses of their own; instead they rented lodge rooms in town. Although the weighty influence of fraternity politics in every campus activity was frequently decried, the system became thoroughly accepted, and student careerists sharpened their manipulative skills in the process of exalting their own and their chapter's prestige. With so many competing organizations, the old literary societies declined in vigor but nevertheless continued to hold a place in the College until the 1890's.

Populated as it now was by a host of student organizations, the campus scene was also enlivened by a variety of forms of student exuberance. Beards came into vogue, Seniors indulged themselves in beaver hats, Sophomores sported canes, the meerschaum pipe was the badge of the elegant gentleman. The velocipede, forerunner of the bicycle, became all the rage. In the slang of the era young females became "ducks," "gumdrops," and "pinks," a student's room was his "shebang," and his roommate might be described, according to his qualities, as a "brick," "cuss," "flat," "slouch," or "trump." The rowdy pranks of the previous era were given new meaning as class warfare and hazing acquired prominence. The Sophomores assumed the role of instilling in the Freshmen a due sense of their utter worthlessness, and class rushes of all sorts, but most especially the cane rush, provided excuses for organized mayhem. Insulting "proclamations" were printed, reciting the puerile qualities of the opposing class, and the old "burlesques" lost none of their savage humor. The Sophomore exhibition produced such wild disorders that it was discontinued as a public exercise by the faculty in 1882.

A new and colorful ritual was the "cremation ceremony." Each spring the Sophomores made elaborate arrangements for interring their most hated textbook—for many years Freeman's *Outlines*. First in the nocturnal procession came the musician, followed by the orator and a poet in white. Next came a bier, supporting a coffin in which reposed the offensive volume, upheld by four costumed pallbearers who also carried torches. Two gravediggers completed the party of dignitaries, after whom the sheeted Sophomores and other students followed in ranks, with a mob of excited "townies" bringing up the rear. "In chill moonlight under the class tree," the oration was pronounced, the poem was recited, songs were sung, and the volume was duly consigned to the flames. If the ceremony did not end in a brawl between "townies" and students, it usually resulted in some equally exhilarating imbroglio.

Some of the more exciting escapades entered the folklore of the College in this era, holding places in the memories of alumni along with the first football game. There was the incident of the destruction of the campus fence in 1867. For months the students had asked in vain that a gate be placed in the fence adjacent to Van Nest in order that they might have convenient access to the halls of the literary societies. On the night of February 2, under the leadership of Tunis G. Bergen—later a highly respected Trustee—a mob of students tore down and utterly destroyed the fence. Weeks of investigation by the faculty fixed the major blame on nine students, all of whom were suspended or dismissed, but in due course, after signing pledges to abide by their matriculation oaths, all were returned to good standing. Even more celebrated was the "cannon war" with Princeton in 1875. Under the mistaken impression that a cannon implanted on the Princeton campus had in the distant past been taken from New Brunswick, a band of Rutgers men stealthily dug up the ancient piece and transported it to the campus, where they were hailed as heroes. This deed occasioned a salty correspondence between the presidents of the two colleges, which did little to diminish tensions, but ultimately a joint faculty committee from Princeton and Rutgers arbitrated the dispute. The cannon was returned, but the Princeton students were to cease their boasts that they had once taken it away from Rutgers.

As college life became increasingly oriented toward athletics, fraternities, clubs, and escapades, the faculty struggled against the current in trying to maintain respect for academic achievement. They gave hearty encouragement for a few years after 1874 to a series of intercollegiate contests in oratory, mathematics, and classical languages, in which undergraduates from several Eastern colleges vied for honors. They installed a chapter of Phi Beta Kappa in 1869—the eighteenth active chapter in the country—to give added recognition to high academic attainments. The list of prize awards was lengthened until by 1880 there were thirteen competitions in as many fields, most of them providing for multiple awards. To judge from the records of grades, student performance was little short of perfection. In a typical class, slightly more than half compiled four-year averages above 90 per cent; only two fell below 80 per cent. A student failing in a single subject was obliged to drop back a class and repeat all his work, but delinquents were invariably given re-examinations, which they usually passed. In common with nearly every other college at the time, Rutgers could ill afford to lose patronage by enforcing rigid academic standards; the same consideration operated to weaken efforts to maintain discipline. So long as colleges remained desperately in need of students, the students would have to be treated with tactful indulgence.

The most heartening evidence of the worthwhileness of the College experience was to be seen in the careers of the graduates. Coming for the most part from relatively humble backgrounds, dozens of them attained positions of the highest prominence in many fields. Garret A. Hobart, 1863, became Vice-President of the United States and Foster M. Voorhees, 1876, served as Governor of New Jersey. Albert S. Cook, 1872, was one of the foremost English scholars of his generation; Ellis A. Apgar, 1866, headed the state's school system for nearly twenty years; Alexander Johnston, 1870, had a brief but brilliant career as an historian. Among the important business leaders were Frederick Frelinghuysen, 1868, president of the Mutual Benefit Life Insurance Company; Haley Fiske, 1871, president of the Metropolitan Life Insurance Company; and Leonor F. Loree, 1877, president of the Delaware and Hudson Railroad. Others achieved prominence as lawyers, physicians, engineers, and teachers. Reflecting both the changing character of American society and the altered emphases within the College, the proportion of clergymen among the alumni declined greatly, and the fields of business and technology claimed the largest numbers of graduates.

After nearly a century of marginal existence, the College in the 1860's gave promise of moving forward rapidly to a new level of eminence among institutions of higher education. In swift succession it acquired a respectable endowment, secured its release from denominational control, established a Scientific School, became a land-grant college, augmented its faculty, erected new buildings, revised its curriculum, instituted post-graduate studies, and spawned a vigorous extracurricular life. In its program and facilities it clearly ranked with the better colleges in the nation. But in spite of all these evidences of healthy progress, the College, instead of growing in numbers, actually experienced a slight decline.

The causes of this frustrating lack of patronage are not difficult to identify. Foremost of all was the fact that American colleges in general had not yet become popular institutions. Although educational statistics for the period leave much to be desired, they present a crude picture of the situation. Between 1870 and 1880 the number of colleges increased from 266 to 364, but the average enrollment remained slightly under 100. The largest college in 1872 was Harvard, with 637 students; Princeton enrolled 369, Columbia 124, and the University of Pennsylvania only 88. Of twenty colleges in Pennsylvania, only one had as many as 200 students and fifteen had fewer than 100. The problems that Rutgers faced, then, were not peculiar; they were inherent in the educational and social structure of the nation. There would not be a marked increase in the proportion of young people attending colleges until public high schools became widely established, funds from private and public sources were enormously increased, and a college education was regarded as essential to improved economic opportunity.

Doubtless it was small consolation to those devoted to the welfare of Rutgers, but within the context of the times the condition of the College was better than most and should not have occasioned dismay. It is difficult to imagine what more could reasonably have been expected from the Trustees, the president, the faculty, the students, and the alumni in advancing the interests of the institution. It is possible, of course, to see in the Rutgers environment certain special limiting factors. Because the College continued to be strongly identified with, and look for support from, one of the smallest Protestant denominations in the country, its constituency remained restricted. Similarly, the extreme conservatism of the State of New Jersey with respect to higher education cut off any hopes of aid from that source. The failure to provide a dormitory and dining hall and thereby enable Rutgers to compete with other colleges in cost of room and board may have been a serious mistake in policy. Even the reluctance to discard entirely the classical curriculum in favor of "practical" courses or extensive electives may seem, in retrospect, to have been an error, but many colleges that followed such experimental policies met with disaster. Here and there an outstandingly able president—Eliot of Harvard, White of Cornell, Angell of Michigan, Gilman of Johns Hopkins—somehow surmounted great obstacles and carried his institution to unprecedented heights of usefulness and strength, but such were the exceptional cases. For Rutgers, as for the vast majority of colleges, the immediate challenge was that of survival.

As Dr. Campbell approached the end of nearly two eventful decades as president, he decided that the time had come to submit his resignation. He had always been very nearsighted, and after 1870 his sight failed so that he was no longer able to read. Aware of this handicap, and discouraged by the failure of recent fund-raising efforts, he told the Trustees in June 1881 that he could no longer discharge his duties as the welfare of the College demanded. He remained in service, however, until his successor was inaugurated a year later. After leaving the presidency, he organized the Suydam Street Reformed Church, of which he was the pastor until shortly before his death in 1890. His students long remembered him as a remarkably effective teacher of moral philosophy, the Trustees and alumni hailed him for his success as a fund raiser, the faculty revered him for his willingness to endorse new ideas, and his closest friends recalled the zeal of his religious faith and the enthusiasm that he brought to every endeavor. "The future of the college looks very bright to me," he told the Trustees as he prepared to leave office. "Under a young and vigorous President, what is to be will far surpass what has been." Of his own contribution he made no mention, but its magnitude was plain to all.

Chapter Six

The Emergence of the State College

The course of development that Rutgers College would pursue in the future was far from clear when Merrill Edwards Gates was installed as president in June 1882. A basis for a possible choice between alternative courses had been laid by certain decisions made during Dr. Campbell's administration, notably the creation of the Rutgers Scientific School and the acceptance of the land-grant designation. The College could develop its private resources, remain largely independent of public support and control, and give continued emphasis to the old classical curriculum, or it might move in the direction of becoming the State College of Agriculture and the Mechanic Arts, in fact as well as in name. Those who were in charge of the destiny of the institution were only dimly aware of these alternatives; hardly in a position to make a clear-cut choice between them, they pursued instead a policy of cautious opportunism. Consequently, by the end of Dr. Gates's administration in 1890, the College had assumed a peculiar, dual character, and this status came to be clearly recognized during the administration of his successor. Rutgers was to be both private and public and was to combine features of the old classical college and the newer land-grant institutions.

When the Trustees sought a successor to President Campbell, they looked for a vigorous young man whose immediate task would be to strengthen the College academically. In selecting Gates, they chose a professional educator, rather than a clergyman or a public figure. Only thirty-four years old, the new president had graduated from the University of Rochester in 1870 with a brilliant record and had achieved notable success for twelve years as the principal of Albany Academy. Imposing in appearance, highly gifted as an orator, of distinguished lineage, he was widely regarded as a young man of remarkable promise. The faculty greeted the news of his election with unanimous approval, and the students celebrated the announcement with wild enthusiasm.

President Gates had decided views about the College and about his

111

own role in its management. The American college, he believed, was "designed to give a liberal education, not to train specialists in any one department of knowledge." Taking a firm stand on the controversial question of the elective system, he argued forcefully in his inaugural address in favor of a strictly prescribed curriculum. "Experience has proved," he stated, "that in developing mental power, certain studies have a far greater effect than do others." Decrying Herbert Spencer's theory that students should pursue those studies which they found most pleasant, he stressed the values of discipline. "A system of education which substitutes for all the disciplinary work of the college course, a seductive and discursive field of elective studies, where a youth at eighteen is told to wander, selecting at his own sweet will . . . is utterly subversive of all self-discipline, and will not develop manly fibre, or give tone and symmetry to intellect or character." In a similar vein he denounced the prevailing notion that a special morality should prevail in college, that undergraduates should be expected to "sow their wild oats." College men, he insisted, should be held to the highest standards of morality and decorum; then "that unlovely species . . . 'the college hoodlum'" would become extinct. Here, albeit in new language, was a reaffirmation of the old collegiate tradition.

President Gates quickly made it plain to the faculty that although he would consult with them on matters of importance, he was fully prepared to accept responsibility for running the College. He was equally imperious in his relations with the Board of Trustees, scolding them on occasion and pointing out to them the nature of their duties. The students soon discovered that unlike his predecessor he was a strict disciplinarian who was not disposed to excuse exuberant indiscretions but who, on the contrary, would deal firmly with offenders while giving them somewhat tedious lectures on Christian ethics.

Gates's zeal to improve the academic and moral tone of the College was reflected in many actions. Admission requirements, formerly administered with a measure of tolerance, were now rigorously enforced. In place of the fairly casual oral examinations given to prospective candidates, written tests were now prescribed, and the president took pride in the fact that as many as one-quarter of the candidates were refused admittance. The passing grade for term work and examinations was raised from 50 per cent to 60 per cent, and after a long interval the old system of having each class examined by a committee of the faculty, in addition to the instructor in charge, was restored. Reversing the trend toward reducing the amount of time spent on the classics, the faculty now required one term each of Latin and Greek in the Junior year. The only concession that was made to the elective system was a slight revision of the curriculum in 1886 to permit Seniors to take two two-hour electives; Juniors were permitted only one. Elective subjects, however, were not to carry grade marks nor to enter into the calculations of the general standing of students.

The new emphasis on high quality of academic performance also resulted in the establishment of an honors program. "The idea," explained a faculty committee, "is to encourage independent reading and study and investigation on the part of the student under direction of the Faculty, who undertake to satisfy themselves as to the character and thoroughness of the work done." Students of high standing could apply to the president for permission to take additional work, for which they would be given "honorable mention" in the College catalogue. Few students availed themselves of the privilege. The list of prize awards continued to grow until by 1890 there were seventeen different competitions. Although the students complained about the increased burden of work and the pressure for high achievement, the president did not relax his campaign but instead took pride in the generally improved standing of the College.

Gates recognized that the success of his program to improve the quality of the College required changes within the faculty. Two men of long service whose effectiveness he questioned were induced to resign and a third was reduced to part-time status. New men with excellent qualifications were brought in, including Austin Scott, who had taken his doctorate at Leipzig and had conducted one of the original seminars in history at Johns Hopkins; Louis Bevier, 1878, a Johns Hopkins Ph.D., who taught first modern languages and subsequently Greek; Edgar S. Shumway, a Latin scholar of high attainments; and Alfred A. Titsworth, a graduate of the Scientific School, who brought new strength to the work in civil engineering. Significantly, not one of the fifteen men appointed during Gates's administration was a clergyman, and nearly all of them held earned doctorates. Clearly, an old academic tradition had ended; hereafter the faculty was composed of trained, professional scholars.

Along with reform of the faculty and the tightening of academic standards came substantial improvements in the condition of the library. In 1884 Irving S. Upson, who held the position of chief clerk of the State Experiment Station, was appointed librarian with a salary of $150, "out of which," in the language of the official minutes, "he may have the privilege of engaging an assistant, the Trustees recognizing the fact that his work will be largely a labor of love to his Alma Mater." Upson, a graduate in the class of 1881, was indeed a dedicated man and soon brought the library to a new level of efficiency. With the strong support of President Gates, the Trustees were induced to appropriate $1,000 or more each year for books while modern techniques of cataloguing and arrangement were instituted. When Upson entered upon his duties, the library contained about 10,000 volumes; augmented by gifts of large collections, such as that by P. Vanderbilt Spader in 1887, it grew rapidly to more than 26,000 volumes by 1890.

Upson represented the appearance in the College of a distinctively new type of functionary, the nonfaculty administrator. Quietly effective, possessed of the complete confidence of the president, the faculty, and the Trustees, he was in time given additional assignments, becoming registrar in 1890, secretary of the faculty in 1892, and treasurer of the College in 1905. His appointment as librarian, a post previously held by a succession of professors, represented the first step in the process by which the faculty gradually divested itself of responsibility for all functions not directly related to teaching. Interestingly enough, Upson was given nonvoting faculty status in 1890 and was viewed as an agent of the faculty in discharging his manifold duties, but in time the separation between "faculty" and "administration" became clearly defined.

Under the new regime, various efforts were made to assume control over the extracurricular conduct of the students. Soon after the new administration began, the students were induced to vote in favor of the abolition of cane rushing, and the faculty resolved "to use discipline to any needed extent to prevent its revival in any form." Despite these pledges and injunctions, there were occasional rushes, usually resulting in the suspension of the ringleaders. The students sought to avoid the letter of the law by engaging in flag rushes, but the faculty promptly squelched this evasion by resolving that "the hanging or displaying in public places about the college grounds or buildings of class insignia manifestly designed to provoke contests" was a punishable offense. There was a similar crackdown on cases of academic dishonesty. The use of what were euphemistically referred to as "adventitious aids" in classroom recitations and examinations had long been tolerated, but in 1889 the students were told that such practices must cease, and the warning was soon followed by the dismissal of two students.

Gates frequently proclaimed that the highest aim of the College was the formation of strong Christian character. His own contribution to the attainment of this ideal was considerable. Each Sunday morning before the regular services he conducted a Bible class, which had been compulsory for all students since the beginning of President Campbell's administration. In addition, he invariably attended the Thursday evening prayer meetings and sought to speak to each undergraduate individually about his religious convictions. He was gratified to be able to report to the Trustees that there were rarely more than a few graduates each year who had not openly professed their faith in Christ. The compulsory Bible class continued until 1893, when President Scott, pointing out that no other college had such a requirement, made attendance voluntary. Chapel attendance, of course, continued to be mandatory.

The emphasis on discipline extended to the military program. Ever since 1866 military drill, required of the scientific and optional with the classical students, had been carried on in lackadaisical fashion, much of the time under the direction of the professor of history. The amount of instruction was increased and grade marks were given in 1887, but, when young Lieutenant Samuel E. Smiley arrived to take command in 1888, the cadet corps still presented a nondescript appearance. "When he lined up the handful of students," it was later recalled, "lo and behold, the man in the middle was a big football center garbed in a sober black frock coat reaching nearly to his knees. Covering his head was a shiny, black silk 'stove pipe.'" His companions in arms wore skullcaps, derbies, tennis blazers and similar apparel. A year later Smiley persuaded his troops to buy the top half of a uniform, consisting of an unlined blue blouse, a cap, and white gloves, and the next year blue trousers were added. Thus nattily attired, the cadet corps increased the numbers of its recruits, took its duties seriously, and became a popular campus organization.

Even the sphere of sports, which had been under the exclusive control of the Athletic Association, was brought under scrutiny. Concerned about the effects of intercollegiate contests on class attendance and academic performance, the faculty placed restrictions on out-of-town games and in rare instances decreed that certain students whose work was deficient must be dropped from their teams. With similar considerations in mind, the Glee Club's schedule of concerts had to meet faculty approval. These actions were extremely significant, for they signalled the beginnings of an entirely new attitude toward extracurricular activities. Increasingly, the domain in which the students had enjoyed almost complete independence and responsibility would be brought under supervision, first by the faculty and then, in due course, by administrative officials.

Concern with the welfare of students, previously confined to the academic and spiritual, was extended to include their health and physical well-being. In 1883 a local physician, Dr. Henry Rutgers Baldwin, was invited to give two brief lectures on health to all the students after morning prayers. Three years later, satisfactory arrangements having been made for the use of the Seminary gymnasium, compulsory physical training was introduced for all Freshmen and Sophomores. An instructor, Archibald Cuthbertson, was hired on a part-time basis, and the students, with manifest reluctance, submitted to one hour of class instruction and three hours of individual exercise each week.

Perhaps the most important of all innovations affecting the students was the erection of a dormitory. From the earliest years of the College there had been discussions of this subject within the faculty and among the Trustees. There had been continual complaints that the cost of boarding in private houses discouraged students from attending Rutgers, and there was considerable substance to the charges. On the other hand, there was strong sentiment against the dormitory system because of its alleged harmful effect on the manners and morals of the students. By 1872, following another thorough study of the matter, the faculty came out strongly in favor of a dormitory, and the Trustees, reluctantly agreeing that such a facility was essential, authorized the president to seek funds for the purpose. Almost no money was obtained, and the project was dropped. Meanwhile the students, through the columns of the *Targum,* continued to urge the need for a dormitory. In 1887 President Gates reported to the Trustees that the faculty, with the exception of one member, believed that the College should have a dormitory, and a poll of the Board "seemed to indicate a prevailing opinion that such a building was necessary." There the matter rested until one day in January 1889 Garret E. Winants of Bergen Point, who had accumulated a vast fortune through investments in shipping and real estate, called on President Gates and, entirely unsolicited, offered to build a dormitory. The Trustees, hurriedly convened in special session, accepted Winants' generous offer. Van Campen Taylor, an alumnus and Newark architect, prepared plans in accordance with the instructions of the donor, and the result was a highly satisfactory building that contained accommodations for eighty-five students, a dining hall, and a lounge. First occupied in September 1890, the Winants Dormitory brought about a fundamental change in the living arrangements of the undergraduates. A related development at about the same time, in 1887, was the erection by Delta Phi of the first fraternity house. Other such houses followed, and soon the vast majority of students were living in compact groups in dormitories or fraternities instead of being scattered among numerous boarding houses in all parts of the city.

The influence of President Gates was clearly evident in every dimension of the College. As might have been expected, his new policies and the firmness with which he implemented them aroused antagonism. A major outburst of resentment occurred in 1886. On April 1 the numerals of the Class of 1889 were discovered daubed in paint on the front of the chapel. When the usual methods of detection failed, the president threatened to turn the matter over to the police, reading the appropriate sections of the criminal code to the students assembled in chapel. This tactic produced results, and seven men were suspended. The president's handling of the incident produced intense excitement and stimulated certain alumni to attack him in the press, charging that he ruled students and faculty with an iron hand, that he had driven two of the best loved men from the faculty, and that enrollments had declined because of his severe measures. When a student meeting was held to adopt resolutions denouncing the published statements, considerable hostility was manifested toward Gates and the resolves were not adopted. The return of the suspended students to the College in May was made the occasion of a tremendous celebration, complete with a parade through town behind a hired band and a pause before the president's house for the utterance of several loud groans. Despite the severity of the attack, Gates retained the support of most of the faculty and the Trustees and made no concessions to his adversaries.

One area in which the president was notably unsuccessful was that of spurring the Trustees to secure additional endowment funds. At the time that he took office, a campaign was announced to raise $100,000, but after three years of half-hearted effort—in which the president took little part—only about half that amount was secured. By 1886 annual deficits were running to nearly $10,000 a year, part of which were met by subscriptions among the Trustees. The difficulties arose in part from the fact that in order to maintain enrollments free scholarships were liberally granted to almost any student who requested them; tuition fees amounted to only 7 per cent of the total budget in 1887. Late in the decade a few substantial gifts added $60,000 to the endowment, but large deficits continued. Gates became increasingly caustic in his pleas to the Trustees. "He suggested," runs the report of one of his tirades, "that if the time and strength so often devoted to the discussion of honorary degrees were to be given to devising methods for increasing the resources of the College, to adding to the number of its students and increasing the efficiency of its work, good results would follow." As if this were not sufficiently pointed, he continued by remarking, "I look with confidence to you, Gentlemen of the Board, representing as you do in your own right some millions of money, and connected as you are, many of you, with men of great wealth, to see to it that ample provision is made for carrying forward the increasing work which God has committed to our care." But, as his successor was also to learn to his sorrow, the Trustees were unable or unwilling to raise money; that chore had to rest with the president.

While the College was having little success in its quest for private resources, President Gates and his associates—notably Dr. Cook—were actively at work to secure increased aid from the state and Federal governments. Although the College was carrying out faithfully the obligations it had accepted in 1864, it had not as yet received any subsidy from the state, and the income from the land-grant fund, never more than $6,900, did not begin to meet the increased expenditures that resulted from the establishment of the Scientific School and the operation of the experimental farm. The efforts to secure state aid met formidable obstacles: the inherent fiscal conservatism of New Jersey, the constitutional barrier against state appropriations to private institutions, the opposition of certain vested interests, and the hostility of farm groups, who decried the fact that the "Agricultural College" was unable to attract students to its course in agriculture. Aid from Federal sources under legislation directed toward providing additional funds for land-grant colleges encountered no such obstacles and was to be of inestimable benefit to the College.

Two such Federal laws—the Hatch Act of 1887 and the so-called second Morrill Act of 1890—more than doubled the operating income of the College and resulted in placing the work in the biological sciences on a new and secure foundation. The Hatch Act provided for the establishment of agricultural experiment stations at land-grant colleges, each of which would receive an annual subsidy of $15,000. In accepting the conditions imposed by the act, the New Jersey legislature reaffirmed the status of the Rutgers Scientific School as the "State Agricultural College of New Jersey." The new "College Experiment Station" was integrated with the existing State Experiment Station, utilizing the same facilities and having Dr. George H. Cook as director. Of greatest importance, the additional funds were used to appoint several remarkable scholars, to be responsible for inaugurating a full-scale program of instruction and research in the biological sciences. This group included Dr. Julius Nelson, a Johns Hopkins Ph.D., who soon achieved distinction in zoology for his oyster research; Dr. Byron D. Halstead, a Harvard-trained botanist of the first rank; and Dr. John B. Smith, an entomologist, who gained an international reputation for his researches on the mosquito.

The second Morrill Act of August 30, 1890, made available to each land-grant college appropriations that started at $15,000 and rose by annual increments of $1,000 to $25,000. These funds could be applied "to instruction in agriculture, the mechanic arts, the English language, and the various branches of mathematical, physical, natural and economic science, with special reference to their applications in the industries of life, and to the facilities for such instruction. . . ." With this substantial new source of income, the College again made several strong appointments. The significance of these two Federal enactments can scarcely be exaggerated; by 1890 nearly three-fifths of the total College budget—exclusive of the experiment stations—came from Federal sources, and that proportion increased as the receipts from the second Morrill Act escalated. Only four professors were paid wholly from the private funds of the College; the others received their salaries in whole or in part from one or another of the land-grant funds.

At the same time that the College was reaping the benefits of its land-grant designation from Federal sources, a determined effort was being made to induce the State of New Jersey to make some contribution to the institution. In 1883, with the hearty backing of the Board of Managers of the State Experiment Station, the Trustees sought an annual appropriation of $3,000 in compensation for the use by the Station of the costly experimental farm and the state laboratories in Van Nest Hall. Instead, the state agreed to pay $500 annual rent for the Station facilities. In 1887, prompted by President Gates, the state-appointed Board of Visitors roused themselves to action and launched a campaign to get the state to build an "Agricultural Hall" to house the work of the Scientific School and the Experiment Station. Declaring that the Trustees had "done much more than the wording of their contract calls for" to provide educational programs of benefit to agriculture and the mechanic arts, they chided the state for its attitude. "Other states have appropriated liberal sums to supplement those arising from the land grant," they stated, "while New Jersey has done nothing for the institution given to her up to this time."

A bill providing state funds for the construction of an "Agricultural Hall" was introduced in the legislature early in 1888 and speedily received the unanimous approval of both houses. But when Governor Robert S. Green made it known that he believed there were insuperable constitutional objections to appropriating state funds for a building at Rutgers, the measure was withdrawn and replaced by a substitute. Under the new scheme, the building was to be erected not for the College, but for the State Experiment Station, provided the Rutgers Trustees would make available a suitable plot of ground. In this form the bill was enacted and received the Governor's approval on April 23, 1888. A site on Hamilton Street, north of the old campus, was deeded to the Trustees by members of the family of James Neilson, which the Trustees in turn proposed to lease to the state for a dollar a year. When the state's Attorney General objected to this arrangement, the Trustees agreed to make an outright conveyance.

The building, which became known as New Jersey Hall, was completed in the spring of 1889. Although it was legally under the jurisdiction of the Board of Managers of the State Experiment Station, it actually housed the College work in the fields of chemistry and biology, as well as Experiment Station activities, thereby freeing space in Van Nest Hall and Geological Hall for other functions. Thus the College in fact acquired an "Agricultural Hall," but the somewhat dubious means by which this end was accomplished left unresolved the crucial question of the willingness of the state to contribute to the support of its land-grant college.

The difficulties inherent in the relationship between Rutgers and the state, first clearly exposed in the attempt to secure New Jersey Hall, did not discourage further efforts to obtain state assistance. In 1888 and again in 1889, the Board of Visitors, prompted by President Gates, was unusually fervent in its annual reports in pleading the cause of the College. Explaining in detail how other states were appropriating large sums annually for their land-grant institutions while New Jersey had done nothing, they again commended the Rutgers Trustees for the heavy expenditures they had made in behalf of the Scientific School and called upon the state to recognize its obligations. In 1889 they recommended a specific plan. The number of free scholarships in the Scientific School should be greatly increased, in return for which the state would make regular annual appropriations toward the operating expenses of the College. This proposal, which was to involve the College in incredible difficulties with the state over the next fifteen years, was at once made the object of a determined campaign.

The College was in a good position to demonstrate the need for additional scholarships. Under the legislation of 1864, it will be recalled, forty scholarships tenable in the Scientific School had been created. For many years it had not been possible to attract sufficient candidates to fill all the available scholarships, but as the result of intense efforts by the College administration, the improved cooperation of the school superintendents, and a general expansion of the public high schools, the number of qualified applicants increased. In 1888 the Trustees agreed to add ten scholarships to the forty that they were obliged to offer and then authorized the granting of free tuition to thirteen additional students who were certified by their county superintendents. Of the eighty-three students enrolled that year in the Scientific School, sixty-three paid no tuition.

With the strong endorsement of county and city school superintendents, as well as the Board of Visitors, a bill was introduced in the legislature early in 1890 to provide for the awarding of one state scholarship each year in each of the sixty assembly districts in the state. Rutgers, in return, was to receive an annual appropriation from general state funds of $12,000. The measure readily passed both houses, but when Governor Leon Abbett raised various objections to it, it was withdrawn and was replaced by a substitute. This bill, entitled "An Act to Increase the Efficiency of the Public School System of the State by Providing for Additional Free Scholarships at the State Agricultural College," differed significantly from the original measure. Instead of getting a lump-sum appropriation, Rutgers was to be compensated at the rate of $174 for each scholarship awarded. More important in terms of subsequent legal entanglements, the money was to come not from general state revenues but from the state school fund, which was derived from special sources and which, under constitutional limitations, was to be devoted exclusively to the support of the public schools.

In its new form the measure seemed destined for quick passage. It got through the Senate without controversy, but when it was called up for final vote in the House certain legislators asked that the vote be postponed pending a public hearing. Princeton, it developed, was strongly opposed to the measure and had a paid lobbyist, Thomas N. McCarter, working for its defeat. The disclosure of this hostility caused a momentary sensation. The friends of Rutgers rallied to her support, charging, not at all accurately, that Princeton had refused to accept the land-grant designation when it had been offered to her and that Rutgers had thereupon accepted and honorably fulfilled its obligation. After a heated debate, the motion to lay the bill over was defeated and the measure was then enacted by an overwhelming majority. One newspaper account, making much of the intercollege rivalry, headlined its story "The Crimson [sic] downs Orange and Black." Governor Abbett, still retaining doubts about the constitutionality of the scholarship bill, permitted it to become law without his signature. Another ominous sign was that the State Board of Agriculture refused to support the measure because of its resentment of the fact that so few students enrolled for the course in agriculture.

President Gates and the Trustees were fully aware that the scholarship act was highly controversial and that it might well be open to objections on constitutional grounds, but after consultation with legal authorities they decided to implement the measure and await any challenge. Accordingly, thirty-three scholarship students were admitted in September 1890 on the basis of competitive examinations administered by the city and county superintendents of education. In due course the College authorities submitted a bill to the state for the tuition charges as authorized by the law. After an initial payment of $1,500 had been made, the state comptroller, without giving any reasons for his decision, declined to approve any further payments. For the next dozen years the competitive examinations continued to be held, successful candidates were awarded scholarships and were admitted to the Scientific School, the College presented its bills to the state, and the state refused to pay. What had promised to be a new era in the relationship between the College and the state had become a legal nightmare. From this time forward, the problem of "state relations," which previously had been of minor importance, loomed ever larger in the affairs of the College.

The effect of the several Federal and state enactments on the basic character of the College was tremendous. Until around 1890 the numbers of classical students had customarily exceeded the numbers of scientific students by two or three to one. But because of the new facilities provided

by New Jersey Hall, the augmented scientific faculty financed by the
Hatch and second Morrill Acts, and, not least in importance, the additional students attracted by the state scholarship program, the numbers
of students in the Scientific School rose sharply and in the decade of
the 1890's exceeded those in the classical curriculum by more than two
to one. Instead of being a classical liberal arts college with an appended
scientific department, Rutgers had almost overnight become a scientific
and technical institution with an appended classical department.

The radically altered situation was immediately reflected in significant
changes in the curriculum of the Scientific School. Almost from its inception, there had been but two curricula—civil and mechanical engineering,
and chemistry and agriculture. Now, in 1888, a new curriculum in electrical engineering was introduced and in 1890 separate curricula were
established in chemistry and in agriculture and a new curriculum in
biology was inaugurated. As in the past, the scientific students all pursued
substantially the same studies during their first two years, embarking on
their specialized programs only in their final two years. The most popular
curricula were those in civil and mechanical engineering, electrical engineering, and chemistry. Biology for many years attracted few majors,
and only occasionally before 1900 did a student enroll in agriculture.
Needless to say, the title "State Agricultural College," by which the
Scientific School was popularly known, was a complete misnomer and
produced widespread misunderstandings of the actual functions of the
land-grant college.

At this important juncture in the development of the College, President
Gates submitted his resignation effective September 30, 1890, to accept
the presidency of Amherst College. During his tenure the quality of
the faculty had been greatly improved, academic standards had been
generally strengthened, student discipline had been tightened, and actions
had been taken which, after many vicissitudes, were to involve Rutgers
in a fundamentally altered relationship to the State of New Jersey. It
was somewhat ironic that although his primary interest was in the old-
style classical college, Gates' major achievement was the strengthening
of the Scientific School and that while he was conspicuously unsuccessful
in increasing the private endowment funds he was extremely influential
in securing public funds. He bequeathed to his successor an excellent
faculty and an expanding student body, as well as vexatious financial
problems and a wide range of critical issues involving relations with
the state.

The man selected by the Trustees as Gates' successor in November
1890, was Dr. Austin Scott, who had distinguished himself as professor
of history and constitutional law in the College since 1883. Scott had
an impressive background. Following his graduation from Yale in 1869 he

had taken a master's degree at the University of Michigan and had then gone abroad to secure his doctorate in history at Leipzig. While in Germany, he assisted the venerable George Bancroft in the preparation of the tenth volume of his monumental *History of the United States*. Returning home, he taught for two years at Michigan and then was called to Johns Hopkins, where he conducted a seminar in history from 1876 to 1882 and worked with Bancroft on his *History of the Constitution of the United States*. Never a productive scholar, Scott scintillated in the classroom, played a leading role within the faculty and in professional organizations, and developed an extensive acquaintance with prominent men in the state. Possessed of a fiery temper and lacking the gifts of an administrator, he found many aspects of the presidential role uncongenial to his temperament, but for fifteen years he struggled to surmount the many difficulties that he encountered, and when he resigned his onerous office to resume full-time teaching he could derive satisfaction from several notable accomplishments.

The entire Scott administration was strongly dominated by concern about relations with the state. Indeed, almost every significant policy decision was directly affected by that concern. At the heart of the problem was the refusal of the state to make the payments anticipated under the Scholarship Act of 1890. Realizing how important the state connection was to the College, Scott and the Trustees were reluctant to take any actions that would sever the relationship; consequently they continued to award the scholarships, at the same time engaging in an intricate series of legal maneuvers designed to secure a favorable adjustment of the issue. Meanwhile, deprived of any income from the scholarship students—who included nearly all of the students in the Scientific School—the College was placed in a desperate financial predicament, which grew even worse when depression conditions after 1893 all but cut off prospects of aid from private sources. Internally, the great imbalance between the Scientific School and the classical division posed many problems that long eluded solution. Although conditions began to improve markedly after 1900, the College under Scott did not make the large advances that had been hoped for on the basis of the favorable developments that had occured in the final years of the Gates administration.

Because of their crucial importance, the issues involved in the state-scholarship controversy require some elaboration. The state authorities made it known to the College that there were two reasons why no payments were forthcoming. The act of 1890 had specified that payments should be made from the dedicated state school fund *only* after all other appropriations authorized from that fund had been met. The simple fact was that there was never such a surplus available to meet the scholarship charges. But even more serious were two constitutional objections. Under Article IV, section 7, paragraph 6 of the state constitution the legislature was strictly enjoined from applying the income from the school fund to any purpose other than support of the public schools. It was also contended that Article I, section 20, barring state appropriations "for the use of any society, association or corporation whatever," was an impediment to the expenditure of general state funds for the purposes contemplated in the scholarship act, inasmuch as the Trustees of Rutgers College were a private corporation. All of these points were made by Governor George T. Werts in 1894 when he vetoed a bill that would have charged the state scholarships to general state funds and were reiterated in opinions of the state's attorney general in 1898 and again in 1901. Various attempts on the part of Scott and the Trustees to resolve these problems through new legislative enactments came to naught, and at length it became apparent that a judicial test—to which the College authorities were loath to resort—would be necessary. Meanwhile, between 1890 and 1901, there were on the average sixty free scholarship students enrolled in the College each year, and the amount due from the state rose steadily to $131,610.

Behind the constitutional and fiscal obstacles lay an equally formidable source of opposition. The agricultural interests of the state, powerfully represented by the State Board of Agriculture and by rural legislators, were hostile to the College because so few students entered from farming communities and because agricultural studies had such a small place in the Scientific School. At the very time that the state scholarship act was before the legislature, President Gates had addressed the annual meeting of the State Board of Agriculture urging support for the measure, but a resolution to that effect was defeated. Several months later a representative of the College spoke with the Comptroller and Governor Abbett about the problem.

> They were both entirely courteous [he reported], but the Governor said "there was a general complaint among the farmers that we had an Agricultural College without Agriculture in it"; and then read to me a communication from the President of the State Board of Agriculture attacking us for not teaching more agriculture.

The point was a delicate one. Until 1890 little agriculture was taught, and that only as part of the curriculum in chemistry and agriculture. On the other hand, the early efforts of the Scientific School, and most particularly of Professor Cook, to build interest in agricultural studies had met with no response. Moreover, it was a distressing fact that the public high schools in the rural areas were so inadequate that they were unable to prepare students to meet even the low entrance requirements maintained by the Scientific School. With the full dimensions of the problem apparent to them, Scott and the Trustees instituted a whole series of measures intended to conciliate the agricultural constituency and gain support generally throughout the state.

One of the first steps that was taken was to create a distinct curriculum in agriculture, which attracted only an occasional student but which evidenced the genuine desire of the Trustees to meet the farmers' demands. Next, a careful search was made for a successor to Professor Cook, who had died in 1889, and the man selected for the post, Dr. Edward B. Voorhees, was an admirable choice. A graduate of the College, he had served on the staff of the Experiment Station and now received the title of Professor of Agriculture. In this position, and subsequently as director of the Experiment Station, he quietly won the respect and confidence of the agricultural interests and laid the foundations for the subsequent growth of the College of Agriculture. When it became apparent that the agricultural curriculum would not be popular, the faculty attempted to salvage the situation in 1893 by requiring every student in the Scientific School to take a course in "Elements of Agriculture."

Consideration was given to various means of providing instruction in agriculture for those who for one reason or another were not prepared to undertake a full four-year course. One proposal was that the Grammar School should offer a year of preliminary training to equip farm boys to enter the College. Serious consideration was given to establishing a special two-year course in practical agriculture, but the means were not available to undertake such a program. The favored solution was to provide a "short course" which farmers or their sons might attend during the winter months. Such a course was actually offered early in 1892, featuring lectures by Professor Voorhees and six other members of the scientific faculty, but the response was so disappointing that the program was discontinued. In common with many other land-grant colleges, Rutgers had yet to solve the problem of how to make the "Agricultural College" fit its name.

Concern with the attitude of the farmers as well as with the general matter of state relations was influential in stimulating another experiment, that of extension education. In his inaugural address, President Scott advocated a program designed to carry scientific and technical knowledge from the College campus to farmers, artisans, and interested citizens in all parts of the state. Citing specifically the success of a comparable scheme at the University of Wisconsin and the work of the American Society for the Extension of University Teaching in Philadelphia, with which he was familiar, he foresaw large benefits to the agricultural and industrial life of the state as well as a greater appreciation of

Rutgers. "By some such form of carefully organized endeavor, wisely directed and persistently pursued," he declared, "the State College, established for the benefit of agriculture and the mechanic arts, will appear to the people of New Jersey in its true character, not merely as the beneficiary, but in continued fidelity to the trust, the servant of the State and the nation."

With the cordial approval of the Trustees, the plan for extension education was at once implemented under the efficient direction of Professor Louis Bevier. In January 1892, courses in agriculture, astronomy, electricity, and chemistry were given in six communities. By 1894–95, ten towns widely distributed throughout the state were involved in the program, and the range of courses included Greek drama, the Eastern question, and Italian and French art as well as agriculture and entomology. The usual course consisted of six or twelve lectures, most of them delivered by outstanding members of the faculty. Students in each course were furnished a useful printed syllabus, an hour for class discussion following each lecture was arranged, and any who elected to take an examination might receive a certificate of their proficiency. Experience demonstrated that those who attended the courses were most interested in such subjects as history and literature, and by 1897–98 the only offerings were in those fields. Indeed, the most popular course in that year was on the literature of India and Persia. For a brief period the extension program flourished, sustained by "extension societies" organized in urban and suburban communities. But after 1895 attendance declined, scientific and technical courses were dropped, and in 1900 the experiment came to an end, not to be revived until 1912. Faculty members were reluctant to travel to remote parts of the state for small remuneration, farmers and artisans displayed little interest in the types of courses that were given, and the College seemingly lacked the resources to engage in energetic promotion of the extension program. Despite its lack of success, however, the effort doubtless had the result of making Rutgers better known throughout the state and demonstrated that the "State College" was casting about for some means of expanding its services to the people.

As the College groped toward a redefinition of its public role, the Trustees were forced to reexamine the historic relationship with the Dutch Church. In accordance with the agreement that had been made in 1864, three-fourths of the membership of the Board were required to be communicants of that church. This restriction not only limited drastically the field from which Trustees could be chosen but increasingly it failed to reflect the altered constituency from which the College drew its students—especially in the Scientific School—and to which it must look for support in the future. An unsuccessful attempt had been made in

1883 to induce the General Synod to change the proportion to two-thirds, and the effort was renewed in 1891. Assuring the Synod that the College did not intend to slight its function of supplying ministers to the Church but arguing that many useful men were ineligible for election to the Board because of the small non-Church quota, the Trustees won the consent of the Synod to the change, which became effective in 1892. The new dispensation did not profoundly alter the composition of the Board, which continued to be composed largely of alumni drawn almost equally from New York and New Jersey, most of those in the latter category residing near New Brunswick. Perhaps of more immediate significance in the functioning of the Board was the creation in 1890 of a small "Advisory Committee" which was invested with "general recommendatory and advisory powers in all matters relating to the management of the College, its business and its affairs." With the president as chairman, this influential committee underwent little change in personnel over the years and was primarily concerned with handling the delicate problem of relations with the state.

The new policies and programs, seemingly so appropriate in view of the circumstances, were not immediately productive of the desired results. The stalemate over the issue of the state scholarships continued. Enrollments, after reaching a peak of 251 in 1893, declined sharply to 182 in 1895. "The recent falling off in numbers," President Scott explained, "is probably due to the hard times of the past two years, as well as to the fact that Rutgers cannot compete in some departments with other colleges owing to its limited means." Large annual operating deficits could be met only by heavy drains on capital funds. Scott, who frequently expressed doubts about his ability as a fund raiser, could report nothing but discouragement in his awkward efforts to enlarge the endowment. As he analyzed the situation, the College faced a dilemma. "We fall between two stools," was the way he expressed it. "We have long been familiar with the objections made by those jealous of our state relations, that viz., we were a church College. And now the indications seem to be increasing that the historic relation to the Dutch Church is slighted, because we have relations to the State." In attempting to serve two constituencies, the College found itself denied by both.

While the president and the Trustees were wrestling with difficult matters involving external relationships, the faculty was deeply involved with the problem of adapting the educational program to meet changed conditions. After extensively revising the courses of study in the Scientific School around 1890, they turned their attention to the classical division. They correctly foresaw that the effect of the state scholarship act would be to channel students into the Scientific School, where no tuition would be required, and away from the classical division. "These influences," read a faculty report in 1892, "together with the general trend of the times toward scientific pursuits, have operated to increase very disproportionately the number of our scientific students and to decrease the relative number of our classical students." The entering class in that year, for example, contained 71 scientific and 25 classical students. In 1896 the graduating class was made up of 40 scientific and 15 classical. The problem, then, was how to save the classical division from near extinction.

Some thought was given to making a complete separation between the two schools, on the Yale model. It was argued that such a division would lessen popular confusion about the public-private character of the College, simplify the management of funds, reduce friction within the faculty, and possibly encourage greater financial support for the classical division. It was also contended that the classical students were superior in ability and preparation because they were required to meet higher admission standards than the scientific students and that therefore they should not have classes together, as was the case in many subjects after the Freshman year. The proposal had much to commend it, but it could not be implemented because there were not adequate funds to support a completely separate classical program. The faculty also urged that free state scholarships be created for students in the classical division, but although the Trustees endorsed this plan, there seemed to be no prospect that the state would adopt it. As an alternative, the president was authorized to award one four-year scholarship tenable in the classical division to any preparatory school that would nominate a suitable candididate. Such scholarships, of course, were not funded; however, they represented a means by which students could be attracted to the classical course.

Some of the difficulties faced by the classical division were no doubt attributable to the excessive rigidity of its program. Few colleges in the nation had been more resistant to the elective system. In 1891 the faculty belatedly undertook a general revision of the classical curriculum, and in line with their recent action in setting up five distinctive curricula in the Scientific School, they provided for choices among four majors in the classical division. Under the new arrangement, all classical students would continue to take the same prescribed courses in their first two years—Greek, Latin, German, English, mathematics, biology, chemistry and history. In the Junior and Senior years there were three prescribed courses each term, including French, mental philosophy, logic, ethics, physics, astronomy, geology, mineralogy, history of civilization, political economy, constitutional law, international law, and art. The remaining two subjects could be chosen from one of four major fields, defined as ancient languages, modern languages, mathematics and science, and history and philosophy. Whatever major field was selected at the start of the Junior year had to be pursued in the Senior year as well. By this arrangement, students were able to exercise some options in their final two years and specialize in fields of particular interest to them. Interestingly enough, no official grades were given for elective courses; the student's standing in his class was determined exclusively by his record in the required subjects. Honors were awarded for distinguished work in the major based on the recommendation of the professors. Leading all other majors in popularity by a wide margin was history and philosophy, followed by ancient languages, modern languages, and mathematics and science.

The courses available to the classical students were much the same as those that had made up the curriculum a generation before. Two new disciplines, however, were soon added. In 1891 John C. Van Dyke, librarian of the Sage Library at the Seminary, was given a part-time appointment as Professor of the History of Art, and the former President's House was made the Fine Arts Building. A prolific author of works on the history of art and art criticism, Van Dyke had previously given occasional lectures at the College, and he was to continue his distinguished services for thirty-five years. The rapid growth of public high schools in the era created a heavy demand for teachers, in recognition of which Eliot R. Payson was appointed in 1891 as Professor of Pedagogy, to give a single course entitled "The Art of Teaching." Payson at the time was headmaster of the Rutgers Preparatory School, as the Grammar School had been renamed in 1883, but subsequently he became fully engaged with College duties, endearing himself to his students as few men in the history of the College have done.

Despite the introduction of the system of majors, the number of classical students continued to decline; in 1899 there were only eight graduates. With obvious reluctance, the faculty at last adopted an expedient that had been under consideration since 1881, when the so-called "Third Course" had been approved but not introduced. Renamed the "Latin-Scientific Course," this curriculum was instituted in September 1901 as an alternative to the classical curriculum. The crucial innovation was that Greek was dropped both as an entrance requirement and as a prescribed subject in the curriculum. In place of Greek, candidates for admission had to offer two years of modern languages and two years of physics and chemistry. The Latin-Scientific course differed from the classical curriculum only in that French and physics were substituted for Greek in the first two years and the degree awarded was that of Bachelor of Letters rather than Bachelor of Arts. No doubt the determining factor in inducing the faculty to set up a rival to the traditional classical curriculum was the increasing difficulty of recruiting from the public high schools students who had any acquaintance with Greek. Students were slow to enroll in the new course. Between 1905 and 1915 only 68 Litt.B. degrees were awarded, as compared with 116 A.B.'s and 400 B.Sc.'s.

That the classical curriculum survived at all in this period was very largely due to the effectiveness with which the old Grammar School, or Rutgers Preparatory School, served as a "feeder" for the College. Still subsidized by the Trustees but managed with a considerable degree of autonomy by its headmaster, the Preparatory School provided facilities for boarding pupils as well as day students. Both Gates and Scott appreciated the vital importance of the School to the College, for the vast majority of classical students were prepared there, and willingly, if somewhat despairingly, they continued to divert College funds to the School.

In retrospect it is easy to be extremely critical of the College authorities for their failure to go further in liberalizing the curriculum. In effect, they were guilty of continuing to offer a product they could not sell and, indeed, could scarcely give away free. All that can be said in extenuation is that they were not alone in their conservatism and lack of vision, although in time they became nearly so. The old classical college had never been a popular institution and had survived in spite of its irrelevance to the needs of society, but by the late nineteenth century, faced with competition from other concepts of higher education, it survived only as an anachronism.

If the College seemed to stagger in the 1890's as it sought to adapt to rapidly changing circumstances, the effects were scarcely apparent on the undergraduate scene. The trend toward a proliferation of extracurricular activities and organizations that had become so evident in the post-Civil War decade continued with accelerated momentum. Hesitant and ineffectual efforts on the part of the faculty to defend traditional academic values did not suffice to stifle the emergence of the new collegiate way of life, with its devotion to athleticism, sociability, and gay adventures. Indeed, by the end of the century the concept of the "well rounded man" had won general acceptance.

Despite the efforts of President Gates to tone down the exuberant quality of undergraduate life, the 1880's saw the emergence of new enthusiasms. Roller skating became a craze, and the rink in New Brunswick was the most popular gathering place for students and townspeople. The undergraduates participated in skating contests and even organized a "polo" team on roller skates to compete with other clubs. Tennis came into vogue, and for a brief period there was intense interest in lacrosse. Elaborate class banquets, often the occasion for interclass frays, won a secure place in the social routine; formal dances were held occasionally, although not until the next decade did the Sophomore Hop and the Junior Promenade become fixtures. Senior class plays, usually farces written by the students, provided a dubious outlet for thespian talents until a short-lived dramatic club was organized in 1897 to produce Robertson's "David Garrick" under the direction of Professor E. Livingston Barbour. The Glee Club, which assumed a permanent status after 1880, was among the most active and prestigious of all student organizations, customarily putting on a score of concerts each year; a dozen years later it was joined by instrumental clubs. Intercollegiate debating was inaugurated in 1899 with a contest with New York University.* The fraternities, still seven in number, grew in strength and substance until by the turn of the century all of them possessed more or less commodious houses in the vicinity of the campus.

As new organizations multiplied on the campus, the two most venerable of them all faded out of existence. The literary societies, Peithessophian and Philoclean, once the focal centers of student interest, sustained a semblance of life through the 1880's but foundered in 1896–97.† Representing as they did the values and traditions of a bygone era, they commanded no support from the students of the Gay Nineties. In 1899 a "College Congress" was organized in the hopes of carrying on the oratorical activity that had once distinguished the literary societies, but after a couple of years it suffered an abrupt demise. To the extent that intellectual discourse held any place in the extracurricular it was to be found in the student Y.M.C.A. and there it had a distinctly religious and social orientation.

Symptomatic of the emphasis on the virtues of the extracurricular was the establishment of secret honorary societies to confer the most coveted of distinctions on undergraduate leaders. For the Senior elite there was Cap and Skull, organized in 1900. The Juniors stood in awe of their classmates in Casque and Dagger (1901); the Sophomores had Theta Nu Epsilon (1892); and even the lowly Freshmen could exchange congratulatory glances if they achieved membership in Serpent and Coffin (1903). Although the faculty continued to add to the long list of academic honors and prizes, the students had their own means of recognizing the kind of achievements they most admired, and they were not unaware that the wider society beyond the bounds of the campus shared their sentiments.

It was entirely appropriate that the only addition to the physical

---

* This first intercollegiate debate had been preceded in 1881 and 1887 by debates between representatives of Peithessophian and the Philomathean Society of New York University.

† Philoclean was revived in 1908 and Peithessophian in 1923. In 1932 the two societies, neither of which was very vigorous, united to form Philosophian.

plant in the 1890's was a handsome gymnasium. The generous gift of Robert F. Ballantine, wealthy Newark brewer and devoted Trustee, the building was designed by Charles A. Gifford and contained a spacious drill room and gymnasium, running track, ball cage, bowling alleys, swimming tank, and locker rooms. In 1913 a swimming pool was added as the gift of Mrs. Ballantine. From the time that it opened in 1894 it became the busiest center of College life, serving as the armory for the Rutgers Cadet Corps and providing facilities for dances, concerts, and lectures as well as catering to classes in physical education and to various athletic teams. Under the direction of Charles E. Adams and, after 1898, of Fred H. Dodge, the gymnasium was the scene of strenuous physical activity, both prescribed and voluntary, as the undergraduates undertook to prepare themselves for physical feats demanding skill and prowess.

Interest in competitive sports, and especially in intercollegiate contests, grew through the years. Football easily retained first place in popularity. By the mid-nineties the varsity played formidable schedules of as many as thirteen games, meeting leading schools throughout the East and even venturing into the South. Usually outmanned by their opponents, the teams continued to be hailed more for their heroic qualities than for their victories. After 1891, the old College Field having become unavailable, Neilson Field provided the arena for all outdoor sports, much to the annoyance of the owner of the adjacent property. The game belonged entirely to the players until in 1899 the first paid coach— William V. B. Van Dyck, 1896—was retained by the Athletic Association. Thereafter a succession of professional coaches followed, usually at yearly intervals, until the renowned George Foster Sanford arrived on the scene in 1913 to inaugurate an era of football greatness. Baseball continued to have its devotees, and new opportunities for participation were afforded by the introduction of track (1899) and gymnastics (1902) as approved intercollegiate sports.

Increasingly aware that the student-run athletic program could seriously disrupt the regular academic routine—for example, the football team in 1893 sought to be excused from classes for five days to play games in Baltimore, Washington, and Charlottesville—the faculty gradually evolved policies to restrain such a tendency. In 1897 these regulations were codified by a special faculty committee. The manager of each team was required to submit to the faculty for its approval a list of proposed games, together with the names of prospective players. Only one game each term was permitted to infringe upon a regular recitation period, and in such cases scheduled work had to be made up in advance. Students whose work was unsatisfactory or who had a deficiency were debarred from competition. Contests with teams from other colleges were favored over those with athletic clubs. Similar restrictions were placed upon the student musical organizations. Within the next few years the regulations were extended to prohibit contests with other than college teams, to require physical examinations of team members, and to tighten the requirements regarding academic eligibility.

Thus the faculty, after having all but ignored the whole area of intercollegiate athletics for more than twenty years, began to take a protective interest in the matter. Meanwhile the alumni, motivated by a variety of considerations, began to manifest their concern. The result was a revision of the constitution of the Athletic Association, heretofore run almost entirely by the students. In 1901 responsibility for directing the affairs of the Association was vested in a board of managers composed of one representative of the faculty, three alumni and three undergraduates, together with the president and the treasurer of the Association, the chairman of its board of trustees, and the physical director of the College. As in the past, the Association continued to bear all the expenses involved in conducting the athletic program, even including the maintenance of playing fields and the hiring of coaches, for it had not yet been established that intercollegiate sports formed an integral part of the College program. For the immediate future it remained uncertain whether these extracurricular diversions would remain largely under the control of the students, come under the domination of the alumni, or become the special concern of a professional athletic establishment.

The gradual intrusion of the faculty into the extracurricular sphere was counterbalanced by the entrance of the students into a field traditionally reserved to the president and the faculty, that of maintaining discipline. The burden of dealing almost constantly with a wide range of offenses against good order, ranging from rushes, "slopes," and fence tramplings to the explosion of firecrackers in classrooms, plagiarism, and inebriety, had always taxed the patience and wisdom of the authorities. Influenced no doubt by the increasingly progressive temper of the times, by his own strong predilections for civic responsibility, and by a desire to find a new solution to a perennial problem, President Scott became a strong advocate of student self-government.

The experiment was first conducted on a limited basis in Winants Hall, where the students from the first had an elected Senate whose responsibility it was to maintain order within the building. Although this venture was not an unqualified success, the faculty was encouraged to proceed further in 1894 and create a joint student-faculty committee, with the president as the chairman, to pass judgment on all disciplinary cases. This body functioned so effectively that in 1895 the faculty decided to enlarge student responsibility for self-government under a temporary plan that was given permanent status a year later in a faculty-approved constitution.

The preamble recited that the experience of the past three years had "confirmed the Faculty's trust in the honor and good judgment of our students, its belief in their capacity for self-government, and in the value of the system as a part of their education in citizenship" and declared it to be the policy of the faculty "to place in the hands of the students the primary responsibility for the good order of the College," subject to the terms of the charter and the rules of the Board of Trustees. An elected student committee, composed of four members from each of the two upper classes and two from each of the lower classes, with President Scott as the nonvoting chairman, was empowered to recommend to the faculty specific penalties for any offenses brought before them. They were also to consider any other matters affecting the College and suggest measures which might tend to promote the general welfare. In the event the faculty should disagree with the judgment rendered by the student committee, provision was made for a final determination by a joint conference committee of three students and three faculty members.

For a time all went well, and the faculty readily accepted the decisions of the student committee. But by 1899 the faculty found it necessary to register its dissent from what it regarded as inconsequential punishments inflicted for serious offenses, and several cases had to be handled by the joint conference committee. The student judges, it appeared, were not disposed to deal severely with their peers. Increasingly complaints arose within the faculty and even from the alumni that discipline within the College was breaking down. Even the editor of the *Targum* acknowledged that self-government had become a farce and in February 1901 urged the appointment of "a cool, clear-headed tactful dean."

Ultimately the problem became so acute that the Board of Trustees, after a careful study by its committee on instruction and discipline, was moved to action. Convinced that student self-government was not the answer and anxious to relieve the harassed president of the burden of maintaining discipline, they decided to create the new office of Dean of the College, effective July 1, 1901. Professor Francis C. Van Dyck, who had been at the College for forty years as student and teacher, was appointed to the office with an addition to his salary of $250 a year and was to "have charge of all matters relating to the government of the students under the supervision of the President and Faculty.

Thereafter the new Dean—affectionately known as "Poppy"—exercised discretion in referring cases either to the student committee or to the faculty but in most instances dealt with matters without recourse to either body. By his appointment the president and faculty were enabled to divest themselves in large part from handling minor disciplinary problems in much the same manner that they had previously allocated certain responsibilities to the librarian and the registrar.

The decade of the 1890's had been an especially difficult one for the College, but with the beginning of the new century there was a general stir of activity and, within a few years, a resolution of some of the most formidable problems that plagued the institution. Much of the initiative for forward-looking measures came from the Trustees, who sensed that they must exert leadership; some came from the alumni body, which was growing in size and influence; and some was supplied by the faculty. The creation of the Latin-Scientific course, the appointment of a dean, and the revision of the management of the Athletic Association were indicative of the changes in the air. But there were other stirrings as well, including a greatly heightened concern with public relations and a definitive move to settle the long-standing issue of the state scholarships.

The matter of bringing the College to the attention of the general public and its special constituencies had been the subject of occasional interest in the past. As early as 1876 a press committee had been appointed within the faculty, but it soon ceased to function. President Scott may have had public relations in mind when he arranged for the observance of "Charter Day" on November 10, 1895, the anniversary of the first charter; this became an annual event in the College calendar. In the same year he appointed a faculty committee to report on how full, prompt, and accurate press reports of Rutgers news might best be secured. In 1899 a standing faculty committee on "Press and Publication of College News" was appointed, and in the same year a pamphlet on the College was prepared for distribution to alumni and to high-school principals. These modest efforts did not satisfy the alumni, who complained that few Rutgers graduates sent their sons to their alma mater because it was so little known and who urged that more determined efforts be made to publicize the College. The Trustees responded to this pressure by authorizing the expenditure of $500 for the appointment of a "Press Agent" within the faculty and for the publication of a special alumni supplement to the *Targum*. After little more than a year, the special appropriation was terminated, but the faculty press committee endeavored to carry on the work by preparing a printed "Rutgers Letter" for distribution to New Jersey and metropolitan newspapers.

Alumni initiative was also responsible for the organization of the short-lived "Rutgers College League of New Jersey," the brainchild of William S. Myers, former faculty member and vigorous alumni Trustee. The

League was especially active and effective in 1902 and 1903 in sending out circular letters urging alumni to give support to pending state legislation vital to the College. Alumni concern about low enrollments in the College led to suggestions that the faculty should aggressively cultivate relations with secondary schools in order to recruit students. Sensitive to growing pressure, the faculty created a standing committee on alumni interests, which sought to assure the graduates of its desire to meet their wishes and explained the measures that were being taken to reach the schools. What was most needed, they urged, was money to appoint a special representative to carry on a systematic program of secondary-school relations, but this proposal could not be implemented for several years.

Nothing better illustrates how the College was expanding the range of its interests, functions, and relationships in these years than the growth in the number of faculty committees. To the handful that had existed in 1890 there were added by 1905 committees on athletics, gymnasium, press, music, alumni interests, employment of students, extension, library, relations to preparatory schools, dormitory, and municipal hygiene examinations. Formerly concerned almost entirely with activities that were centered in the classroom and the chapel, the faculty now found itself involved in such strange fields as advertising, hotel management, sports, and adult education. Increasingly it seemed to be necessary to assign specific tasks to designated individuals. Thus Irving S. Upson, the first "administrator" in the College, had been assigned the posts of librarian and registrar, to which he added the office of secretary of the faculty in 1891 and that of treasurer in 1905. Thus, too, Dean Van Dyck had assumed responsibility for student discipline. Initially most of these administrative posts had been created by the faculty to serve their convenience, but, by a subtle and interesting process that came to fruition in the 1920's, there emerged ultimately a body of administrative personnel that was not responsible to the faculty but rather to the president and the Trustees.

The adjustment of the stultifying deadlock with the State of New Jersey and the inauguration of a new relationship that promised a bright future for the state college constituted the final and most significant achievement of the Scott administration. Repeated efforts over the years to work out with state officials some solution of the snarled legal situation that impeded payment of the state scholarship claims were fruitless until in 1902 Governor Franklin Murphy agreed to recommend to the legislature that a three-man commission be appointed to seek an adjustment of the issue. The legislature responded with an act that recognized that the state was "under a moral obligation, at least, to compensate the college," authorized the Governor to appoint three commissioners, and charged them not only with determining what ought to be paid but also sought their recommendation with respect to the continuance of the scholarship plan.

The claims commission, made up of Amzi Dodd, William H. Corbin, both eminent citizens of wide experience, and Charles J. Baxter, State Superintendent of Schools, found that the College had more than met its obligations under the law, brushed aside constitutional objections, and recommended that the state should pay the full amount of $131,610. They also insisted that in accepting the benefits of the Morrill Act the state had assumed an obligation to make the land-grant college a part of its system of public instruction and contribute to its support. Accordingly, they endorsed a continuance of the scholarship plan. However, responsive to a strong case made by Baxter, they recommended that in order to obviate future constitutional objections, the "State Agricultural College" should be placed under the supervision of the State Board of Education, through which agency state funds would be channelled to the College.

The Rutgers Trustees were gratified by the unequivocal directness with which the commission sustained their claims, but they were greatly perturbed at the proposal that supervisory powers over the State College should be transferred from the Board of Visitors to the State Board of Education, foreseeing threats to the authority conferred on them by their charter. Through their extremely able attorney, Richard V. Lindabury, and through other channels as well, they strove to avert such a development. The legislature, after some intricate bargaining, seemingly decided to honor its "moral obligation" to the College by passing an act authorizing the payment of $80,000 (rather than the full amount recommended by the commission) to the Trustees. But in the subsequent appropriation act it attached the proviso that there must first be a judicial determination of the validity of the act of 1890. What the College authorities had long sought to avoid was now inescapable, and a suit was instituted in the State Supreme Court. In directing its advisory committee to proceed, the Trustees empowered them "to take such steps as they may deem advisable to adjust and collect the claims of the College against the State, without changing substantially existing relations between the College and the State."

The Supreme Court decision, rendered by Justice Bennet Van Syckel on February 3, 1904, completely upheld the case presented by the College. The justice found no constitutional barrier to the establishment of a state college nor to appropriations for its support. Taking the position that it was immaterial whether the mode of payment prescribed by the act of 1890 was legal in view of the subsequent legislation of 1903, he found that authority existed for the payment of the $80,000.

The acceptance of the federal endowment with its accompanying terms [he held] led to legislation which clearly committed the State to the intention and purpose of paying out of State funds such sum in addition to the federal endowment as would be necessary to secure and maintain the proposed scholarships provided for in the said several legislative acts.

Heartened by this extremely crucial verdict, the Trustees remained in suspense for yet another year while the case was carried to the Court of Errors and Appeals. Finally, on March 6, 1905, this highest court in the state affirmed the decision of Justice Van Syckel. Amid the general rejoicing, some astute observers noted that three of the six judges voting in the affirmative were alumni of Rutgers, while four of the five who voted in the negative were alumni of Princeton. Five members of the court, including three Rutgers alumni, refrained from voting.

These historic decisions, establishing the fact that the Rutgers Scientific School had been adopted and established as the "State Agricultural College" and that the legislature might legally contribute to its support, left unanswered many questions about the precise relationship of Rutgers to the state that were to be raised in the future, but it immediately cleared the way for legislation beneficial to the College. The $80,000 offered in payment of the claim for $131,160 was gratefully accepted by the Trustees and was followed by an additional $27,600 to satisfy claims arising between 1902 and 1905. In 1905 the legislature provided for the continuance of the state scholarships, authorizing payments to the College at the rate of $120 for each such scholarship up to a maximum of $15,000 a year. Much to the relief of the Trustees, the legislature ignored the recommendation of the claims commission with respect to giving supervisory powers to the State Board of Education.

While the matter of the scholarship claims was awaiting adjustment by the claims commission, the legislature had taken another extremely significant step toward establishing Rutgers as the State College. In 1901 William S. Myers, then an assistant professor of chemistry, conceived the idea of establishing a course in clay working and ceramics, closely resembling that which was being offered at Ohio State University and two other institutions. With the approval of the Trustees, he proposed to seek an appropriation from the legislature to provide the facilities for such a course and for its annual maintenance. Myers, who soon left the College to become a professional propagandist, conducted an intensive campaign in behalf of his bill, utilizing circular letters, pamphlets, and the personal influence of friends and leaders of the ceramic industry. The favorable result was the passage of an act in March 1902 requiring the "trustees of the State Agricultural College of New Jersey" to establish a department of ceramics and providing $12,000 to equip a suit-able laboratory and $2,500 for annual operating expenses. The Trustees promptly honored the mandate of the legislature, arranged for the con-struction of the necessary facilities, and instituted a four-year course in ceramics in the Scientific School as well as a two-year course. Modest though this act was in its scope, it was of considerable significance, for—aside from the partial payment of $1,500 that had been made in 1891 under the scholarship act—it involved the first actual expenditure of funds by the state in behalf of the College.

The Ceramics Act had a profound effect on the Trustees, or, more particularly, on their policy toward the state. William S. Myers, who joined the Board as an alumni trustee in 1902, argued effectively that in the future Rutgers should not seek general grants from the legislature because of the risk of encouraging state control of the institution. He urged that "a policy for the future guidance may be laid down, which seeks only to secure Legislative appropriations for Special Purposes and for Special Departments." In substance, this was the strategy of the Board during the next two decades. It was successfully tested in 1905 when the legislature "required" the Trustees to establish a department to pro-vide short courses in agriculture, and in the following year funds were appropriated for a building to house this department and for operating costs. After more than forty years, it seemed, Rutgers and the state had discovered a mutually satisfactory formula whereby the land-grant college could be aided.

While the issue of state relations was thus being fortunately resolved, the College was able to rejoice over an important private benefaction. Early in 1902 Mrs. Ralph Voorhees, whose numerous philanthropic gifts had aided many institutions associated with the Reformed Church, offered to provide funds for a new library. The old library, still housed in the chapel, had grown nearly fivefold since Upson assumed the li-brarianship in 1884; it contained approximately 50,000 volumes. Through-out much of that period both Gates and Scott had repeatedly urged the need for a new building because of the intolerably crowded condi-tions in the existing quarters. The Voorhees Library, of which Henry Rutgers Marshall was the architect, was formally dedicated on Charter Day, 1904, and the books were moved to it during the following sum-mer. Affording adequate space at last for the expanding collection, the new library could now extend its services to the students and faculty by remaining open eleven hours a day. Upson, who had made the library his "labor of love" for over twenty years, soon resigned as librarian and in 1907 was succeeded by George A. Osborn, who had become Upson's assistant shortly before his graduation from the College in 1897.

The construction of the new library and the final adjudication of the scholarship claims brought to an end one of the most trying periods in the history of the College. Exhausted by the strains of his office, President Scott submitted his resignation on the day after the Court of Errors and Appeals handed down its decision. "That decision," he later explained, "and the subsequent amendment of the [Scholarship] Act by the Legislature seem to me distinctly to mark the close of an epoch, and to open a future full of promise in the career of our College." It was his conviction that a change of administration would "stimulate fresh hopes and endeavors for a greater measure of success." The Trustees granted Scott an extended leave of absence and appointed William H. S. Demarest as acting president. When Scott persisted in his intention, his resignation was accepted in October 1905, but he retained his post as Voorhees Professor of History and commanded respect and affection as a great teacher until his death in 1922. Plagued with difficulties as his administration had been, it represented a pivotal era in the development of the College. The position of the Scientific School as the state college had at last achieved tangible recognition, the character of the College had been drastically altered as Federal and state enactments created an imbalance between the classical and scientific divisions, and the recognition of new responsibilities and new relationships had given the College new perspectives on its role and function. Under Scott's able successor, his hopes "for a greater measure of success" were to be abundantly realized.

Chapter Seven

Progress toward an Uncertain Future

As alumni and friends of Rutgers gathered on the campus in June 1906 to participate in the inauguration of President William H. S. Demarest, they shared the feeling of expectancy common to such occasions that a promising new era lay ahead. There was a general awareness that the circumstances were unusually favorable for a movement forward as well as an urgent feeling that the College must advance rapidly if it was to retain its stature in the academic world. What course future development would take still remained unclear. Rutgers had lost much of its original identity as a tightly integrated classical college, but it had not yet taken on the identity of a state university. The decade that lay ahead was to be rich in accomplishments—an unprecedented expansion in numbers and in facilities, an elaboration of the academic program, a spectacular increase in state support, substantial private benefactions. But the problem of identity, brought ever more sharply into focus, was not resolved and soon assumed the proportions of a crisis.

Despite the gains that had been made over the preceding twenty years, Rutgers in relative terms had lost ground. It had always been a small college, but now in 1906, with only 235 students, it was conspicuously small. Princeton had more than five times that number; Harvard, Columbia, and several state universities exceeded 4,000; and even such traditionally small institutions as Amherst, Colgate, and Lehigh enrolled around 500 students. Amidst the tremendous ferment that reshaped American higher education in the late nineteenth century, bringing forth full-fledged universities with their graduate and professional schools, sprawling public universities eagerly turning their energies to new objectives, coeducation on an unprecedented scale, and curricular experiments without number, Rutgers had yielded but slowly to the forces of change, partly through choice and indecision but also because of such factors as its peculiar state relationship. Now, if ever, the time had arrived for an energetic effort to bring the College abreast of the times.

The times were highly favorable for such an effort. The Progressive Movement was in full tide and in New Jersey its local manifestation—the "New Idea" movement—created a political environment sympathetic to enhancing educational opportunities and expanding the role of government. During the first decade of the new century the public high schools of the state were at last placed upon a secure foundation, assured of adequate financing, and so expanded in size and numbers that by 1911 the Commissioner of Education could boast that every youngster might aspire to a high-school diploma. The state's fiscal structure was extensively overhauled, particularly in the field of railroad taxation, with the result that vastly increased revenues suddenly became available. Private foundations with enormous resources were created to pour millions into the nation's colleges and universities and to exert irresistible pressures for reform and standardization. National educational organizations were formed to promote the collective interests of higher education, set standards, and chart the course of the future. Alumni, often stimulated by the athletic prowess displayed by the sons of their alma mater, exhibited a new strength of loyalty and expressed it with financial contributions. Above all, young men and women were flocking to college to obtain the degrees that now were becoming recognized as essential to success in business and the professions.

The man who led the College in this exciting period of development possessed unusual attributes for the task. The first alumnus to occupy the presidency, Dr. Demarest was the personification of old Rutgers. His ancestors through four generations had been Trustees; his father had graduated from the College in 1837 and had been the secretary of the Board of Trustees for thirty-two years while serving as a professor at the Seminary. Reared in New Brunswick, Dr. Demarest had graduated with the Class of 1883, taught for three years at the Preparatory School, and then proceeded to the Seminary and to a pastorate in the Reformed Church. In 1901 he was called to the professorship in church history at the Seminary. Meanwhile, he had been elected to the Board of Trustees and in 1904 became its secretary. Having served as acting-president since May 1905, in February 1906 he was chosen to succeed Scott.

With his strong ties to the old College, to the Dutch Church, and to traditional values, Dr. Demarest was not disposed to equate change with progress or to embrace the fad of the moment. Yet in an eminently practical manner he recognized that the College must be "liberal in adjustment to the life and exigencies of the times while not swayed by every wind of educational doctrine." Even stronger than his loyalty to the past was his desire to enhance the stature of Rutgers, and to accomplish that objective he was prepared to be tolerant of innovations. Although it was his ardent hope that with enlarged private resources Rutgers could achieve an honored position as a college of the historic type, emphasizing liberal culture and Christian character, he cultivated relations with the state with conspicuous success and brought into being the "State University of New Jersey," in fact as well as in law and title.

To the faculty, which reciprocated his feelings of respect with loyalty and affection, he gave freedom and encouragement for the development of new programs and defense against influences that threatened academic values. In his relations with the Trustees he was rigorously but tactfully insistent in proposing measures for the advancement of the institution. He made extensive tours to visit colleges and universities in all regions of the country in search of ideas that might be fruitfully applied at Rutgers. He acquired a keen understanding of political tactics and dealt with remarkable effectiveness with legislators and Governors. Never reticent about begging for funds, he tirelessly presented the College's cause to prospective benefactors, especially to those within the Dutch Church. His devotion to the College was remarkable, and, despite his occasional misgivings about the trend of its development, his constant policy was one of "immediate and rigorous and broad advancement."

Among the earliest achievements of the new administration were the complete overhauling of the admissions system and an extensive revision of the curriculum. A special faculty committee worked for a year on these complex and related matters, obviously seeking to bring practices at Rutgers into line with those at other institutions. In this endeavor they were successful, although so rapid was the pace of change in the academic community in that era that within little more than a decade another major modernizing effort was required.

The problem of admissions procedures was particularly intricate because it had so many facets. When all colleges had essentially the same curriculum and private academies prepared students to meet the simple entrance requirements, there was little difficulty. But as the colleges introduced new curricula, each with distinctive entrance requirements, and as public high schools, exceedingly varied in quality and program, sent increasing numbers of students to the colleges, chaos resulted. By the turn of the century, through the combined efforts of national and regional educational organizations, a process of standardization was under way. The high schools were forced to offer similar programs, uniform entrance examinations were administered through such agencies as the College Entrance Examination Board, and entrance requirements came to be expressed in terms of standardized units.

At Rutgers the admission problem involved both the questions of what requirements to demand and how to administer them. The requirements for admission to the Scientific School had always been much lower than those for the classical school. Repeated recommendations from the faculty that they be raised were rejected by the Trustees, who were extremely sensitive to the criticism that boys from rural areas could not meet the existing requirements. The situation became embarrassing when the New York State Board of Regents refused to recognize a bachelor of science degree from Rutgers and the Carnegie Foundation would not admit the College to its approved list. Some progress was made in 1906 when a knowledge of two foreign languages was added to the requirements. Meanwhile, the rapid growth of the high-school system and the provision of short courses to meet the most insistent pressure of the farmers opened the way for a solution of the problem.

Beginning in 1908 admission requirements were defined in "units," rather than in terms of detailed bodies of subject matter. For admission to the bachelor of arts or bachelor of literature courses, fifteen prescribed units were required. For the bachelor of science curricula, only twelve and one-half units were needed, but this number was gradually increased to fourteen by 1912. However, students might be admitted with as many as three "deficiencies," all of which had to be made up within a year. Candidates for admission could establish their qualifications by taking entrance examinations through various agencies, but most were accepted on the basis of certificates from approved schools. After 1912 certificates were accepted only from four-year high schools. In 1918, largely as the result of strong pressure from certain alumni Trustees, the requirements were liberalized. Five distinct sets of requirements—each involving fifteen units—were established for various curricula and approximately one-third of the units might be in optional subjects. Heretofore a matter of small consequence, the whole area of admissions had now assumed great importance and reflected many of the new influences that were operative in the field of higher education.

The major revision of the courses of study in 1907 had many ends in view, the chief of which was to build up enrollments in the non-technical curricula. The most important innovation was the creation of a so-called "General Science" course, which in effect permitted students to pursue a liberal, nontechnical curriculum without having to study either Latin or Greek. In order to sustain the faltering bachelor of arts curriculum, provision was made for students who lacked Greek to begin the study of that language in their Freshman year. In the three non-technical curricula (A.B., Litt.B. and General Science), there was a prescribed program of Freshman subjects, but in the three subsequent years approximately half of the program consisted of electives. These measures, and especially the establishment of the General Science course, had the desired results. Whereas in 1905 only 25 per cent of the undergraduates were enrolled in the nontechnical curricula, by 1915 the proportion had risen to 44 per cent.

The sharp rise in the proportion of nontechnical students was due

Governor William Franklin, who granted Queen's College its first charter on November 10, 1766, and its second charter on March 20, 1770.

CHARTER
OF A
COLLEGE

To be erected in

NEW-JERSEY,

By the Name of

QUEEN'S-COLLEGE,

For the Education of the Youth of the said Province and the Neighbouring Colonies in true Religion and useful Learning, and particularly for providing an able and learned Protestant Ministry, according to the Constitution of the Reformed Churches in the United Provinces, using the Discipline approved and instituted by the national Synod of Dort, in the Years 1618, and 1619.

NEW-YORK,
Printed by JOHN HOLT; at the EXCHANGE,
M,DCC,LXX.

Title page of a printed copy of the Queen's College charter of 1770.

1

Old Dutch Parsonage, Somerville. Built in 1750–51 by John Frelinghuysen, son of Theodorus Jacobus, the parsonage was later the home of Jacob Rutsen Hardenbergh, first president of Queen's College, and of his stepson, Frederick Frelinghuysen, the first tutor at the College.

Frederick Frelinghuysen

John Taylor

The first tutors of Queen's College

Transactions of the Athenian Society.

1776.

June 29th

General Howe with the British Fleet arriving at Sandy Hoo[k] All the Members of the Athenian Society who were able to bear Arms immediately marched to oppose the Enemy.

Matters being thus in Confusion. July the 27th the College was suspended to the 21st of October. And,

Wednesday Evening November 13th the Athenian Society met Mr Dewitt in the Chair, and proceeded to Business.

Mr Vanartsdalen opened the Society by speaking from Sallust

Composers.
{ Mr Taylor read a Letter to a Tory.
{ Mr Bogart read on Retirement.
{ Mr Vanartsdalen on Lying.
        Mr Bogart spoke from Cato.

Readers.
{ Mr Van Wyck read from Suetonius.
{ Mr Grandin read from Suetonius.
        Mr Taylor spoke from Shakespear's Brutus.

Mr Scheurman absent.

Then the Society was dismissed.

Minutes of the Athenian Society. The Revolution brought "Confusion" to the College in 1776.

4

Rev. Dr. Ira Condict

Rev. Dr. John H. Livingston

Two pillars of Queen's College. Dr. Condict, president pro tem, 1794–1810, led the movement for the erection of Old Queen's. Dr. Livingston, having twice declined the office, served as president, 1810–1825.

QUEEN's COLLEGE, NB.

Old Queen's. The earliest known sketch, showing the building before the present cupola was erected around 1826. Professors lived in the two wings; the central portion contained classrooms and a library.

Rev. Dr. Philip Milledoler

Col. Henry Rutgers

Queen's becomes Rutgers. The College was revived under Dr. Milledoler, president from 1825 to 1840, and was renamed in honor of Col. Rutgers, philanthropist and churchman of New York City.

Theodore Strong, Professor of Mathematics and Natural Philosophy, 1825–1861.

Lewis Caleb Beck, Professor of Chemistry and Natural Philosophy, 1830–1853.

James Spencer Cannon, Professor of Metaphysics, 1826–1852.

Alexander McClelland, Professor of Languages and of Evidences of Christianity, 1829–1851.

The early faculty of Rutgers College

A. Bruyn Hasbrouck, president, 1840–1850.

Theodore Frelinghuysen, president, 1850–1862.

Abraham Van Nest, trustee, 1823–1864

Jacob J. Janeway, trustee, 1830–1850; vice president and professor, 1833–1839.

Van Nest Hall

LITH. OF SARONY & MAJOR, N.Y. CLINTON ST. N.Y.

Presidents House

RUTGERS COLLEGE in NEW BRUNSWICK N. JERSEY.

PUBLISHED BY THE GENERAL SYNOD'S, SABBATH SCHOOL UNION OF THE REF'D PROT' DUTCH CHURCH.

The Class of 1859 in front of Van Nest Hall

Rev. Dr. William H. Campbell, president, 1862–1882.

George H. Cook, Professor of Chemistry, Geology, and Agriculture, 1853–1889; vice president, 1864–1889.

David Murray, Professor of Mathematics, Natural Philosophy, and Astronomy, 1867–1876.

Jacob Cooper, Professor of Greek, 1866–1893, and of Logic and Mental Philosophy, 1893–1904.

COLLEGE MATTERS.

Nota Bene.—It is an established custom in all institutions of learning, for the students to raise their hats to the Professors, as an act of recognition and due respect. "It is a poor rule that won't work both ways," and common civility and politeness demand that the compliment should be *always* returned. We hope that our attention will not be directed to this again, and that "a word to the wise" will prove sufficient.

A SCHOLASTIC and erudite Freshman deigned to bring his acute and lofty faculty of criticism to bear upon J. G. Whittier's "*Garibaldi*," which we published in our last issue, and pronounced it considerably below par. If the illustrious poet should see this how badly he would feel. Perhaps this luminous friend will hereafter supply our poetical column from the rich effusion of his gigantic and symmetrical brain. We fear that the names of Whittier, Longfellow, Tennyson, and Bryant, may yet be eclipsed by this rising star.

WHAT WE WANT.

EVERY one is willing to admit the power of music; the feelings and emotions which it is capable of producing; how it softens and subdues. Music speaks to us in tones of gentleness and love; it steals its way into the innermost soul, and the whole being soon gives way to its potent influence. And yet, in the face of all this, how few cultivate this art. How sensibly do we feel the want of it in our College. Brothers, we are greatly deficient in this respect; we have scarcely musical talent enough to sustain our College choir. Out of one hundred and fifty students, we verily believe that ten cannot be found who understand the first principles of music. Where are our glee clubs? our college songs? Sophomores, awake! let us hear your voices. Don't be afraid of College Professors—they won't hurt you. Give us "Three black crows," if you can't do any better. Oh, that the dignity and self-respect of *seniors* would encourage them to sustain "their choir," instead of bringing disgrace upon it and themselves, as a certain few of them have done and are attempting to do.　　　　'70.

HERTZOG HALL.—In pursuance of the action of the Standing Committee on Hertzog Hall, the Rev. P. J. Quick has taken his place as Rector of the building, and is discharging his duties in an earnest, faithful, and efficient manner.

Ample provisions have been made for the care and comfort of the students, and good board provided for those desirous of taking their meals in the building. A well prepared table, and a genial company invite thither, and the kind demeanor of the "Pater Familias," gives dignity and a home-like influence to the "Hertzog Family."

O TEMPORE! O MORES!—The Senior Class, before THE TARGUM reaches the public, will have appeared in beaver hats, thus establishing a precedent which we hope will be followed by the classes coming after. We anticipate that this will be-a-ver y imposing affair if the weather proves propitious. 1869, *Annus Mirabilis*.

HITHERTO, in Rutgers, it has been a custom for the Freshmen to treat the upper classes with some degree of respect, in deference to their (supposed) advantage in years and scholarship. But this is a progressive age, and, behold, we now have a Freshman class whose chief characteristic is the remarkably high-handed manner in which they conduct themselves toward the upper classes. Do you see an airy youth taking up the whole sidewalk, and treating every one with an ease of manner which would betoken intimate acquaintance—it is a Freshman. Another style of Freshman goes around as if the College was run for him, and him alone; he answers all questions, either with an easy stare, or as if his breath was too precious to waste on Seniors or Juniors. A third type, travels decidedly on his muscle—goes around like a prize fighter; swaggers through the halls, vowing destruction and death on any one who may in any way offend him, and turns out, as such gentry generally do, a much worse barker than biter.

Now, gentlemen of '73, just accord to the poor upper classmen a degree of respect nearly equal to that which you wish for yourselves. Treat them personally with a moderate degree of civility, and they will be contented. The Sophomores must take care of themselves.

THE FOOT-BALL MATCH.

ON Saturday, November 6th, Princeton sent twenty-five picked men to play our twenty-five a match game of foot-ball. The strangers came up in the 10 o'clock train, and brought a good number of backers with them. After dinner, and a stroll around the town, during which stroll billiards received a good deal of attention, the crowds began to assemble at the ball ground, which, for the benefit of the ignorant, we would say, is a lot about a hundred yards wide, extending from College Avenue to Sicard-street. Previous to calling the game, the ground presented an animated picture. Grim-looking players were silently stripping, each one surrounded by sympathizing friends, while around each of the captains was a little crowd, intent upon giving advice, and saying as much as possible. The appearance of the Princeton men was very different from that of our own players. They were almost without exception tall and muscular, while the majority of our twenty-five are small and light, but possess the merit of being up to much more than they look.

Very few were the preliminaries, and they were quickly agreed upon. The Princeton captain, for some reason or other, gave up every point to our men without contesting one. The only material points were, that Princeton gave up "free kicks," whereby a player, when he catches the ball in the air is allowed to kick it without hindrance. On the other hand, our practice of "babying" the ball on the start was discarded, and the ball was mounted, in every instance, by a vigorous "long kick."

Princeton won the toss, and chose the first mount, rather oddly, since it had been agreed to start the ball against the wind. At 3 P. M., the game was called. The Princetonians suffered from making a very bad "mount," or "buck" as they call it; the effects of which were not remedied before the sides closed, and after a brief

struggle, Rutgers drove it home, and won, amid great applause from the crowd. The sides were changed, Rutgers started the ball, and after a somewhat longer fight, Princeton made it a tie by a well directed kick, from a gentleman whose name we don't know, but who did the best kicking on the Princeton side.

To describe the varying fortunes of the match, game by game, would be a waste of labor, for every game was like the one before. There was the same headlong running, wild shouting, and frantic kicking. In every game the cool goaltenders saved the Rutgers goal half a dozen times; in every game the heavy charger of the Princeton side overthrew everything he came in contact with; and in every game, just when the interest in one of those delightful rushes at the fence was culminating, the persecuted ball would fly for refuge into the next lot, and produce a cessation of hostilities until, after the invariable "foul," it was put in straight.

Well, at last we won the match, having won the 1st, 3d, 5th, 6th, 9th, and 10th games; leaving Princeton the 2d, 4th, 7th, and 8th. The seventh game would probably have been added to our score, but for one of our players, who, in his ardor, forgot which way he was kicking, a mistake which he fully atoned for afterward.

To sum up. Princeton had the most muscle, but didn't kick very well, and wanted organization. They evidently don't like to kick the ball on the ground. Our men, on the other hand, though comparatively weak, ran well, and kicked well throughout. But their great point was their organization, for which great praise is due to the Captain, Leggett, '72. The right men were always in the right place.

After the match, the players had an amicable "feed" together, and at 8 o'clock our guests went home, in high good spirits, but thirsting to beat us next time, if they can.

PRINCETON vs. RUTGERS.

THE second of the three games of Foot Ball between Princeton and Rutgers was won by the former at their ball-grounds, on Saturday, the 13th inst. Eight out of fifteen was the game, but as Princeton won the first eight the other innings were not played. The style of playing differs, materially, in the two Colleges. A fly, or first bound catch, entitles to a "free kick," a la Princeton. We bat with hands, feet, head, sideways, backwards, any way to get the ball along. We must say that we think our style much more exciting, and more as Foot Ball should be. After the regular game two innings were played after our fashion, and we won them. It is but fair to our twenty-five to say that they never have practised the "free-kick" system. At half-past six we sat down to a very fine supper, prepared for us by our hosts. Speeches and songs, accompanied, of course, by the study of practical gastronomy, passed the time pleasantly until the evening train bore us Brunswickwards. We hope soon to welcome Princeton to New-Brunswick for the third game, and beat them. Their cheer, sounding as if they meant to explode, but for a fortunate escape of air, followed by a grateful yell at the deliverance of such a catastrophe, still sounds in our ears as we thank them for their hospitality. If we must be beaten we are glad to have such conquerors.　　　　D.

Targum reports the first football game

The Rutgers crew, about 1864

Dr. Merrill E. Gates, president, 1882–1890.

Dr. Austin Scott, president, 1890–1906; Professor of History, Political Economy, and Constitutional Law, 1883–1922.

The faculty of Rutgers College, 1892. First row: E. T. Middleton, E. L. Barbour, Julius Nelson, E. S. Shumway, I. S. Upson, J. C. Van Dyke. Second row: unidentified, F. C. Van Dyck, Austin Scott, Wm. R. Duryee, A. H. Chester, Carl Meyer. Third row: E. A. Bowser, Jacob Cooper, Byron Halstead, E. B. Voorhees, Louis Bevier, A. Atkinson. Rear row: C. E. Adams, A. E. Titsworth, J. B. Smith, R. W. Prentiss. E. L. Stevenson.

Winants Hall, the first dormitory, 1890

17

Ballantine Gymnasium, built in 1894; destroyed by fire in 1930

New Jersey Hall ablaze, 1902

String Group, 1897—soulful but gay

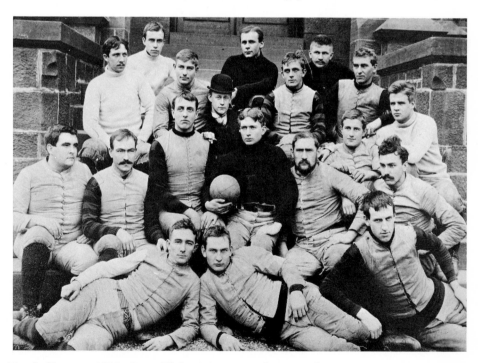

Football team, 1891. Capt. Philip M. Brett, who served as acting president, 1930–1932, is in the center.

Rev. Dr. William H. S. Demarest, president, 1902–1924.

The College celebrates Dr. Demarest's acceptance of the presidency, February 8, 1906.

R.O.T.C. drill, May, 1917

Mabel S. Douglass, Dean of the New Jersey College for Women (now Douglass College), 1918–1933.

Dr. Jacob G. Lipman, Dean of the College of Agriculture and Director of the Experiment Station, 1914–1939.

Leonore F. Loree, trustee, 1909–1940, who fostered the growth of the College for Women.

James Neilson, trustee, 1886–1937, and generous benefactor.

Aerial view of the Rutgers College campus, 1923. Visible on Queen's Campus in the foreground are (left to right) Winants Hall, Van Nest Hall, Geological Hall, Old Queen's Kirkpatrick Chapel, the Alumni-Faculty House, and the Schanck Observatory. Beyond, on the former Neilson Campus, are Ford Hall, New Jersey Hall, Voorhees Library, Engineering Building, Chemistry Building, Ballantine Gymnasium, and Ceramics Building. Beyond is the New Brunswick Theological Seminary, with College Field in the left background and Neilson Field in the right background.

College Hall

Cooper Hall (original portion at extreme right)

The first buildings of the College for Women. Classes were held in College Hall; and Cooper Hall, with its later extensions, served as a dining hall and dormitory.

Aerial view, College of Agriculture. The major buildings shown, from the left foreground, are the Short Course Building, greenhouses, Horticulture Building, Poultry Building, Administration Building, and Dairy Building. In the background is the College Farm.

Dr. John Martin Thomas, president, 1925–1930.

Dr. Philip Milledoler Brett, acting president, 1930–1932.

Dr. Robert C. Clothier, president, 1932–1951.

President Clothier and administrative officers, 1932. Left to right: Col. John T. Axton, Chaplain; Albert S. Johnson, Comptroller; Parker H. Daggett, Dean of Engineering; Norman C. Miller, Director of Extension Division; Fraser Metzger, Dean of Men; Walter T. Marvin, Dean of Arts and Sciences; Luther H. Martin, Registrar; Harry J. Rockefeller, Graduate Manager of Athletics; President Clothier; Edward H. Brill, Purchasing Agent; Carl R. Woodward, Assistant to the President; George E. Little, Director of Athletics; W. T. Read, Dean of Chemistry; Arthur C. Busch, Secretary of the Alumni Association; and Earl Reed Silvers, Director of Public Information.

Rutgers vs. Lafayette at Neilson Field, 1932

Victory over Princeton at the Stadium dedication November 5, 1938

Football in two eras. Neilson Field was in use from the 1890s until 1938

A.S.T.P. (Army Specialized Training Program) unit at mess in the Gymnasium, 1943.

Veterans enrolled in overwhelming numbers in 1945

Commencement at the Stadium, June 9, 1951

University Choir performing with the Philadelphia Orchestra

The Institute of Microbiology, dedicated 1954

Professor Selman A. Waksman, Nobel laureate, 1952

Dr. Robert C. Clothier and Dr. William H. S. Demarest welcome Dr. Lewis Webster Jones, newly elected to the presidency of the University.

Dr. Lewis Jones, president, 1951–1958.

Dr. Mason Welch Gross, president, 1959–

The Rutgers University Library, 1956

Frelinghuysen, Hardenbergh, and Livingston (now Campbell) dormitories, 1956.

Science Center, University Heights, 1964. Shown clockwise (from left) are the Nelson Biological Laboratories, the Center for Alcohol Studies, the Wright Chemistry Laboratory, the Engineering Center, and the physics complex, including lecture hall, Physics Building, and (under construction) accelerator facility. In the background are the former temporary science facilities and storage buildings and the faculty housing project. In the extreme left background are the Davidson dormitories.

Douglass College Library, 1961

Hickman Hall, Douglass College, 1964

A new campus emerges for the Newark Colleges—Law Center (right foreground), Boyden Hall, Conklin Hall, and Dana Library.

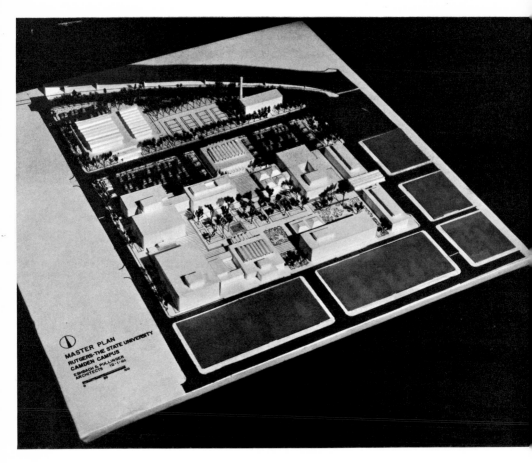

Model of the projected campus for the College of South Jersey, Camden.

The undefeated football team of 1961. Captain Alex Kroll is in the center; Coach John Bateman at the extreme right, front row.

The Class of 1936 marching in the Bicentennial Alumni Reunion Parade, June 1966.

only in part to the changes in the curricula. Even more influential was the institution of an extraordinary arrangement whereby students in all curricula were made eligible for state scholarships. In an extremely significant action taken in January 1909 the Trustees, with the approval of the Board of Visitors, resolved: "That the several courses leading to the degrees of B.A. and B.Litt. respectively, already established by the Trustees of Rutgers College, be and hereby are also established as courses in Rutgers Scientific School, the State College for the benefit of Agriculture and the Mechanic Arts." By this daring but simple device—the implications of which are best left unpondered—the Scientific School was made coextensive with the College in order that liberal arts students might share the scholarship privilege with the scientific students.

Several other changes were incorporated in the reform of the academic program. The old three-term calendar was replaced by the two-semester system, a shift which in itself occasioned a drastic reordering of individual courses. The college catalogue, now grown to over 200 pages, was completely revised in 1907, and courses were for the first time given numbers and arranged in logical sequence by departments. Mechanical engineering, previously combined with civil engineering, was now constituted as a distinctive course.

The new arrangements were maintained with slight modifications down to 1916, when the faculty undertook another major review of its offerings and restructured the entire program in accordance with currently popular trends. The technical curricula underwent little revision, although they were now differentiated, beginning with the Freshman year, and provided less time than formerly for nontechnical subjects. Military science was made a requirement for all Freshmen and Sophomores and might be elected by upperclassmen. The liberal arts curricula were subject to the most extensive revision. Group requirements, arranged in seven fields, were introduced, and students had to take varying numbers of hours in each group, depending on their curricula. The old elective arrangement was modified by a new system that required concentration on "majors" and "minors" in the Junior and Senior years.* It was also

* The specific group requirements were 8 hours in English; 14 to 22 hours in foreign languages; 14 hours in science and mathematics; 10 hours in history and political and social science; 8 hours in philosophy, psychology, and education; 2 hours in art and architecture; and 4 hours in military science. A major consisted of six hours of work in one subject through two years. The minor involved two related subjects carried through two years. The majors in 1917–18 were botany and plant physiology, chemistry, classical languages, English, German, Greek, history, Latin, mathematics, physics, political science, Romance languages, and zoology and physiology. A total of 136 term hours was required for graduation, except that honor students might qualify with 124 hours. In the technical courses the credit-hour requirements varied between 144 hours in biology to 146 hours in agriculture.

contemplated that, after the Sophomore year, a limited number of honors students would be designated, for whom special courses would be offered; but for various reasons this plan could never be fully implemented. The students appreciated the widened latitude of choice now offered to them, but they were especially jubilant over the introduction at the same time of a "cut" system that permitted them occasional indulgence in the luxury of missing a class. Representing as it did an effort to curb the evils inherent in the free elective system, to encourage a degree of specialization in the upperclass years, and to present stimulating offerings to outstanding students, the new program, which became effective in September 1917, demonstrated the willingness of the faculty to adopt what were deemed to be the best contemporary theories and practices.

While the general academic structure of the College was being modernized, a notable expansion was under way in particular fields and entirely new programs were being added. Most remarkable was the rapid development of instruction in agriculture, under the stimulus of new Federal grants, increasingly generous state support, and the able direction of one of the most brilliant and energetic men ever to serve the College—Dr. Jacob G. Lipman. The Experiment Station, staffed by excellent scientists under the direction of Dr. E. B. Voorhees had for many years been conducting valuable programs of research and issuing informative bulletins, but no solution had been found for the problem of building an instructional program. A turning point occurred in 1906 when the legislature appropriated funds to establish a program of short courses. After a building was constructed at the College Farm, a series of twelve-weeks' courses in such areas as general agriculture, horticulture, dairying, and animal husbandry were arranged, and in January 1907 forty students enrolled for the first session. The program was a success and grew steadily in succeeding years. Meanwhile, Federal appropriations for the Experiment Station were doubled by the Adams Act of 1906, and in 1907 Congress provided for doubling the subsidy granted under the second Morrill Act. With these enlarged resources, the agricultural staff was augmented and course offerings in the four-year agricultural curriculum were multiplied.

In 1911, when Dr. Voorhees was stricken with a fatal illness, Dr. Lipman became director of the Experiment Station. A graduate of the College in the class of 1898, Lipman had taken his doctorate at Cornell and joined the staff of the Station as soil chemist and bacteriologist. A man of incredible energy, unusual foresight, and great personal charm, he soon gained an international reputation as a scientist, which he retained when he turned his varied talents to developing and administering the burgeoning program in agriculture. With the short courses well established, he zealously promoted interest in the regular agricultural cur-

riculum, with remarkable effectiveness. Prior to 1908 there were usually
no more than five students enrolled; by 1914 agriculture was by far
the most popular of the seven technical curricula, with sixty-eight students, although the three engineering curricula together enrolled seventy,
exclusive of Freshmen. A new dimension was added to the program
in agriculture in 1912 when the Department of Extension was organized
in the Experiment Station and the first county agent was appointed in
Sussex County. Encouraged by state legislation enacted in 1913 and by the
Federal Smith-Lever Act of 1914, the extension work quickly grew to
large proportions. By 1918, as a result of the Smith-Hughes Act, there
was also a program for training teachers of agriculture for the high
schools.

With this vast expansion of activities went physical growth. The size
of the College Farm was more than doubled, new structures were built
for the Experiment Station, and in 1914 a large administration building
was erected with a state appropriation of $100,000. Housing most of
the agricultural departments, which had long since outgrown the facilities
of New Jersey Hall, the new building represented a decisive step toward
the development of a major campus devoted exclusively to agriculture.
In the same year, in recognition of the great importance that this field
had acquired, Dr. Lipman was named to the newly created post of
Dean of Agriculture, with administrative responsibility for all phases of
the varied program.

Another area that experienced marked growth was that of education.
The expansion of the New Jersey high-school system in the early 1900's
created a heavy demand for qualified teachers. The single State Normal
School at Trenton prepared only elementary teachers, with the result
that the high schools had to look chiefly to colleges and out of the state
for their staffs. When in 1911 new state rules required that applicants
for secondary-school teaching positions must be college graduates and
that they be certified only in the subjects they were properly qualified
to teach, the need for measures to increase the supply of eligible candidates became acute. Rutgers had instituted courses in pedagogy in
1891, and small numbers of graduates had entered the teaching profession. But in 1911 the College authorities decided to give new emphasis
to work in that field, for they saw that it would "mean not only a growing
service for Rutgers students, but as well an even more sympathetic and
influential relation with the secondary education of the State than has
ever before maintained."

As a first step, Professor Alexander James Inglis was appointed Professor of the Science of Education, to join Professor Payson in that department. A Columbia Ph.D., Inglis was at the College for only two
years before leaving to accept a post at Harvard, but he prepared the

foundations for an ambitious and effective program. Course offerings in the College were expanded, but even more important was the establishment in 1913 of a summer session under Inglis' direction. Offering a wide range of courses, most of which were intended to serve the needs of teachers, the first session enrolled over 300 students, more than twice the number that had been anticipated. By 1915, when Professor Charles H. Elliott had succeeded Inglis, 101 courses were presented to 567 students, the overwhelming majority of whom were teachers or prospective teachers. In a related move, extension courses were revived in 1912 under a faculty committee headed by Professor Inglis. Although the initial plans contemplated the arrangement of vocational and cultural courses for interested adults, in fact the emphasis soon came to be placed almost entirely on teacher training. College-level courses in education and in content fields, for which credit was approved by the State Board of Education, were offered at convenient times in New Brunswick and elswhere. Through these various endeavors, the College made a major contribution to the state's educational system.

The developments in agriculture and education added large, new dimensions to the functions of the College, but there was also a decided strengthening of established departments. Engineering and chemistry, which had always been the leading fields in the Scientific School but which were severely handicapped by cramped and makeshift physical facilities in Geology Hall and New Jersey Hall, were raised to new levels of effectiveness with the erection of the Engineering Building (1909) and the Chemistry Building (1910). Under the leadership of Professor Alfred A. Titsworth, who was named Dean of Mechanic Arts in 1914, and Dr. Ralph G. Wright, who became Professor of Chemistry in 1907, undergraduates received excellent training. The biological sciences, well supported because of their relationship to agriculture, included the most distinguished scientists on the faculty. With expanded quarters in New Jersey Hall and the adjacent Entomology Building, they were equipped to build on the fine reputation that had been established by Nelson, Halstead, and Smith.

Graduate work, which had been carried on in desultory fashion for over thirty years, achieved new status. With cordial support from President Demarest, departments that possessed the requisite staff and facilities were encouraged to accept graduate students, and in 1912 a faculty committee redefined the requirements for the doctoral program to include three years of study, knowledge of French and German, a general examination, and a thesis. Within a few years, aided by numerous industrial fellowships, there were a score of graduate students in residence, most of them in the field of agriculture but some in chemistry and biology as well. Simultaneously, the faculty—especially in the sciences—

became increasingly concerned with research and scholarly publication.

The expansion and elaboration of the academic program, notable as it was in the sciences, agriculture, and education, did not yet extend to the social sciences and the humanities. In spite of the fact that enrollments in the liberal disciplines were growing at a more rapid rate than those in the sciences, course offerings underwent little change. History, under the colorful Professor John H. Logan, remained a one-man department until 1916. Dr. Scott taught all that was offered in the fields of political science and economics; Professor Walter T. Marvin represented the field of philosophy and psychology; and Latin, Greek, and art each occupied the time of one professor. The English department was staffed by three men and there were six in modern languages, while agriculture alone boasted a dozen instructors, engineering eight, and chemistry four. The problem essentially was that Federal and state funds were available for scientific and technical departments but not for the liberal arts departments.

The determined efforts of the president, faculty, and Trustees to advance the College met with a heartening response. For thirty years there had been little growth in the size of the student body, but between 1906 and 1916 enrollments soared from 236 to 537, exclusive of the summer session, short courses, and the extension program. Many factors contributed to the advance, including the modernized educational program, the proliferation of public high schools, the availability of state scholarships, and the general acceptance of the worthwhileness of a college education. But there was also an extremely active campaign to recruit students. President Demarest travelled throughout the state, addressing high school audiences and educational organizations, to publicize the opportunities available at Rutgers, and carried on a voluminous correspondence with school principals and superintendents. Professor Louis Bevier, who served as State Inspector of High Schools from 1905 to 1909, lost no opportunity to promote the College and delivered lectures, illustrated with slides, on the advantages of the institution. The faculty committee on relations with schools presented framed photos of College buildings to state high schools, circulated thousands of illustrated pamphlets, and solicited the names of prospective students.

The young men who responded to these appeals reflected the change that was taking place in the educational environment. Of the students who had matriculated in 1886, nearly 80 per cent had attended private preparatory schools, but by 1916, 82 per cent of the entering Freshmen were graduates of public high schools. Although there continued to be a trickle of candidates from the old Dutch Church strongholds in the Hudson Valley, the undergraduates were drawn primarily from New Jersey, and especially from the more densely populated northern portion of the state. Approximately 40 per cent of them held state grants and many of the remainder were aided by College scholarships. The ethnic and religious composition of the student body altered perceptibly as the children of recent immigrant groups, Catholics, and Jews claimed the privileges of higher education at the State College.

Even more marked than the rise in student enrollments was the growth in the teaching staff, which went from thirty-one members in 1906 to eighty-one in 1916. Among those who entered the faculty in this period were several notable men, most of whom devoted the remainder of their academic careers to Rutgers and made large contributions to the College and their departments—Walter T. Marvin, Professor of Philosophy and Psychology and later the first Dean of the College of Arts and Sciences; Charles H. Whitman, for three decades head of the English department; John H. Logan in history; Ralph G. Wright in chemistry; Stanley E. Brasefield in mathematics; Edmond Billetdoux in Romance languages; Walter R. Newton in German; Robert C. H. Heck, Albert R. Johnson, and Harry N. Lendall in engineering, and Maurice A. Blake, Thomas J. Headlee, John P. Helyar, and Lyman G. Schermerhorn in agriculture. Professional academicians, they nevertheless gave their first loyalty to the institution, and together with their senior colleagues, they gave Rutgers a remarkably strong and effective faculty.

There were, however, subtle but significant changes taking place in the status and orientation of the faculty. As the academic profession acquired a new sense of self-consciousness and moved toward agreement on standards of training and competence, as disciplinary boundaries took on increasing clarity and rigidity, and as the number of teachers grew in magnitude, a new academic order emerged. Hierarchy of rank assumed importance. Before 1900 the occasional faculty member at Rutgers who was not a full professor was in the minority, but as the staff expanded precise categories of instructor, assistant professor, associate professor, and professor came into vogue, to recognize levels of status and achievement. After 1909 instructors had no voting privilege in faculty meetings, which they were permitted to attend only by invitation. Advanced degrees, not yet the *sine qua non* for appointment or promotion, were highly desirable badges of distinction; it was a moot point whether to address someone with the title of "doctor" or "professor." Perhaps out of a consciousness of their loss of individuality but more probably to give dignified expression to their new corporate identity, the faculty adopted academic regalia for College ceremonies. First worn at President Demarest's inauguration, the quaint medieval costumes gained complete acceptance in 1913 when the Trustees, who themselves had first donned doctoral robes in 1905, agreed to purchase gowns for all members of the faculty.

Almost inevitably, growth was attended by ever more elaborate organization, increasingly involved procedures, and additions to the administrative staff. Meetings of the whole faculty, presided over by the president, were held regularly twice a month, but the impossible burden of dealing with innumerable special cases led to the creation in 1906 of a "Committee on Administration," composed of the president, the dean, the registrar, and Professors Bevier and Titsworth. This committee effectively administered the increasingly intricate regulations governing admissions, scholastic standing, and schedule changes. In a process that was repeated in other areas, the faculty in 1908 empowered the Committee on Administration to handle all admission matters; the Committee promptly delegated this authority to the registrar, subject to its final approval. Departmental structures had yet to receive official definition, but the boundaries were gradually becoming established as the various disciplines, influenced by their national professional associations, staked out their claims to the particular spheres of knowledge that they would zealously promote and jealously defend against all rivals.

Symptomatic of the new academic order, too, was the appearance in the College catalogue for 1916 of a category of personnel labelled "Officers of Administration," which included twenty-one individuals. The faculty had taken the lead in creating the posts of librarian and registrar and the Trustees had added a dean. In 1914, recognizing that certain units within the College required administrative direction, the Trustees appointed a dean of agriculture, a dean of mechanic arts, a director of short courses, a director of agricultural extension, and a director of summer session. When the loyal and efficient Irving S. Upson died in 1915, he was succeeded as treasurer by Henry P. Schneeweiss, 1877; and Luther H. Martin, 1909, became registrar and secretary of the faculty. As matters of public relations and alumni affairs assumed increasing importance, young Earl Reed Silvers, 1913, became assistant to the president with special responsibilities for those areas. Thus did a fourth force—the administration—come to share with the Trustees, the president, and the faculty the conduct of College affairs.

No mere description of curricula or tables of organization can communicate an understanding of what the College was. It was the sum of many individual personalities, and if one had to be selected to represent the archetype of the Rutgers professor and administrator of the period it would be Louis Bevier. Bevier was a native of Marbletown, New York, where his Huguenot ancestors had long been identified with the Dutch Church. After graduating from Rutgers with the first honor in 1878, he had taken his doctorate in the classics at Johns Hopkins and then had spent two years in study abroad before joining the College faculty in 1883. A brilliant linguist, he taught modern languages and

Latin before becoming Professor of Greek in 1893. Several monographs in philology evidenced his high attainments as a scholar, but his intellectual interests and his concern with the welfare of the College, his church, and his community carried him into many fields of action. As a classroom teacher he had few peers, for he understood young men, liked them, and won their interest along with their affection. He was the mainstay of the Athletic Association, serving as its treasurer and always giving encouragement and guidance. Through this interest he became one of the founders of the National Collegiate Athletic Association and one of its first officers. He was deeply involved in alumni affairs, holding the post of treasurer of the Alumni Endowment Fund for many years. Interested in education at all levels, he was a member of the State Board of Education and then State Inspector of High Schools, in which role he wrought incalculable improvement in standards and in the articulation of high school and college programs. He organized the first extension program in 1892. He was a popular successor in 1912 to F. C. Van Dyck as Dean of the College and broadened the scope of that office to include academic as well as disciplinary problems. He was an enthusiastic promoter of a women's college and was among the first to volunteer to teach without compensation when the fledgling institution came into being in 1918. His long, drooping mustache gave him a rascally appearance and was responsible for the kickname of "Greaser," used with sly irreverence by generations of students. An incorrigible rhymster, he composed poems and hymns for every occasion and submitted his offerings to every likely publication. As a member of the consistory of the Second Reformed Church, he was its main pillar, as he was of the faculty. Death came to him one afternoon as he sat engaged in his favorite recreation, playing chess in his home with a student. The old-time professor brought up to date, learned in his discipline, serving in every capacity where his talents might be useful, he epitomized Rutgers to his colleagues and students.

The rapid development of the College in these years owed much to the favorable relationship it maintained with the state. After the decisions on the scholarship claims, the constitutional objections to appropriating funds for the College were stilled, and Governors and legislators alike were disposed to be sympathetic to requests for support. Moreover, the state's fiscal position was greatly improved, notably by a revision of the system of railroad taxation, with the result that vast new sums suddenly became available for new purposes.* By 1906 regular appropriations for scholarships, ceramics, and short courses had become established, and

---

* General state revenues rose from $4,830,000 in 1905 to $12,063,000 in 1915; in the same period income from the state railroad-tax mounted from $940,000 to $4,663,000, chiefly because of the Perkins Act of 1906.

thereafter the College pursued a cautious policy of seeking to add specific items to the list. President Demarest took the leading role in dealing with Governors and legislators, always confining his requests to what he felt assured could be obtained but constantly pressing the state authorities to give to Rutgers recognition and support comparable to that bestowed on state colleges elsewhere.

Year by year the legislature increased its commitment to the College. In 1908 special funds were appropriated to equip the new Engineering Building and two years later there was a similar grant for the Chemistry Building. Encouraged by the ready response to their modest requests, the Trustees reexamined the whole question of state relations and decided that the future looked promising. "They further conclude," read their report, "that the way is open for new details of legislation as any year may suggest and that occasional efforts for larger cooperation and special appropriation seems advisable." Pushing forward with this strategy, they were successful in 1911 in obtaining state funds to provide equipment for courses in entomology and physics as well as an increase in the number of state scholarships.

An important change in the procedure by which the College obtained funds from the state was made in 1912. Previously it had been necessary to secure first an act of the legislature authorizing an expenditure for a particular object—such as the short courses—and then to endeavor to persuade the appropriations committee to include the item in its annual appropriations act. The College secured a law which, in effect, exempted it from the first step and enabled it to deal directly with the appropriations committee. This procedure unquestionably facilitated matters. One of the first fruits of the new arrangement was an appropriation in 1912 of $100,000 for the Agricultural Administration Building, the second building at the College erected with state funds. Over the next several years the list of specific items in the appropriations for the College steadily lengthened. Appropriations for reference books and periodicals and for the summer session were added in 1913, "long courses" in agriculture in 1914, and College Farm maintenance and additional equipment for engineering and chemistry in 1915. A major advance was made in 1916 when appropriations were obtained for supporting the regular courses in engineering, sanitary science, chemistry, and military science. A year later courses in education entered the subsidized category, but efforts to have physics, biology, and botany included were unsuccessful. By 1917 the state appropriation of $120,700 accounted for approximately one-third of the total income of the College, with another third coming from Federal sources.

Obviously the relationship between the state and the College had undergone a fundamental transformation since 1902. Appropriations were now being made not only for scholarships, buildings, equipment, and programs especially authorized by the legislature but also for the support of several teaching departments in the sciences and education. As state support grew in magnitude and in breadth, questions were raised in some quarters about the precise status of Rutgers. Much confusion resulted from the fact that legislation affecting the College usually referred to the institution as the "State Agricultural College." President Demarest grasped the essence of the problem as early as 1908:

> It may not be out of place [he told the Trustees] to add our sense of regret that the title "Agricultural College" has come into the legislation touching our Scientific School. . . . It is so distinct a misnomer, suggesting but a single part of the manifold work committed to the college and carried on by it, and misleading people not well informed, that some amendment of such legislative phrasing, if possible, would seem very desirable.

The matter was the subject of consideration for several years, until finally in 1917 the legislature enacted a bill drafted by College authorities that was designed to clarify the situation. The act simply stated that the "Rutgers Scientific School, being the State Agricultural College, the State College for the benefit of agriculture and the mechanic arts, maintained by the 'Trustees of Rutgers College in New Jersey'" would now be designated "the State University of New Jersey." Confusing as it may seem, the State University of New Jersey was a division of Rutgers College. Although the new title was added to the College stationery and was influential in securing for Rutgers admittance to the National Association of State Universities in 1918, its consequences were minimal. For one thing, no one knew which portions of Rutgers were included in the Scientific School. Moreover, in subsequent enactments and in the annual appropriations bill the old name of "State Agricultural College" held on and legislators retained the impression that the special responsibility they had to "agriculture" did not extend in the same degree to the "mechanic arts" or to "other scientific and classical studies." Neither did the new designation clarify the status of Rutgers. On the contrary, the nature of the state relationship was to become increasingly a source of controversy after 1917, both within the Board of Trustees and at the governmental level.

As the College moved toward a closer relationship with the state, it severed its ties with the Reformed Church. Under the agreement with the General Synod, as revised in 1891, two-thirds of the Trustees had to be communicants of the Reformed Church. This restriction seemed increasingly inappropriate, and when the Carnegie Foundation ruled that the College was ineligible to participate in its pension plan for professors because of the denominational connection, President Demarest initiated a successful appeal to the Synod to rescind the quota in 1909. There still remained in force the sections of the College charter requiring that the president be a member of the Reformed Church and that there should be a professorship of divinity. Critics charged that such provisions were entirely inconsistent with the new character of Rutgers as a state university, and in 1920 the Trustees acted to amend the charter to eliminate those requirements as well as "all provisions of the said Charter of a sectarian character . . . to the end that this College shall be in law and in fact non-sectarian in all respects." For some, the complete break with the denomination that had brought the College into existence and helped to sustain it for a century represented a final, tragic concession of defeat, the death blow to the old ideal of the Christian classical college. But the decision seemed to be inescapable, for the new Rutgers that was emerging had long since ceased to be the child of the Covenant and was becoming the ward of the state.

When Dr. Demarest began his presidency he had little reason to anticipate that within a decade the state, which had so long neglected the College, would be its main source of support. Although he pressed vigorously for the state appropriations that he felt the College needed to fulfill its land-grant obligations, he continued to envision a dual Rutgers. Along with the state college, there was the old foundation, the private Rutgers, with its responsibility for maintaining and strengthening what the president termed in his inaugural address "ideals of education exalted by the fathers and found worthy of enduring honor." State and Federal funds would be available, it seemed, only for limited purposes in technological and scientific areas. If the College was to continue its historic mission it must look to private sources for an adequate endowment and enlarged physical facilities. The president shared with the Trustees the belief that unless the private assets of the institution grew in proportion to the public subsidy, the old foundation would crumble and Rutgers would pass completely under public control.

The circumstances seemed to be favorable for securing large benefactions. Universities throughout the nation were successfully cultivating multimillionaire philanthropists, fabulously endowed foundations, and their own numerous and loyal alumni. Always the hope was to discover a large donor—a Duke, a Vanderbilt, a Gould, a Sage, or a Rockefeller; the old methods of selling perpetual scholarships or preaching in the churches to obtain small subscriptions would no longer suffice. President Demarest was more than willing to practice the new art, and despite the cruel disappointments that were to be experienced he clung doggedly to the quest.

Immediately upon taking office he informed the Trustees that the endowment should be increased by $500,000 and received their encouragement to undertake to raise it. Several individuals responded with gifts of $5,000, but interest quickly dwindled and only about $50,000 was added to capital funds. To meet recurring annual deficits the president induced a number of friends and Trustees to contribute annually to his "Administration Fund," which usually amounted to about $4,000. Wealthy alumni in New York City, under the leadership of Trustee Leonor F. Loree, were prevailed upon in 1910 to organize a "Graduates' Committee" for the purpose of raising $100,000 for the new Chemistry Building, but they were able to do no more than pay the interest on the loan that financed its construction. Meanwhile the Alumni Endowment Fund, launched in 1892 to stimulate annual giving, grew at the rate of a few thousand dollars a year.

Interminable negotiations with the great foundations produced frustration. For more than a decade the president had sought to have the Carnegie Foundation place the College on its approved list in order that retiring faculty members might have the benefits of the Foundation's pension plan. To meet the Foundation's standards of eligibility, admission requirements were raised, accounting procedures were revised, and the denominational requirement respecting Trustees was eliminated, all to no avail. The Rockefeller-endowed General Education Board was also disappointing. When the College first made its appeal in 1904 it was turned down, presumably because of its connection with the state. After it was announced in 1909 that a grant had been made to the University of Vermont, President Demarest again made application, but the College was told it must first pay off all its debts before it could be considered for a matching grant. Still later, when a drive was launched in connection with the 150th anniversary, the president made the strongest possible presentation to the Board, but again there were difficult questions about the public-private character of Rutgers and no grant was forthcoming. This refusal came as an especially severe blow, because the foundation grant was expected to stimulate the matching gifts that would enable the College to raise $1,000,000 for its anniversary. Valiant efforts were made and an intensive campaign was conducted among the alumni, but only about $270,000 had actually been secured when the entrance of the United States into the war brought a halt to the effort.

Although increments to the endowment were meagre, the assets of the College were augmented by very substantial additions of property and buildings. James Neilson, alumnus and Trustee and a member of a wealthy New Brunswick family that had been identified with the College almost since its origin, took the occasion of Dr. Demarest's inauguration to present deeds for much of the land north of the old campus, between

Hamilton Street and Seminary Place, requesting that it be named Neilson Campus in memory of his father. In the course of time several parcels within the block were acquired from other owners, chiefly with funds supplied by John Howard Ford, and a second major campus was developed. The old College Field, site of the first football game, was also obtained through private gifts, as were extensive tracts for the enlargement of the College Farm.

New buildings were desperately needed to keep pace with the rapidly growing student body. The engineering program was hampered by totally inadequate facilities in Geology Hall and chemistry was being crowded out of New Jersey Hall because agriculture and biology needed all the available space. In 1905 the College had approached Andrew Carnegie with a request for $100,000 with which to erect a science building. Carnegie replied that a $50,000 building should be adequate and offered to give half of that amount. There the matter rested for more than a year because some influential Trustees felt that the chief need was for increased endowment rather than for a building that would diminish capital funds. Carnegie was then asked to donate the full cost of the building on the condition that the College would raise an equal amount for endowment, but when this proposal met a cool response, the Trustees with some reluctance decided to accept his original offer and apply it to the construction of an engineering building. The balance of the cost could be met by drawing upon the $80,000 that had recently been received from the state in settlement of the scholarship claims. Located on the new Neilson Campus, the building was completed early in 1909 at a total cost of $95,000, of which $20,000 represented the state appropriation for equipment.

No funds were in sight for the erection of a chemistry building, but so critical was the need that in 1909 the president urged that construction be authorized with borrowed funds. The Trustees sanctioned this extreme measure, and the new structure was erected north of the Engineering Building at a cost of $85,000, of which $25,000 came from the state. For many years the interest on the bank loan was carried by the New York City "Graduates Committee," but the heavy investments in the two science facilities reduced the income-yielding funds of the College and thereby diminished the prospects for giving enlarged support to the nonscientific disciplines. Through state grants for equipping a physics laboratory in the basement of Geology Hall, for adapting a building in the rear of New Jersey Hall for the work in entomology, and for the erection of the Agricultural Administration Building the physical requirements of the scientific and technical departments were satisfactorily met.

Among other notable additions to the physical assets of the College from private sources was a handsome dormitory, the gift of John Howard Ford. He and his brother, James B. Ford, were the two greatest benefactors of the College in this period. John Ford had many ties to New Brunswick and joined the Board of Trustees in 1912 after accumulating a fortune in the rubber industry. The dormitory was begun shortly after his death in 1914 and completed the following year. Ford Hall contained admirably arranged accommodations for eighty students and set a standard of excellence not to be matched in the period of this history. In a related effort, three spacious "cottages" were erected on upper George Street to house students in the Preparatory School, replacing the outmoded "Trap" on Hamilton Street. By 1916, the physical appearance of the College had changed considerably as the new Neilson Campus, with New Jersey Hall, Ballantine Gymnasium, Voorhees Library, the Engineering Building, the Chemistry Building, the Entomology Building, Ford Hall, and the new President's House complemented the old Queen's Campus. At the other end of the city the Short Course Building, Agricultural Administration Building, and numerous structures for the Experiment Station formed the nucleus of a new complex.

Although the total assets of the College were being multiplied and state and Federal appropriations were rising steadily, the Trustees were confronted with a disheartening financial prospect. Annual deficits averaging nearly $15,000 and loans to finance plant expansion produced an indebtedness of $165,000 by 1917. A gift of $100,000 from James B. Ford, the largest single benefaction up to that time, was used to reduce the debt, but the heavy annual deficits remained. The crux of the matter was that while state and Federal funds were largely sustaining the technical and scientific departments, the private resources of the College, given the existing tuition structure, were inadequate to support the fields that did not receive governmental subsidy. When the million-dollar endowment campaign of 1916 met with failure, the cherished vision of bringing the old, private foundation to a position of equality with the state college dimmed, and in the succeeding years the Trustees were brought face to face with agonizing decisions about future policies.

Remarkable as were the transformations wrought in the College in the first decade of the Demarest administration, they scarcely extended to the way of life of the undergraduates, although new elements were added, and the subtle process continued by which the autonomy of the students was undermined and restricted. As the new Freshmen arrived on the campus in ever increasing numbers, they were effectively—if somewhat rigorously—indoctrinated in what was expected of them if they were to become acceptable members of the undergraduate social order. The Sophomore's "Proc" proclaimed the rules the Freshmen must obey in their abject role as "greenies" and specified the dire penalties that would be meted out to the disobedient. The Freshmen soon acquired a sense of class spirit, which they manifested in a series of jousts with their Sophomore tormentors—the Proc Scrap, Flag Rush, Rope Rush, and athletic contests. Ultimately they expressed their sense of having arrived at full undergraduate status with a class banquet, provided their arrangements could be made with sufficient secrecy to insure that the affair would not be totally disrupted by the Sophomores. Meanwhile, they were anxiously hoping to receive a bid from a fraternity or, if they had arrived with the reputation of being fine fellows, they might submit to an extravagant round of courting before making their choice. Representatives of the football team, the glee club, the Y.M.C.A. or the *Targum* would look them over appraisingly, and those who quickly distinguished themselves as men of affairs could aspire to membership in Serpent and Coffin. For the shy ones, the grinds, or the social rebels, the process of assimilation to this hearty, masculine, group-oriented world might be agonizing; but for most, the feeling of acceptance that came from joining in the class yell, exchanging a secret grip, or sharing in a team effort produced deep satisfactions.

New activities and organizations entered the College scene, reflecting in some instances new interests or concerns. The Dramatic Association, formed in 1908, had a somewhat erratic career and was succeeded in 1914 by Queen's Players, which attempted with some success the staging of serious drama. The College Orchestra made a brief appearance in 1915, but it attracted much less attention and support than did the College Band, organized a year later under the aegis of the military department. The Debate Team, which compiled an extraordinary record of victories, was a source of considerable pride to the institution, as were the four winners of the prestigious Rhodes Scholarships in this period. The long-dormant Philoclean Society was revived in 1908 and in addition to holding occasional debates and engaging in discussions of contemporary issues undertook the sponsorship of an interscholastic debating league that soon grew to embrace scores of secondary schools. The Y.M.C.A., now provided with quarters in Van Nest and staffed by a salaried executive secretary, had a large membership and took on the role of a social service agency. To the list of secret honor societies Chain and Bones was added in 1906 for prestigious Sophomores, and a new event on the social calendar after 1910 was the Military Ball. As yet there was little evidence of pronounced political or social awareness among campus groups, although there was an active Prohibition League, dedicated to advancing the cause of temperance. Perhaps the most significant newcomer to the campus was the Menorah Society, organized in 1913 by the small group of Jewish students for the purpose of promoting the study of Jewish history and culture.

Student government, which had been in a stage of arrested development for more than a decade took on a new complexion in 1914 with the introduction of an elective Senior council. Composed of seven men, the Council concerned itself with problems of general interest to the undergraduates and submitted recommendations for the approval of the Assembly, which consisted of the entire student body. The Council's first major proposal was that an honor system should be adopted, but the Assembly rejected this innovation in 1915 and again in 1917. Meanwhile the innocuous Self-Government Board lingered on, although it rarely had any disciplinary matters placed before it.

The number of fraternities on the campus had remained stable since 1879, when Chi Psi was founded, but between 1904 and 1914 six new houses appeared—Omega Pi Alpha (1904), later (1913) Pi Kappa Alpha; Queen's Club (1909), later (1918) Kappa Sigma; Scarlet Club (1909), later (1918) Phi Gamma Delta; Ivy Club (1913); Lambda Chi Alpha (1913); and Theta Pi (1914), later (1915) Phi Epsilon Pi. The increase kept pace with the enlargement of the student body, and about half of the undergraduates continued to be fraternity members. Until 1914 the fraternities were subject to no rules or regulations whatsoever by the faculty or Trustees; a thoroughly laissez-faire policy prevailed. An interfraternity council had been organized on an informal basis in 1911, with graduate and undergraduate delegates from each house, but it possessed no legislative or executive powers and functioned on the basis of mutual consultation.

The emergence of a new policy toward fraternities was indicated by a faculty resolution late in 1913 suggesting to the Trustees that in the best interests of the College a limitation should be placed on the number of fraternities and local residence clubs and that hereafter all proposals by local clubs to affiliate with national fraternities should be subject to faculty approval. The Trustees somewhat ambiguously resolved that these recommendations should be "in general approved" and advised the president to disapprove the formation of any additional fraternities or clubs. The matter continued to be troublesome, and in 1917 the Trustees formulated a new policy: no residence clubs or fraternities could be established without their sanction.

Involved in the whole issue of curtailing the number of fraternities was the delicate and bewildering problem of anti-Semitism. There had been only occasional students of the Jewish faith at Rutgers before 1900, but a decade later they had become sufficiently numerous to arouse the deep-rooted prejudices of the traditionally Christian student body. In an age not distinguished for racial and religious tolerance, it was predictable that the Jewish students would be the victims of gibes and discrimination. In 1914, when the faculty and Trustees had committed themselves not to approve new clubs or fraternities, a group of Jewish students formed Theta Pi, which affiliated with the national fraternity, Phi Epsilon Pi, in 1915. An extremely awkward and unpleasant situation then developed. The Trustees would not approve the fraternity, but neither were they disposed to order its dissolution. Student sentiment was strongly hostile to the chapter, which was not admitted to the interfraternity council, and the *Scarlet Letter* pointedly ignored its existence. Ultimately—in April 1919—the Trustees granted Phi Epsilon Pi formal permission to continue in existence, but not until 1922 did the *Scarlet Letter* confer its recognition. Efforts of other Jewish students to secure recognition for their organization, the Campus Club, met with decided opposition from the undergraduate body and the administration, and the group disbanded with considerable bitterness in 1918. Probably the prevailing student opinion was summarized in an anonymous letter to *Targum* on March 9, 1920, which asserted that Rutgers men believed "that everything should be done to discourage Jews from coming to Rutgers. We have a fear, deep in our hearts, that Rutgers may suffer the fate of C.C.N.Y. and New York University." In time these sentiments were to moderate and finally wither, but they were an inescapable part of the American climate of opinion.

The one sphere of undergraduate activity that underwent a dramatic transformation was football. In the fall of 1913 "Sandy" suddenly arrived on the scene, introducing big-time football, a period of gridiron glory, and alumni control of the game. A small but highly influential group of graduates under the aggressive leadership of Trustee Leonor F. Loree determined that Rutgers should become a major football power and formed a syndicate to underwrite the development of the sport. Whereas formerly the Athletic Association had hired the coach, arranged the schedule, and maintained the football field, the Syndicate now took over these responsibilities. It was Loree who prevailed upon George Foster Sanford to coach the team. A graduate of Yale, where he had been an outstanding lineman, Sanford had demonstrated his considerable coaching talents at Columbia and West Point, among other schools, before taking the helm at Rutgers. The campus had never known such a personality. Articulate, commanding, colorful, dynamic, he immediately became an idol to his players and to the vast majority of the students as well. Preaching clean sportsmanship, maintaining constantly that "football is method, not men," and demanding complete dedication, "Sandy" brought the whole College under his spell.

He soon demonstrated that he was capable of producing the success that he promised. In his first season the team won six of nine games, and in 1915 it achieved unprecedented success, losing only to Princeton and scoring 352 points to thirty-three for the opposition. Games at the Polo Grounds in New York City with such major opponents as Washington and Jefferson, Syracuse, Nebraska, and West Virginia attracted national publicity. The Syndicate refurbished Neilson Field, erecting stands and a field house as the home games drew ever larger throngs. Whatever else the consequences, Rutgers men now thrilled with pride at the achievements of Sandy's teams and hailed as heroes such outstanding players as Robert A. Nash, 1916, Harry J. Rockafeller, 1916, Howard P. Talman, 1917, and John P. Toohey, 1916. To the president and a segment of the faculty, these developments were not entirely welcome, but so great was student enthusiasm and so strong was alumni influence that they were obliged to conceal the concern they felt. If the undergraduates in the Athletic Association experienced any regrets at seeing football pass from their control and take on a status different from other sports, they gave no sign of it.

New forms of intercollegiate athletic competition gained approval along with football, baseball, track, and gymnastics. Basketball was introduced by members of the Class of 1908 in their Freshman year, at first on an informal basis but by 1907 with faculty approval. After two indifferent seasons, the sport was dropped until the winter of 1914, when it assumed a permanent place on the athletic roster. When Frank Hill began his long tenure as coach in 1916, basketball grew in stature and popularity, and in 1920 the team went to the finals of the national championships. The opening of the swimming pool in the Ballantine Gymnasium in March 1915, under the supervision of swimming instructor James Reilley, quickly led to the organization of a swimming team, which engaged in its first meet in February 1916. Tennis, similarly, acquired new status with the construction in 1908 of five courts on Seminary Place, and soon a tennis team received the limited recognition of a minor sport.

The whole realm of intercollegiate athletics continued to be regarded by the Trustees and faculty as tangential to, rather than an integral part of, the College's program. Through its Committee on Athletics the faculty exercised a negative kind of control over team schedules and sought to prevent the encroachment of athletics on the academic curriculum, but the Athletic Association, in which the faculty was represented, bore the entire managerial and financial responsibility for the teams. These policies commanded general support, although Professor Louis Bevier, from his vantage point as treasurer of the Athletic Association and secretary-treasurer of the National Collegiate Athletic Association, was an advocate of change. In his view, the direction of athletics should be vested in an officer of the College "and not in irresponsible outside coaches, hired from season to season to develop a special team." With extraordinary foresight, he recommended in 1908 the engagement of a director of athletics and the assumption by the College of financial responsibility for all sports. In part because of financial reasons, this proposal was not fully implemented for another quartercentury. In the meantime the faculty extended its supervision to encompass standards of eligibility, setting forth in 1915 detailed regulations to insure that only students who were taking a full-course schedule and who were not failing or deficient in more than five hours of work could play on teams. Not surprisingly, the faculty's concern with academic standards was not entirely consonant with the views of football-minded alumni, who often expressed anguish about the high mortality rate among promising athletes and even contended that eligibility for sports should have no disciplinary relationship to scholastic standing. These attitudes did not sway the faculty, which was also cool to an alumni plea that there be no classes between two and four o'clock in order to facilitate team practice. After all, they could point out, arrangements had been made in 1910 to end all classes by four o'clock in the interest of athletics, a move that necessitated Saturday classes.

Whether their interest in the College was largely focused on athletics or derived from other sources of loyalty, the alumni increasingly assumed the status of an organized and vocal constituency. Looking to them for support of various kinds, the president and his associates fostered this development. A movement was launched to form alumni clubs in various localities, and by 1910 there were fourteen such clubs in New York and New Jersey and as far afield as Boston, Cleveland, Chicago, and Southern California. Largest of all was the New Brunswick Club, which enjoyed the facilities of the former President's House—which was converted into an alumni-faculty club. With the appointment of Earl Reed Silvers as presidential assistant in 1913, a new era in alumni relations began. Silvers was chiefly responsible for bringing to fruition the plans of the Alumni Association for a magazine. Under his extremely able editorship, the *Alumni Quarterly* (which became a monthly in 1921) first appeared in October 1914. Admirable for its extensive coverage of every phase of College activities, the *Quarterly* more than achieved its announced purpose of strengthening the bonds between Rutgers and her sons. In 1916, after a study of practices in other colleges, the Alumni Council was created to coordinate all areas of alumni activities. Made up of the officers of the Association, nine members-at-large, the alumni Trustees, and representatives of each class and local club, the Council worked through numerous committees, primarily to strengthen alumni loyalty, cultivate relations with secondary schools, and publicize the College. With the appointment in 1921 of William P. Garrison, 1910, as Alumni Secretary there was a decided expansion of the alumni program, and the annual Alumni Loyalty Fund was established. Alumni also increased their dominance of the Board of Trustees; of twenty-four Trustees elected in the decade after 1905, all but four were Rutgers graduates. The theory that the College somehow belonged to its alumni, first given definite form in the 1880's with the movement for the election of alumni Trustees, was now widely accepted.

In these momentous early years of the Demarest administration the College had indeed made a tremendous surge forward. Pride in its recent accomplishments, as well as in the ancient origins of the College, found timely expression in 1916 in the celebration of the 150th anniversary of the first charter. For the hundreds of returning alumni, the undergraduate body, the visiting academic dignitaries, and the loyal townspeople, the observances early in October signified that the College, first called Queen's, had more than justified its struggling existence and had grown to impressive stature. As the incidents of the past were recalled in the moving address by President Demarest at the commemorative exercises in the old First Reformed Church and brought vividly to life in the elaborate pageant at the College Farm, reverence for the old foundation and for the worthies who had built it united Rutgers men and confirmed their sense of a common heritage. On Saturday afternoon, led by ten white-haired survivors of the historic first football game, alumni and students paraded through the town with songs and cheers and up College Avenue to Neilson Field for the football game with Washington and Lee. In a sense, the great celebration represented a final tribute to the old Rutgers—the Rutgers of the Dutch Church; of the Hardenberghs and Frelinghuysens, Milledoler, and Campbell; of Strong, Bowser, Cooper, and Van Dyck. A year ahead lay the designation of the Scientific School as the State University, and beyond that a series of developments that were to give to the institution an identity radically different from that which the celebrants hailed in 1916.

Punctuating the end of an era in the life of the College as well as of the nation was American involvement in World War I. Superficially, the impact of the war on the College did not appear to be as catastrophic or disruptive as might have been expected, at least down to the final months. To most observers it seemed that the academic routine was following its usual pattern. But in surprising ways the war, and the altered attitudes and conditions that followed in the wake of the war, marked a significant break with the past and gave accelerated momentum to the forces of change.

Immediately following the declaration of war, the faculty convened in a solemn mood to pledge their unqualified support to the Government and arrange to grant full credit for the semester to students who might be called into service. Except for providing two additional hours a week for military instruction, no adjustments seemed to be required in the academic program. Shortly the Rutgers League of National Defense was organized, headed by the president, chiefly for the purpose of preparing a detailed registry of the training and skills of all alumni and faculty, in order to assist in meeting the manpower needs of the Government. Plans were also made to promote the sale of Liberty Bonds among faculty and students. Within the next two months, classes were seriously depleted, as 215 of the total of 512 students withdrew, most of them to engage in farm work, but 63 of them to enter the military forces. Four members of the faculty—John H. Logan, William B. Twiss, Edmond W. Billetdoux, and David Fales—also left for war service.

When the next academic year began in September 1917, the editor of the *Alumni Quarterly* noted a serious tone among the 446 students, but no major dislocations. "The life of the college," he observed, "is going on very much as usual." By shortening the Christmas vacation and eliminating the Easter recess, the faculty planned to end all classes by May 21, which necessitated some curtailment of the spring sports schedule. The only alterations in the curriculum were the addition of a course in radio communication, given at the request of the War Department, and two short courses in the care and maintenance of farm tractors. A severe fuel shortage in January occasioned some inconvenience and resulted in the temporary suspension of chapel services. In the second semester there was some decline in enrollments as thirty-four men enlisted or were called in the draft.

With the growing number of Rutgers men in uniform, Earl Reed Silvers established the War Service Bureau and undertook to send frequent newsletters to all those in service and to publish in the *Quarterly* the scores of letters he received in return. Patriotic fervor was at a high level. When a Freshman made himself obnoxious in April by refusing to advocate the sale of Liberty Bonds in a public-speaking class, he was seized by an irate group of students, held for several hours in a room in Ford Hall, and in the evening was turned over to a mob to be stripped, covered with molasses and feathers, and paraded through town. Such incidents were exceptional, as fraternities, clubs, and teams maintained their accustomed activities. No doubt to many undergraduates the year remained memorable for the success of the football season. A remarkably strong team, led by Captain Kenneth M. Rendall, 1919, and Paul Robeson, 1919, defeated some of the strongest college and service teams in the East and lost only to Syracuse by the slim margin of 14–10.

Everything changed in September 1918, with the establishment of the Students' Army Training Corps. Early in September President Demarest returned from a conference of college presidents at Plattsburg, New York, to announce plans for the S.A.T.C. Every student in the College over seventeen years of age who met the physical standards would be enrolled in the Corps on October 1. The Government would provide for tuition and subsistence and pay students thirty dollars a month. Students under eighteen might also enter the Corps but would receive no subsidy from the Government. Circulars went out to the secondary schools advertising "A College Education Without Expenses," and the largest Freshman class in history, 274 in all, reported when classes began on September 18. Another hundred had been turned away because of a lack of facilities.

Garbed in khaki and crammed into two dormitories and three fraternities, the boys were subjected to military discipline under the command of Lieutenant James C. Torpey, assisted by seven second lieutenants. Reveille at 6:30 was followed punctually by mess, cafeteria style, at 7:00 in Winants Hall, classes from 8:00 to 10:00, and drill from 10:00 to 12:00. After lunch, there were four hours of classes; then came retreat, supper, three hours of study, and taps at 10:00 o'clock. Adding to the rigors of this experience was the terrible epidemic of influenza that struck soon after College opened, forcing scores of students to return to their homes and causing the death of four. The regular academic curricula had to be completely revised to provide fifteen hours each week for required courses in military practice, military theory, and war aims. As a consequence, electives were drastically restricted in favor of standardized programs. Because of the rigid military schedule, extracurricular activities were all but suspended.

This regimen had scarcely become fully operative when the Armistice was announced, and on December 13 the S.A.T.C. was formally demobilized. The faculty immediately resolved to return to the normal schedule, insofar as possible, with the start of the second term, but the transition was complicated by the withdrawal of more than 100 of the Freshmen who had entered in September and by the return of seventy-six upperclassmen whose work had been interrupted by war service. Looking back on the recent, tumultuous events, Earl Reed Silvers expressed a common feeling of bewilderment:

> The past few months have seen unusual changes on the college campus. The military has taken precedence over the academic; patriotism has overshadowed college spirit. The establishment of the S.A.T.C. has been a splendid thing for Rutgers; it has assured us an adequate student body, and has permitted us to preserve our faculty organization intact.

It is not without a tinge of regret, however, that some of us have watched the passing of old traditions. The morning chapel service has been discontinued; various college organizations can find no time for the customary meetings; fraternity life is at its lowest ebb. The future is uncertain.

The war had demanded heavy sacrifices from a generation of Rutgers men. Exclusive of the S.A.T.C., 838 alumni and students had served in the armed forces, and more than 3,000 of their letters received by the War Service Bureau recorded their experiences in every camp and theatre of war. Half of them were commissioned as officers, most of them of company grade, but two as major generals and one as brigadier general. Twenty-one died in service, and an equal number were wounded in action. A solemn memorial service to honor those who had given their lives in the nation's cause was held in the chapel in February. Elaborate preparations were made for a "War Commencement" in June, and over 600 alumni—many of them recently returned from France—attended the War Service Dinner. Although not untouched with sadness for those who would never return, the occasion was marked by ardent expressions of patriotism and devotion to the College. It was especially stirring because it had been preceded by a victory over Princeton in the baseball game, the first triumph over the ancient rival since that famous football game in 1869. So, with appropriate observances, the College turned from its preoccupation with the war to the uncertain future.

Chapter Eight

From College to University

In the years immediately following the Armistice there was a general awareness in America that nothing was ever to be quite the same again. Restlessness, uncertainty, and experimentation dominated the postwar scene. For Rutgers, as for the nation, the war seemed to mark a break with the past, although it would be difficult to assign the same causes to explain both developments. Quite suddenly, Rutgers ceased to be a college, and after a few turbulent years of readjustment it took on the structure and the name of a university. The transformation under any circumstances would have occasioned difficulties, but the temper of the times and the eruption of clashing opinions within the ranks of those charged with guiding the destiny of the institution added formidable complications. In a remarkable degree, there was a disposition to challenge long-held concepts and traditional policies and to venture into new roles and try new methods. Not all of the innovations were well advised, and the direction in which the College was to move was less than clear, but there was obviously impatience with things as they were.

Despite the many significant developments that had taken place since 1825, Rutgers had remained a college. New fields of instruction had been introduced, curricula had been multiplied, and administrative deans and directors had been appointed, but the College had retained its unity. The faculty all met together in a single body, the oversight of the president and the Trustees extended equally to all departments, and the students all thought of themselves as members of one collectivity. Physically, too, the College was closely integrated, for with the important exception of the Administration Building at the College Farm, academic facilities were concentrated on Queen's Campus and Neilson Campus. Within a short span of years—by 1925—the picture had altered radically. There were now three major campuses, several colleges endowed with varying degrees of autonomy, two completely distinct student bodies, and special agencies to whom the Trustees delegated

168

extensive responsibilities for particular colleges. Rutgers College had become Rutgers University.

The transformation was bound to occur, for many influences were combining to reshape the institution. Of central importance, however, was the founding of a women's college. Not only did this action represent a radical departure, because traditionally Rutgers had been exclusively dedicated to educating men, but it also resulted in the establishment of a completely new type of organizational unit, the creation of a new management agency, and the addition of a significant new factor in the already complex formulation of relations with the state. The founding of the women's college, then, is of unusual interest because of the bearing it had on the broader problems of university structure and state relations as well as because of its inherent importance. The story is an extraordinary one, too, because it reveals how a remarkable success was achieved by employing singularly unorthodox methods.

The general backwardness of New Jersey in the field of higher education was especially glaring with respect to facilities for women. As late as 1918 there was only the small College of St. Elizabeth at Convent Station, although there had been other short-lived institutions elsewhere. Throughout the West, coeducation had become the rule. In the Northeast numerous women's colleges had been founded after 1860, and late in the century several of the older and more prestigious men's colleges, with Harvard taking the lead, established what were termed affiliated or coordinate colleges for women. As early as 1881 the Rutgers faculty had proposed to the Trustees that young women should be admitted, but this overture was coldly rejected. A similar rebuff had been given in 1895 to a plea from the Rutgers Female Seminary in New York City that it be adopted as an annex of the College. When in the same year an inquiry was received as to whether women might compete for state scholarships under the law of 1890, the question was referred to a special committee of the Trustees and discreetly buried. From time to time there were other such rumblings, but no action.

The effective movement for a women's college began late in 1911 at a district meeting of the State Federation of Women's Clubs, when sudden enthusiasm was manifested for the proposition that women should be admitted to Rutgers. Present at this meeting by invitation was the president of the College Club of Jersey City, Mrs. Mabel S. Douglass, a Barnard graduate and a woman of extraordinary energy and capacity. Her ardor aroused by the prospect of a challenging opportunity, Mrs. Douglass soon became the chairman of a Federation committee to work in behalf of the cause. With amazing industry, she collected relevant information from all parts of the country, enlisted the support of numerous influential men throughout the state, formed an impressive advisory council, lectured extensively to stimulate popular interest, and entered into negotiations with the president and the Trustees of Rutgers.

President Demarest early took the position that, while coeducation was out of the question, Rutgers would look with favor on the establishment of an affiliated women's college, provided the necessary funds could be assured from private or public sources. He continued to urge this view on the Trustees and to give such encouragement as he could to Mrs. Douglass. Finally, in June 1914, the Trustees approved in principle the proposal for an affiliated women's college and authorized its Advisory Committee to confer with Mrs. Douglass and her associates. The conference revealed that although considerable interest had been aroused, little money had actually been raised. Late in 1914 the prospects brightened when James Neilson offered a small tract of land and a house, and the women made a determined effort to secure $75,000 to launch the projected college, again without success. At this point, in January 1915, Mrs. Douglass was compelled to withdraw from the movement because of personal afflictions, and although others attempted to carry on the campaign, her driving spirit was sorely missed.

The groundwork had been laid, however, and the movement now acquired support from many quarters. Organizations like the State Grange and the New Jersey Education Association lent their strong endorsement. The State Board of Education, concerned about increasing the supply of high-school teachers, manifested interest. Then, in 1917, the passage of the Smith-Hughes Act promised Federal financial assistance for courses in home economics. At the same time the Carpender estate, admirably located near the College Farm and well adapted as a site for a women's college, came on the market. President Demarest now took the initiative, backed by the faculty and interested townspeople, and recommended that the Trustees act immediately without regard to the availability of funds. At his urging, it was resolved on April 12, 1918, "That the Trustees of Rutgers College do establish a Woman's College as a department of the State University of New Jersey maintained by the Trustees."

At this momentous April meeting the Board set in motion plans to open the new college in September and created a special committee of seven to implement them. The next few months were ones of remarkable activity. The Carpender estate was acquired, and shortly thereafter the nearby Cooper property as well. A course of studies for the Freshman year, to be offered mainly by enthusiastic volunteers from the Rutgers faculty, was arranged. At the invitation of Dr. Demarest, Mrs. Douglass in May accepted the position of Dean, and immediately set to work in makeshift quarters in Van Nest Hall to prepare for the September opening. Overseeing the renovation of the college buildings, canvassing for urgently needed funds, determining teaching schedules, and finally bringing the hastily contrived college to the attention of prospective students demanded enormous energy and devotion. It had been decided to launch the college even if no more than fifteen students enrolled, but on registration day, September 18, the surprising total of fifty-four young women presented themselves, and an exciting year of improvisation and achievement got under way.

With the college—somewhat informally named the New Jersey College for Women and best known as N.J.C.—in operation, the Trustees grappled with problems of finance and organization. Contrary to expectations, private benefactions failed to materialize, and the Trustees were obliged to advance substantial sums—amounting by 1922 to $166,000—for initial operating expenses and for the acquisition and rehabilitation of properties. The policy had been established at the outset that the finances of the women's college were to be completely separate from the regular Rutgers funds, and the advances were therefore in the form of interest-bearing loans. The financial situation was eased considerably in the second year when a state appropriation of $50,000 was secured for operating expenses, and in subsequent years this appropriation was increased, reaching $150,000 by 1924.

In a highly significant development, responsibility for the affairs of the college was vested in a board of managers in November 1919. Made up of five trustees and five prominent women of the state, with the Dean and the President as ex officio members, this board possessed extensive authority. It supervised the expenditure of all funds, had charge of all N.J.C. property, engaged members of the teaching and clerical staff, prescribed the curriculum, and generally directed policies and management. Although nominally subject to the control of the Board of Trustees, the Board of Managers in fact enjoyed almost complete autonomy. Meeting each month in the New York office of Leonor F. Loree, the Board was extremely effective in bringing about the rapid development of the new institution. Loree, who believed that colleges should be run like businesses but whose views had encountered strong resistance within the Board of Trustees, made the most of the freedom he enjoyed with respect to N.J.C. and devoted himself to its advancement with extraordinary zeal.

Installing an extremely able member of his own organization as business manager and supervisor of buildings and grounds, Loree soon had N.J.C. producing huge annual surpluses, which were used to acquire additional properties. He was favored in his economical management by the fact that for several years the teaching staff was made up largely of members of the Rutgers faculty, who were willing to accept

very modest remuneration. Frowning on small classes, avoiding a proliferation of courses, and financing dormitory accommodations with
first and second mortgages, he seemingly accomplished financial mir-
acles. Few fully appreciated his handiwork, for neither the Trustees
nor the Board of Managers ever saw the annual budgets of N.J.C. It
was Loree's belief, and he was doubtless correct, that if it were generally known how large the operating surplus was, the state would reduce
its annual appropriations and thus deprive the college of the funds it
desperately needed to expand its plant. President Demarest found these
financial policies extremely disturbing, especially when Loree prevailed
upon the Trustees in 1924 to assume responsibility for some $275,000 of
mortgage indebtedness on the cottage-type dormitories that had recently
been erected. Ultimately, as it developed, Dr. Demarest's forebodings
were to be confirmed.

By whatever means the ends were achieved, N.J.C. was from the
outset a remarkable success. When the first class graduated in 1922, the
student body had grown to 283, and the quality of the program was
adjudged to be sufficiently high to merit the establishment of a chapter
of Phi Beta Kappa. As the college developed, its educational program
became increasingly differentiated from that of the men's colleges, placing heavy emphasis on courses in home economics, education, dramatics,
music, and art, and relatively less stress on the sciences. There was also
notably more concern with the individual welfare of the students, as
evidenced by the appointment of numerous resident counsellors and by
the encouragement given to faculty members to join actively in the
extracurricular life of the college. By resorting to imaginative expedients,
such as building a gymnasium out of discarded wooden packing cases,
converting the former Carpender barn into a science building, and con-
structing a series of additions to the Cooper house to provide dining
and dormitory facilities, elemental physical requirements were met
adequately. In 1922 Federation Hall, erected with funds raised by the
Federation of Women's Clubs, provided quarters for work in the biological sciences. There was a major advance in 1924 when the state
legislature appropriated $250,000 for a large classroom building; similar
appropriations followed in 1926 and 1927.

Imbued with the sense that they were engaged in the pioneering experience of building a completely new educational community, the
students, faculty, and administrators developed an intense *esprit de
corps*, which inspired them to heroic endeavors and welded them into
a proud and zealous fellowship. This feeling made them jealous of their
autonomy; they were a part of the State University of New Jersey, but
they came to regard themselves as a very special and distinctive entity
having only a remote connection with the men's institution across town.

To this feeling of separateness there was one conspicuous exception. The social relationships between the girls at the "Coop," as it came to be known, and the boys at Rutgers became predictably close and cordial, adding an especially pleasant facet to life on both sides of the town.

In terms of the overall development of Rutgers, the founding of the New Jersey College for Women had many significant consequences. It represented, first of all, a long-overdue recognition of the right of women to educational opportunity and thus added an entirely new dimension to the services that Rutgers was providing to the people of the state. Because it was the first element in the emerging university to receive separate collegiate status under its own board of managers, with control over its own finances, it precipitated difficult questions about the future internal structure of the institution, questions that were to reverberate for decades. Similarly, the peculiar relationship of N.J.C. to the state was a factor of some confusion. Whereas state appropriations had been restricted to certain departments in the men's college, N.J.C.— which was technically a "department" of the State University of New Jersey—received a lump-sum annual appropriation to finance all phases of its program. It also enjoyed special favor with respect to state funds for classroom buildings. The full implications of its unique status were not immediately perceived, but as they gradually became apparent, notably after 1931, there were drastic redefinitions of its place within the University.

While the New Jersey College for Women was securing its autonomous position within the university structure, a comparable process was under way with respect to the Agricultural College. Because of its relevance to this development, some explanation must be given of the matter of nomenclature. In a legal sense, the State Agricultural College was the land-grant college of agriculture and the mechanic arts, together with such other departments—notably ceramics—as had been specifically created by legislative action. The "State Agricultural College" was also, by the legislation of 1917, the State University of New Jersey. Following this line of analysis, the actual work in the field of agriculture was the responsibility of a department of the State University, as were also engineering, ceramics, and the New Jersey College for Women. However, to its devoted friends, to influential farm groups, and even to the Board of Visitors, the "State Agricultural College" was commonly viewed as constituting only the agricultural department presided over by the Dean of Agriculture, Dr. Lipman. The Board of Visitors, for example, whose powers of "supervision and control" legally extended to all elements of the State University, in fact confined their interest almost entirely to the work in agriculture. This curious viewpoint, together with the dynamic leadership supplied by Dean Lipman, the energetic pres-

sure applied by the agricultural constituency, and the cordiality manifested by legislators from rural areas had remarkable consequences in
the decade after 1918.

The first rumblings of what was to be a major upheaval occurred late
in 1918 when a self-constituted "committee of farmers" met to voice
numerous complaints about Rutgers in general and the agricultural
department in particular. Several of the questions they raised will be
dealt with in another connection, but among their chief proposals was
that the "College of Agriculture" should be separately organized under
its own board of trustees, on which farmers' representatives should have
a majority. The Rutgers authorities, after conferring with the committee,
rejected this demand, taking the position that the Board of Visitors insured that the interests of the state were adequately protected. At this
point the Board of Visitors, whose president was James Neilson, a leading member of the Board of Trustees but a fervent champion of the
agricultural department, emerged from a long period of quiescence and
began to press vigorously for changes along certain of the lines proposed by the "committee of farmers."

Following a series of conferences between committees of the Board
of Visitors and the Trustees early in 1920, agreement was reached on
several important issues. In October the Trustees resolved to organize a
college of agriculture, work out a plan to permit direct participation by
the Board of Visitors in the management of this college, and give their
full support to "A Program for the Advancement of Agriculture." This
"Program," which had been formulated by Dean Lipman, projected a
ten-year construction schedule involving six major buildings and a
total expenditure of nearly $1,000,000. Decrying the limited means then
available for instructional, research, and extension work, the "Program"
stressed the importance to the state of efficient agricultural production
as a justification for enlarged facilities. President Demarest was reluctant
to see the creation of a distinct college of agriculture, for he feared that
it would mean an undue concentration of state support on that unit
of the State University, but the forces favorable to the proposal were
so strong that they could not be resisted.

Accordingly, on June 14, 1921, "in order to organize more completely
as a department of the State University of New Jersey the work in
agriculture," the College of Agriculture was formally created by the
Board of Trustees. Acting upon a suggestion that had been advanced by
Leonor F. Loree, the College was placed under a "Managing Committee," very similar in its powers to that which had been constituted
for the New Jersey College for Women. Made up of five Trustees, five
members of the Board of Visitors, with the Dean and the President as
ex officio members, this committee—like its counterpart—was given con-

trol of property, expenditures, and personnel, subject to the general direction of the Board of Trustees. Undoubtedly this new status contributed to the rapid advancements that the College made in the next few years. Going before the state legislature as a distinct entity, with the support of a vocal and organized constituency and a clearly defined program of development, the College secured the Horticultural Building in 1919, the Poultry Building in 1921, and the Dairy and Animal Husbandry Building in 1922. Then it graciously stood aside to give priority to the successful efforts of the New Jersey College for Women to obtain three classroom buildings.

With its enhanced facilities and steadily augmented operational funds, the College of Agriculture entered upon its most brilliant period of growth and service. Oddly enough, in this time of marked expansion, there occurred an abrupt decline in its undergraduate enrollment—from 109 students in 1921 to eighty in 1924. Agricultural colleges throughout the nation experienced similar declines, largely attributable to depressed conditions in the industry, but the drop-off at Rutgers was considerably higher than the national average. Graduate enrollments, however, remained fairly stable, at around thirty students. But it was through its programs of research and extension that the College performed its greatest services, bringing scientific knowledge to bear upon every problem of concern to the New Jersey farmer. Its well-publicized achievements, representing as they did a direct economic contribution to the state, won for the College wide popular support and sympathetic consideration from the legislature.

The sudden development of the New Jersey College for Women and the College of Agriculture gave particular urgency to the large problem of devising a suitable organizational structure for the emerging university. For nearly five years the president, the Trustees, and the faculty grappled with this problem, having in mind not only the issues that were brought to the fore by these developments but also complex considerations involving state relations, economy, and educational efficiency. Also to the fore were crucial decisions regarding the role of the faculty in the conduct of the institution. As if these matters did not present sufficient difficulties, solutions were further influenced by sharp disagreements over basic principles. One faction, led by Leonor F. Loree, contended strenuously for a "businesslike" plan of organization and for a more vigorous cultivation of public support. The opposing faction, led by President Demarest, defended traditional practices within the academic community and favored adherence to established policies with respect to the state.

Attention was first focused on the problem of internal organization by an economic crisis. The faculty, whose salaries had undergone slight change since the 1870's, suffered serious losses in real income as a result of the inflationary trend that began in the war years, and in 1920 they appealed to the Trustees for substantial increases. At the same time, however, with undergraduate enrollment at an all-time peak of 710, the College confronted alarming annual deficits. In response to the faculty's plea, the Trustees in April created a special committee, headed by Loree, "for the purpose of determining what changes can be made in the organization to enable the College more adequately to meet its responsibilities toward faculty and students."

The Loree committee did its work promptly, presenting in June a detailed report with recommendations. It took the position that salaries could be increased only if drastic economies could be effected. Accordingly, it called for the elimination of classes with small enrollments, the weeding out of duplicating courses, a higher ratio of appointments at the ranks of instructor and assistant professor, increased use of graduate students as teachers, and the removal of any rules or traditions limiting the number of teaching hours of faculty members. The committee also insisted that a detailed annual budget be prepared in such a way as to facilitate thorough scrutiny of costs. With respect to organization, it was urged that a college of agriculture be created and that all other instructional work in the men's division be grouped into five departments. The heads of these five departments, together with the deans, would have charge of all matters relating to the curriculum. Finally, the report recommended the appointments of a dean of the College, a dean of men, and a Freshman student counsellor, all of whom were to have teaching duties as well.

Beyond these specific proposals, the report reflected Loree's conviction that the powers of the faculty must be curbed. "To a very considerable degree," it was said, "authority has passed from the Board of Trustees to the Faculty and is exercised by them, while, on the other hand, to a considerable degree, college instructors no longer consider themselves as generally in the service of the institution but rather as specialists whose activities are only at the command of the institution for the limited degree in which they may be utilized in their self-determined field." An expert in running railroads, Loree saw no reason why the same management principles could not be applied to running a college.

Shocked and angered by the report of Loree's committee, President Demarest, bespeaking also the sentiments of the faculty, prepared a lengthy rejoinder. "It is quite essential," he pointed out, "that the fundamental difference between a college or university and a purely business corporation be recognized. It would be entirely inappropriate and educationally disastrous to attempt to define the teaching service by the hours and pay-system which may maintain in factory, mine or store." Discreetly, perhaps, he did not mention railroads. While he acknowledged the desirability of an annual budget and conceded that economic considerations should be kept in mind in arranging curricula or making new appointments, he found himself in disagreement with virtually every recommendation in the report, as well as with the philosophy that inspired it. So long as funds were needed for faculty salaries, he was reluctant to create additional administrative posts. As for the respective powers of the faculty and the Trustees, he correctly observed "that authority has been disposed between the two quite as it is now for generations: the Faculty has been in all our colleges and universities the executives of curriculum and of the details of teaching arrangement." The problems facing the College, he felt, could best be met by adding to its resources.

These two clashing viewpoints were aired at a stormy special session of the Trustees in June, and for the moment it appeared that President Demarest might retain support for his position. The committee's recommendation with respect to an annual budget was adopted, but all other proposals were referred to various committees for further consideration. In the succeeding months a Freshman counsellor, Professor Charles Hale, was appointed, there were some changes in course arrangements, and most new appointments were made at the rank of instructor. At the request of Dr. Demarest, Charles H. Elliott, Professor of Education, undertook to prepare a comprehensive plan of organization.

This first struggle over reorganization reached a climax at the Trustees' meeting in June of the following year. The Board had before it a plan prepared by Elliott that provided for four colleges—arts and sciences, engineering, agriculture, and women, together with a school of education, a summer session, and a division of extension teaching. Within the College of Arts and Sciences there were to be thirteen departments. Loree had numerous objections to this plan and was also strongly opposed to the proposal that Dr. Louis Bevier should be named Dean of the College of Arts and Sciences. In the final outcome, the Elliott plan was shelved, although in accordance with previous agreements the College of Agriculture was created. Moreover, in line with the original recommendations of Loree's committee, the new posts of Dean of the Faculty and Dean of Students were established. Bevier having resigned his deanship, Dr. Walter T. Marvin was named Dean of the Faculty and Professor David Fales was appointed Dean of Students. Disheartened by the recent trend of affairs and worn down by the intense pressures to which he was subjected, Dr. Demarest requested and received a year's leave of absence. Frederick Frelinghuysen, one of Demarest's staunchest supporters on the Board of Trustees was named president pro tem, although the actual direction of the College was to rest with the new Dean of the Faculty.

A second major effort to develop an overall plan or organization for the emerging university got under way in October 1921, when the faculty appointed a committee of ten, headed by Dean Marvin, "to consider and report to the Faculty on the problems of internal organization of the institution in all its schools and departments with a view to expressing the Faculty's point of view on these matters." The comprehensive report of the committee, after undergoing thorough discussion and some revision in five special meetings of the faculty, was submitted to the Trustees in June 1922. It envisioned a university made up of colleges of arts and sciences, engineering, agriculture, and women, together with a school of physical and biological science, a school of education, and a graduate school. Departments were to be organized within schools and colleges, but each would be a university department. That is, there would be a single department of mathematics (within the College of Arts and Sciences) to serve students in all schools and colleges. Each college faculty would be empowered to formulate curricula and deal with matters of instruction, research, and discipline within their colleges. To provide for coordination among the several schools and colleges the report recommended the creation of a university assembly and a university council. The Assembly, which would include all faculty members of professorial rank, would have powers of legislation and review on all matters of "internal relations." The Council, made up of deans, directors, and two faculty representatives from each college, was to possess what were termed "advisory, coordinating, and discretionary" powers. Finally, in order to centralize university administrative functions, the report called for the appointment of a university registrar, a university treasurer, and a university superintendent of buildings and grounds. To a remarkable degree, subsequent developments over the course of several decades validated the wisdom of these far-reaching proposals.

The faculty's report was referred to the Trustees' committee on instruction and discipline, where it was the object of considerable discussion and behind-the-scenes controversy for a year and a half. Not until October 1923 was the Board prepared to act, and even then their action was not definitive. The faculty's recommendations with respect to creating colleges, schools, and university departments were adopted with some modifications. Specifically, the Board accepted the faculty's proposal for colleges of arts and sciences, agriculture, women, and engineering and a School of Education, but rejected the proposal for a school of physical and biological sciences and a graduate school. Consideration of the remainder of the faculty's report, dealing with the powers of the several faculties and the creation of a university assembly and a university council, was deferred, and nearly a decade passed before the subject was revived. For various reasons, official notice of the Trustees' actions in authorizing the creation of colleges, schools, and departments was not communicated to the faculty until January 1925, at which time Dean Marvin recommended that the faculties of the College of Agriculture and the College of Engineering should organize. Meanwhile, in recognition of the new status that had been created by the extensive internal reorganization, the Trustees had authorized the adoption of the title of Rutgers University and without any ceremony it was first employed at commencement on June 14, 1924.

The last step in the implementation of the modified plan was taken on October 9, 1925, when the College of Arts and Sciences—"said College to consist of all departments not administered by other Colleges or academic divisions, except the Department of Military Science and Tactics"—was brought into existence. Walter T. Marvin, heretofore Dean of the Faculty, became Dean of what was at once the oldest and the youngest college within the University.

Among the major reasons why there was so much contention and delay over reorganization plans was the continual insistence of Loree and his adherents that the institution must effect economies by installing business-like procedures. After frequently voicing complaints that the recommendations made by his "Committee of Five" in 1920 had never been implemented, Loree had the Committee revived in January 1924, to renew its demands for heavier teaching loads, elimination of small classes, and the like. In response to this challenge, a faculty-administration committee made an exhaustive inquiry and produced a detailed analysis of all of the points that had been raised. They found that the average cost per student was $387 in liberal arts courses, $547 in technical science courses, and $808 in agriculture, for an overall average of $518. This figure, they maintained, was not in excess of the costs at comparable schools; indeed, they contended that Rutgers must expect to increase its expenditures per student. One by one they examined and rejected Loree's proposed economy measures, pointing out how they would impair educational quality. The solution, they concluded, lay in "the securing of a greater income, an adequate plant, and a larger body of students rather than in the immediate reducing of average costs and contracting of our curriculum." They concluded by again recommending the appointment of a superintendent of buildings and grounds and the adoption of a salary scale—to be effected gradually—that would have minimum salaries of $3,500 for assistant professors, $4,500 for associate professors, and $6,000 (minimum and maximum) for full professors. The Board of Trustees responded by resolving to appoint a super-

intendent of buildings and grounds and expressing its desire to put the
proposed salary scale into effect if and when funds became available.
In the meantime, they urged the faculty to effect every possible economy
by reducing the number of departments, avoiding expansion of staff,
and raising to the maximum the number of teaching hours.

Out of the stress and anxiety of these troubled years a new university
structure had emerged. Molded by divers considerations, influenced by
sharply differing viewpoints, reflecting the clash of personalities, it
hardly represented the ideal solution to a complex problem. Moreover,
it left one large aspect of that problem, namely, the role of the faculty,
in total confusion. The structure that it created was oddly out of balance.
Two colleges—the College for Women and the College of Agriculture—
were clearly distinguishable from the others by their autonomous positions under special managerial boards, by their favored relationship to
the state, by their avid partisans on the Board of Trustees, and—not
least of all—by the extraordinary effectiveness of their leadership. Furthermore, because of delays in creating a genuine university-wide administrative staff, certain benefits that might have been derived from
the university-type organization were not realized and the institution
functioned essentially as a collection of schools and colleges. It was
doubtless unfortunate, too, that at an especially critical period, when
many pressing issues demanded attention, so much of the energy of
the president, the Trustees, and the faculty was absorbed in the tedious
and sometimes bitter struggle over organizational reforms. And it was
sad that two men so utterly devoted to Rutgers as President Demarest
and Leonor F. Loree should have disagreed so fundamentally about
what was in the best interests of the institution.

The internal readjustments that were necessitated by the changing
character of the institution were paralleled by comparable alterations
of policy with respect to relations with the state. From the time of the
settlement of the scholarship claims in 1904 until 1918, Rutgers had
met an increasingly favorable response from Governors and legislators
as it pursued a moderate policy of seeking adequate support for those
departments or programs that fell within the vague orbit of the "State
Agricultural College." After 1918, with the establishment of the College for Women as a department of the State University and the rapid
physical development of the College of Agriculture, the state was
even more liberal with its appropriations than in the past. But as Rutgers
assumed increasing prominence within the state and as public funds for
its support grew, it became the object of pointed criticisms, which the
Trustees had to meet. Moreover, by 1923, because of the course of
development in the preceding five years, the time had seemingly ar-

rived for a complete reappraisal of the future relationship of Rutgers to the state.

Around 1918 attacks on Rutgers in its public role had focused on two main issues. There were charges, emanating chiefly from Roman Catholic sources, that the charter requirements that the president must be a communicant of the Dutch Reformed Church and that there should be a professor of divinity made Rutgers a denominational institution. There were also unfavorable comments about the high proportion of Dutch Church members on the Board of Trustees and the total absence of any Roman Catholics. There is no question that the charge of denominationalism carried weight even with legislators who were generally well disposed toward Rutgers, and it was one of the major points raised by the self-constituted "committee of farmers" late in 1918. It was, in fact, in response to the farmers' criticism that the Trustees set in motion the necessary legal steps to amend the charter to eliminate every denominational reference. When this was finally accomplished in November 1920, there remained the question of Roman Catholic representation on the Board of Trustees. Informally, a good deal of pressure had been exerted in behalf of such a move, and Leonor F. Loree regarded it as a matter of utmost importance. Finally, in October 1922, William B. Gourley, a prominent Roman Catholic layman from Paterson, who at one time had served as chairman of the Democratic State Committee, was elected to membership on the Board.

The second issue was less explosive but equally critical to the maintenance of good state relations. It involved the matter of title to lands on which the state erected buildings. When New Jersey Hall had been built, the state had insisted upon and had received from the Trustees a deed to the plot of land on which it stood. Later, however, in the cases of the Administration Building (1912) and the Horticultural Building (1919), the state had not required a conveyance of title to the sites. But both in and out of the legislature there were those who felt that it was improper for the state to erect buildings on lands owned by the Rutgers Trustees. Again, the "committee of farmers" had pressed this contention in their correspondence with the Trustees. The matter came to a head in the legislature in 1920, when an appropriation of $100,000 for a ceramics building was made conditional upon the Trustees' giving a deed for the proposed building site. The Trustees were for a time reluctant to accede to this condition, in part because of legal opinions to the effect that they might be violating their fiduciary responsibilities. But when it became clear that no funds would be forthcoming from the legislature for other needed buildings unless the condition was met, the Trustees in February 1921 resolved to execute deeds to the state for lands "necessary in connection with buildings to be erected, or heretofore erected" with state money.

Although the settlement of these issues did not entirely abate critical questioning of Rutgers' peculiar relationship to the state—the *Trenton Times*, for example, continued to manifest hostility—the legislature steadily increased its support. In order to account for the generous treatment accorded to Rutgers and establish the background for grave difficulties that were to arise later, it is essential to explain certain relevant features of New Jersey's odd fiscal arrangements. When the state's system of railroad taxation was revised in 1906, it was provided that so-called "main stem" railroad property—essentially the property over which the trains ran, as distinct from sidings and freightyards—would be taxable by the state at the average tax rate in the state and that after a certain share of these revenues one-half of 1 per cent of the assessed valuation) had been reserved for general state purposes the remainder would be apportioned among the counties to be applied to the support of free public schools. With the passage of the years, the yield from this "main stem" tax increased beyond all expectations. Very soon the legislature began to "divert" portions of the fund from the counties to other designated educational purposes in order to reduce the strain on ordinary state revenues. This policy dated from 1909, when the appropriations for state scholarships at Rutgers as well as for the state normal schools, the state School for the Deaf, and similar agencies were charged to the "main stem" tax. President Demarest was quick to see the potentialities in this arrangement. In December 1909, he wrote Governor Fort to inquire whether all of the appropriations to Rutgers might be charged to the railroad fund. "I mention this" he explained, "in the thought that if the money can be so charged, its appropriation might be made more willingly and unanimously than otherwise, and the way be clear for later and more liberal provisions for the college's use and development." Although his suggestion was not immediately adopted, Dr. Demarest correctly foresaw that the main-stem tax would be a bonanza and that the legislature might be induced to apply it to general educational purposes.

That time had arrived by 1920. Revenues from the main-stem tax had soared from around $3,500,000 in 1907 to over $7,389,000. Even after making what was regarded as fair provision for local school districts— over $4,000,000—a very sizable surplus remained. President Demarest had continued to urge that all Rutgers appropriations be charged to the fund, and in 1918 and 1919 had even proposed that a fixed amount should be appropriated over a period of five or ten years. "It will relieve the annual uncertainty of things," he argued, "and make possible a consistent, continuous program of maintenance and advancement so much more advantageous to the higher education of the State." This ideal arrangement was not adopted, but, in the appropriation bill enacted in March 1920, all of the funds for the College were charged to the main-stem tax, along with a host of other educational agencies, including the State Board of Education, the State Board of Examiners, the three normal schools, and the teachers' retirement fund.

This action had two very important consequences. For the next several years, as the railroad taxes mounted, the legislature distributed its largesse with a ready hand. But soon difficulties arose. All of the public educational agencies in the state were in vigorous competition for the main-stem revenues. In time, those that were directly under the State Board of Education became increasingly resentful of the large sums that were being channelled to Rutgers, which found itself under attack by other educational interests. Equally disastrous, receipts from the railroad tax levelled off after 1930, and consequently all the agencies and institutions—including Rutgers—that were dependent on that source found themselves in a financial straitjacket.

For the immediate future, however, access to the railroad revenues brought enlarged benefits to Rutgers. Legislative appropriations rose from $263,240 in 1919 to $971,748 in 1925. In accordance with long-established practice, the funds for operating expenses were designated for specific departments, chiefly in the scientific and technological fields but including education and the College for Women. The liberal arts courses, in which the largest numbers of students were enrolled, received no direct subsidy, and it was chiefly because of this circumstance that Rutgers was obliged to observe rigorous economies in those areas. Only a small measure of relief was afforded when state scholarship stipends were increased in 1920 from $160 to $200. The greater portion of the increased funds after 1919 went to the College for Women and toward a building program that provided new facilities for horticulture (1919), ceramics (1920), poultry (1921), dairy and animal husbandry (1922), and physics (1925–26), and three classroom buildings for the College for Women (1923, 1925, and 1926). The magnitude of the state-financed building program in this period can be better appreciated when it is understood that for the ensuing two decades no state funds were available for capital construction at the University.

Not all of the needs of the expanding institution were met by state appropriations. President Demarest continued to envision a dual Rutgers made up of both the State University and the old foundation, each looking for support to its own constituency. Through the years he never lost sight of his cherished goal of strengthening the old foundation by adding to the endowment and obtaining special funds for buildings and other objectives that lay outside the scope of state activity.

The 1916 endowment fund drive, interrupted by the outbreak of war, had fallen far short of the announced goal, but in 1919 conditions suddenly became favorable for a new campaign. August Heckscher, the multimillionaire philanthropist of New York City, became interested in Rutgers and offered to give $200,000 if the College succeeded in raising a total of $1,000,000. Accepting the challenge implicit in this generous offer, the Trustees in October 1919 resolved to make the effort, and President Demarest assumed the chairmanship of the special committee in charge of the campaign. An immediate appeal was made to the General Education Board, which responded with a conditional pledge of $100,000. With such an auspicious start, the campaign was carried forward with great determination. Area committees were organized, a thorough canvass was made of the alumni, and the president was indefatigable in soliciting individuals. For the final stages of the effort the services of a professional fund-raising organization were retained.

The response was generally heartening. The citizens of New Brunswick, who had so loyally sustained the College in its early years, contributed nearly $200,000, and more than half of the graduates responded to the appeal. By June 1920, the total of $1,000,000 had been subscribed, although many subscriptions were payable over a period of five years. Moreover, the College debt—amounting to about $52,000—had to be discharged before the $100,000 from the General Education Board became payable. It fell to the lot of the president to find donors for this unappealing purpose, and only after intensely frustrating efforts was he at last able to report success in January 1924. With the exception of approximately $160,000 devoted to property purposes, the remainder of the $1,000,000 fund was added to the endowment. Benefactions from other sources—most notably the $100,000 bequest of Margaret Olivia Sage in 1919, the gift of Elizabeth Rodman Voorhees for the enlargement of the library in 1923 and the grant from the estate of John Rogers Hegeman for a dormitory in 1924—sustained the hope that the private sector of Rutgers could be strengthened.

Additions to the endowment helped to relieve the threat of recurring annual deficits, but there remained an urgent need for more buildings. By 1921 both the College for Women and the College of Agriculture had formulated well considered plans for their physical development, and there was the prospect that their needs would be met largely from state sources. As yet, however, there had been no attempt to prepare an overall projection of the physical requirements of the expanding institution. The faculty had urged that such a comprehensive plan be prepared, and in October 1921 the Trustees authorized a special faculty committee under Dean Marvin to undertake such an assignment.

This earliest attempt at large-scale planning was based on the assumption that within twenty-five years there would be at least 2,350 students in the men's colleges. In general terms, the committee listed as among the most pressing needs an auditorium and armory, a general classroom building, an infirmary, substantial additions to the engineering and chemistry buildings and the library, and new buildings for physics, biology, and fine arts. With respect to dormitory accommodations, it proposed residential units of 500 students modelled on the Oxford college plan. Acknowledging that these projections were "preliminary and tentative," the committee strongly urged that the Board of Trustees engage a supervising architect to prepare thorough, coordinated plans, as well as a superintendent of buildings and grounds. Significantly, too, the question was raised as to whether future growth should take place on the old campus or whether consideration should be given to concentrating all educational operations in the vicinity of the College of Agriculture and the College for Women. This question was to be raised in various forms in the future, but it lost some urgency when the six-acre Martin property, north of the Seminary campus, became available in 1924. Foreseeing that this tract would be an admirable location for future dormitories, thus permitting the full use of the Neilson Campus for classroom buildings, the Trustees hastened to acquire it. With this general conception in mind, and on the basis of the proposals that had been prepared by the faculty committee, the architectural firm of York and Sawyer in 1924 prepared a "suggested layout" to serve as a guide to the development of the whole area north from Somerset Street to Huntington Street. Although this design was never to be implemented fully, it did exert influence on development plans for the next twenty years.

Because of the lack of funds, little progress could be made in meeting the faculty's estimate of physical requirements. The capacity of the Voorhees Library was doubled with the completion of a well-designed annex in 1926, but there was to be no addition to living accommodations for men students until the Hegeman Dormitory was erected in 1926 and no expansion of classroom facilities on the old campus aside from those provided in the Ceramics Building and the Physics Building. For many years to come most departments operated under serious handicaps with facilities that had been deemed to be adequate for a college of 500 men.

Deeply involved though they were in dealing with the problems of internal reorganization and campus planning and in fending off the

drastic proposals that were being urged on them in the interests of economy, the faculty continued to experiment with changes in the several
curricula. No clear-cut philosophy guided the reforms, which tended
to be piecemeal in nature and represented responses to various stimuli.
On the whole, however, there was a discernible effort to adjust the
educational offerings to a student body that was not only growing in
number but was also displaying different interests, aptitudes, and degrees of preparation from the prewar generation.

The group system, combined with majors and minors, that had been
installed in 1917 in the liberal arts courses underwent little revision
before 1926. Greek was dropped as a major after 1919 and economics
was added in 1922. Honors courses were established for highly qualified
upperclassmen, and Dean Marvin was an earnest advocate of an
honors school, somewhat on the English model; but economic considerations militated against the implementation of this proposal. As a means
of encouraging more than minimal academic performance, the widely
approved system of quality credits was introduced in 1922, at first for
the Freshman class but in due course for all classes. Perhaps to most of
the students and many of the faculty the most radical alteration in the
academic routine was the introduction in 1919 of eight o'clock classes,
a heritage of the Spartan S.A.T.C. schedule.

More important than the structural changes in the liberal arts curricula was the rapid expansion of certain departments. As a reflection
of the generally heightened interest in social studies observable in all
universities after the war, there was a sudden expansion of the fields of
history, political science, and, above all, economics. In 1917 all of the
instruction in these subjects was carried on by three men. By 1924 the
Department of History and Political Science had a staff of eight men,
teaching a dozen year-courses in history and three in political science.
The Economics Department, organized in 1922, by 1924 had four instructors, offering the surprising total of thirty-six semester courses in
economics and business management. The Department of Education,
which grew from two members to seven in these years, was entering
upon a period of tremendous development, largely because of the burgeoning extension program. Sociology, taught by Professor Fales, made
its first appearance in the catalogue in 1919. Howard Decker McKinney,
1913, who had assumed the recently created post of Musical Director in
1916, introduced the first courses in music in 1919, meanwhile managing
the highly successful concert series and bringing the campus musical
organizations to new standards of performance.

Almost unnoticed, certain courses and requirements that had survived as vestigial remnants of the old College now disappeared. Especially notable was the ending of the age-old requirement of both

Greek and Latin for the A.B. degree; after 1919 one classical language sufficed. The traditional course in evidences of Christianity, the universal hallmark of the Christian college, was offered for the last time in 1916–17, but it was succeeded by a course in Bible and ethics that remained a requirement for all Juniors in liberal arts courses as late as 1926. Hebrew, offered almost exclusively for students preparing to enter the ministry, was dropped after 1920. Civics became American Government. Also abandoned were the time-honored English term essays, the bachelor's theses, and the long list of commencement orators. In the interests of symmetry and efficiency, a determined effort was made to purge the curricula of courses with varying credit awards in favor of a standard three-credit basis.

In the several technical curricula there was clearly a continuance of the trend to multiply highly specialized courses and to impose ever more burdensome requirements. Agriculture, for example, now offered its students a choice among five curricula and required 151 credit hours for graduation, three less than were required in ceramics. In 1919 the Trustees requested the faculty to investigate the "advisability of increasing literary training in the Scientific Course [*sic*] and of diminishing laboratory hours." "The demands made upon graduates by scientific industries," explained the faculty, "the insistent choice by entrance candidates of institutions giving technical instruction in large detail, and the virtually universal practice of technical institutions discourage an increase in the proportion of literary studies at the present time." One result of this discussion, however, was the decision to increase the training in English composition by six semester hours, with a corresponding reduction in the foreign language requirement. The most striking fact with respect to the technical curricula was that they actually enrolled fewer students in 1925 than in 1920, despite the overall increase in the men's colleges from 641 to 753.

The most serious problem that confronted the faculty with respect to the academic program was that of Freshman failures. By the early 1920's it was not uncommon for nearly one-third of that class to fall by the wayside. One solution to the problem was to improve admissions procedures, to the end that those of inferior capacity would be excluded. Under the procedures prevailing in 1919, any graduate of an approved school who offered the requisite number of units could be admitted quite simply on the basis of a certificate. Except for those who took the fairly rigorous state scholarship examinations, most applicants chose to avail themselves of this so-called certificate privilege.

Considerable study was given to the use of intelligence tests as a means of screening candidates for admission. Intelligence testing had been employed on a large-scale basis by the armed services during the war, and almost at once the test devised by Professor Edward L. Thorndike of Columbia University was utilized by the colleges. On the initiative of Professor Marvin, the Thorndike test was administered to the entering Freshman class on an experimental basis in September 1919 and was made a regular part of the admission requirements two years later. The tests disclosed that about 15 per cent of those admitted scored below 60 per cent, which was regarded as the minimal standard for prospective college students. It was considered significant that of those students who had entered on the basis of examinations, not one fell below the standard. Marvin proposed that any applicant who scored below 50 per cent in the Thorndike test should be refused admission, but the faculty refused to approve the erection of this type of barrier. Instead, a revised form of certificate was adopted, effective September 1923, which required a statement of the candidate's rank in class, his grades, and a letter of recommendation from his principal. It was agreed that no applicant who ranked in the bottom quarter of his class would be accepted. When this new procedure was applied, the entering Freshman class declined in size from 312 in 1922 to 240 in 1923. The new entrants—the Class of 1927—were adjudged to be a highly superior group, scoring far better in the intelligence test than any previous class. However, in spite of these promising indications, the class suffered a casualty rate of 22 per cent in its first year, which was lower than that of its predecessors but still disturbingly high. Obviously, the selective process had not yet attained perfection.

Another solution to the mortality problem was so to revise the Freshman program as to minimize failures. Leonor F. Loree insisted that the fault lay in the grading system. He pointed out that in the 1880's the average grade of all the students in the College was slightly over 90 per cent, whereas by the 1920's the average had declined to about 77 per cent. Clearly, the professors were guilty of setting impossibly high standards. The faculty rejected this implication, as well as Loree's charge that the wide variation in grades given by different professors evidenced the unreliability of the whole grading system. To Loree's contention that the College should adapt itself to the high schools of the state, the professors responded with the counterview that the schools should be brought up to the standards set by the College. Although they rejected Loree's approach, the faculty did appoint a special committee to study the Freshman curriculum to determine whether it could be made to bridge the gap.

This committee's report, which was adopted as of September 1922, was notable for the fact that it recognized the need for a specially designed Freshman program as well as for its detailed proposals. The committee discovered that the better students felt that the Freshman courses presented little challenge, that many entering students did not know how to study or think independently, and that most students were deficient in their ability to use the English language. Accordingly, the required Freshman English course was revised to stress the principles of composition and rhetoric. At the beginning of the year, a proficiency test was given, and those in the top quarter of the class were placed in special sections while the poorest students were obliged to take a remedial course. At the end of the first year there was another examination, in which students had to attain a grade of 75 per cent; if they did not reach that standard in the first or subsequent attempts, they could not graduate. Placement tests were introduced also in mathematics and modern languages in order to segregate students of varying ability.

To provide a "different" kind of intellectual experience for the Freshman, the report called for the introduction of an entirely new type of survey course. This innovation had its origins in the "War Issues" courses that had been included in the S.A.T.C. programs across the nation and that had led in turn to the formulation of the widely acclaimed contemporary civilization course at Columbia University. At the request of the faculty the Department of History devised such a course, "designed to introduce the student to the controlling ideas and institutions which constitute the framework of our civilization," and in 1922 presented it as a Freshman elective. Dean Marvin, an ardent advocate of this approach, contemplated similar courses in "General Evolution" and "General Literature" and was instrumental in having a course in general physiology introduced in 1923 as an elective for Freshmen. Partly in order to accommodate the new program, Freshmen entering in 1922 had to take five three-hour courses rather than four four-hour courses as in the past. Whatever evaluation may be made of the virtues of the reformed Freshman curriculum, the faculty had made a serious attempt to achieve well-defined objectives and had embraced what seemed to be the best practices current in other universities.

During these critical years of transition, so disruptive of old patterns and so beset with internal tensions, the faculty faced peculiar trials. Their role in the new university structure was left undefined, and many of the policies promulgated by the Trustees aroused grave apprehensions about their declining status. Salaries remained deplorably low, ranging from $1,700 for instructors to $3,750 for full professors, and many felt obliged to take on additional duties at the College for Women or in the extension division in order to supplement their incomes. Because of the emphasis on economy, ever higher proportions of the faculty were in the two lower ranks, promotions were rare, and staff turnover was very high by comparison with previous periods. Efforts to secure an improved salary scale, a group insurance system, a pension plan, and an arrangement for sabbatical leaves, all met with rejection. Symptomatic, perhaps, of the growing feeling of anxiety and insecurity was the establishment in 1922 of a chapter of the American Association of University Professors.

The major responsibility of the faculty was classroom teaching; research and graduate instruction as yet received little emphasis. There were those, however, who sought to carry on scholarly investigations, and in May 1921 a special faculty committee on research presented a notable report that for the first time called attention to the importance of research and set forth several recommendations of means to encourage and facilitate such activity. "The function of an institution of learning is equally to conserve the acquisitions of the past and to create new knowledge," declared the committee. "In its best sense the one function cannot survive without the fulfillment of the other. Creative scholarship is therefore as legitimate and as necessary to the life of the college as is teaching." Accordingly, the committee urged that adequate time and facilities be provided for research and proposed the creation of an annual research fund of $1,000 to be used for the purchase of books and apparatus. The time had not yet arrived for a general advance in this area, but the faculty did create a standing committee on research, and beginning in 1922 arrangements were made to collect published writings of the faculty, to be bound and issued annually as the *Rutgers College Studies*. Another sign that scholarly inquiry was achieving recognition as an important function was the formation of a chapter of Sigma Xi in 1922. In spite of adverse conditions, in 1923–24 more than 100 articles and books were published by twenty-three members of the faculty—most of them concerned with agriculture or the biological sciences.

If the realm inhabited by the faculty was undergoing a great transformation, the general structure of undergraduate life seemed to be strangely static. After the interruption occasioned by the war, the normal pattern of activities—sports, fraternities, clubs, and class rivalries—was speedily reestablished. Curiously, there was scarcely any sign of innovation, of the introduction of strikingly new interests or organizations. But in this unsettled age of the flapper, jazz, and Prohibition, of the automobile, radio, and movies, of F. Scott Fitzgerald, H. L. Mencken, and John Held, Jr., there was a different air about the campus. Dean Bevier sensed it as early as 1920. "The same restlessness which characterizes the population at large and may be a natural consequence of the war has been manifest in other ways also," he noted. "While the general attitude of the undergraduates has been one of reasonableness, still a certain impatience with long standing regulations, important in the orderly processes of all educational institutions, has been somewhat in evidence, and has made the work of the year a little more difficult than in normal times." Others shared the same feeling that the students had changed, that there was less intellectual interest, less seriousness of purpose than they had remembered before the war. More than ever the students were engrossed in their bustling extracurricular world, but even beyond that they were highly sensitive to the popular culture, which insistently shaped their manners, their taste, and their values. Leaders of jazz bands rivalled football captains in popularity; Norma Talmadge and Douglas Fairbanks were far more vivid figures than Evangeline or Horatius; a speakeasy possessed an allure not associated with the old barroom; and a Stutz Bearcat, or even a Model T, conferred undreamed-of satisfactions.

With these changing attitudes and the growth in the number of students came what President Demarest termed "some relaxation of highest standards of good order and of respect for the best amenities of life, compelling somewhat greater concern of college authorities with things which should not tax their attention." As a consequence, increasingly formal arrangements were made for supervising the conduct and safeguarding the welfare of the students. Earlier, in 1912, a system of Freshmen counsellors—ten Freshmen to a faculty member—had been instituted, but it did not prove effective, and in 1919 Professor Charles Hale was named Freshman Counsellor. Two years later, at the insistence of the Trustees, the post of Dean of Students was created, with Professor David Fales as the first incumbent. Concern with the physical well-being of the undergraduates occasioned the appointment of a College physician in 1916, who, in addition to conducting physical examinations of all students and holding daily consultations at his office in Ballantine Gymnasium, also taught a course in hygiene. Under revised requirements for physical training, all students were obliged to devote an hour on two afternoons each week to participation in some organized sport or in exercise under the supervision of the R.O.T.C. instructors. Even the faculty wives showed their interest by arranging a reception and dance for the Freshmen.

The students themselves were aware that new and not wholly desirable influences pervaded the campus. In particular, there was an alarming increase in cases of dishonesty, leading to disciplinary action that strained relations between the faculty and the undergraduates. Sentiment grew for a student-administered honor system, and after a two-year campaign led by *Targum* and the Y.M.C.A. the Student Assembly in May 1920 adopted an elaborate set of rules for introducing an honor system. During the next few years constant difficulties arose over the issue of students "squealing" on one another and over the precise procedures that should be used to try offenders. Attempts were made to surmount these difficulties by frequent changes in the regulations, but it did not seem possible to contrive a workable plan. As a last resort, the system was made optional in particular courses. Finally, in November 1925, the last vestiges of the unsuccessful experiment were abolished by an almost unanimous vote of the student body. As had been the case in the 1890's, student self-government had displayed its limitations, and it fell to the deans and the faculty to enforce discipline.

Undergraduate enthusiasm for athletic competition remained high. Teams were organized in cross-country running (1919), lacrosse (1920), and rifle shooting (1920), bringing to nine the number of sports in which there were intercollegiate contests. Gymnastics, once highly popular, was not revived after the war. In football, after several indifferent years, the 1924 team led by the All-American Homer Hazel, 1925, was victorious in eight games before bowing to Bucknell by the close margin of 12–7. As emphasis upon sports grew in intensity, the faculty sought to tighten the eligibility rules to avoid abuses. Especially aggravating was the extremely high mortality rate among Freshman football players, until finally it was decreed that beginning in September 1924 Freshmen would no longer be eligible for varsity competition.

The growth in the number of sports, among other things, necessitated changes in the organization of this phase of College activity. Following a pattern that had long since become familiar at other institutions, a graduate manager—William P. Garrison, 1910—was appointed in 1920 to manage all the business affairs of the Athletic Association. After a few years it became apparent that this arrangement was defective, in part because there were several different bodies involved in the athletic scene. On Garrison's recommendation, and with the approval of the faculty, a new plan was instituted by the Trustees. Full control over the athletic program was centralized in a council on athletics, made up of three Trustees, three alumni, three students, and three faculty members, to whom the Graduate Manager reported. The Council was supposed to operate the program at no expense to the trustees but in accordance with general rules governing such matters as eligibility and scheduling laid down by the faculty. As yet, then, intercollegiate sports were to be conducted jointly by students, faculty, and alumni and remain partly outside the defined framework of the College.

So crowded were these hectic postwar years with fateful policy decisions and urgent adjustments to novel conditions that the large accomplishments tended to become obscured. But no previous era had brought such advancements as were represented by the founding of the College for Women, the rise to prominence of the College of Agriculture, the securing of unprecedented appropriations from the state, and the attainment of the $1,000,000 fund. These were successful years, but success bred problems. The very progress that was being made gave rise to conflicting views as to whether more might have been achieved and whether long-established policies should continue to obtain. Because so many of the recent developments were intimately involved with the relationship of Rutgers to the state, that moot topic came increasingly to the fore as an object of controversy.

President Demarest's convictions never wavered. In January 1923, in response to the question of how far Rutgers should go in making concessions to the state in return for greater appropriations, he restated his position. Arguing that the legal relationship between the state and the College had in no way been altered since 1864, he contended that the Trustees should not yield to the state any more jurisdiction than it then possessed. Rather, he insisted on the wisdom of "quiet, and moderate and gradual dealing with the State in securing the support desirable for [the] progressing work of the State College." Such support should be confined to the land-grant elements of the institution; the Trustees should find the funds to sustain the other departments. At the same time he repeated an earlier suggestion that the title of Rutgers University should be adopted to supersede the title of State University of New Jersey.

There were contrary opinions. As early as 1918, Leonor F. Loree had urged that the title of State University be given prominence in all College publications. "My own feeling," he wrote President Demarest, "formed out of my early experience and strengthened with each year that has gone by, is that Rutgers cannot look forward to any assured future except by strengthening its relations to the State and Federal Governments." The tangible evidence of what state support accomplished for the College for Women and the College of Agriculture drew others to support Loree's view, most notably James Neilson, who was as devoted to the College of Agriculture as Loree was to the College for Women.

The issue erupted into what appeared to be an irreconcilable conflict in April 1923, when Neilson prepared and circulated to the Board of Trustees a twenty-seven point attack on the president and his policies. His criticisms dealt with a great many deficiencies in the College that had long been recognized but which for one reason or another, chiefly financial, had not been corrected. But the main burden of his complaint was that the administration had failed to formulate a general plan of development and press vigorously for state funds with which to implement it. In his reply to this sweeping indictment, President Demarest answered every point that was raised, summarized the considerable achievements of his administration, and defended the "quiet and moderate and gradual" approach that he had taken to the state. Rather than present the state with a huge program and thereby risk stirring up opposition, he had believed it prudent to make specific requests year by year. He explained, too, that because the College received its funds from the main-stem tax, it must proceed with some delicacy in order to avoid antagonizing the other educational interests that were also dependent on that source.

The Trustees were now brought face to face with a choice of alternatives. At the same meeting at which Neilson's communication was presented, the Advisory Committee was directed to make a thorough study of all state and Federal legislation relating to the College and recommend "what in its opinion should be the policy of the College in regard to its future relations to the State and the nation." The final report, largely the handiwork of Philip M. Brett, 1892, surveyed the tangle of laws and concluded that the state, especially after 1912, had "entered on a broader educational policy and one not limited by the narrow scopes of the contract embodied in the United States Act of 1862 and the State Act of 1864." In other words, the state had evidenced its willingness to extend support to fields beyond those of "agriculture and the mechanic arts." At the same time, Brett found no evidence that the obligation of the College to the state was other than that of a trustee for public funds. He also pointed out that "the work of the old College and of the so-called State College in New Jersey [*sic*] are interwoven and how difficult it would be to attempt to untangle or differentiate the work of the different departments." He concluded that the prevailing cordial relations with the state and Federal governments "should be continued and expanded, looking towards increased Governmental aid, with consequent increased usefulness of the College in its influence and in carrying on the work of higher education." At the same time he cautioned that the utmost care should be taken to preserve in the Board of Trustees "the ultimate powers of supervision, administration and control vested in them" by the College charter. Finally, "for the protection of the prestige of the original foundation," his report recommended the adoption of the title of Rutgers University.

Superficially, this comprehensive analysis seemed to represent a compromise between the major opposing points of view, but in that it called for expanded state support and strongly implied that such support should be sought for all departments, it forecast an entirely new policy. The strategy of seeking appropriations for very specific objects, originally formulated by William S. Myers two decades before, was to be set aside in favor of a campaign for public funds with which to develop the entire institution. How the state would respond to this approach could not, of course, be foreseen. Neither could it be foretold how the Trustees would react if large-scale public support were to be made conditional on increased state participation in the management of the institution.

For several years President Demarest had considered laying aside the burdens of his office, and in October 1923 he submitted his resignation, to become effective June 30, 1924. "The pressing need of the college for certain additional buildings and additions to certain buildings, and for increased income, making possible a higher standard of salary for the teaching staff," he wrote, "convinces me that, unaware of donors able and ready to provide the needed new resources, I ought not remain longer in my executive position." He had but recently recovered from a serious illness, he had become aware that he no longer had the united support of the Trustees, and he felt that he had done all that he could for the College. His zealous hopes that the old foundation might be so strengthened as to assume equality with the State University had not been realized, and it now appeared that Rutgers must abandon its dual role and reshape its destiny as a public institution. Distressed by the new trend, Dr. Demarest's major concerns during his final year in office were to bring to completion the history of the College, on which he had labored for many years, and to raise the money to relieve the College of its indebtedness. His retirement became effective in June 1924, and while the search for his successor proceeded, Trustee William E. Florance, 1885, served as president pro tem, although the actual management of affairs was entrusted to the Dean of the Faculty, Dr. Walter T. Marvin.

President Demarest's administration outshone that of all his predecessors. Quietly effective in his dealings with state officials, cordial and respectful in his relations with the faculty, diplomatic but insistent in his guidance of the Board of Trustees, he wrought well for the college that so fully commanded his affection and his talents. He could take pride in the growth of the institution from a small college of 243 men to an aggregate of colleges and schools enrolling six times that number of undergraduates. The endowment had been tripled in size, the physical plant had expanded at an even greater rate, and the annual state appropriations had risen from $52,000 to $750,000. The academic program had been expanded and strengthened, entirely new fields of educational service had been inaugurated, and the difficult transition from a college to a university had been accomplished. Following his retirement, Dr. Demarest served for ten years as president of the New Brunswick Theological Seminary and from his residence on the campus continued to be actively interested in the welfare of the University until his death in 1956. No son of Rutgers had ever been privileged to serve his alma mater with such loyalty and distinction.

Chapter Nine

The Premature State University

"I understand that the Trustees of Rutgers University desire the institution to meet the demands of public higher education in New Jersey in a broad and generous spirit," wrote Dr. John Martin Thomas, "and it is this challenge to constructive work, in many respects unique in the United States, which is attracting me to Rutgers." In thus indicating his acceptance of the presidency in June 1925, Dr. Thomas made it quite clear that Rutgers was to take on a new, unambiguous identity as the "State University of New Jersey." "While every effort should be made to retain and merit the loyalty of alumni and friends who love the great traditions of historic Rutgers, with which I am in full sympathy," he explained, "the college has accepted a great responsibility in becoming a land-grant college of the State and in permitting the designation of the State University of New Jersey."

At his inauguration, held on October 14 under the elms on Neilson Campus, he elaborated on his view of the mission of the state university. Taking as his theme "The Expansion of Public Education in New Jersey," he demonstrated that New Jersey needed a full-fledged state university and detailed what Rutgers must do to meet the requirements of that role. "I would keep back nothing Rutgers has from the service of the Commonwealth by whose support and encouragement she has grown from a college of a few score students to the commanding institution she is today. . . . What any state institution has done for any state, in research, in extension, in any field of education, that Rutgers will gladly do for her state, if the need arise and if resources permit." Here was a new voice, pledging a new Rutgers. Fittingly enough, the pages of the ancient leather-covered matriculation book of the College, in which 6,800 students had signed their names—beginning with Isaac Alstine Blauvelt, Class of 1828 and ending with John M. Grossman, Class of 1928—had become filled, and a new volume was now begun.

Having searched for more than a year to find the right man to lead

Rutgers along a new path, the Trustees believed that in Dr. Thomas they had an ideal choice. He possessed extensive experience as a college president, having served from 1908 to 1921 as the head of Middlebury College, his alma mater, and from 1921 to 1925 as president of Pennsylvania State College. A native of New York but spiritually a Vermonter, he was not unfamiliar with New Jersey, for he had been pastor of a Presbyterian church in East Orange from 1893 to 1908. Vigorous, decisive, and knowledgeable, he quickly familiarized himself with conditions at Rutgers, determined his course of action, and with manifest impatience set about the task of reshaping the institution. "That difficulties exist need not be denied," he conceded. "That a college socially selective in its clientele, scornful of vocational curriculum, insistent above all on the maintaining of tradition, cannot serve the purposes of a state institution may be freely admitted. That a university responsive to the needs of a great industrial commonwealth may lose some of the amenities of a strictly private institution must be frankly faced."

Soon after taking up his new duties on September 1, having consulted with Trustees, deans, and prominent state officials, Dr. Thomas sat at his desk to outline a "Program for 1925–26." Starting with "Build partition in President's Office, to provide room for Secretary," the list ran to forty-six items and covered virtually every aspect of the University. Not all of his goals could be achieved within a year—some remain yet unrealized—but within the space of months he had put through a host of measures that shook the old college to its very foundations. Merely to summarize these innovations will suggest their impact.

At Dr. Thomas' first official meeting with the Board of Trustees, several significant actions were taken. The rules of the Board were revised to reorganize the standing committees and to create an executive committee. Made up of the president and seven other members appointed by the Board, this committee was to have general "recommendatory and advisory powers in all matters relating to the management of the University," limited powers during intervals between Board meetings with respect to matters not entrusted to other committees, and full power to act with reference to appointments, courses of study "and in general whatever pertains to instruction and instructors." In this latter area it replaced the old committee on instruction and discipline. Perhaps the most important consequence of this change was that the full Board no longer dealt with matters of personnel and curricula. Moreover, the Executive Committee, working closely with the president, came to wield predominant influence within the Board.

At the same session, the post of Dean of the Faculty was abolished and Dr. Marvin was named Dean of the newly created College of Arts and Sciences. The title of Dean of Students was changed to that of

Dean of Men and Dr. Fraser Metzger, formerly chaplain at Pennsylvania State College, assumed that office on November 1. The Administration Committee of the faculty was replaced by a University council, made up of the president, the five deans, and the registrar. It met weekly to plan and coordinate University policy. A new "University Faculty," ostensibly made up of the faculties of all the colleges but with little participation from the faculty of the College for Women, was brought into existence.

This eventful Trustees' meeting also gave approval to new educational offerings. An industrial extension division, destined to have an extraordinary growth under its director, Norman C. Miller, was authorized. Sanction was given also to a new degree, that of Bachelor of Science in Education, and this step forecast the development of an immense program for thousands of in-service teachers. Reflective, too, of the decided trend toward vocational curricula was the inauguration of a four-year course in journalism and a comparable course in business administration.

Other innovations followed swiftly throughout the year. An engineering experiment station, intended to afford to industry the kind of research services so well provided for farmers by the Agricultural Experiment Station, was founded. The tuition fee in the College of Agriculture was cut from $260 to $140 in an effort to stimulate larger enrollments. Plans were made for a Freshman week in September 1926, in order to orient incoming students to their new academic and social environment; it was highly successful. In yet another attempt to reduce Freshman failures, a special program was introduced whereby those who were failing took but three courses, all taught by department heads. Slight revisions were made in entrance standards, lowering the requirements for the College of Arts and Sciences and the School of Education. In response to the argument that students would perform better if they had some vocational motivation, certain combinations of courses were now grouped and labelled "Business," "Pre-Legal," "Pre-Theological" and the like.

The campus swarmed with the largest Freshman class (339) and the heaviest total enrollment (853) ever, but with construction under way on the Hegeman Dormitory, the addition to the Voorhees Library, and the long-awaited Physics Building, there was the promise of relief from cramped facilities. At N.J.C. the imposing chapel—the gift of Elizabeth Rodman Voorhees—and the second recitation building moved toward completion. For the first time the state appropriation rose above $1,000,000 and included funds for the College of Arts and Sciences in addition to the usual items. There were substantial salary increases for members of the faculty. Driving forward toward the goals set forth in his inaugural address, President Thomas delivered sixty speeches in all parts of New Jersey, setting forth the needs of the University and expounding the economic advantages that would accrue to the state in return for its support of public higher education. Already, many within the faculty felt misgivings about aspects of the president's program and his manner of implementing it, but the Trustees, the alumni, and interested citizens responded favorably to the energetic administration.

The innovations of this first year, significant as they were, did not add up to a long-range development program. Before such a program could be formulated, comprehensive and detailed studies were needed, and Dr. Thomas immediately made preparations for them. In looking to the future a plan for physical facilities was essential, and soon after taking office the president invited the distinguished city planner, Harland Bartholomew, 1911, to undertake this assignment. He also entered into negotiations with the United States Bureau of Education to have that agency make a general survey of the University.

Previous efforts at campus planning had been neither comprehensive nor definitive. As early as 1915, Albert D. Taylor, the noted landscape architect of Cleveland, Ohio, had prepared an interesting plan for the development of the property at the College Farm to include not only projected buildings for a college of agriculture but also facilities for a woman's college, athletic fields, and a men's dormitory group. Subsequently, the Board of Managers of the College for Women had retained architects to devise an overall plan and had then systematically acquired property in accordance with that plan. In 1921 a special faculty committee had made a valiant effort to project future building requirements but had not attempted to plan the location of buildings, and in 1924 Louis D. Ayres, 1896, of the firm of York and Sawyer had sketched a general plan for the utilization of the properties between Somerset Street and Huntington Street.

The central problem with which Bartholomew grappled was that of deciding at what location future expansion should be concentrated. The old campus in the vicinity of College Avenue comprised about thirty-five acres, and adjacent properties could be acquired only at considerable expense. The campus of the College for Women embraced forty-four acres, the College Farm area included 410 acres, and there were large undeveloped tracts in the immediate vicinity. In May 1926, Bartholomew presented his preliminary conclusions to the Trustees. He recommended that future expansion at the College Avenue site should be limited and that additional acreage should be acquired in the College Farm area with a view to bringing all units of the University together there in the future. "To add $3,000,000 in buildings where there is now but $1,000,000," he stated with reference to the old campus, "and then scrap all in ten years would not be good economy." This reasoning was sufficiently impressive for the Trustees to authorize Bartholomew to proceed with detailed studies. In the summer of 1927 members of his staff spent three months in New Brunswick accumulating data, and in November 1927 Bartholomew presented his final report.

"It is believed," his report began, "that a change of location for the Men's Colleges and development of a centralized university is inevitable and since it must come some time, had better be anticipated at the earliest possible moment." The College Avenue site, in his judgment, could be made to serve a maximum of 5,000 students, provided lands for recreational purposes could be secured across the river or north of Buccleuch Park. Alternatively, an admirable site for a concentrated university of 10,000 or more students could be developed on the south side of the city in the area bounded roughly by Nichol Avenue, the Raritan River, and Lawrence Brook and incorporating the lands of the College for Women and the College Farm. Although he indicated what might be done to develop the old campus to its maximum potential, he strongly urged that consideration be given to the proposed new location. Unfortunately, at the very time this bold and attractive plan was being formulated, the State Highway Department decided upon the route of a new highway—Route 1—and it bisected the area that Bartholomew envisioned as the new University campus. Efforts to alter the route were unavailing, and Bartholomew was directed to study the best means of utilizing the old campus as the nucleus for future expansion. This whole venture in planning, despite its abortive ending, was extremely important, because it compelled the University authorities to think broadly about long-range policies. Furthermore, many of the principles and objectives set forth at this time were to influence decisions affecting the development of the University for decades to come.

Even more influential was the survey made under the auspices of the United States Bureau of Education. President Thomas wanted a systematic and thorough study of the needs of New Jersey in higher education to provide a basis for the full development of the University. With the approval of the Trustees, and with the endorsement of the Commissioner of Education and the Governor, he arranged for the Bureau of Education to conduct the investigation. Under the direction of Dr. Arthur J. Klein, Chief of the Division of Higher Education of the Bureau, a survey team of fourteen highly qualified specialists drawn both from the Bureau of Education and several universities worked intensively during the fall of 1926 and presented its final report in March 1927. This objective and thorough analysis, contained in a volume of 258 printed pages, searchingly examined New Jersey's needs in the field of higher education and made detailed recommendations as to precisely what the University must do to meet those needs. The entire report was based on the assumptions that New Jersey would want a full-fledged state university, that the state would utilize Rutgers for that role, and that the Trustees would commit themselves fully to developing Rutgers as an instrumentality of the state.

The survey documented New Jersey's shocking deficiencies in public higher education. Because of generally inadequate facilities and the total lack of educational programs in such fields as commerce, medicine, dentistry, and law, only 7 per cent of New Jersey students attending college were enrolled in the University. Even more striking was the revelation that nearly 80 per cent of New Jersey students went out of state for their college education, a far higher proportion than in any other state. The conclusion seemed obvious: the University must be expanded and developed with a view to accommodating around 7,000 students by 1937. With these goals in mind, the report offered a clear guide to their attainment, dealing with organizational and administrative reforms, the projected requirements of existing schools and colleges and of those undergraduate, graduate, and professional schools that should be established, and thoughtful recommendations with regard to personnel policies, student welfare, library services, research, and extension activities. It was an authoritative blueprint for the future, and it left no doubt that there was an enormous gap between the services currently being provided by Rutgers and those which should be provided by an adequately supported state university.

More than a blueprint was needed. If New Jersey was to boast a real state university, the state would have to appropriate funds on a heretofore unprecedented scale. Moreover, the survey team recognized that a new level of state support might well be contingent upon increased participation by state representatives in the management of the institution and upon the complete dedication of Rutgers to the role of a state university, even to the extent of adopting the name of "State University of New Jersey." Finally, the attitude of those responsible for the institution, the Board of Trustees, could be crucial in determining whether the blueprint would be translated into reality. These were the imponderable factors upon which the destiny of Rutgers hinged. To President Thomas they represented problems for which he could find solutions, and he now devoted himself fully to the effort.

Already it had become apparent that the legislature must be induced to provide some alternative to the main-stem tax as the source of the University's annual appropriation. The counties were complaining because their share of the tax was declining. Other educational agencies, foremost of which was the Teachers' Pension Fund, were clamorous for more money, and all joined in protesting that Rutgers was not a state institution and should therefore not be among the recipients of the main-stem taxes. At best, it seemed, Rutgers could not hope for much more than $1,000,000 a year from this source, and far greater sums would be required to bring the projected state university into being. The solution urged by President Thomas was a half-mill state-property tax, which could yield around $2,000,000 a year for the support of higher education. Governor George S. Silzer recommended such a tax in his annual message in January 1926, and a bill to that effect was introduced, but it remained buried in committee.

Preparations were made to launch an intensive campaign in behalf of the special mill tax during the 1927 session of the legislature. Thomas delivered speeches throughout the state, the alumni were mobilized, literature to promote the measure was circulated extensively. Meanwhile, the attacks on the University rose to a new crescendo, with the *Trenton Times* in the forefront and the educational interests in the background. The nub of the criticism was that because Rutgers was governed by a private board of trustees, it was not in fact a state university and was not entitled to receive state funds. Never had these charges been pressed so vigorously, and with the campaign for the mill tax under way and the vast plans for an expanded university in jeopardy, it seemed essential that steps be taken to meet criticisms.

In this crisis, President Thomas relied heavily on the guidance of Edward L. Katzenbach. As Attorney General of New Jersey, Katzenbach was one of three ex officio Trustees, and he was the first Trustee in that category ever to take a deep interest in the institution; he regularly attended Trustee meetings. He was thoroughly acquainted with fiscal and political aspects of the situation, deeply concerned about the hostility of the educational interests, and anxious to find some solution that would assure the development of the state university. It was his personal judgment that nothing less than an arrangement that would give state representatives a majority on the Board of Trustees would suffice to meet the problem. This question came to the fore when the Trustees held a three-day session in January 1927 to hear the report of the Klein survey and reexamine the University's relations to the state. The survey had taken cognizance of the complaints about the composition of the Board of Trustees and had suggested the addition of five more representatives of the state. Accordingly the Board appointed a special committee to consider the constitution of the Board and relations with the state.

President Thomas and Katzenbach were disposed to give state representatives a majority on the board, but Trustee Alfred L. Skinner, 1883, and the members of his committee did not agree that such a drastic revolution was necessary. After a few weeks of intensive activity, the

Board was convened in special session on February 18 to act on an amendment of the charter. A resolution declaring that it was "deemed advisable that there should be a closer cooperation in educational work between this Institution and the other educational agencies of the State" and providing for the addition, ex officio, of the Chancellor, the president of the Senate, the Commissioner of Education, and the president of the State Board of Education to the Board of Trustees was speedily passed and became effective three days later. In a closely related move, Katzenbach, as Attorney General, issued an opinion on March 7 that was designed to explain the relationship between Rutgers and the state. He found that the relationship was a contractual one and that the state, through the Board of Visitors and the appropriation committees of the legislature, exercised effective control over the institution, whose services to the state he commended in the highest terms.

Intended to placate the educational interests, strengthen the public character of the institution, and influence the legislature to enact the mill tax, the hasty action of the Trustees produced none of these results. The mill tax again went down to defeat, attacks on the University continued as vociferously as ever, and the educational interests remained hostile. Moreover, the legislative appropriation in 1927 was cut to $828,930, of which $120,000 was taken from general state funds. An impasse had been reached. The University could not move forward without vastly increased resources, but so long as it remained under attack as a "private" institution, those resources would be denied to it.

The prospect of a solution was seen with the recommendation by Governor A. Harry Moore that the legislature appoint a commission "to examine the existing relations of the State with Rutgers University and to recommend to the present Legislature such re-organization and means of adequate support as may be deemed to be to the best interest of the State." Thomas and Katzenbach had both concluded that only through such a move could the impasse be broken, and they expected that the commission and the Trustees would readily come to some satisfactory agreement. Together, they worked out the draft of a bill designed to give the state majority representation on the Board of Trustees, and Thomas drafted a new version of his mill-tax measure.

When the commission, headed by Edward D. Duffield, president of the Prudential Life Insurance Company, held its first meeting on February 23, 1928, in Newark, it was presented with a document prepared by President Thomas that he intended to be the commission's final report! To Thomas' dismay, the commission declined to accept this ready-made solution and decided instead to make its own thorough study of the problem. Meanwhile, the public information campaign, under the able direction of Carl R. Woodward, 1914, was given new impetus, and in February 1928 the *Rutgers Alumni Monthly* put out a "State University Number" to stir enthusiasm for Thomas' program. In an article, "Our Present Opportunity," Thomas stated: "I have done my best to defend Rutgers as a State institution on the present basis of contractual relation with the State and supervision by a Board of Visitors. . . . But I have come to see that that line of battle had become untenable before I took the field. . . . We must find the courage to trust the people of New Jersey with a larger and more direct voice in our affairs."

The response was not what he had called for. A small faction within the Board of Trustees, thoroughly aroused by the radical nature of Thomas' proposal, set about rallying opposition sentiment and a similar movement was launched among the alumni. Among other arguments, Thomas' opponents insisted that there was absolutely no guarantee that giving the state a majority on the Board would mean increased financial support. Others, citing the Dartmouth College Case, maintained that there was no legal means by which control could be vested in the state. Most decried the potential evils of political domination and foresaw the desecration of the old foundation. The Trustees had never taken a position on Thomas' proposals, but as the months went by it became increasingly apparent that they were not prepared to endorse them.

As the Duffield Commission continued its deliberations and its consultations with Trustees, alumni, and other representatives of the University and the state, it soon discovered that the problem was exceedingly complex and that the University was not united on a solution. In addition to the disagreement over the degree of control to be given to the state, Leonor F. Loree and Dean Douglass were actively seeking an autonomous status for N.J.C. Unable to reach any conclusions in time to present them to the 1928 legislature, the commission received an extension of time. In November 1928, it conducted a public hearing, hoping to receive some constructive ideas, but it learned nothing. President Thomas, meanwhile, was "lying low," for after his initial *faux pas* at the first meeting of the commission he deemed it best to remain in the background.

Finally, early in 1929, the fog of confusion and controversy lifted. Sentiment among the Trustees had crystallized in opposition to the Thomas-Katzenbach plan. Philip M. Brett, 1892, who a year earlier had expressed tentative approval of the president's approach and who now sought to reflect the consensus of opinion within the Board, explained to Thomas in January how he viewed the situation. He had reached the conclusion that a way could be found by which a fair contract could be made with the state, "reserving to the trustees not only control of its own property, but also the management and control of the University." "I confess I look with the utmost apprehension," he added, "towards any arrangement with the State under which the management and control of the University, the selection of its courses and entrance requirements, the selection of faculty and employees of the institution, would be in any way even remotely under State control and subject to the obvious evils resulting therefrom. To my mind, the real opposition has been not through any fear that the State was not receiving a *quid pro quo,* but has arisen from the fact that we were receiving any monies at all from sources to which other interests were looking as their base of supplies." With the position of the Trustees clarified, the Duffield Commission, guided by its able counsel, Edward M. Colie, brought its deliberations to a conclusion and issued its report on February 11, 1929.

The commissioners found that Rutgers had rendered valuable services to the state, that it had been efficiently administered by the Trustees, and that any disturbance of the existing relationship would be unfair to Rutgers and injurious to the state. They rejected as costly and unwise the notion that the state should establish a completely new state university. Also rejected was the proposal that the state should be represented by a majority of the Trustees. "We have been unable to find any method by which this may be done legally." The best solution, they concluded, was to retain the present arrangement, whereby the state utilized Rutgers as a public instrumentality on a contractual basis. The major defect in the current relationship was that the state had no proper agency to give comprehensive consideration to the needs of higher education and to discover how Rutgers could best be utilized and developed to meet those needs. Accordingly, they proposed the creation of a state board of regents to perform those functions. Other major recommendations were that the state scholarships be ended and the sums appropriated for them be applied to reducing the tuition fees of all New Jersey residents; that the title of State University of New Jersey— conferred by the act of 1917—be repealed; and that the Board of Regents, when created, study the anomalous position of the College for Women and determine what its proper status should be. Not least in importance, they strongly urged that the allocation of the Rutgers appropriation to the main-stem tax should be ended and that a direct tax should be levied for public higher education.* To President Thomas,

* The commission was not unanimous. J. Albert Dear, Jersey City newspaper publisher, prepared a minority report calling for the creation of a state university entirely separate from Rutgers. Another member, Patrick V. Mercolino, also favored a new state university, with free tuition for all students, although he did not fully accept either the majority or the minority report.

this report represented a "bitter disappointment"; the reaction of the Trustees was generally favorable.

The legislature promptly passed a series of measures implementing the commission's recommendations, with the conspicuous exception of that relating to a special tax for higher education. The state scholarships were phased out, the title of State University was repealed, and a board of regents was created. Made up of the Commissioner of Education and seven other members appointed by the Governor, the Regents were "charged with the duty of determining the State's needs in connection with public higher education, and determining to what extent institutions of higher education, other than State institutions . . . [should] be utilized to meet such needs in whole or in part. . . ." The Regents were to recommend each year to the State Budget Commission the amounts to be appropriated for such institutions and contract on behalf of the state for educational services. Seemingly, this arrangement would regularize and clarify the relationship of Rutgers to the state, create an agency that would devise long-range plans for developing Rutgers to meet the needs of the state in higher education, and provide every assurance that state monies appropriated to Rutgers would be expended properly. Such was surely the expectation of the Trustees, and it was no doubt the expectation of the Duffield Commission, the legislature, and the Governor as well.

Unfortunately for all parties concerned, affairs did not proceed as expected. When the Board of Regents formally organized in September 1929 with Henry W. Jeffers as chairman, they made it clear, in Jeffers' words, that "Rutgers is not swallowing the Board of Regents." They decided to take quite seriously their duty to study how the state's needs in higher education could best be met. Very soon they concluded that the status of Rutgers required "clarification," and that in the meantime they could recommend no further appropriations for buildings. As their thinking progressed, they sought some feasible means to separate the "private" Rutgers from the "public" Rutgers, and by September 1930 they were ready to propose a scheme to the Trustees whereby Rutgers would be "delimited" to a college of liberal arts; all other units would be taken over by the state. Rutgers, then, would operate as a private college within a federated state university. Only through some such clear-cut separation of public from private elements, the Regents reasoned, could the way be opened to the full development of a real state university. At the same time, President Thomas outlined a comparable plan for a "geographical separation," the "private" Rutgers to retain the old campus and the "public" university to be developed in the vicinity of the College for Women and the College of Agriculture.

The Trustees found these novel proposals completely unacceptable.

Meeting in special session on November 21, 1930, they heard the report of a committee that had been conducting discussions with the Regents and then approved the draft of a statement in reply. They declared flatly that they could not "consistent with their charter, contractual, and fiduciary obligations enter into any arrangement that would result in delimiting the College to a College of Liberal Arts." Citing the injunction of the Duffield Commission against any disturbance of the long-established relationship between Rutgers and the state, they urged that any modifications be worked out within the existing framework and offered to continue discussions within this context with the Regents. Here was another impasse.

For the next dozen years the Board of Regents continued to evolve various schemes for creating a "genuine" state university, none of which ever approached acceptance, while all plans for expanding Rutgers were held in abeyance and the awkward reliance on a share of the main-stem tax kept old animosities alive. The entire experience of the preceding few years had a sobering effect on the Trustees; their early enthusiasm for the state university ideas championed by President Thomas had cooled, and they could see no tangible gains to Rutgers from all the efforts that had been put forth. On September 19, 1930, Dr. Thomas announced that he was resigning, effective October 31, in order to accept a position with the National Life Insurance Company, and Trustee Philip M. Brett was named acting president.

Amidst all the tumult created by the agitation of the state university issue, the University proceeded on its uneven and uncertain course of development. Until the Great Depression struck the University, these were years of continued growth. By 1929 enrollments in the men's colleges had risen to 1,401 and, even more amazing, there were 1,159 women at N.J.C. No less significant than the increases in numbers was the expansion into new fields of educational service.

The Industrial Extension Division, with strong backing from President Thomas and under the driving leadership of Norman C. Miller, was remarkably successful. It was created to have charge of all extension activities other than those in the fields of agriculture, home economics, and education; among its objectives was that of securing good will and support for the entire University. Miller, who had conducted a similar program at Penn State, was a masterful organizer and promoter, and within a few years there were more than 3,000 students enrolled in formal classes and about half that number in correspondence courses. The most popular courses were those in foreman training, engineering, business administration, and public speaking, but there were also special programs such as postgraduate courses in medicine, graduate-level work in petroleum technology, and an advanced management institute. In addition, Miller's division ran the New Jersey League of Interscholastic Debating, sponsored radio broadcasts, conducted a lecture bureau, and arranged numerous special institutes. Classes were organized in factories and in several centers throughout the state in accordance with popular demand and were staffed in large part by other than members of the regular academic faculty. There was some friction resulting from the feeling that the division often trespassed in fields that more properly belonged in other jurisdictions, and many faculty members looked askance at what they deemed the crass vocationalism of the variegated program, but the division—renamed University Extension in 1927—continued to flourish.

In terms of sheer numbers, the largest division of the University was the School of Education. The state normal schools, which did not become four-year teachers' colleges until 1935, were quite inadequate to meet the demands for schoolteachers, especially at the high-school level. As late as 1928 high-school graduates who took additional work in six summer sessions might be certified as elementary school teachers. In order to serve these high-school graduates and also provide courses leading to the bachelor's degree for normal-school graduates, the School of Education conducted a thriving summer session and a far-flung extension program, which moved into high gear after the Trustees in 1925 authorized the granting of the degree of Bachelor of Science in Education. Candidates for this degree could enroll for classes in professional and academic subjects offered in the late afternoon or evening, on Saturdays, and in the summer session. By 1930 the extension programs of the School of Education enrolled 5,375 teachers in forty-two centers throughout the state and there were nearly 2,000 students in the summer session. Dean Clarence E. Partch, who succeeded Dr. Elliott in 1928, guided this extraordinary development, and in 1930 introduced graduate programs leading to the degrees of Master of Education and Doctor of Education.

So rapid was the growth that the University faculty became concerned about the quality of the program and its effect on the entire institution. A special faculty committee in 1930 determined that the major problem was that far too many members of the regular academic staff were teaching inordinately heavy overtime schedules for the School of Education extension in order to supplement their incomes. Accordingly, various reforms were instituted to improve the standards of the courses, and regular staff members were restricted to teaching not more than two extension courses. Throughout the 1930's the in-service teacher programs conducted by the School of Education, in addition to the resident undergraduate curricula for high-school teachers, filled a great need within the state until the four-year teachers' colleges became fully operative.

Another notable innovation in this era was the incorporation of a college of pharmacy into the University. Courses in pharmacy had been started in Newark in 1892 by an interested group of men, and in 1894 the New Jersey College of Pharmacy, a nonprofit educational corporation, was chartered. By 1927 the College had a faculty of fourteen, a student body of 270, and an excellent new building at Lincoln Avenue and Arlington Street. Dedicated to raising the standards of pharmaceutical education, the Trustees of the institution as early as 1922 sought affiliation with Rutgers. In part because of unsettled conditions within the University, no affirmative action was taken, but there had been negotiations from time to time. New impetus was given to the consideration of the matter in August 1926, when Robert W. Johnson—president of Johnson and Johnson—made a strong representation in favor of the merger proposal, stressing the good effect such a move would have on the pharmaceutical industry of the state. At about the same time, Dr. Ernest Little of the Department of Chemistry was granted a leave of absence to become acting dean of the College of Pharmacy. These circumstances, together with the disposition of President Thomas to extend the services of the University into new areas, created an environment favorable to the merger.

Conferences between representatives of the two institutions produced agreement on a plan for integrating the College of Pharmacy, which received the final approval of the Rutgers Trustees on January 14, 1927. All of the assets of the school were taken over by Rutgers, and a new five-man committee of Trustees was created to have special oversight of the enterprise, in cooperation with a nonvoting advisory committee of men interested in pharmacy. The Trustees announced that their action was motivated by the conviction that they had the duty of "maintaining and increasing standards of pharmaceutical education," but they were mindful, too, that by conducting work in Newark the University might receive stronger support in that quarter for its general program. Also involved was the consideration that the College of Pharmacy Building was well adapted to use for the extension programs of Dean Partch and Director Miller. The College instituted a three-year course of studies in 1927, and five years later adopted a full four-year curriculum leading to the bachelor's degree. The first of the outlying branches to become affiliated with Rutgers, the College of Pharmacy established a high reputation in its field and suggested the model for later expansion in Newark and Camden.

Continuing its phenomenal growth, the College for Women strengthened its internal organization, elaborated its educational program, and completed the first great stage of its physical development while at the same time pursuing its peculiarly independent relationship to the rest of the University. In 1928 Dean Douglass was able to boast of a larger graduating class than that of the men's colleges. Each summer additional dormitory facilities were hurriedly constructed to accommodate the increment of students anticipated in September. By 1930 the College possessed an unusually attractive campus of over 100 acres, three large groups of cottage-type dormitories, the splendid new Jameson Dormitory, Cooper Hall, an excellent infirmary, three state-financed classroom buildings, Federation Hall, the imposing Voorhees Chapel, and a well-appointed music building, half of the funds for which were raised by the Federation of Women's Clubs. Except for a library and a gymnasium, the College was more than adequately equipped to cope with the steadily mounting enrollments.

The academic program, meagre in the first years, grew to include a wide range of academic, vocational, and pre-professional curricula, comparable to that of any woman's college of equal size. The teaching staff, drawn originally very largely from the men's colleges, changed rapidly after 1927, when Dean Douglass concluded that it would be desirable for many reasons to have a separate faculty. Whereas in 1926 half of the instructors were from Rutgers, by 1930 all but fourteen of the 102 faculty members taught exclusively at the College for Women. Accompanying this change were the organization of separate departments and the beginning of formal faculty participation in the conduct of the College. Largely in spite of the omnipresent Loree and his unorthodox educational theories, admission standards were raised and—for better or for worse—the College became increasingly conventional in its policies and procedures. Whatever his peculiarities—which included organizing a memorable drum and bugle corps of students to lead the procession in celebration of the College's tenth anniversary—Loree was indefatigable in his zeal for the physical development of the College and was ever concerned to promote its welfare.

The autonomy that the College enjoyed under its highly independent Board of Managers presented vexatious problems for the Rutgers administration and Trustees. The Board of Managers, which in practice had become a self-perpetuating body, assumed complete responsibility for the College, except when the Rutgers Trustees were called upon to make loans to underwrite the construction of added facilities. Diplomatically couched reminders by President Thomas that the College budget should be submitted to the Trustees were ignored. Similarly, the efforts of the president to oppose the establishment of separate departments and the creation of a library school in 1927 were unavailing.

When Dr. Thomas related his difficulties to a knowledgeable Trustee he was told, "You are undoubtedly correct, except for the difficulty of trying to do anything with respect to the College for Women which does not originate with its Board of Managers and which is not exclusively for the benefit of such College."

The Klein survey had called attention to the excessive authority wielded by the Board of Managers and had questioned whether the Trustees could legally delegate such extensive powers. The Duffield Commission, also, had recommended that the position of the College should be clarified. While its study was in progress, Dean Douglass, Loree, and powerful women's groups conducted a campaign to secure an autonomous, or even independent, status. "We were created as a department of a State University," Dean Douglass declared before a public hearing of the commission. "We never were created as a part of old colonial Rutgers." Contributing, no doubt, to the zeal with which the College sought to maintain its autonomy were deep-seated animosities toward President Thomas and a decided aversion to any interference by the University faculty in College affairs.

Ultimately there had to be some kind of showdown, and it was precipitated by the Board of Regents. In a letter of May 3, 1930, the Regents explained that any funds appropriated for the University must be expended in accordance with a contract between the Regents and the Trustees. Noting that the Trustees assumed "practically no direct control over the financial and other affairs of the New Jersey College for Women," the Regents asked that "pending any change in the relations of the New Jersey College for Women from its present status as a department of Rutgers University to an independent legal entity" the Trustees take appropriate action to bring the College under their "more immediate supervision and control."

This directive led to the appointment of a special committee, headed by Edward L. Katzenbach, which spent a year considering the problem before presenting its report in June 1931. After coming out strongly in favor of a separate women's college, with its own faculty, departmental organization, and administration, the committee recommended that five women should be added to the Board of Trustees and that the Board of Managers should be replaced with a Trustees' committee on the College for Women, to include the women Trustees, five other Trustees, and the president of the University. Through this device the virtues of the old arrangement might be retained at the same time that the legal responsibilities of the Board of Trustees would be properly discharged. After several months of further discussion and controversy, these recommendations were adopted. The charter was amended in April 1932 to provide for the five women Trustees, and in June the new college committee held its first meeting. The authority conferred on the committee approximated that which had been bestowed on the Board of Managers, with the extremely important exception that now the Trustees required the submission of an annual budget, in which no changes could be made without their approval.

There were other difficulties. Like his predecessor, President Thomas was gravely concerned about the mounting loans to the women's college. Because of a business failure, a large donor was unable to advance sums that he had pledged for dormitory construction, and the Board of Managers in June 1930 sought to borrow $340,000 on mortgages from the Trustees. An unusually sharp controversy split the Board, but in the end the loan was approved, bringing to $893,950 the amount of college indebtedness held by the University Trustees. In his final published annual report, the president with evident bitterness detailed these financial arrangements and voiced his "serious concern" about them. He then proceeded to attack the policy of running the college to produce an annual surplus, criticized the low salaries and the attendant high turnover in staff members, and intimated that high academic quality could not be achieved under such circumstances. Another blow descended in 1932 when the Regents ruthlessly pruned the asking budget of the college, eliminating or reducing individual items in such a way as to affect seriously the academic program.

By this time it was apparent that the first brilliant and constructive period in the life of the College for Women had come to an end around 1930. For the next two decades there would be little growth in numbers or in physical facilities but rather a consolidation of the position at which the College had so swiftly arrived. Broken in health, Dean Douglass was granted a year's leave of absence in September 1932, but since her health did not improve she submitted her resignation in May. A few months later the college mourned the death of its founder. Dean Douglass had succeeded even beyond her own lofty vision in creating and developing a major college for women within the brief span of a dozen years. In the wake of the changes made in the control of the College in 1932, the overweening influence of Leonor F. Loree declined. Under greatly altered conditions, both within and outside the University, a new administration took over. After Professor Albert E. Meder had served in the interim as acting dean, Margaret T. Corwin was installed as dean in January 1934. In retrospect, one might be disposed to be critical of some of the irregular methods, defiant attitudes, and dubious fiscal practices associated with the building of the College, but the final results represented a great success story, a story that might never have happened if conventional procedures had been employed.

Within the men's colleges, the most significant developments were in the area of curricular reform. Ever since 1891, when the rigidity of the old classical curriculum had been modified by provision for certain elective majors in the two upper classes, a decade had not gone by without some major reorganization of the programs of studies. In 1901 the nontechnical students had been offered an alternative to the classical curriculum in the form of the so-called Latin-Scientific course, leading to the degree of Litt.B. Then, in 1907, a third alternative had been introduced, the General Science course, for which the degree of B.S. was offered. The distinctions among these three courses had faded in a sweeping revision in 1916, when the new system of group requirements was adopted and students were permitted large freedom in the choice of electives and in the selection of majors and minors. Now the pendulum swung away from the elective principle toward an arrangement of courses of study, not in terms of the degree to be awarded, but rather in terms of vocation, profession, or specialized academic interests as the penultimate step on the road to departmentalized majors.

The new orientation, which reflected a general trend in American higher education, was facilitated by the recognition of the College of Arts and Sciences as a distinct entity and was championed by President Thomas and Dean Marvin. Both believed that student motivation would be strengthened if, instead of pursuing a loose "general" course, as most of them did, they were enrolled in well-structured curricula that fitted some specific career objective. Accordingly, in 1926, although the old group and major requirements were retained, appropriate courses were packaged and "recommended" under the labels of Economics, Business Administration, Pre-Legal, Pre-Theological, Pre-Medical, Journalism, Chemistry, and Sanitary Science. This expedient arrangement was obviously a half-way measure, and for the next two years the faculty of the College of Arts and Sciences wrestled with the problem before producing a solution that represented a further break with patterns dating back to the 1890's and earlier.

In a comprehensive reform, which became effective in September 1929, the old group and major requirements were abolished, and all students entering the College of Arts and Sciences were obliged to choose among eleven curricula.* All curricula were designed in accordance with the principle that during the first two years students should pursue a general course of studies, embracing work in English, mathematics, science, foreign languages, and social science, although the programs

---

* These were: Language and Literature, History and Political Science, Economics, Pre-Legal, and Pre-Theological, all leading to the A.B. degree; Journalism, for which alone the Litt.B. was awarded; and Mathematics and Natural Science, Pre-Medical and Biological, Business Administration, Chemistry, and Sanitary Science, all leading to the B.S. degree.

were not identical. In the two upper classes, students would normally take two courses in their major field, two related minors, and an elective. This pattern was an adaptation of the idea that a distinction should exist between "junior college" and "senior college" as had been recommended by the Klein survey. It clearly represented a revolt against the elective principle and an attempt to strike some balance between general education and specialized preparation for some career. "Thus the college discourages four years of aimless wandering," the 1929 catalogue explained, "and assumes that a young man by the age of eighteen should be sufficiently mature to recognize at least the general direction of his vocation." Knowledge could best be acquired when the purpose to which it was to be applied supplied motivation; this was indeed a far cry from the old days of discipline, piety, and ornamentation. A final tie with the past was snapped when no acquaintance with the classics was required of a candidate for the hallowed A.B. degree. Also in keeping with current thinking was the endeavor to provide some special opportunities for the most highly qualified students through the organization of an honors school, but, again, there never seemed to be the resources available to bring this ambitious plan to fruition.

The unashamedly vocational and pre-professional orientation of the curricula distressed many purists within the faculty, who mistakenly blamed President Thomas for what was in reality a belated capitulation to a national trend that had long since captured other citadels of learning. In another sense, it was the triumph within the liberal arts college of the land-grant concept of "useful knowledge." The Thomas administration openly, vigorously, and insistently advocated this concept, as evidenced by such moves as the establishment of the Industrial Extension Division, the expansion of programs for in-service teachers, and the acquisition of the College of Pharmacy, as well as by pushing curricular reform within the College of Arts and Sciences.

There were other signs of the new orientation. On the initiative of the New Jersey Press Association, a legislative appropriation was secured to institute a single course in journalism in 1925, and Dr. Allen Sinclair Will was appointed to head the work. A year later a full four-year curriculum in that field was approved. Pressure to equip students for careers in business led to the designing of a program in business administration, which was regarded by some of its advocates as the prelude to the establishment of a full-fledged school of commerce. There was also, for a brief period, a special one-year "short business curriculum," frankly designed for marginal students. In a related action, the Bureau of Economic and Business Research was founded in 1927 under the direction of Professor Eugene E. Agger, the new head of the Department of Economics, to conduct studies that might be of service to New

Jersey business. Similar concern with organizing research directed toward serving the state was a factor in the creation of the short-lived Bureau of Bacteriological and Biochemical Research—supported initially by a grant from Johnson and Johnson; of the Psychological and Mental Hygiene Clinic—set up in response to the urgent request of the state's Department of Institutions and Agencies; and of the Engineering Experiment Station.

The shining example of practical usefulness was, of course, the College of Agriculture and its related Experiment Station. So vast was its varied program of instruction, research, and extension activities that even the barest summary would require many pages and then fail to communicate the extent of its services. In 1930, a representative year, it gave resident instruction to 118 undergraduates and forty graduate students, the latter drawn from eighteen states and several foreign countries. In addition to dozens of investigations directed toward meeting specific problems affecting New Jersey farmers, research of fundamental significance was being carried forward by Dean Lipman, Professor Selman A. Waksman, and their associates in soil microbiology; by Professor Frederick P. Beaudette in poultry pathology; by Professor Thomas J. Headlee in mosquito control; and by Professor Thurlow C. Nelson in oyster culture—to cite but a few examples. In this one year seventy-one articles were written for scientific and technical journals, including the internationally esteemed *Soil Science,* edited and published at the College. Developing new varieties of plants, discovering effective means to control pests and eliminate diseases, demonstrating efficient tillage techniques, perfecting improved marketing arrangements, the agricultural staff worked with remarkable dedication to translate the results of scientific investigation into practical benefits for New Jersey farmers.

Through wide-ranging extension programs, staffed by county agents and extension specialists in many fields, the educational program was carried directly to individual farmers and their families. The statistics are impressive. In the single year of 1930 a total of 34,250 visits were made by extension agents to more than 13,000 farms, nearly 800,000 circular letters were mailed, and over 9,000 meetings were arranged. The College and the Station issued seventy-nine different publications, ran several series of newspaper articles, and maintained a constant flow of news stories. No division of the University was better known or more highly regarded throughout the state. Indeed, in the popular understanding, the College of Agriculture was thought of as a distinct entity, abundantly fulfilling the role of a state university, while the rest of Rutgers remained somehow "private," relatively remote, and unfamiliar.

As President Thomas strove to make Rutgers over, to transform it rapidly into the conventional model of the service-oriented state university, the faculty shared in the general sense of turmoil. In some respects their lot was improved. In part because of the substantial increase in state appropriations, and especially because state funds were now allocated to the College of Arts and Sciences, there were regular salary increases in varying amounts every year from 1926 through 1931. With opportunities to supplement their regular incomes by teaching additional courses in the burgeoning extension divisions or in the summer session, the faculty actually experienced a level of affluence they had been denied in the preceding decade. Another decided gain was the institution in 1929 of a system of contributory group insurance for all employees. The matter of sabbatical leaves, which had met such resistance in the past, was again pressed, and in 1930 the Trustees evidenced their approval of the principle and adopted a plan to be implemented when financial conditions permitted. No approach had yet been made to the vexing problem of retirement allowances, although with the new status of the University under the Board of Regents there was a momentary hope that employees might be permitted to enroll in the state retirement system. There were signs, at least, of concern with the development of personnel policies.

Economic gains notwithstanding, there was manifest discontent within the faculty over administration policies. The trouble began with the first faculty meeting of the new regime, when the president sought to lighten the requirements in certain curricula, only to encounter unyielding resistance from the biology faculty, led by Professor Arthur R. Moore. Moore, an able scholar who had recruited an outstanding group of associates, was promptly told by President Thomas that he should seek another position because of his uncooperative attitude. Moore was forced out, but not before many of the leading men in the faculty had rallied to his defense and had made it plain to the Trustees that they feared that Thomas was impairing academic standards by his highhanded actions. There were other clashes and resignations, most notably those of Edward H. Rockwell, the Dean of Engineering, and Dr. Ralph G. Wright, the respected head of the Department of Chemistry. Animosities were created by the apparent partiality of the president for several associates that he had brought with him from Pennsylvania State College, by disagreements about the quality and management of the extension programs, by controversies over the manner in which graduate work was conducted at the College of Agriculture, and by antagonism to some of the methods employed to reduce the number of those not completing the Freshman year. Basic to much of the discontent, however, was the conviction on the part of the faculty that they were being denied their rightful role of participating in those decisions that affected the academic affairs of the University.

When, in 1923, the Trustees had adopted a new structure for the University, they had deferred any action on those sections of the organizational plan that defined the powers of the faculty. Until 1925 the faculty met in one body to transact its business in accordance with traditional practices that had evolved over many decades, but with the creation of separate faculties for each of the colleges, it was unclear what relationship—if any—the University Faculty would have to the college faculties. On October 7, 1925, President Thomas convened the first meeting of the University Faculty. With a view to clarifying its role, he appointed a committee in November to prepare a constitution and bylaws, and a month later the committee reported. In essence, the University Faculty was to include the president, all deans and directors, and faculty members above the rank of instructor. It was to formulate general educational policy, fix minimum requirements for admission, make recommendations respecting the organization and rearrangement of the work of the schools and colleges, and determine educational questions affecting them jointly. It also defined the composition and powers of the several college faculties. The constitution was supposed to be presented to the faculty for approval in December, but instead, after conferring with certain Trustees, the president decided the matter should be referred to a joint faculty-Trustee committee for further study.

There the effort bogged down. Several months later Dr. Thomas explained to Leonor F. Loree that the joint committee "was really appointed to head off a movement in the Faculty which I feared might lead to definitions of practices which would be impracticable. The situation in the Faculty last year was such that it did not seem wise to hasten action of the committee, and I think you expressed to me your judgment to that effect." Operating without a constitution, the University Faculty met monthly, heard reports from its standing committees, and was far from being inactive. However, representatives from N.J.C. were rarely in attendance, and there existed a tacit understanding that the University Faculty, in which the College of Arts and Sciences had the largest contingent, would not interfere unduly either with N.J.C. or the College of Agriculture. The Klein survey had been critical of this makeshift arrangement and had recommended the establishment of a representative University senate to provide a body through which there might be effective faculty participation at the University level, but nothing was done.

Almost immediately following the departure of President Thomas, the long-pent-up concern of the faculty with the issue of their powers exploded, and in December 1930 a five-man committee, headed by Professor Thurlow C. Nelson, was elected to draft a constitution. A month later the University Faculty met to receive and act on the document, which generally resembled that which had been prepared five years earlier. It was apparent to astute observers that something unusual was about to transpire, for Dean Lipman and Dean Douglass were both in attendance, marshalling their respective faculties. The constitution was presented, Dean Lipman moved that it be tabled, and after a brief, irregular discussion, the motion was easily carried. A motion that a new committee be appointed was then defeated, and the meeting adjourned in confusion. Dean Lipman and Dean Douglass and the loyal members of their staffs, it appeared, had no desire for a strong University faculty; they much preferred to retain their autonomy than to risk domination by the "downtown" faculty. On this issue the move to establish a well-defined role for the faculty again foundered.

The changing role of the faculty was conditioned by the growth of what was now casually labelled "the administration." As the University expanded, the functions of the faculty, once all-encompassing, became restricted to the realm of the classroom and the laboratory and administrative officers were appointed to handle specific responsibilities. In addition to the several deans and directors, the roster by 1925 included a librarian, a registrar, a treasurer, a physician, a director of publicity and information, a graduate manager of athletics, and a superintendent of buildings and grounds. The appointment of a full-time dean of men in 1925 and of a University chaplain a year later enabled the faculty to divest itself of virtually all involvement with matters of discipline and also heralded a general extension of student welfare services. The most important administrative development of the decade, however, involved the complete reorganization of the business management of the University. The Klein survey had been highly critical of the loose arrangements then prevailing and had recommended a centralization of control over budgeting, purchasing, auditing, clerical personnel, dormitories and dining hall, and buildings and grounds. Accordingly, the Trustees created the new post of comptroller and treasurer, in which Albert S. Johnson was to serve with great effectiveness, from August 1927 until his death in 1957. Because of the nature of his responsibilities, the comptroller at once assumed a position of great influence within the University, second in importance only to that of the president. Where once the president had only the faculty to look to for advice and for the discharge of specific duties, within the span of a decade he had a vast corps of administrative officers, who shared with him much of the responsibility for conducting the affairs of the University.

"That the Rutgers of 1930 is not the Rutgers of 1920 is in no sense news." This simple observation might have been applied to any aspect of the University, but it was, in fact, the introductory statement to a searching report on profound changes that were taking place in the communal life of the students. Prompted by concern about the decline in what was vaguely termed "college spirit," a committee of students and faculty in 1930 made a thoughtful inquiry into the phenomenon and brought into perspective the hidden revolution that had been under way for more than a decade.

In the pre-Civil War period, students had identified themselves with the College through their membership in the two literary societies; later, class organizations had come to the fore and provided a basic structure within the student community. Now the classes were losing their hold on student loyalties. Class warfare, which took the form of several types of traditional rushes, came to an end in 1929. Interest in these manifestations of class spirit had been dwindling, and a tragic incident that resulted in the death of a student prompted the Student Council to decree the abolition of all rushes. Class banquets were also passing from the scene; the Freshman banquet in 1930 had to be cancelled when not enough tickets were sold. What had happened? Why were class loyalties disintegrating, and what might take their place?

The investigating committee correctly divined that "the University and the individual student life have become a complex of many activities, leading to a diffusion of interests and loyalties." Between 1920 and 1930, the number of men students increased from 614 to 1,401. These students were dispersed among twenty-three fraternities and three major dormitory units, as well as among accommodations in town and at home. They were divided among three colleges and, within the colleges, they followed dozens of curricula. They participated in scores of organized activities or passed their four years on the campus without becoming involved in any activities outside the classroom. In 1920 the entire student body met together almost daily in chapel; now each class met but once a week, and the entire student body never assembled. The faculty had grown in size and had "less real existence as an entity in the student mind than ten years ago." Less obvious, but, in the findings of the committee, most important of all, was the "increase in distracting activities, social and otherwise, outside the college life, including the increased frequency of week-end and other trips facilitated by easy transportation." Finally, the student of 1930 was "less cloistered, more out in the world; less 'collegiate,' more cosmopolitan" than his counterpart of a decade before.

To those who advocated determined efforts to resuscitate the class warfare that had served to build spirit and loyalty in the past, the committee replied that not only at Rutgers but throughout the nation this form of group expression was outmoded. The larger and more hetero-geneous the group, they found, the less likelihood there was for any adequate form of mass expression. In the future, loyalty to the University would be derived from the sense of comradeship engendered by par-ticipating in worthwhile activities, academic and extracurricular. They did propose various means of instilling group loyalty, such as opening the University year with a ceremonial function in which all would join, having Freshmen live and dine together, and deferring rushing by fraternities until a basis had been laid for broader loyalties, but they could not escape the conclusion that an era had ended. "The committee realizes that this report will perhaps be a little disappointing to those whose minds are set on stirring up the old 'college spirit' in the old way," they concluded. "We urge such individuals to reread this report, noting again the evolution which is taking place in other institutions, and the real meaning of some of the changes that have occurred at Rutgers, and then see if they can logically come to any conclusions other than those here set down."

Simultaneously with this subtle transformation of the student com-munity, there was a broad extension of control over student affairs. Al-though the able and considerate Dean of Men, Dr. Fraser Metzger, re-peatedly declared that it must be the major goal of the University to build men, it seemed to be necessary to bring every student activity under close supervision. Whereas once the extracurricular realm had been almost completely outside the bounds of faculty concern and had afforded wide latitude for students to exercise initiative and assume responsibility, new concepts of student welfare dictated that every phase of student life should be guided, directed, safeguarded, and regulated.

This process, of course, was well under way before 1925. It had begun when the College faculty established regulations to prevent intercol-legiate athletics from interfering unduly with the academic program, and had proceeded through such steps as the erection of a dormitory and dining hall, the creation of the office of Dean, the appointment of a College physician, the restrictions on the formation of new fraternities, and the establishment of the Council on Athletics. Other steps fol-lowed. In 1925 a set fee for the support of student activities was added to the term bill, bringing to an end the old system under which each student organization had to undertake to raise its own funds. Later in the same year the full-time office of Dean of Men was established. Soon there was a student business activities committee, made up of three students and three representatives of the administration, to exercise control over all student business concessions and audit the accounts of the various student organizations. House mothers were installed in the dormitories, and subsequently in some of the fraternity houses. New influences were brought to bear on fraternities following the formation in 1929 of the Interfraternity Alumni Council. Initiated by Dean Metzger, its purpose was to advise and cooperate with the chapters in the conduct of fraternity affairs and work with the administration in the best interests of the University and the fraternities. Among its earliest actions it instituted inspections of fraternity houses with a view to improving sanitation and cleanliness, sought to reform hazing practices, and brought about the first limitations on rushing. The last vestiges of student participation in the management of intercollegiate athletics ended in 1932 when the Council on Athletics was abolished. The Trustees assumed full responsibility for financing the athletic program, which was to be conducted by the newly created Division of Physical Education. Once students had recruited professional coaches; now professional coaches were to recruit students.

There were marked changes in the composition of the student body. Early in the century it was still overwhelmingly Protestant, scarcely reflecting the heterogeneous demographic characteristics of New Jersey. By 1929 a survey of religious preferences showed that Jews made up nearly 20 per cent of the student body and Roman Catholics about 15 per cent. Children of immigrants who had arrived in the late nineteenth century were becoming a major element in the student population. The student who was working his way through also became a common phenomenon in the 1920's. For some years the Y.M.C.A. ran an employment bureau to place men in part-time jobs, and in 1928 this function was taken over by the University Chaplain, Colonel John T. Axton. In that year more than 200 students sought his aid in obtaining employment; a large number made their own arrangements. Some indication of the taste and temper of the students of this generation may be gleaned from a Senior poll conducted by *Targum* in 1928. The venerable E. R. "Dutchy" Payson was voted the most popular and most humorous professor; public speaking and money and banking were tied for the designation of most valuable course. The best book of the year was *The Bridge of San Luis Rey,* and *Strange Interlude* was hailed as the best play. Hoover was the overwhelming choice for president, Lindbergh was the outstanding American, and Mussolini was the leading world figure.

The altered character of the University and its student body was reflected in only a modest degree in the range of organized extracurricular activities. Among the notable innovations were the formation of clubs closely related to curricular interests—the History and Politics Club, the Economics Club, the French Club, the Spanish Club, the German Club, and the like. Similar organizations brought together students in agriculture and the several branches of engineering. As yet, there were no signs of campus groups dedicated to political or social causes. In the literary field a humor magazine, *Chanticleer,* enjoyed considerable popularity for a few years after its initial appearance in 1923, until its irreverent and sometimes tasteless style brought about its suppression. On the serious side, *Anthologist* was launched in 1927 to provide a vehicle for those who were interested in poetic and literary expression. Debating, under the dynamic Professor Richard C. Reager, became one of the most popular of campus activities, offering to dozens of students the opportunity to acquire experience in practical public speaking.

Student government remained a relatively weak force. The Senior Council, which dated back to 1914, was reconstituted as the Student Council in 1923. Made up of elected Seniors and the heads of six major student organizations, it exercised some oversight of student activities, arranged mass meetings, supervised elections, and made recommendations to the administration. Campus politics, organized chiefly on the basis of rival "combines" of fraternities, was a frequent target for denunciation but continued to control elections or appointments to virtually all student offices, from team managerships and prom chairmanships to the editorial posts on campus publications. Nonfraternity men, relegated to something of a second-class status under this system, became sufficiently aroused under the leadership of Earl S. Miers, 1933, to organize in 1931 what was called the Neutral Council, but the fraternities maintained their dominant role in campus affairs.

On the athletic scene, new emphasis was placed upon affording to the maximum possible number of students opportunities for team competition. The Department of Physical Training assiduously promoted an ambitious program of intramural competition to complement the increasing list of varsity, junior varsity, and Freshman teams. Wrestling (1927), boxing (1928), fencing (1928), water polo (1929) and soccer (1930) were added to the sports schedule. Football in these years produced more defeats than victories, despite modest alumni efforts to recruit promising players and the creation of Upson scholarships to attract young men of character and physical vigor. The formation of the "Middle Three" in 1929—Lafayette, Lehigh, and Rutgers—provided a new basis of athletic rivalry with nearby schools of comparable standards. While football was in the doldrums, the swimming team enjoyed an excellent record, climaxed in 1929 by a season that was marred only by an extremely controversial loss to Yale. Lacrosse, too, achieved great success; the 1928 squad lost but one game in the regular season and participated in the playoffs to select the team for the Olympics. The extent and success of the athletic program was especially remarkable in view of the severely limited physical facilities. For outdoor sports there were only Neilson Field and the even less adequate College Field; indoor sports taxed the capacity of the aging Ballantine Gymnasium.

A crippling blow to the athletic program, and the most memorable event to those who were attending the University at the time, was the almost total destruction of the Gymnasium by a fire of unknown origin on the night of January 7, 1930. Through nearly four decades, the building had served as the center of campus activity, the scene of dances, concerts, rallies, and meetings, as well as sports competitions, physical education classes, and health services. Three days after this disastrous loss, the Trustees met and determined to raise $600,000 for a new and larger building. Because of the depressed economic conditions, only about half of this sum could be obtained, but ground was broken for the new gymnasium in December, and by January 1932 it was sufficiently near completion to house a capacity audience for a concert by Paul Robeson, Class of 1919.

The five eventful years of Dr. Thomas' administration can be viewed as a premature and unsuccessful effort to convert Rutgers into a full-fledged state university. Initially encouraged by the Trustees to embark on such a course, the president instituted new policies that brought about a rapid rise in enrollments, an emphasis on those programs of education that seemed especially appropriate to a state institution, and a thorough public airing of the legal and fiscal relationship of Rutgers to the state. In terms of its objectives, the Thomas program was a failure, for by 1930 it was apparent that the establishment of the Board of Regents did not produce the long desired clarification of the status of the University. Neither had any progress been made in resolving the financial problems occasioned by the reliance on a share of the main-stem tax.

There can be no simple assignment of blame for the failure. It might be said that New Jersey, with its notoriously conservative attitude toward state-supported services and its traditional resistance to taxes, was not yet ready to accept responsibility for higher education. The Trustees, who had somehow failed to understand that increased state control would be a concomitant of increased state support, drew back when realization of this fact dawned on them. President Thomas, because he was often lacking in tact and candor in his dealings both with the Trustees and with state officials, seriously impaired his own effectiveness in handling a complex situation. For the University generally, the failure revived old questions about the identity of the institution. Where did its future lie? Was it to be "public," "private," or something in between? Whatever the eventual answer to these questions, it had to be recognized that during the Thomas regime the entire educational program of the University was reoriented toward the goal of service to the state. To the limit of its resources, and even beyond them, Rutgers with its sprawling extension divisions, its newly created research bureaus, its democratic admissions policies, its popular College of Agriculture, and its newly revised curricula had indeed taken on much of the appearance of a state university.

The somewhat abrupt resignation of Dr. Thomas served to highlight the crisis facing the University. While the Trustees pondered their future policies, they turned to Philip Milledoler Brett and prevailed upon him to accept the office of Acting President. A descendant of the Rutgers president whose name he bore, Brett had been extremely active and popular as an undergraduate in the Class of 1892, had become a successful lawyer in New York City, and had served on the Board of Trustees since 1906. He possessed not only high ability and deep devotion to Rutgers but also a rare personality, of such warmth, generosity, and charm as to win the affection of all who knew him.

Taking office at a time when the University was encountering the first onslaughts of the depression, when relations with the Board of Regents were verging on disaster, and when the morale of the faculty was at low ebb, Brett in his calm and kindly manner tackled the problems he confronted with tact and wisdom. Beyond the routine management of University affairs, his greatest achievement was to restore the confidence of the faculty and the alumni in the institution by his humane and considerate attention to their feelings and views. So fully did he win their esteem that the faculty addressed to him an unanimous petition imploring him to accept appointment as president, and the Alumni Council took similar action. Deeply appreciative of these tributes, Brett nevertheless felt obliged to decline what he referred to as "the greatest honor which has come to me during my life." After eighteen months of dedicated service, he relinquished his office to his successor, Dr. Robert C. Clothier, but continued to manifest his devotion to Rutgers by his long and fruitful subsequent service on the Board of Trustees.

Chapter Ten

Depression and War

For a quarter of a century Rutgers had been in the throes of transformation from a small college to a multi-dimensional university, from an essentially private institution to an instrumentality of the state. The Rutgers that President Thomas bequeathed to his successor was vastly different in size, organization, and scope from that which Dr. Demarest had found on his accession to the presidency in 1906. Now, abruptly, the rapid pace of growth and innovation was interrupted by an interval of relative quiescence. For more than a decade the University seemingly stood still, experiencing little or no expansion in numbers of students, in staff, in buildings, or in the extent and variety of its academic programs. Its progress was brought to a halt by the devastating economic effects of the Great Depression and by the persistence of a stalemate in relations with the state under the ill-fated Board of Regents. Having weathered the depression, the University next confronted the even more abnormal conditions created by the nation's total involvement in World War II. The dominant theme of these years, then, is not that of rapid development but rather of a struggle to adapt to severely adverse external circumstances.

At the very time that the full extent of the predicament confronting the University was becoming apparent, Dr. Robert Clarkson Clothier took up the duties of the presidency. A member of a distinguished Philadelphia family, Dr. Clothier had spent several years in personnel work following his graduation from Princeton University in 1908. He had entered the field of education in 1923 as assistant headmaster of Haverford School and had become Dean of Men at the University of Pittsburgh in 1929, from which post he had been called to Rutgers. He was elected president in December 1931 and assumed his official responsibilities on March 1, 1932.

In his educational philosophy, Dr. Clothier consistently stressed his concern with the whole character of the student. "Our objective in educational work," he declared in his inaugural address, "is not the development of men and women of high intellectuality alone, but men and women who are well-balanced, who are inherently honest and reliable. . . . I hold that if we are charged with the development of the individual to his full social stature, we cannot ignore our responsibility for the development of these social-cultural-spiritual qualities." Embodying in his own personality the virtues and qualities of a gentleman, he held before faculty and students the ideals of integrity of workmanship, social decency, and individual responsibility. Distinguished in appearance, gracious in manner, and warmly sensitive to human relationships, he was to be especially effective in sustaining the morale of students, faculty, and alumni during an exceedingly trying period. Within the severe limitations imposed by financial considerations, he gave strong encouragement and support to proposals emanating from the faculty for strengthening and developing the academic program.

The new president was neither by temperament nor background a "state university" man, and he correctly sensed that with state relations in the hopeless impasse that had been reached by 1932 the Trustees were disposed to consider alternative policies to those that had been pressed so vigorously by President Thomas. In an extremely important statement to the Board of Trustees in October 1932, President Clothier outlined his conception of the direction in which Rutgers should move:

> I feel that eventually this Board will have to make its decision as to whether, in the end, Rutgers is to be a state university under state control or a private institution under private control. So far as my own judgment goes, I cannot bring myself to accept the idea of Rutgers turning its back on the tradition of the last 150 years and accepting the status of a state university with all the educational perils and threat to educational ideals which it involves.
>
> Instead, I think of Rutgers continuing in its present cooperative relationship with the state, adapting itself as best it can to the handicaps and difficulties which that relationship involves, since there has evolved over the last fifty years a definite dependency on state support. But I think, too, of Rutgers having the courage to depart from this course of least resistance, to strike out for itself, to enlist the aggressive interest of the alumni and friends, to develop in them the habit of giving and giving generously, to build endowments—as gradually or as quickly as conditions permit—until twenty years from now (or less) Rutgers will be so splendidly equipped with plant and endowed with funds that the State will recognize the overwhelming advantage of cooperating with her,

talk of an independent state university will cease, our prestige in the University-State relationship will be dominant, and we shall be in control of our own destiny.

Acutely conscious of the highly unsatisfactory relationship that obtained with the state and aware that the most determined efforts of his predecessor had not brought forth the desired results, President Clothier, with the cordial support of the Trustees, saw as the only alternative the enhancement of the resources of the "private" Rutgers. On one occasion he was moved to exclaim to the Board, "Rutgers cannot continue to live half slave and half free." For eight years—until 1940—the president adhered to this basic philosophy, which profoundly influenced many aspects of University policy.

Whatever the long-range goals of the University might be, its immediate future was bound up with the state through the Board of Regents, and that relationship proved to be distressingly unfruitful and frustrating. Not content merely to administer the contractual relationship that had long maintained between the state and the University, the Regents endeavored to formulate somewhat grandiose plans for the complete reorganization of higher education in New Jersey. In 1931 they retained as their educational consultant, Dr. Albert B. Meredith, who had served as Commissioner of Education in Connecticut for a decade before becoming head of the Department of School Administration at New York University in 1930. After some preliminary studies, Dr. Meredith proposed the creation of a "University of New Jersey," modelled generally on the New York system of organizing public higher education.

The state university that he envisioned would include the state teachers' colleges and normal schools, projected junior colleges, and certain other agencies, as well as Rutgers. With respect to Rutgers, however, the so-called state units were to be segregated from the "private" units under some arrangement comparable to that which existed at Cornell University. Management of this complex educational structure would be vested in a state board that would possess certain of the powers of the State Board of Education and of the Board of Regents. In successive annual reports from 1932 down to 1941 the Regents continued to champion this blueprint for higher education. However, the public response to these proposals was one of indifference, the legislature was negatively disposed, and the State Board of Education was decidedly hostile.

The preoccupation of the Regents with schemes for a "University of New Jersey" placed the Rutgers authorities in a quandary. Aside from its radical character, the plan obviously enjoyed little support, and moreover its precise application to Rutgers was never clearly elucidated. Consequently the president and the Trustees could not regard it as a practical and satisfactory alternative to the existing contractual arrangement. On the other hand, because it was vital to attempt to maintain some semblance of cooperative and amicable relations with the Regents, Rutgers could not take the position of adamantly rejecting any proposals looking to a "clarification" of its status. Accordingly, there were from time to time polite conferences between representatives of the Regents and Rutgers, but not until after 1941 did they lead to any common understandings. Meanwhile, the Regents remained critical of the contractual relationship, declined to recommend capital improvements at Rutgers, and exerted minimal influence with the legislature in behalf of annual appropriations for the University.

There were other difficulties. On the recommendation of Dr. Meredith, the Regents in 1932 announced a policy of eliminating state appropriations for the support of undergraduate educational courses at Rutgers and the College for Women on the grounds that such work duplicated the efforts of the state teachers' colleges. The University unsuccessfully protested this edict and then found other means to continue the teacher-training programs. The Regents also came forth in 1933 with a highly controversial plan to reorganize activities in the field of agriculture by integrating the State Experiment Station with the College Experiment Station and the College of Agriculture and transferring to the Regents the supervisory powers and duties of both the Board of Visitors and the Board of Managers. President Clothier and the Trustees took the position that this was essentially a matter to be worked out by the Regents with the Visitors and the Managers. The latter two bodies stoutly refused to surrender their functions, and after prolonged negotiations the Regents had to admit defeat. These two cases are illustrative of the kinds of questions raised by the Regents, questions that posed serious and time-consuming problems for the Rutgers authorities without, in most instances, producing constructive consequences.

Continual difficulties with the Board of Regents did not represent the only aggravation in the area of state relations; the University authorities were constantly on the defensive against proposals looking to the establishment of a "Free State University." This movement derived its strongest support from Hudson County, where J. Albert Dear, publisher of the *Jersey Journal* and former member of the Duffield Commission, gave it unstinting support. Ostensibly the proponents wanted a university wholly under state control, possibly based on the existing teachers' colleges, in which there would be no tuition charges for New Jersey residents. Bills to accomplish this objective were introduced in the legislature as early as 1931 and occasioned considerable interest and controversy between 1935 and 1944. Whenever the matter came up, the "Free State University" forces spent more time in attacking state support for Rutgers than they did in elaborating their own position, lending credibility to the charge that they included many elements whose chief motivation was hostility to Rutgers. The movement never approached success, but it did constitute a worrisome annoyance and created a factor of discord within the legislature, against which the University officials had to contend. The threat was deemed to be of such importance that in 1938 the University's public relations program was revised and strengthened in order to stress the wide range of services that Rutgers was providing for the state.

Even more critical in its impact on the University was the drastic curtailment of state appropriations. In common with other states, New Jersey by 1932 found itself confronted with staggering costs for the relief of the unemployed at the same time that government revenues were being curtailed by the effects of the depression. Of special relevance to the financing of education was the decision of the railroads to "withhold" nearly 40 per cent of the taxes assessed against them, which meant, of course, a sharp drop in receipts from the main-stem taxes from which the University and other educational agencies received their funds. Consequently, in 1932 the Rutgers appropriation was cut by 20 per cent, and in the following year there was a further reduction of 10 per cent. Taken together with declining income from student fees and from gifts, these slashes created a crisis of major proportions for the University.

In meeting the situation, salaries were reduced in 1932 and again in 1933, and, far more serious, over fifty staff members lost their appointments. Several special bureaus, including the School for Child Study, the Engineering Experiment Station, the Short Courses in Engineering, and the Psychological and Mental Hygiene Clinic, had to be discontinued temporarily, and there was a considerable reduction in the number of regular undergraduate course-offerings. Every expense item was pared to the barest minimum, and even regular maintenance work was postponed. Rigid economy was the watchword. Clerical salaries fell as low as $600, and faculty members struggled along on salaries that might be as little as $1,800 for an instructor and $3,150 for a full professor.

Until 1932 the University had not approached the legislature directly on appropriation matters, leaving that function to the Regents. But, confronted with the disastrous cutback of 1932 and convinced that the Regents could exert little pressure, Rutgers mobilized its supporters and thereafter waged a campaign in behalf of its budget requests in every legislative session. Dr. Clothier and a group of administrators known as the "Board of Strategy" directed their efforts with increasing effectiveness. In 1934 the downward trend was reversed and the state appropriation was increased by 15 per cent; two years later it was brought up to the pre-1932 level of slightly more than $1,000,000 dollars. Although these hard-won advances brought some alleviation of the financial stringency and made possible a restoration of salaries, conditions of austerity continued to prevail and there seemed to be no prospect of additional funds with which to expand the physical plant or the educational program. Quite obviously budgetary considerations dictated that these were to be years of retrenchment rather than of growth. It is against this background, then, of deadlock with the Board of Regents, uncertainty over the future public role of Rutgers, and—above all—deep concern about conditions engendered by the depression that the affairs of the University in this period must be viewed.

In no dimension of the University were the effects of the depression more obvious and pervasive than among the undergraduates. As a direct consequence of the hard times, enrollments declined sharply in the men's colleges, falling from 1,401 in 1929 to 1,200 in 1933, before starting a rapid upward climb.* Increasing numbers of those who were struggling to continue their studies were forced to live at home and commute to the campus, with the result that scores of dormitory rooms remained vacant and many fraternity houses were half empty. Because hundreds of students found themselves without the resources to meet their college expenses, student loan funds were entirely exhausted by 1932 and available scholarships were quite inadequate to the demand. Part-time employment became a desperate necessity, but it was hard to come by. And among those who survived to obtain their degrees, the quest for a job was apt to be grim and discouraging.

In order to meet these unprecedented conditions, the University administration instituted several emergency measures. In a manner reminiscent of an earlier stage, an intensive campaign was launched to recruit students and reverse the downward trend of enrollments. A "Prep School Week End," first held in May 1933, brought hundreds of prospective students to the campus annually, and alumni were urged to join the "Send-a-Boy-to-Rutgers Club." Similar considerations prompted the decision in September 1933 to admit applicants who did not meet admission requirements as "unclassified" students. Even more in keeping with the temper of the times was the announcement in January 1933 that unemployed men over the age of thirty who possessed the

---

* Enrollments in the College for Women declined from a high of 1,159 in 1929 to a low of 940 in 1934 and remained near the level of 1,000 until after 1945. The men's colleges recovered their losses by 1936, and by 1939 had over 1,700 students in attendance.

necessary qualifications would be admitted without any tuition charges; twenty were enrolled the following month.

Along with intensive recruitment went various efforts to lighten the financial burden on the students. In 1932 and again in 1934 dormitory rents were reduced substantially, in part because nearly 40 per cent of the rooms were empty. In the same period, at the urgent request of the dean of men, the Trustees authorized the granting of one hundred additional $100 scholarships to needy students. Although these expedients represented the best the University could do with its available resources, they scarcely met the critical situation. More scholarships were essential, and in a surprising development they were obtained from the state in 1937.

Acting on the recommendations of the Duffield Commission, the legislature in 1929 had terminated the state-scholarship program that had been instituted in 1890. The depression underscored the problems that beset qualified young men and women who desired a college education, and when the University administration proposed to the Appropriations Committee early in 1937 a revival of state scholarships the response was immediate and enthusiastic. Under the vigorous leadership of Samuel Pesin, chairman of the committee and assemblyman from Hudson County, $50,000 was designated in the appropriation act to initiate the program. The University had not anticipated such prompt and affirmative action, and, when the measure was finally enacted in June, extraordinary efforts were required to create the machinery for making the awards. Altogether, 178 full-tuition scholarships, distributed in proportion to legislative representation, were awarded to entering students in both the men's colleges and the College for Women on the basis of financial need, personal qualifications, and a competitive scholastic aptitude examination. In subsequent years the scholarship appropriation was increased to $200,000, making it possible to establish four-year scholarships on a continuing basis. The Board of Regents condemned the scholarship plan but cooperated in its administration. The program was of inestimable importance and served not only to bolster enrollments but also to attract students of superior quality to the University.

For a large proportion of the students, part-time employment was a necessity if they were to remain in college. Early in 1933 all student employment was centralized under an able and aggressive assistant dean, Edward H. Heyd, 1931, who worked wonders in finding jobs on the campus and in the local community for impecunious undergraduates. Indispensable assistance was afforded also through Federal relief programs. In March 1934 funds became available under the Federal Emergency Relief Administration (F.E.R.A.) to employ two hundred men and women students in various tasks at which they were able to earn as much as fifteen dollars a month. With the establishment of the National Youth Administration in 1935, the student-aid program was vastly expanded and placed on a continuing basis. The fund allotments amounted to fifteen dollars a month for 12 per cent of the total enrollment, and students were employed—usually at forty cents an hour—on clerical, research, or library projects that were, insofar as possible, relevant to their disciplinary interests. In the estimate of University administrators and the N.Y.A. beneficiaries themselves, this program worked admirably to realize its main objectives. As late as 1941 there were 461 students employed with N.Y.A. funds; by 1943, when the program was terminated, that number had dwindled because more lucrative opportunities had become available through private employment.

Finding employment for graduates was a new responsibility assumed by the University in this anxious period. A poll of Seniors in May 1933 revealed that only about half of them expected to obtain employment after graduation; in actuality one-third were still unemployed six months after receiving their diplomas. Concern about this alarming situation led to the establishment of a new bureau of personnel and placement in 1935, with Heyd as director. In addition to supervising student employment, the Bureau developed an effective program for placing graduates in positions. With the cooperation of numerous alumni and industrial experts, a special course, "How to Get a Job," was offered to all interested Seniors; company representatives were brought to the campus to interview job applicants; and skilled counselling service was provided to assist students in determining their career aptitudes. The results were impressive. Ninety per cent of the 1936 graduates either found employment—at an average salary of $100 a month—or entered graduate schools. Although the depression persisted, such measures as these assuaged its worst effects.

Not surprisingly, the collapse of the American economy gave students a new perspective on the world they were about to enter and stimulated discussion of radical solutions for contemporary problems. The first major indication of a new tone of protest was the organization in 1930 of the Rutgers Forum, which conducted meetings throughout the year on such subjects as conscription, censorship, and socialism. A year later the Liberal Club made its appearance and attained prominence for its sponsorship of currently popular causes. Often in cooperation with such groups as the Rutgers Christian Association, the League for Independent Political Action, the League for Industrial Democracy, and the local branch of the Socialist Party, it arranged popular series of lectures that featured such speakers as Earl Browder, Norman Thomas, Scott Nearing, and Harry Laidler. Although due interest was manifested in the

"Roosevelt Revolution," the burning issues of the day centered around the problems of war and fascism. Compulsory R.O.T.C. was a favorite target for attack, and various types of "peace pledges" were ardently circulated. In 1935 over 300 students gathered on the Seminary campus under the sponsorship of twenty student organizations to conduct a peace strike as part of a national movement of protest. By 1935 the most active phase of the radical movement had largely subsided, although the campus was never again to be quite so complacent and conservative about contemporary problems as it had traditionally been. In 1936 there was momentary enthusiasm for the Veterans of Future Wars, an organization that had originated at Princeton and spread like wildfire throughout the nation's campuses. Dedicated to securing a bonus in advance for future veterans, it represented both a satirical attack on the regular veterans groups and a weirdly humorous aspect of the students' aversion to war. Despite the self-proclaimed radicalism of a small number of highly vocal leftists, the mass of the undergraduates remained faithful to inherited political loyalties, and by 1938 they were more absorbed in mastering the intricacies of the Big Apple—or in improving their manners and morals by attending voluntary courses in Etiquette and Right Living—than in elucidating Marxian dialectics.

There were other subtle but significant changes in the patterns of undergraduate life in the depression decade. Among the more notable was the elimination of the time-honored custom of petty grafting. It had long been accepted practice for undergraduate politicians who managed dances, class banquets, or various concessions to pocket large sums for which no accounting was ever made. "Those were the days," one alumnus recalled, "when the class treasury might pay $800 for an orchestra for which the dance chairman paid $400, or when a $4.00 class assessment paid for a $1.00 class banquet." Perhaps because of the hard times, the undergraduates became resentful of such campus rackets and supported the efforts of the Dean of Men's office to enforce a rigorous accounting of all student funds. In a related area, campus politics underwent something of a revolution. The fraternities, long the complete masters of positions of prestige and profit, suffered serious losses in numbers because of economic considerations. At the same time the non-fraternity men, reorganized in 1935 as the Scarlet Barbarians, grew in strength and leadership. By the spring elections in 1938 they were fully mobilized to contest with their fraternity rivals, and they captured all but two of the class offices and three of eight Student Council seats. Although the fraternities made a strong comeback the following year, their dominance had been broken, and it had become evident that fraternity membership was no longer a prerequisite to high campus position.

The twenty-one campus fraternities, three of them local clubs, faced problems other than the political challenge of the neutrals. As one observer put it, "No one felt the depression more keenly than Brother Greek, who wrapped himself in his chapter mortgage and determined to weather the storm." Dwindling memberships, unpaid bills, and mounting criticism of fraternity practices plagued most chapters. In an effort to reform one of the worst evils of the existing system, a plan for deferred rushing—which meant that no Freshman could be pledged between the start of the term and Thanksgiving—was instituted in 1936. Although the reform had many salutary effects, especially for the Freshman, its economic consequences were nearly disastrous to many houses. The feeling that the entire fraternity system faced a crisis was intensified by the political victory scored by the neutrals in 1938. At this point the alumni, roused by a series of articles in the *Alumni Monthly*, interested themselves in the problem, and in 1939 the old practice of "cut throat" or unrestricted rushing was reinstituted. Whatever their failings, the fraternities retained their appeal both to undergraduates and alumni and somehow muddled through this difficult period.

The depression years brought genuine distress to innumerable students and left its mark on many aspects of undergraduate life, but, paradoxically enough, its sombre tone did not extend to campus social activities. In part because students were virtually obligated to remain on the campus for economic reasons, the social calendar had never been more crammed with events. A notable innovation was the Freshman Reception, held early in the year to bring together the entering classes of men and women at Rutgers and N.J.C. Another popular event was the annual winter weekend at the Inn at Buck Hill Falls under the sponsorship of the Glee Club. The major formal dances, featuring the big bands of Tommy Dorsey, Hal Kemp, or Duke Ellington, drew capacity throngs, and informal dances—held on most Saturday nights on either side of town—were well patronized. To the excellent dramatic productions offered by Queen's Players were added spectacular "Varsity Shows" in 1938 and 1939, reviving a tradition of musical comedy that had begun in the 1880's. The repeal of Prohibition, of course, offered new opportunities for conviviality, and such haunts as the Corner Tavern, Norm's, and Strickland's were largely taken over by student clientele. Still, the most popular diversions remained the movies, often combined with a date at the "Coop."

On the athletic scene, too, there was little evidence of gloom or austerity. Under George E. Little, who was brought from the University of Wisconsin in 1932 to direct the newly created Division of Physical Education, the entire athletic program was expanded and strengthened. With the vastly improved facilities afforded by the new gymna-

sium and—after 1938—by the several playing fields in the University
Heights area, intramural competitions acquired increased popularity,
and intercollegiate teams gained new laurels. With strong encouragement from Little, crew was revived after a hiatus of several decades.
The first shells took to the water in April 1933 and, coached by Edward
H. Ten Eyck, were prepared to engage in intercollegiate competition a
year later. Another new sport was 150-pound football; under coach
Harry J. Rockefeller the team for several years dominated the league in
which it played. Junior varsity football and boxing were also accorded
recognition at this time, thus further multiplying opportunities for participation, in line with the stated goal of "athletics for all." Later golf
and soccer joined the list. Basketball teams under Frank Hill and swimming teams under James Reilly—both veteran coaches—compiled excellent records, but J. Wilder Tasker's football teams disappointed the expectations of avid fans.

Unquestionably football acquired added attraction when the ancient
rivalry with Princeton, which had lapsed in 1915, was resumed in
1933, and perennially there were high hopes that the victory achieved
in that first contest in 1869 would at last be repeated. The long-awaited
day came on November 5, 1938. Directed by a new coach, Harvey
Harman, and inspired by the ceremonies attendant upon the dedication
of the new stadium, an indomitable Rutgers team fought to a 20–18
victory. No moment in the long annals of Rutgers sports was more
memorable, and, whether rightly or not, the triumph had an incalculable and lasting psychological impact on all who were identified
with Rutgers.

In one way or another the University succeeded in sustaining and
even increasing its undergraduate enrollments, and the students in turn
adapted themselves remarkably well to the conditions of the times. Although as alumni many of the graduates of the depression decade encountered cruel disappointments in their ambitions and a large proportion of students concluded that prudence dictated the choice of a job
offering security rather than alluring but uncertain prospects of wealth,
confidence in the worthwhileness of higher education remained unim-
paired. If anything, the experiences of these years, with the intense
competition for available economic opportunities, seemed to confirm the
practical value of a college education. As never before, students directed
their thoughts toward the problem of "How to Get a Job," and most of
them felt a sense of gratitude to the University for the manner in which
it equipped them to meet that problem.

The depression also left its mark upon the faculty. Through 1931 there
had been increases in salaries, steady growth in numbers, and equitable
advances in rank. Then came the drastic budget cuts of 1932 and 1933,

with accompanying reductions in salaries, and, worse still, dismissals from the staff. After 1935 salaries were gradually restored to the pre-1931 levels, but in part because of legislative edict salaries could not be advanced until 1941. Since the University administration was averse to granting promotions that did not carry with them some increase in income, for fear of weakening the existing salary scale, most members of the faculty remained frozen in their ranks throughout the decade. Difficult and even disheartening as their plight was, they counted themselves fortunate to have relatively secure employment, and they understood the futility of engaging in any drastic efforts to advance their positions. For ten years the faculty remained stable; few teachers resigned or retired and fewer still were added, with the result that after 1945 there was a profound gap in both age and attitude between the older faculty and the new corps of instructors that joined the staff in the era of postwar expansion.

One of the major problems that had plagued the faculty for many years was the ambiguous definition of its role in the University structure. Attempts to secure a faculty constitution in 1925 and again in 1931 had met with frustration, and the so-called "University Faculty" continued to function even though its composition and powers remained undefined. Early in his administration President Clothier perceived the need for clarifying and reforming the entire University organization, and a special committee that he appointed produced a comprehensive set of "Rules and Regulations of the Faculty," which were approved by the Trustees in June 1933 and became effective in September.

In addition to defining the duties of administrative officers and the composition and powers of the several college faculties, the regulations created new agencies through which the faculty might participate at the University level in the determination of policy. The old University Faculty was replaced by a University Council, made up almost equally of designated administrative officers and elected faculty representatives. The Council was to "exercise advisory and legislative powers pertaining to all academic matters except those which have been assigned by the Trustees or the President to designated officers, faculties, committees and boards, and shall make provision for the coordination of the activities of the several branches of the University." Associated with the Council was the University Assembly, made up of all administrative and academic personnel, which was empowered "to consider the legislative enactments of the Council and of the several faculties, and to request their reconsideration or to advise the President concerning them." More than a decade was to pass before the Assembly was called into session; in actuality it was to be useful only in extreme emergencies.

The Council, which was not conceived or constituted as an agency of the faculty, was hardly a vigorous or effective body. Usually meeting but twice a year, its infrequent actions dealt with such matters as admission requirements, grading systems, and academic standards. After the first few years it became customary to devote a portion of each session to the general discussion of such topics as "The Student, the Teacher, and the Library," or "Educating the Whole Person." Not until around 1943, when intensive studies were launched relating to personnel procedures and postwar educational policies did the Council demonstrate its real potentialities, but subsequently this momentum was not sustained. Regardless of its shortcomings, and they were evident, the Council did provide a forum for a limited discussion of University affairs and, on occasion, could generate action leading to significant innovations.

Although some definition had now been given to the roles of the faculties, the status of the individual faculty member remained curiously indistinct and even insecure. The principle of tenure had not yet been explicitly recognized; in theory if not in fact all appointments were on a yearly basis. In criticizing the notion that professors should have formal assurance of tenure, Dr. Clothier argued that the teacher's best guarantee of his position lay in the possession of certain desirable personal qualities. The president compiled a list of eleven such qualities covering teaching capacity, loyalty to the institution, wholesomeness, active participation in extra-classroom activities, and attractiveness of appearance and manners, but—interestingly enough—did not emphasize what was soon to become known as "research accomplishments." There were no formal criteria for appointments or promotions and no provisions for faculty participation in either action. Older members of the staff looked forward with apprehension to retirement, for there was no real pension system.

Remarkably enough, morale remained strong, and beyond their devotion to their teaching duties the faculty manifested an unusual *esprit de corps* and a constant willingness to devote themselves to the betterment of the institution. Most of those who were members of the staff in 1932 were to remain at Rutgers until the end of their careers, and they were no less dedicated to promoting the welfare of the University than they were to their special disciplines. Gifted scholars and popular teachers—among them Edward M. Burns, William H. Cole, John J. George, Albert R. Johnson, William H. F. Lamont, Howard D. McKinney, Richard B. Morris, Thurlow C. Nelson, Houston Peterson, Richard C. Reager, James J. Slade, and Selman A. Waksman—commanded the respect and affection of several undergraduate generations. Mingling after lunch in the Alumni House, or joining enthusiastically in the jaunts of the Outing Club, or sharing the concerns of neighbors in Highland Park, the faculty was a closely knit social group, a consideration that undoubtedly ameliorated some of the less pleasant aspects of their position.

Harmonious though relations were between the faculty and the University administration, the campus was thrown into a furore in 1935 by an incident that not only involved questions of academic freedom but touched as well on some of the most sensitive issues of the day. An instructor in the German Department at the College for Women, Lienhard Bergel, was informed that his appointment would not be extended, both because declining enrollments made his services unnecessary and because his performance had not been entirely satisfactory. Subsequently, Bergel charged that he was being dismissed because of political differences with the department's head, Professor Friedrich J. Hauptmann, whom he accused of disseminating pro-Nazi and anti-Semitic propaganda among the students. These charges were aired publicly, and numerous groups and individuals espoused the cause of the young instructor. In the face of mounting pressure, President Clothier appointed a special Trustees' committee, with J. Edward Ashmead as chairman, to conduct a thorough investigation of the explosive situation.

Ashmead's committee conducted a series of twenty-nine all-day hearings between May 21 and July 23, at which 110 witnesses were heard, and produced a lengthy printed report summarizing the evidence with the committee's conclusions. There was no question that Hauptmann and some of his colleagues in the department entertained favorable views of Hitler's Germany, a position that Bergel and many members of the college faculty and students as well found intolerable. The Ashmead committee judged, however, that Hauptmann had not abused his role in the classroom and that he and his associates were entitled to hold their own political opinions. They found no evidence that Bergel's failure to secure reappointment was based on other than routine academic considerations. Accordingly, they recommended that no further action be taken in the matter.

In concluding their report, the committee set forth a position on academic freedom. "The very existence of our universities and colleges," they declared, "depends upon free and open discussion, including discussion of controversial matters. . . . This freedom, however, carries with it a corresponding responsibility. No teacher may claim as his right the privilege of discussing in his classroom controversial topics outside his own field of study." All persons are entitled to their own opinions on all subjects, and all might express those opinions freely, subject only to restrictions imposed by law, by common decency, and by the nature of the occasion.

The committee's findings were denounced by those to whom Nazism was intolerable and by those who saw Bergel as the victim of political persecution. Leading the attack was the American Civil Liberties Union, which, although it characterized the investigation as "probably the most searching and certainly the most lengthy public inquiry of its sort in academic history," disagreed entirely with the conclusions reached. Other critics threatened to carry the matter to the legislature unless the committee's findings were reversed. Meeting in this highly charged atmosphere on October 17, the Trustees reviewed the various documents relating to the controversy and after prolonged discussion affirmed the conclusions of the Ashmead committee. For obvious reasons, the incident had a detrimental effect on the University, and its repercussions lingered on for many years. There was a sensational revival of interest in the matter early in 1941 when it was disclosed that Hauptmann had disappeared, presumably to return to his native Germany. These rumors were verified at the close of the war when Hauptmann was apprehended by Allied military authorities for having served as a minor functionary under the Nazi regime.

In spite of the oppressive limitations imposed by financial considerations, to say nothing of the difficulties attributable to the attitude of the Board of Regents, the University was able to move forward in several areas. Many important innovations, especially those having to do with promoting scholarship, had their origins within the faculty, but President Clothier displayed both sympathy and ingenuity in advancing such projects to fruition. Other developments, notably those relating to physical expansion, occurred almost fortuitously and represented the seizure of opportunities rather than the deliberate implementation of long-laid plans. In broad terms, perhaps the most significant achievements of these years were those that established the foundations for a genuine University program of graduate work and research.

A major landmark in the emergence of Rutgers to full university status was the creation of the Graduate Faculty in 1932. Provision had been made for graduate study as early as 1876, but until 1912, when new regulations were adopted and the ancient practice of conferring master's degrees on graduates of three year's standing was ended, only a few candidates presented themselves for advanced degrees. Thereafter, there was a slow but steady growth in numbers, at first in the College of Agriculture, then in the biological departments, and finally in the social and humanistic disciplines. In 1930, fifty-one advanced degrees were conferred, exclusive of those in the field of education. Such coordination and direction of graduate work as existed was supplied by the Committee on Graduate Work of the University Faculty, but as fields multiplied, consideration had to be given to some improvement of means of formulating and executing general policies.

The faculty at first recommended the creation of a graduate school, headed by a dean, but when it appeared that economic and organizational considerations militated against this proposal, they advanced as an alternative the formation of a graduate faculty. This plan was approved by the Trustees in June 1932. The new faculty, composed of those professors who offered graduate courses, was given full jurisdiction over graduate instruction leading to the degrees of Master of Arts, Master of Science, and Doctor of Philosophy. This action not only gave distinctive recognition to the importance now attached to graduate work at the institution but also provided an effective agency for guiding its sound development. Thurlow C. Nelson, who played the leading role in bringing the new faculty into being, served as its first chairman. At his suggestion, and because of the mounting administrative burdens associated with the graduate program, the post of Executive Secretary of the Graduate Faculty was established in 1935, and Dr. Walter C. Russell was named the first incumbent on a part-time basis. With the new organization and the conscientious guidance of Dr. Russell, graduate instruction assumed increasing stature and importance. Furthermore, the Graduate Faculty became an important force in advocating improved conditions for research, adequate recognition of scholarly achievement, and the adjustment of teaching burdens to facilitate both investigation and graduate instruction.

The trend toward an increased interest on the part of the faculty in productive scholarship was also clearly evidenced in the establishment of the Rutgers University Press. After careful study by two committees of appropriate methods to insure the publication of contributions to knowledge resulting from faculty research, a well-conceived plan was adopted early in 1936. There was to be a series of Rutgers University Studies, the monographs to be selected by a faculty committee headed by Professor Donald F. Cameron. At the same time, the Rutgers University Press was founded to publish the Studies and such other books as might be eligible. The program actually got under way a year later with Cameron and Earl S. Miers—then a member of the Department of Alumni and Public Relations—overseeing the publication of four books, all by members of the faculty. The Press was reorganized in 1938 when Miers was named manager and the former Committee on the Rutgers University Press was transformed into an advisory board. Within the succeeding year, nine titles were issued, and the Press had established itself as a flourishing institution and as a source of prestige to the University.

As attention turned toward scholarly activity, a new appreciation of the need for improving the library developed. Adequate for the purposes of undergraduate instruction, with nearly 250,000 volumes, the library was housed in a building that had long since become crowded to capacity and was handicapped by inadequate staff and a miniscule book fund. Although many years were to pass before these grave problems could be solved, they were at least given recognition by those who foresaw that the growing emphasis on graduate instruction and research would require library facilities and resources vastly larger than those available. One evidence of this new awareness was the organization in 1937 of "The Associated Friends of the Library of Rutgers University," which sponsored the publication of a journal that featured excellent articles based on library materials and generally constituted a vocal constituency in behalf of the library's needs.

There was obviously a new pattern of interests emerging within the faculty during these years, and the key to it was a heightened concern with research as a proper and necessary function of a university professor. There had always been those on the staff who were dedicated to productive scholarship, but they faced the fact that Rutgers had not as yet adopted the policy of recognizing research as a function coordinate with teaching for which explicit provision must be made in terms of time and facilities. Except at the College of Agriculture, where state and Federal funds had long been available, research was essentially an "overtime" activity, carried forward with whatever meagre equipment could be found. The faculty, through its Committee on Research, had repeatedly called attention to these unfortunate conditions ever since its inception in 1921, with little effect. There was promise, however, in the statement of the president in 1934: "Scholarly research, as well as instruction, is an essential function of the University."

In spite of discouraging handicaps, ways were found in several departments—notably in Ceramics, Chemistry, Engineering, and Biology—to carry forward modest research programs, and individual scholars in the non-scientific disciplines were also active. Especially enterprising and successful were the dozen staff members in the five biological departments who in 1936 organized the Bureau of Biological Research. Dedicated to the principle of cooperative research, the Bureau was able to augment a modest University subvention with funds from foundations and private industry to build up an extensive investigative program that complemented admirably its graduate and undergraduate curricula.

With the sudden expansion of the national defense program after 1939, university research assumed critical importance, and Rutgers, in common with other institutions, was queried by Federal agencies regarding the contributions it might make. It was at this time, early in 1940, that consideration was first given to the formation of a research council to coordinate and develop research, but no immediate action was forthcoming. Subsequently, with America's entrance into the war, a decided impetus was given to research in certain fields, with the result that an activity that had long been regarded as marginal now came to be viewed as essential. Influenced by Professor William H. Cole and others, President Clothier became an advocate of enlarged research opportunities, and in 1943 found the means to initiate a major breakthrough. Because of an abrupt decline in enrollments, a portion of the funds appropriated by the state for instruction could not be spent. With the hearty approval of the Board of Regents, $35,000 was allocated for the support of research. This action, in the words of Dr. Clothier, implied at last "a more realistic recognition of the place of research in the University's program."

The University Research Fund, as it was called, was at first administered by a special committee appointed by the president, with Dr. Walter C. Russell as chairman. Several members of the faculty were granted either leaves of absence or funds to acquire equipment in order to facilitate their studies. Almost at once the committee formulated plans for a continuing agency to promote research, and their vision led to the establishment of the Research Council in May 1944. Financed by annual state appropriations, the Research Council awarded grants to faculty members and undertook the formulation of general policies governing research activities and also worked efficiently under its able director, Dr. Cole, to stimulate interest in research in all departments of the University. In the postwar era, it was a force of inestimable importance in transforming the whole temper of the University.

While these significant steps were being taken to strengthen graduate work and research, the undergraduate programs remained virtually unchanged. With minor exceptions, such as the establishment of a special curriculum in government service in 1935, the academic arrangements that had been adopted in 1929 persisted until 1945. For reasons of economy, there was some curtailment of offerings—courses in art and Italian were eliminated for an interval after 1933—but the overall academic program was not seriously impaired. After 1934, as enrollment grew, admission standards were raised. Whereas only about one-third of the men students admitted in the early 1930's had ranked in the top quarter of their high-school classes, by the end of the decade that proportion had risen to over 50 per cent. At the College for Women the proportion was decidedly higher. Beginning in 1939 all applicants were required to take a scholastic aptitude test in order to provide additional information for the admissions officers. With considerable pride, the president was able to report in 1940 that of the 355 colleges whose students took the test, Rutgers ranked fourteenth, or in the top 5 per cent.

The most striking change at the undergraduate level was the decided shift in student interest toward practical or vocational courses of study. Between 1930 and 1940, the number of students in the College of Arts and Sciences remained nearly stationary, while the College of Agriculture increased by 250 per cent and the School of Education, the School of Chemistry, and the Department of Ceramics more than doubled. No doubt much of the expansion in the College of Agriculture was attributable to the lower tuition fees and the less rigorous admission requirement in that college. Within the College of Arts and Sciences, students turned toward such curricula as Business Administration and Journalism and away from the humanistic courses. Preoccupied with the problem of "How to Get a Job," they deliberately chose those courses that would seemingly increase their qualifications.

In contrast to the stability that marked the regular undergraduate programs, a major transformation was under way in the activities of the Extension Division. Students in increasing numbers were seeking courses of full college status, and studies revealed that many would be interested in working toward degrees on a part-time basis, both in New Brunswick and Newark. The prospects seemed to be especially promising in Newark, but there were complications as well, for both New York University and Columbia University were operating extension programs there, and the facilities available to Rutgers—in the College of Pharmacy building—were already taxed to capacity.

Various means were considered for expanding Rutgers' activities in Newark, including a daring plan to acquire control of what were then known as the "Dana group" of colleges. In 1908 Richard D. Currier had founded the New Jersey Law School as a proprietary institution, adding to it a pre-legal division, which in 1930 became Dana College, and the Seth Boyden School of Business. These schools utilized a large building owned by Currier at 40 Rector Street. After numerous conferences between the two parties, the executive committee of the Rutgers Board of Trustees approved in principle a plan to purchase the building and take over the three colleges but later rescinded this action and referred the entire matter to the full Board. Meeting in January 1933, the Trustees heard President Clothier present the pros and cons of taking the momentous step of acquiring an urban affiliate. Affirmative action would forestall the creation of a separate university in Newark which might ultimately compete with Rutgers for state funds and would enable Rutgers to seize a great educational opportunity and—not incidentally—provide facilities for the expanding Extension Division. On the other hand, there were financial hazards involved, and adverse publicity might result if Rutgers was to undertake a major new project at a time when economy was the watchword. After extended discussion, the whole matter was referred to a committee, and ultimately the plan was abandoned, not to be revived for a dozen years.

The problem of organizing and housing a part-time, evening, degree-granting program in Newark remained. The solution adopted in 1934 was to establish University College, separate from the Extension Division but with Norman C. Miller as its director. This action revived old controversies over the standards maintained in extension courses and evoked hostile criticisms from many members of the faculty and even some Trustees, who felt that the Rutgers degree would be "cheapened" if it were to be awarded for part-time, evening study. University College was authorized to grant the degree of Bachelor of Business Administration, additional facilities were acquired adjacent to the College of Pharmacy, and in 1935 over a thousand students enrolled for work toward their degrees both at Newark and in New Brunswick. Degrees were awarded to the first graduates in April 1938. The new college, whose academic standards were carefully regulated by an advisory board drawn from the older faculties until a University College faculty was organized in 1940, was a highly successful venture, enabling men and women who were fully employed during the day to acquire a college education through years of night-time attendance.

Yet another new venture, which was to redound greatly to the credit of the University, was the establishment in 1935 of the Graduate School of Banking. Sponsored by the American Bankers Association under the immediate direction of Dr. Harold Stonier, the school offered home-study courses throughout the year and an intensive two-weeks' session on the Rutgers campus each June in cooperation with the Extension Division. Candidates who successfully completed the three-year course received diplomas issued jointly by Rutgers and the Association. Two hundred bankers from thirty-five states attended the first session, and within a decade that number had multiplied several times. Among other consequences, the admirably conducted school gave Rutgers a remarkably enthusiastic body of alumni, scattered throughout the nation, that was to manifest its loyalty through many generous gifts.

While these new ventures were being launched, old problems involving the relationship of the College for Women to the rest of the University continued to demand attention. The addition of women to the Board of Trustees and the creation of the Committee on the College for Women in 1932 had given new form to the relationship but had not greatly altered the peculiarly autonomous position of the college. Loree continued to be the chairman of the committee, and the Trustees were not disposed to interfere in what was assumed to be his domain. Although major expansion in buildings and in student body had ended by 1930, the college took advantage of the ensuing decade of stability to strengthen its faculty and its academic program, raise its admission standards, and enhance its reputation as an outstanding women's college. Its jealously guarded autonomy was firmly maintained until certain crises, both financial and personal, led to changes in its special status.

The financial affairs of the college, which had been a source of apprehension to successive presidents, had reached the point of disaster by 1936. The University Trustees were accountable for a mortgage indebtedness of slightly over one million dollars, which had been incurred in the erection of dormitory facilities. Now the mortgages were maturing at the rate of $50,000 a year, and—in part because of the decline in income at the college resulting from the effects of the depression—there were no funds on hand to meet the payments. Consequently, the Trustees were obliged to borrow money, thereby increasing their indebtedness. This situation could not continue indefinitely, and in 1937 a series of actions were taken to cope with the crisis. The bulk of the mortgage indebtedness was refinanced on favorable terms with a $600,000 loan from an insurance company. More important, the University comptroller assumed full control of the finances at the College for Women and immediately instituted various economy measures.

Having by these actions lost its cherished financial autonomy, the college soon experienced further losses. Leonor F. Loree, now in his eightieth year, after nearly two decades of unique and effective service, found it necessary early in 1938 to resign his position as member and chairman of the Committee on the College for Women. His resignation was the occasion for a wholesale redefinition of the powers of the committee. Henceforth, the president was to serve as chairman, and the committee's authority over property and funds and non-academic personnel was rescinded. Although the implications of these revisions were not at once fully apparent, it was clear that the University, through the president and the Trustees, would be in full control of all matters relating to finances, buildings, and clerical employees.

Understandably, these radical revisions in the status of the College for Women were productive of internal tensions and differences in interpretation over policies and procedures. A major crisis erupted in 1940 when the Committee on the College for Women and the Committee on Buildings and Grounds clashed over the issue of which body was responsible for developing plans for a new library at the college. Dean Corwin took the occasion to address a lengthy letter to President Clothier, reciting the many difficulties she encountered under the existing set-up and requesting that a special committee be appointed to review and clarify the relationship of the college to the University. Dr. Clothier acquiesced and named a fourteen-member committee, headed by Philip M. Brett, which held several meetings over a period of nearly two years.

In essence, the champions of the College for Women expressed resentment at the manner in which control over buildings and grounds, business management, and finances had been assumed by the comptroller and certain Trustee committees. In its final report, the special committee sought to clarify the status of the College for Women: "It is part of the University and is coordinate with the men's colleges of the University, all of them together comprising the University." It added, however, that "the College has and should continue to have discretion over its own internal affairs consistent with University policy." In the interest of clarifying procedures and reducing friction, several revisions were made in the University regulations. It was specified that the various Trustees' committees, when dealing with matters affecting the College for Women, must consult with the Committee on the College for Women, and the position of certain administrative officers who reported both to the dean of the College and to University officials was redefined. The significant point, however, was that the actions that had been taken in 1937 and 1938, limiting the autonomy of the college, were reaffirmed. The college was to retain considerable independence with respect to the management of its internal affairs, but its actions must accord with general University policy, especially with regard to matters related to property and finance.

Although the times were not propitious for the realization of great plans, those who constituted the University—the president, the Trustees, the faculty, the students, the alumni—seemed constantly desirous of pressing forward wherever resources and ingenuity permitted. Once the initial impact of economic adversity had been dealt with—in 1932 and 1933—efforts were directed not merely toward recouping the losses that had been suffered but to improving, developing, and expanding the University. The results of these efforts could be seen in an enlarged student body, improved conditions for graduate study and research, broadened educational services, and strengthened internal organization. Even in the realm of physical expansion, where for many years the prospect seemed utterly hopeless, opportunities suddenly presented themselves and gratifying progress was made.

For many years the University authorities had been acutely aware of the deficiency of adequate space for outdoor athletic activities. No vacant areas were available near the main campus, and although the studies of Harland Bartholomew had suggested that the only feasible course would be to acquire acreage across the river, no steps had been taken to implement this plan because of financial considerations and the unavailability of a desirable tract. Suddenly, late in 1934, a new situation presented itself. The president informed a special session of the Board of Trustees that 256 acres—120 of which comprised the nine-hole golf course of the defunct New Brunswick Golf Club—could be obtained for about ninety-three thousand dollars. Located on River Road less than a mile from the main campus, the area could be developed, possibly with the assistance of Federal funds, to provide several playing fields. The president also foresaw that at some time in the future the site might become the main undergraduate campus of the University, with professional schools taking over the old campus. It was, in the circumstances of the times, a daring enterprise, but the Trustees responded affirmatively, and the purchase was made.

Over the course of the next several months imaginative plans were formulated for transforming thirty acres of the new area into a vast athletic plant. George E. Little, Director of Athletics, devoted himself to this project with great energy and foresight, and the eventual success of the enterprise owed much to his determination and oversight. Meanwhile, negotiations were under way with officials of the Works Progress Administration, which culminated in November 1935 in the announcement of a grant of $321,000. Soon nearly four hundred men were at work, grading and constructing twelve athletic fields and making a huge excavation that was intended to be the site of a stadium, if funds should ever become available. The relationship between the University and the state W.P.A. officials was cordial. President Clothier confided to the Trustees in October 1936 that the agency wished to complete the project and would recommend to Washington an additional allocation of $413,000 to build the stadium if the University would contribute about one-quarter of that amount for materials. Again the Trustees were venturesome, and in due course the second phase of the huge project was under way. Eventually the total cost came to nearly $1,300,000, of which about one-fifth was supplied by the University. On November 5, 1938, when the stadium was formally dedicated on the occasion of the football victory over Princeton, Rutgers could take pride in a splendid athletic complex, well planned to combine beauty with utility. And looking further to the future, vast acreage remained available as a possible site for a new University campus.

The prospect of Federal funds for the construction of other desperately needed University buildings seemed bright late in 1934 when, at the request of the Public Works Administration, a list of projects totalling $5,000,000 was prepared. Subsequently, this proposal was scaled down to $2,000,000, and included a biology building, an addition to the Voorhees Library, a soil science building, an agricultural control laboratory, and a library for the College for Women. Under the terms of the

Federal program, 45 per cent of the funds would be available as an outright grant; the remainder would be in the form of a loan at 4 per cent interest, subject to amortization in twenty-five years. In presenting this proposition to the Trustees, the president especially stressed the need for a biology building to replace the inadequate and antiquated New Jersey Hall, pointing out that the total costs involved would amount to less than $20,000 a year. The Trustees agreed that the building was essential, but they were reluctant to increase the already considerable indebtedness of the University unless some means were in sight to underwrite the carrying charges. Efforts both to secure such private underwriting and to induce the Federal Government to grant 100 per cent of the cost met with failure, and thus the opportunity to launch a large building program was allowed to pass.

As a poor alternative, the president induced the Trustees to purchase the Ricketts Building, a factory structure with eighteen acres of land adjacent to the campus of the College of Agriculture. It was available at a modest price, and it could be financed on a mortgage basis. The acquisition of this less-than-ideal building made it possible to relieve the overcrowding in New Jersey Hall by moving the State Chemist and the Department of Entomology there, together with other departments of the College of Agriculture. The purchase of several former residences along College Avenue and their conversion to academic purposes was also undertaken during these years.

With the marked increase in enrollments in the late 1930's, the long-recognized deficiencies in classroom and laboratory space became more critical than ever. Engineering, which had acquired sudden popularity, was especially hard pressed. After weighing various possibilities, it was decided that the most economical solution to the problem would be to construct a large, three-story wing at the rear of the old Engineering Building, with the cost of labor on the project to be met by the Works Progress Administration. Work was begun in 1939 and completed two years later, and although the addition was not destined to meet the long-range needs of the College of Engineering, it almost doubled the space available and therefore represented a decided improvement in the immediate situation.

In addition to the stadium complex and the Engineering Annex, the University benefitted in a modest degree from other Federal relief projects. As early as 1934, under the Civil Works Administration, scores of men were put to work repairing buildings, improving lands, and building roads at the College of Agriculture. In 1936 Neilson Campus was transformed and beautified immeasurably by a well-directed Works Progress Administration project. For many years W.P.A. personnel carried on projects in the library, cataloguing, repairing, and binding books and pamphlets, and in several other departments as well. In retrospect, the University may be charged with having failed to take the maximum advantage of Federal programs, especially to acquire more buildings. Had private donors, or the state legislature, come forward with the requisite matching funds, much might have been accomplished. But already overburdened with debt, the Trustees followed a course that fell somewhere between prudence and conservatism, and after their commitment to the River Road development, they were extremely cautious about further ventures.

Throughout these uncertain and difficult years, the question of the ultimate identity of the University remained unresolved. At the outset of his administration, President Clothier had set forth the goal of a Rutgers so strengthened through private endowments that it could, while retaining a cooperative relationship with the state, control its own destiny. For eight years this concept exerted a dominant influence on University policy. The failure of the state to provide the means for implementing President Thomas' vision of a state university seemingly left no other alternative, and the new administration immediately set in motion programs designed to bolster the private character of Rutgers.

Because the alumni would be expected to play a large part in realizing the new vision, special efforts were made to enlist their interest and support. In 1933 the Department of Alumni and Public Relations was created, bringing the direction of alumni affairs under an officer of the University administration. Earl Reed Silvers, who had long been Director of Public Information, headed the new agency, with Ernest E. McMahon, 1930, in charge of alumni activities. Working through the Alumni Council and the Alumni Association, new clubs were established and old ones were reinvigorated, a homecoming day was instituted, class reunions were vigorously promoted, and considerable stress was placed on a program designed to attract promising secondary school students to Rutgers. The *Alumni Monthly*, reduced in size because of financial stringency, was brilliantly edited for several years by Earl S. Miers, 1933, and by emphasizing alumni achievements, stories of the "old" Rutgers, athletic triumphs, and improvements under way on the campus—and giving little attention to state relations—it served to strengthen the alumni's image of a "private" Rutgers.

In a related move, the Rutgers Alumni Fund Council was established in 1934 to place the function of securing annual contributions from alumni on a broader and more effective basis than formerly. Although initial apathy and the effects of the depression proved to be early handicaps, the Fund grew steadily in numbers of contributors and financial returns over the years and constituted a tangible link between individual alumni and their university. Another innovation was the authorization in 1934 of the Rutgers University Award, an honor to be conferred on alumni and others who had distinguished themselves in service to the University.

These measures were regarded as secondary to the principal aim of increasing the University's endowment, which in 1933 amounted to about four and a half million. President Clothier believed that $35,000,000 should be the goal over a period of twenty-five years if Rutgers was to assume a commanding position in its partnership with the state. But he urged on the recently constituted Endowment Committee of the Trustees, headed by Philip M. Brett, an immediate objective of $10,000,000 within ten years. Because of poor economic conditions, the Endowment Committee was averse to undertaking at once a general campaign. Instead, meetings were held with lawyers who were friendly to the University to lay the groundwork for encouraging future bequests, and plans were made to cultivate potential benefactors.

By 1936, when the endowment had shrunk to $4,000,000, and the University's indebtedness totalled nearly half that amount, the president made an eloquent plea to the Trustees to launch a determined fund-raising effort. In response to his specific requests, the board officially resolved to try to raise $10,000,000 in ten years and to appoint an executive secretary—J. Harold Johnston, 1920—to assist the Endowment Committee. Despite the urgings of Dr. Clothier, voiced at almost every meeting, the Trustees seemed unable to produce any results. The next step, taken in 1938, was to engage the firm of John Price Jones to study the situation and suggest how it might be dealt with.

In its report, the Jones organization gave the opinion that at the heart of the difficulty lay a familiar dilemma. "Because of the conflict of the state university idea with the ideals of the older Rutgers," they found, "the Board of Trustees has been unable to reach a clear-cut definition of Rutgers' course. The consequent confusion of purpose has handicapped the administration, particularly in developing Rutgers as an endowed University." It was their contention that Rutgers "must perform the functions of an endowed university as well as those of a state university. It must enter into a partnership with the State to serve its community, and it should glory in that partnership." Recommending that the University should boldly chart what it termed "The Rutgers Plan," the report suggested that an immediate campaign be undertaken to raise funds for four buildings and that plans be developed to secure $25,000,000 by 1966. The report met a chill response when it was presented to a Trustee group. "Why do we need these outsiders to tell us how to run our affairs," one Trustee exploded. This remark set the tone of the discussion, and produced no agreement on a course of action. The endowment drive limped along, never really getting off the ground.

Even with the stimulus of the 175th anniversary observance in 1941, an attempt to raise $500,000 produced only one third of that amount. Dr. Clothier was by temperament averse to asking for contributions, and no one among the Trustees could supply the energy needed to direct a successful campaign.

It was somehow appropriate that during these financially barren years the single major benefaction should have represented the final act of complete dedication of a man whose forebears had been associated with the College almost from its inception and who himself had served as a Trustee for fifty-one years. James Neilson, 1866, whose numerous gifts of land to Rutgers have been noted frequently and who was so instrumental in the development of the College of Agriculture, the Experiment Station, and the College for Women, died on February 19, 1937, and except for some specific bequests left his entire estate to the University. Included were valuable tracts of land and his beautiful home, "Woodlawn," which became a gracious meeting place for many years under the custody of the Associate Alumnae. A patrician of singular individuality, often at the center of controversies, Jimmie Neilson was a man about whom legends clustered, but in his complete identification with Rutgers he had few peers.

By 1940 Dr. Clothier was prepared to abandon his early vision of a richly endowed Rutgers in control of its own destiny. In an extremely significant confidential memorandum to the Trustees that August, he reflected on the experience of eight years in office and acknowledged that his thinking had changed.

> We have felt for years [he explained] that the panacea for all our troubles would be the creation of an endowment so large that the yield would free us from so great reliance on state appropriations. This would mean an endowment of some $30,000,000. It is not so clear now that this would be an unmixed blessing. Certainly we would accept it with alacrity if some wealthy angel should provide it, but there are signs that the university or college depending solely upon student fees and upon yields from endowments is going to face troublous years and that those which have some measure of governmental support will enjoy relative security (if that word has any meaning at all these days).

As subsequent developments were to make clear, this statement heralded a reappraisal of Rutgers' future relationship to the state and the virtual abandonment of the concept of a Rutgers "liberated" from dependence on the state.

More lay behind this statement than discouragement over fund-raising efforts. After many years of strained or distant relations, a new spirit of harmony and cooperation was observable in the dealings between the University and the Board of Regents. So long as the Regents persisted in their plans for a "University of New Jersey" and the Trustees responded by standing pat on the existing contractual relationship, there seemed to be little possibility for a genuine mutual effort to arrive at an agreement that would advance the cause of public higher education in New Jersey. This impasse began to give way in December 1939, when Dr. Clothier met with two of the Regents, who explained in some detail the resentment they and their associates felt because of what was characterized as the "uncooperative" attitude of the University. It was explained that the Regents wanted "to see something worked out gradually, through which Rutgers would be installed at the top of a pyramid of the educational machinery in the State of New Jersey, and that . . . [they had] no thought whatever of depriving the Trustees of their sovereignty in the administration of the University's affairs." The frank discussion seemed to clear the air. It also produced an understanding that there would be further discussions between representatives of the Regents and the University in an effort to discover some plan for attaining common objectives.

Such conferences were held, and those involved gave detailed study in particular to the application of a plan that would place Rutgers in a position analogous to that held by Cornell University in the New York system of higher education. The more searching this study became, the more it revealed that the situations were not, in fact, analogous. Meanwhile, the discussions were broadened to include the whole future scope of public higher education in New Jersey. For more than two years they proceeded amicably and in good faith. In concrete terms, they did not lead to the formulation of any new blueprints for the future, but they did produce in the Regents the conviction that the University was performing a splendid service to the state and a complete change in their attitude toward the institution.

This radically altered posture was revealed in the Regents' annual report, issued in April 1942. Extolling the great contributions that Rutgers was making, at small cost to the state, the Regents swept aside their own frequently reiterated plans for a reorganization of public higher education "in view of the greatly changed conditions which have developed since these suggestions were made." Now, the report announced, "your Board feels that the State's interest would be well served for the years ahead, both efficiently and economically, by continuing its existing relationship with Rutgers, at least until more definite clarification of its interests appears justified." Even more surprising, the

Regents declared that the state should provide capital funds for buildings at Rutgers, a policy they had strongly opposed since their inception.

At this juncture then, just as the University was to commit all its resources to the support of the nation's war effort, the long stalemate with the state seemed to have ended. Beyond the failure of the endowment hopes and the cordial understandings that developed from the frequent conferences between the Regents and the University, other influences had contributed to the new accord. The state scholarship program, which commanded wide support and approval, strengthened the image of Rutgers as the state university. The improved fiscal position of the state after 1937 revived the prospects of generous appropriations. Beginning in 1938, partly spurred by concern about the "Free State University" movement, the University had placed increased emphasis on cultivating good relations with legislators and other public officials. Moreover, consideration of how the pressing needs for new buildings, increases in faculty salaries, and a comprehensive pension system for staff members could be met all pointed to the conclusion that more public funds were indispensable. In sum, those responsible for directing University policy now saw that the future of Rutgers depended on strengthening the partnership with the state rather than on securing vast endowments; as this concept emerged, it stimulated a new course of action.

Although the full significance of the occasion could not be grasped at the time, the University paused at this crucial moment in its history to observe the 175th anniversary of its founding. In 1941, on the verge of World War II, Rutgers was also in the throes of transition from an old role to a new. Because of the critical temper of the times and in keeping with the University's growing commitment to scholarly excellence, historical pageantry and festive celebration were laid aside in favor of a year-long program of serious intellectual discussion. A series of student convocations featured lectures by distinguished authorities in varied fields. In October, the observance was climaxed by two days of symposia addressed by leading scholars from the humanities, social sciences, and sciences and attended by representatives of scores of universities and learned societies. Certainly the emotional climax of the proceedings was the conferral of an honorary degree on Queen Wilhelmina of the Netherlands, who, speaking to the assemblage by radio from her place of refuge in London, made vivid to all the terror of the war that had brought her nation under the yoke of tyranny.

Notable though the symposia were for their diverse contributions to learning and their exemplification of the virtues of freedom of inquiry, the predominant theme that was stressed by speaker after speaker, reflecting the tragic concerns of the times, was the need to revive and strengthen moral values.

> In summary [recorded an unusually astute commentator] these educators were facing the fact that this mechanized accelerated materialism has already undermined some of the virtues of a more rugged day, softened and weakened the moral fiber and destroyed the dynamic of faith. They were appealing to the academic world to turn once more to inspiration and discipline as the chief instruments to cultivate the strength and will which this and succeeding generations will need if they are to preserve the possibility of intellectual freedom and progress.

Now the war would intervene, but when peace returned, this theme would inspire an attempt to reorient American higher education.

Within two months of the anniversary observance the attack on Pearl Harbor brought America into the war, ending a dreadful period of suspense and projecting the University on an uncertain course. For more than two years the war in Europe had ever more insistently intruded upon the campus. At first, strongly under the spell of the anti-war phobia of the 1930's, faculty and students viewed the conflict as remote from American concern, supporting neutrality policies that were supposed to insulate this nation against becoming involved. Then, following the fall of France, as Governmental policy shifted toward providing assistance to beleaguered England and her allies, the campus was caught up in the violent debate between isolationists and interventionists. Even as late as June 1941, although the students strongly favored an Allied victory and supported the "measures short of war" that were then being taken, they remained overwhelmingly opposed to American entry into the war.

To President Clothier, who viewed the conflict as "a revolution in human affairs comparable with the extinguishment of the Roman Empire," the prevailing cynicism among the undergraduates was a matter of concern. "We all dread the thought of war," he was saying in mid-1941, "but there comes a time in the life of every nation, as in the life of every man, when we must be willing to fight for those things in which one believes." When the University Council convened in December 1940 to discuss "Rutgers and the National Defense," several speakers expressed alarm at the apathy and indifference that prevailed on the campus. There was one suggestion that a special course in National Defense should be developed and another that the president should address all the faculty meetings "in order to arouse the active thought of all faculty members and to encourage them to use every effort to direct the thinking of their students along sound lines." Whatever divisions of opinion there were, they disappeared on December 7, and the entire University community accepted the zealous and vigorous leadership of President Clothier in devoting every resource to the nation's service.

Already there were many signs that the University was being caught up in the national emergency. One of the first was the establishment in September 1939 of a unit of the Civil Pilot Training Program, which provided basic flying instruction to nearly two hundred students, many of whom proceeded directly into military service. As the Army began to expand, increasing numbers of R.O.T.C. graduates accepted commissions and went on active service. On October 16, 1940—Registration Day—334 students registered in the Gymnasium under the recently enacted Selective Service law. To meet the rising demand for skilled personnel in New Jersey's booming defense industries, the College of Engineering, in association with the Extension Division, launched in January 1941 the vast government-financed Engineering Defense Training Program. Another sign of the approaching crisis was the decline in male enrollment by about 8 per cent when the new academic year opened in September 1941. The signs were there, but few read them so perceptively as Dr. Clothier, who foresaw with remarkable clarity the role that the University would have to play, at first in the defense program and then in the total war effort.

When at last war became a reality, immediate measures were taken to place the University in a position to meet any eventuality. Dr. Clothier addressed each of the classes in chapel, urging upon them a calm attitude rather than hasty or impulsive actions, and the same message was communicated by faculty members in their classrooms. Regulations were quickly adopted to assure that students who were called into service should receive credit for work they had begun or, if they were in their final term, that they should receive their diplomas. A defense council was organized to safeguard University property in the event of an emergency, another committee undertook to handle problems connected with requests for deferment from the draft, and the Bureau of Personnel and Placement assumed responsibility for advising students about alternative service opportunities. Plans were made to alter the regular curriculum by introducing certain courses, chiefly of a technical nature, that would be of direct usefulness in war service. The second term was shortened by five weeks and an expanded summer session, in which the faculty volunteered to teach without compensation, was scheduled in order that students might be able to graduate in three years. With a view to the demands of military service, a compulsory physical education program, rigorous in its standards, was instituted. Having taken these steps, the Rutgers authorities then looked to Washington for further guidance, still unsure what policies would govern the wartime role of American universities.

Along with other university presidents, Dr. Clothier journeyed to Washington in January 1942 to attend a conference that cast little light on this grave question. Months went by, during which the University adhered substantially to the normal routines. Finally, in May 1942, the situation seemingly was clarified when both the Navy and the Army announced their reserve programs, which held out the prospect that students who enlisted in the programs would be able to continue their education. When the new college year began in September 1942, the upper classes had lost more than a quarter of their members, but the largest Freshman class in history kept total enrollments near peak level. Suddenly the whole scene altered. The Selective Service Act was amended in November to make eighteen- and nineteen-year-olds eligible, and it was announced that those in the enlisted reserve program would be called into service. In the second term withdrawals proceeded at an accelerated rate, until by May there were fewer than 800 civilian undergraduates remaining in the men's colleges, about half the number that had started the year. The decline continued in the two succeeding years, reaching a low point of 516—most of them underclassmen—in 1944–45. National policy decreed that college students, with rare exceptions for those in certain technical and scientific fields, would not be permitted to complete their education as civilians; instead, the military would make limited use of the universities to provide special training for men who had been inducted into service.

For a time, early in 1943, it appeared that the University would lose most of its civilian students, and plans were made to reduce the staff in proportion. But, again, there was a sudden change. The Army Specialized Training Program was announced, Rutgers was selected as one of the pilot schools, and in March the first contingent of several hundred A.S.T.P. trainees began to arrive. Selected on the basis of tests and educational background from Army enlisted personnel, these men were to receive basic and advanced training in civil, mechanical, electrical, and sanitary engineering or advanced training in foreign area and language studies. Later pre-medical and pre-dental groups were added. With little time for adequate planning, the University had to adapt its personnel and facilities to these new assignments. By the fall of 1943, with over 1,300 A.S.T.P. students in residence, the men's colleges had the heaviest enrollments in their history—1,855. Then, as final preparations were made for the assault on Europe and manpower requirements changed, all but a fraction of the trainees were withdrawn from the campus. The program did not terminate until December 1945, but after

April 1944 it was of minor importance, except to the College of Engineering.

Meanwhile, in August 1943, the Army Specialized Training Reserve Program was inaugurated. High-school graduates who had not attained the age of eighteen were eligible to enroll and continue their education at the college level in a uniform program of studies pending their induction into the Army. The first of these reservists arrived in January 1944, and by early 1945 there were over four hundred attending classes in English, history, geography, mathematics, and science. This program was continued until March 1946. Altogether Rutgers provided training for 3,877 men in the A.S.T.P. and A.S.T.R.P

As male civilian enrollments plummeted and constantly shifting programs for military personnel were introduced, the University was compelled to revise its entire mode of operation. In April 1943, in order to adapt to the A.S.T.P. routine, all of the men's colleges went on a schedule of four twelve-week terms. The regular curricula were largely set aside and replaced with two standardized basic curricula for entering students. The dwindling numbers of upperclassmen were hard pressed to find courses and of necessity many attended classes at the College for Women. New students entered at the start of any of the four terms, and, beginning in January 1943, diplomas were awarded to graduates whenever they had completed their requirements. As conditions altered from month to month, regulations were revised or interpreted liberally to meet the exigencies of the moment.

Almost every vestige of normal undergraduate life disappeared from the campus. By the end of 1943 virtually all student organizations, including the Student Council, had been disbanded for the duration and even *Targum*, which had been published continuously since 1869, went into eclipse in February 1944, after a dispute over editorial policies. All but a handful of the fraternities suspended operations, and several of the houses were taken over to provide accommodations for the Army trainees, who at the peak enrollment occupied all of the dormitories as well. The Gymnasium was converted into a mess hall. The athletic program survived only on an extremely limited basis, and intercollegiate competition was confined chiefly to contests with nearby colleges and military installations in football, basketball, baseball, track, and swimming. The four-term system, together with heavy class schedules, afforded little opportunity for extracurricular activities. Moreover, many civilian students devoted such spare time as they found to working part-time in local war industries or in various volunteer services.

For the faculty the war years brought insecurity, unfamiliar burdens, and bewilderment, along with an often-frustrated eagerness to make a positive contribution to the nation's war effort. Within a year over fifty members of the teaching and administrative staff had entered military service, and others left to take posts with civilian war agencies. In many instances those who remained on campus added to their own assignments the duties of those who had departed. Because the University authorities never knew how many students there would be even a month or two ahead, or what courses of study they would be pursuing, teaching assignments changed constantly, as did staff requirements. At almost any time, there might be mass dismissals. In the late spring of 1944, following the withdrawal of most of the A.S.T.P. cadre, there was a moment of near panic when it seemed that all of the instructors and assistant professors—and some of the senior staff as well—would be without employment. Although many were let go before the crisis passed, others were held on by being assigned to non-teaching duties, and shortly the increase in A.S.T.R.P. students and a trickle of returning veterans turned the tide.

Because the wartime academic program stressed particular fields, many men found themselves in unfamiliar disciplines; historians, botanists, or classicists struggled with classes in mathematics, mechanical drawing, and navigation. As an example of fluctuating requirements, there were seventeen instructors teaching mathematics in the fall of 1943; by the spring of 1944 there were but four. The Economics Department, which numbered twelve men in 1941 and carried the largest teaching load in the College, was reduced by 1944 to three men, one of whom taught in other fields. Hardest hit of all were the humanities, which had little place in the war-oriented curricula and which all but disappeared from the list of courses. Along with their academic duties, most faculty members gave liberally of their time to service as members of civil defense units and similar agencies, and some worked at night in nearby war industries.

The services of the University were not confined to undergraduate training programs. Through the Engineering, Science and Management War Training Program (E.S.M.W.T.), conducted by the College of Engineering with staff drawn largely from the Extension Division, college-level courses designed to enhance the effectiveness of engineering, scientific, and management personnel in New Jersey's war industries were offered beginning in January 1941. During the four and one-half years the program was in operation, over 90,000 men and women from more than 1,500 industries received training in every part of the state. The fourth largest program of its kind in the nation, this enterprise owed much of its success to the accumulated experience of the Extension Division and especially to Professor Maurice A. Chaffee and his associates.

The College of Agriculture and the Experiment Station directed their energies toward encouraging the farmers of New Jersey to increase the production of agricultural commodities. Through the Extension Service, and particularly the County Agents, farmers were furnished with information on crop needs, aided in meeting critical manpower requirements, and advised on the solution of specific problems. The agricultural staff also played a leading role in promoting food conservation and in spurring the planting of "Victory Gardens." In the latter effort, Professor Charles H. Nissley's useful book, *Home Vegetable Gardening,* attained the status of a best seller.

The exigencies of the war permitted little opportunity for research in most fields, but in a few areas significant projects were carried forward. Members of the Bureau of Biological Research, for example, made important studies on the diagnosis and prevention of traumatic shock. Investigators at the College of Agriculture worked on problems involving the fouling of ships' bottoms at the request of the Navy Department and developed mosquito repellents for the use of the armed forces. In the College of Engineering a highly secret project in electrical engineering was conducted with staff recruited in part from other universities. In addition, many University scientists served as consultants in aiding war industries to solve technical problems. Unquestionably, the importance attached to research during these war years elevated that function to a new level of acceptance within the University.

Although outwardly the College for Women seemed to be little affected by war conditions, for its enrollment remained stable and the regular academic schedule was maintained, in actuality it was very much involved. A highly effective War Service Committee mobilized students and faculty for participation in fund appeals and for volunteer service in a host of community projects. A program of non-credit courses in such subjects as engineering drawing, nutrition, and radio and auto mechanics met an enthusiastic response. In addition, there were added to the regular curriculum courses in German, French, and Spanish for translators and censors, in laboratory techniques, and in surveying and mapping. The students also enrolled in courses that would enable them to qualify as U.S.O. hostesses, in Red Cross training courses, and in courses to prepare them for work in occupational therapy. Instead of the conventional social activities, the young women eagerly devoted their time to wrapping bandages, knitting sweaters, and packing gift boxes for veterans' hospitals, while faculty members served as air raid wardens, ration board members, Red Cross workers, and nurses aides. So zealous and effective was the participation of the college in war projects as to win high commendation from the American Council on Education.

The real impact of the war on the University, of course, can never be understood in terms of disrupted routines, radical new undertakings, or even large educational accomplishments. Its impact was intensely emotional, for it touched everyone with the agony of death and the fervor of sacrifice. The entire University community in February 1942 shared with President and Mrs. Clothier their sorrow and shock at the death of their son while in training as an Air Cadet. Soon every issue of the *Alumni Monthly* added to the sense of grief and incredulity as it reported the deaths of intimate friends, fellow classmates, former students, admired heroes. One remembered young Frank J. Holden, 1939, a fellow townsman, killed in the attack on Pearl Harbor; the gallant and virile Parker Staples, 1939, the victim of a Japanese bomb off the Solomon Islands; the Reverend Clark V. Poling, 1933, who perished with his fellow chaplains in the Atlantic; and scores of others who were not merely names on a casualty list but vivid personalities. One read of the heroic exploits of Rutgers men in every theatre of operations; mingled with the feelings of pride went the prayer that they might survive and return. Even the fact that so much of the news of the war came through Rutgers correspondents—Martin Agronsky, 1936, with his terse reports radioed from every scene of action, Clark Lee, 1929, reporting the fall of the Philippines, F. Raymond Daniell, 1924, with his *New York Times* dispatches on the bombing attacks on England—gave each disaster, each triumph, a special relevance.

Meaningless though the bare statistics are in communicating a sense of the involvement of the University, through its men and women, in the holocaust, they must be recorded. Altogether, 5,888 Rutgers men—1,700 of them undergraduates whose college careers were interrupted—served in the armed forces, approximately 36 per cent of the total living alumni body. In addition, 173 women, alumnae, or students of the College for Women entered military service. Inscribed in the Service Book in Kirkpatrick Chapel are the names of 234 men and two women who gave their lives in the line of duty. In fitting tribute to them, Gold Star scholarships were established by the Alumni Association, to be awarded to the sons and daughters of all graduates who died in service. As in the first World War, undergraduates and alumni in service were kept informed of developments on the campus and of the activities of other Rutgers men around the world through the conscientious efforts of the Alumni Office and the specially created office of the Secretary of Undergraduates on Leave. To judge from the response, in the form of thousands of letters from men in every camp and combat area, the tie to their alma mater was a meaningful one, and their correspondence, together with the brilliant reports in the *Alumni Monthly* by Earl S. Miers on the war as seen from the campus, constitute the truest and most vivid history of Rutgers in the war years.

In almost every sense the war represented a disaster for the University. Its students, and many of its staff, were scattered to every corner of the globe. Its academic program, built up over the course of decades, was changed beyond recognition. The traditional humanistic values that gave it meaning were discarded in favor of courses designed to give men the technical training needed to win a war. Freedom of inquiry became irrelevant when the practical task of survival assumed uppermost importance. Whether wiser policies might have inflicted less damage on the universities in this time of national crisis can, no doubt, be debated. Fortunately, the damages proved not to be irreparable. Fortunately, too, the ultimate victory, to which Rutgers and all other institutions of higher education had contributed so much in terms of men and knowledge, more than redeemed the losses that had been incurred.

What is perhaps most remarkable about the war experience is that while the University was struggling to cope with disaster, it was at the same time confidently planning for the future. Looking far beyond the troubled present, administrators and faculty committees were never more energetic or more imaginative in developing plans that were to eventuate after 1945 in the complete transformation of Rutgers. The war, then, was to bring a sharp break with the past, but the break was not the sterile interlude of a disaster. It was rather the result of well-conceived decisions arrived at during a period when change was easy to contemplate and when thought about the meaning of the war's sacrifices spurred positive action toward large goals.

Chapter Eleven

Instrumentality of the State

As the war entered its final stage, with the promise of a victorious peace seemingly assured, the American people were conscious—even determined—that a different and better world must follow the holocaust. There was to be no return to the ill-fated policies and attitudes of the prewar generation; rather, a brave new world, united in peace and inspired by a common concern for the welfare of all men, was envisioned. Long before the firing had ceased, a host of Governmental planning groups were at work, initiating the studies that would eventuate in the United Nations, the Fair Deal, and even in daring proposals for a vast expansion of American higher education. State and private agencies similarly sought to chart new paths to the future; the urge to break with the past was widespread and genuine. Shortly, however, the atmosphere changed. Confidence and hope were replaced by frustration and fear. The "iron curtain" descended, the Cold War raged, China came securely under Communist control, and the awful terror of nuclear destruction threatened the extinction of civilization. Finally, the nation found itself enmeshed in a costly conflict in Korea. At home, bewilderment and despair gave rise to the ugly phenomenon of McCarthyism.

It was in this tumultuous and uncertain environment that the University was to seek its proper role in the postwar decade. More than ever before, remote external influences were to affect its course profoundly from year to year. But the jarring events that lay ahead could scarcely be foreseen when, in the midst of war, ambitious plans were made for the years ahead. Rather, there loomed the immediate task of providing for the returning veterans and at the same time strengthening the University both internally and in its relationship to the state in order that it might increase its usefulness and enhance its stature.

No problem seemed to be more urgent than that of clarifying the status of Rutgers as a state university. Although after 1942 relations with the Board of Regents were harmonious, they gave no promise of becoming productive, for the Regents did not possess the confidence of the legislature. Moreover, the doubts that the Regents had cast upon the existing status of Rutgers would presumably have to be removed by instituting some alternative plan. The University was also concerned about the perennial threat posed by the League for a Free State University and by the move on the part of private colleges in the state to share in the state scholarship program. Most of all, it wanted the assurance of increased and continuing support for all units of the University and freedom from the restrictive types of control imposed on it by the Board of Regents. As President Clothier phrased it, Rutgers would favor an arrangement that would "free the University from its present shackles and enable it to develop progressively as a great state university with a broad program serving all the people of the state."

A peculiarly favorable opportunity for securing such an arrangement arose late in 1943 when Governor Walter E. Edge set in motion plans to reorganize the executive departments of the state government in conjunction with his effort to obtain a new constitution for the state. Russell E. Watson, an alumnus and prominent attorney who enjoyed a confidential relationship with Governor Edge and who was deeply involved with the movement for constitutional revision, was the first to perceive the opportunity. If there was to be a reorganization of the Department of Education, there might at the same time be a redefinition of the relationship of Rutgers to the state. After discussions with administrative officials and leading Trustees in December 1943, Watson was retained to advise the University on the course that it should follow, and he was to be the key figure in the subsequent developments, ably assisted by the Secretary of the University, Albert E. Meder.

Progress was rapid after March 1, 1944, when the University accepted the invitation of the Governor's Commission on State Administrative Reorganization to prepare a comprehensive plan for the reorganization of the state's educational structure. Watson and his associates at the University at once secured the collaboration of the presidents of the Board of Regents and the State Board of Education and the Commissioner of Education. Within a few weeks broad agreement was reached not only on a series of proposals designed to strengthen the central authority of the Department of Education but also on a new status for Rutgers. By April three bills had been drafted for submission to the legislature, and the Rutgers Trustees had given their approval to the proposals. Because the legislature was nearing adjournment, it was understood that no action would be taken until January 1945; in the meantime there would be an opportunity for public discussion of the measures.

The problems that confronted Watson and his associates were delicate ones. The University wanted to solidify its position as an instrumentality of the state and thereby obtain increased public support, but it did not want to be "shackled" by the Board of Regents or any other state agency. The original proposal advanced by the Rutgers authorities was that full control over the University should be vested in the Board of Trustees, to which additional public members would be added, and that the Board should deal directly with the governor and the legislature on a contractual basis. But there was strong support outside the University for a plan that would consolidate responsibility for all public education in the State Board of Education and place Rutgers under the authority of that agency. Ultimately, after the bills had gone through many drafts, a compromise was reached, whereby Rutgers was, in effect, given a status coordinate with the State Board of Education. It was neither to be directly subordinate to the State Board nor was it to enjoy complete independence.

The legislation in its final form declared that the several units of Rutgers were to be "collectively designated as the State University of New Jersey to be utilized as an instrumentality of the State for providing public higher education and thereby to increase the efficiency of the public school system of the State." In accepting this designation, the Trustees were to recognize that the property and educational facilities under their control were "impressed with a public trust for higher education of the people of the State." Four state officials—the speaker of the assembly, the comptroller, the treasurer, and the commissioner of taxation and finance were to become, ex officio, members of the Board of Trustees, and there were also to be added five public Trustees, appointed by the governor for five-year terms. The state was to appropriate "just and reasonable sums" annually to compensate the University for its services, and this compensation was to be made on the basis of an annual written contract "executed by the State Board of Education in behalf of the State of New Jersey" with the Trustees. Employees of the University secured an important benefit when they were made eligible for inclusion in the State Employees' Retirement System.

Extremely significant and intricate provisions defined the manner in which state control was to be exercised over the University. Both the Board of Regents and the Board of Visitors were abolished, and the powers of the latter agency, which had been created in 1864, were transferred to the State Board of Education. These powers were defined as "visiting the State University of New Jersey to examine into its manner of conducting its affairs and to enforce an observance of its laws and regulations and the laws of the State." The functions, powers, and duties of the Board of Managers of the State Experiment Station were transferred to the Trustees, who were to appoint a similar board to act as their agents in managing the Experiment Station. The University was obliged to "advise with" the Board of Education regarding the utilization of its facilities, and the State Board was to "investigate and jointly with" the University make recommendations to the governor and the legislature respecting the needs for facilities and services of the State University and, most particularly, with respect to annual budget requests. The State Board was also directed to survey the needs for higher education generally in the state and recommend to the legislature procedures and facilities to meet such needs.

During the year that intervened between the submission of the bills and their final enactment they were the subject of some public controversy and the object of considerable behind-the-scenes opposition. They were endorsed by more than eighty organizations, but they were attacked by the New Jersey Taxpayers Association, the League for a Free State University, and by the New Jersey Association of Colleges and Universities. The latter group, representing most of the smaller private colleges in the state and given vigorous leadership by the President of Seton Hall University, maintained that the proposed legislation would not create a genuine state university and objected especially to the denial of public funds to church-related institutions and to the Rutgers "monopoly" of state scholarships. The active campaign waged by the Association caused many influential newspapers to waver in their support of the reorganization proposals and even induced Governor Edge to adopt a neutral attitude toward them. The University countered with its own public relations effort, mobilizing its alumni and other interested groups, and also received strong support from the Board of Regents and the Board of Education. When the bills were finally brought to a vote, they passed both houses by substantial margins and were approved by the governor on March 26, 1945. On April 13 the Trustees adopted the necessary resolutions accepting the new status.

Rutgers had now achieved legal recognition as the State University of New Jersey, seemingly bringing to a culmination an evolutionary process that had begun in 1864 with its designation as the land-grant college of New Jersey. It had also succeeded very largely in preserving its autonomy. To President Clothier the new relationship to the state was best described as a "partnership of two self-respecting and mutually respecting entities." "The State has not taken over Rutgers," he explained to the Trustees, "but it has now given Rutgers full recognition." He envisioned increases in state appropriations both for operating expenses and for urgently needed buildings to enable Rutgers to meet its obligations as the State University in the critical years that lay ahead. But the question that remained to be answered was whether an auton-

omous university controlled by a Board of Trustees only a minority of
whom were public appointees could, in fact, win support as a state
university.

While the University was in the process of acquiring a new status it
was entering into negotiations that were to give it entirely new dimensions. Several years earlier—in 1933—consideration had been given to
absorbing the so-called "Dana group" of colleges in Newark. Nothing
came of those discussions, and by 1936 the "Dana group" had merged
with the Newark Institute of Arts and Sciences and the Mercer Beasley
Law School as the University of Newark. Housed in the former Ballantine brewery at 40 Rector Street, the urban institution had demonstrated signs of promise but encountered difficulties when war-time
conditions resulted in decreased enrollments. Because Rutgers, through
its College of Pharmacy, Extension Division, and University College,
had substantial interests in Newark, it was regarded as a rival, and
even a competitor, by the local institution, but there also existed the
possibility of developing cooperative relationships.

When it appeared that the authorities at the University of Newark
would welcome such an overture, President Clothier in February 1945
suggested to Franklin Conklin, the President of the Board of Trustees
of the University of Newark, that they might confer about developing a
cooperative program to provide educational services in Newark. The
response was cordial and soon resulted in a series of conferences in
which administrative officials of the two institutions participated. Out of
these discussions there emerged by July agreement on a complete
merger of the University of Newark with the State University. After the
plan had fully matured, it was approved in principle by the Trustees'
Executive Committee in September. At this point President Clothier
found that several influential Trustees looked askance at absorbing an
urban affiliate, but he tactfully employed his powers of persuasion and
secured the approval of the Board in January. Legislative sanction was
readily obtained in April, and the merger became effective on July 1,
1946.

The Newark Colleges of Rutgers University included a College of Arts
and Sciences, a School of Business Administration, a Law School, and
the College of Pharmacy, with a total enrollment at the start of the new
academic year of over 2,200 students. Under the terms of the merger
agreement, they enjoyed the same status as other colleges of the University, and members of their faculties had the same salary scale and retirement privileges as their counterparts in New Brunswick. The assets
of the former University of Newark, including the building at 40 Rector
Street and a meagre endowment fund, were transferred to the Trustees
of Rutgers. To the Rutgers authorities, the merger would enable the

State University to strengthen public higher education, particularly urban education in the Newark area; and to the extent that students from that area would attend the Newark Colleges, additional spaces would become available in New Brunswick for students from other parts of the state. It was recognized, however, that there would have to be a considerable upgrading and expansion of the physical facilities at Newark if the colleges there were to meet even the minimal demands that were anticipated.

The State University Act and the absorption of the Newark Colleges profoundly affected the external character of the University. There was also an internal ferment under way between 1943 and 1945 that was to reshape curricular patterns, personnel procedures, and administrative structures. With normal routines disrupted by the exigencies of war conditions, several University committees grasped the opportunity to formulate plans for the future on the assumption that new and enlarged responsibilities lay ahead for Rutgers. Remarkably enough, much of the initiative for innovation came from the University Council, which neither previously nor subsequently was distinguished for its effectiveness.

The Council's Committee on Educational Policies, under the chairmanship of Professor J. Milton French, was especially productive. It undertook to reexamine the educational objectives of the University, and after noting with concern the long trend toward the proliferation of specialized pre-professional and pre-vocational curricula it came out strongly in favor of a liberal education for all students. Such an education, in the Committee's definition, "sets before the student . . . the skills and techniques, the arts and crafts, and the systematized knowledge of man in his natural and social environment, in order that they may make him fit to live a useful and satisfying life. By its appeal to the emotions and ideals of the student it looks toward the high goal of building character." Distressed by the seeming decline in respect for traditional moral and social values among undergraduates of the recent generation but also inspired by the conviction that a broad acquaintance with the major disciplines of knowledge was indispensable to an educated man, the Committee declared its faith in "general education," to use the term that was coming into vogue at the time and that was to acquire wide acceptance after the publication of the influential Harvard report, *General Education in a Free Society*, in 1945.

Accordingly, French's committee recommended that every candidate for the bachelor's degree should be required to take two full-year courses, not both in the same department, in each of three areas—the humanities, the social sciences, and mathematics and science. It was contemplated that each department involved would designate, or design, courses suitable for election by students from other disciplines. Although the University Council somewhat surprisingly endorsed these proposals, their implementation was, to say the least, partial. The faculty of the College of Arts and Sciences adopted in full the general education requirements, effective July 1, 1945, and the College for Women, whose faculty had already moved toward such a plan, adhered to the tenor of the recommendations. But the other colleges, most notably Engineering and Agriculture, took no action to modify their highly specialized and technical curricula to provide for general education. Within the College of Arts and Sciences, the chief effect of the new requirements was to increase markedly the enrollment of students in the humanities and thereby promote the growth of the departments in that area. Modest as were the actual results of the recommendations of the Committee on Educational Policies, the succeeding twenty years did not produce another comparable attempt to redefine the overall educational philosophy of the University.

The Committee also produced a significant report on the relationship between teaching and research that sought to clarify the function of a professor in a university. Whereas previously research had been viewed as an activity in which some members of the faculty might choose to engage, scholarship was now recognized as an essential function, complementary to that of teaching, and it was declared to be University policy to afford to each professor adequate time and facilities for his research interests. This new policy was not unanimously acclaimed, for there were many, especially among the older members of the faculty, who believed their responsibilities were confined to teaching and who resented the new emphasis on scholarship. But within a very few years the concept that at a university the professor should be both teacher and scholar acquired dominance and produced, among other consequences, new criteria for the appointment and promotion of faculty members and an extraordinary expansion of research activity.

Concerned as the faculty was with projecting educational policies that would give new directions to the development of the University, they were acutely aware that their own position within the institution must be defined and improved if genuine progress was to result. During the preceding period of depression and war the security, the status, and not least of all the financial position of the faculty had been impaired, and with the steady growth of an administrative bureaucracy the traditional role of the faculty in shaping policy had diminished. Concerned about a wide range of grievances and problems, the University Council late in 1943 approved a motion by Professor Thurlow C. Nelson that called for a general study of personnel procedures and policies. President Clothier responded by appointing a special committee, headed most effectively by Albert E. Meder, which solicited statements from the several faculties and ultimately produced a comprehensive report covering such topics as faculty participation in the formulation of educational policies, departmental organization, tenure, appointments, promotions, and salaries. With only slight modifications the numerous recommendations of this "Committee on Personnel Procedures" were approved by the Trustees and embodied in the University statutes as revised in January and October 1945.

With respect to organizational problems, slight changes were made in the composition and mode of operation of the University Council in order to enhance its effectiveness as an instrument in shaping University-wide policies, but the result was hardly successful. Of considerably more importance were innovations at the levels of the college and the department. Provision was made for a committee of review in each college to act as a general grievance committee, hold hearings in dismissal proceedings involving personnel on indefinite tenure, and serve in an advisory capacity to the dean on appointments, promotions, and dismissals. Departmental procedures were democratized when the system of having appointed "heads," whose authority was absolute, was replaced by a new arrangement whereby a chairman nominated by the members of a department served for a limited term and with the obligation to consult his colleagues on matters relating to planning and personnel. In an effort to encourage coordination among departments in different colleges engaged in offering instruction in the same field, "divisions" were constituted.

Personnel policies, long ambiguous or outmoded, were set forth with considerable precision. Instructors held annual appointments and could not serve longer than four years in that rank. Assistant professors were appointed for three-year terms and if under exceptional circumstances they were continued in that rank after six years they acquired tenure. Associate and full professors enjoyed indefinite tenure. For the first time the criteria that would govern promotions in rank were set forth—"scholarly activity, teaching effectiveness, research accomplishments, competence, experience, and general usefulness to the University." A revised salary scale, ranging from a minimum of $2,400 for instructors to a maximum of $6,000 for professors and including provisions for regular annual increments, was especially welcomed. Because University employees were now eligible for membership in the state retirement system, this contingency, long a source of concern to older professors, could now be met, and the normal retiring age was fixed at seventy. Altogether, the new regulations resulting from the work of the Committee on Personnel Procedures represented a major advance on several fronts and were, indeed, absolutely essential as the University embarked upon a new stage of growth and development.

The intense awareness that the University was about to assume a new role was reflected not only in the acceptance of the designation of the State University of New Jersey, the Newark merger, and the several internal reforms that have been mentioned but in many other actions as well. A special Trustees' committee on development elaborated a plan for the expansion of physical facilities that envisioned the immediate erection of five major academic buildings, all of which had been urgently needed for twenty years. With the absorption of the Newark Colleges, an entirely new structure, the Alumni Federation, was brought into existence in 1947 to weld together the alumni organizations of all the colleges of the University. The public relations department was expanded, and, among other ventures, in 1945 it launched a radio series, the Rutgers Forum, as a means of making the University better known to the citizens of New Jersey. In a related endeavor, dozens of faculty members lectured throughout the State in behalf of a "New Jersey Meets Her World Neighbors" project. In order to enable members of the staff to keep informed of new developments within the University, the *Faculty News Letter* made a timely first appearance in August 1944.

The individual colleges shared in the adventure of girding themselves for the anticipated new era. Arts and Sciences adopted general education, the College for Women experimented with "area studies," the College of Agriculture completely overhauled and simplified its curricula, the College of Engineering braced itself for unprecedented numbers of students, and University College prepared to recruit its own faculty, thus becoming fully autonomous. The Research Council, foreseeing enlarged support for research from industrial sources, the Federal Government, and the state sought to encourage departments to initiate projects. Meanwhile department chairmen, their faculties depleted by war conditions, were scouring the graduate schools and other likely sources to obtain the faculty that would be needed when the veterans began to return. Heightening the sense of transition that pervaded the atmosphere were new administrative appointments—Albert E. Meder as Dean of Administration, Donald F. Cameron as Librarian, Earl Reed Silvers as Dean of Men, Wallace S. Moreland as Director of Public Relations, Earl S. Miers as Director of the Press, and Harry G. Owen as Dean of the College of Arts and Sciences—to mention only the more prominent. The University had come through a long period of trial and frustration, but now, fortified by its status as the State University and the attendant expectation of generous financial support, strengthened internally, and stimulated by a general determination to expand rapidly in size and improve in quality and capacity for service, it faced the future with exceptional zeal and hope.

At the forefront of all considerations as the University administrators prepared for peacetime operations was the determination to meet the needs of the returning veterans. President Clothier declared that the University "recognized a moral responsibility to accommodate all qualified veterans and high school graduates for whom it is possible to provide, not just those whom it is convenient to take." In discharging this obligation, the equated full-time enrollment soared from its prewar maximum of 7,000 to nearly 16,000 by 1948. In the men's colleges alone the student population went from 750 in September 1945 to over 1,800 by the following June, reached 3,200 in September 1946 and attained a peak of 4,200 a year later. Such an explosive rate of expansion required the improvisation of all types of temporary physical facilities, a sudden multiplication of staff, and extraordinary administrative effort. It produced that peculiarly hectic and dynamic period in the history of the University best labeled the "Era of the G.I."

Remarkable ingenuity was displayed in expanding the physical plant. As the vanguard of the demobilized veterans descended on the campus early in 1947 temporary arrangements were made to house a contingent of them at Camp Kilmer, and in the following year some 900 were living in barracks at nearby Raritan Arsenal, which continued to provide accommodations for dwindling numbers until 1950. Because about ten per cent of the returning servicemen were married, a semi-permanent trailer village, known as Hillside, was hastily improvised in the stadium area. To meet the critical shortage of housing for the hundreds of new staff members, 300 flimsily constructed apartment units were erected at University Heights with subsidies from the state and Federal governments. But perhaps the best known symbol of the period was the University Commons, familiarly known as "Reconversion Hall." An enormous prefabricated corrugated iron structure that had been destined for use as a factory in Russia, it was brought in crates from the Belle Mead Army Depot and erected in 1947 on what had formerly been the Neilson Athletic Field. With a floor area of 60,000 square feet, it contained a vast field house in addition to a cafeteria that could seat 850 people.

Drastic expedients were employed in meeting the need for classrooms and laboratories. A score of demountable aluminum buildings, once army barracks, were set up along upper George Street to provide forty highly unsatisfactory but serviceable classrooms. In a similar fashion, the demand for vastly augmented laboratory space in engineering, chemistry, geology, and biology was met by utilizing over sixty barracks-type buildings at what was hopefully termed the "future science center" at University Heights. By late 1947, 1,000 students were commuting across the river daily to the improvised facilities. Meanwhile a dozen or more former residences along College Avenue, together with several fraternity houses, were pressed into service as offices and classroom buildings. In one way or another, rudimentary temporary accommodations—most of them still in use twenty years later—were provided. Although Federal grants afforded some assistance and much war surplus property was acquired at nominal cost, the Trustees by 1947 had been obliged to borrow $2,500,000 to meet the costs of the emergency expansion program.

Equally striking was the recruitment of a vastly augmented faculty. In 1940 the faculty of the College of Arts and Sciences had numbered slightly more than 100. When classes began in September 1946, sixty-two new instructors joined the staff, and a year later there were an additional fifty-two appointments. By 1948 it was a rare department in which the newcomers did not outnumber those who had been members of the prewar faculty. Because few appointments had been made in the years between 1930 and 1945, the gap between the prewar and postwar faculty produced in most departments a cleavage between "old hands" and "young Turks" that at its best compelled a reexamination of traditional practices and stimulated innovation. The sudden infusion of a new generation was not without its problems, but the level of quality of those who remained at Rutgers was such as greatly to strengthen the faculty.

When it became apparent that not all of the students who were clamoring to be admitted could be accommodated at New Brunswick and Newark, five emergency "Off Campus Centers" were created in Morristown, Englewood, West New York, Trenton, and Atlantic City. Housed in local high schools and offering a limited range of first- and second-year courses in the evening, the Centers were operated by the University Extension Division and served over 2,000 students between 1946 and 1949. At the same time University College, which opened a branch at Paterson in addition to its main centers at New Brunswick and Newark, attained peak enrollments. To enable veterans to proceed toward their degrees as rapidly as possible, a double summer session was offered for three years and proved to be highly popular.

In spite of the frantic preparations that were made, the flood of demobilized servicemen threatened to engulf all the campuses. Increasing numbers were admitted in September and November 1945 and in February 1946, and the following September the largest wave of all—over 1,200—hit the men's colleges. At the crest of the tide in 1948–49 there were 8,569 full-time undergraduates at New Brunswick and Newark, and Rutgers discovered that suddenly it had become one of the twenty largest universities in the country. Excluding the College for Women, nearly 70 per cent of those enrolled were veterans. In June 1949, when the commencement exercises were first held at the Stadium, 1,666 degrees were awarded, and a year later there were 2,278. Without doubt the heavy influx of veterans was facilitated by the G.I. Bill of Rights, more formally known as Public Law 346, under which honorably discharged veterans were entitled to a payment for tuition, books, and supplies, together with a monthly allotment of $65 for single men or $90 for those with dependents.

The campus scene during these hectic years of reconversion presented a bewildering appearance. Long lines at registration, at the bookstore, and in the Commons; overcrowded classrooms; a frustrating shortage of parking spaces; time-consuming trips to and from the barracks at Raritan Arsenal, the trailer village at Hillside, or the science laboratories at University Heights; and not least of all the anxieties produced by the failure of monthly subsistence checks to arrive on schedule, all set the tone of campus life in New Brunswick. With more than a third of the students in the men's colleges commuting from their homes in all parts of the state and with others living at the Arsenal and Hillside, the student body lacked a sense of unity; many felt deprived of a full college experience. For most veterans, and especially those with families, the great urge was to complete their requirements in the minimum amount of time in order that they might get on with their interrupted careers.

In spite of the radical changes in campus conditions and in the make-up of the student body, most of the elements of campus life that had been familiar to the prewar generation were speedily revived. Among the first group of veterans to return, a sizable proportion had been at Rutgers before entering the service, and with amazing vigor and dedication they set about restoring the environment they had known previously. By June 1946, most campus organizations—Student Council, *Targum,* Cap and Skull, Scarlet Barbs, Glee Club, the *Scarlet Letter,* and various curricular clubs—had been revived, and both the Soph Hop and the Junior Prom had been staged with the customary formality. Far from being indifferent to extracurricular activities, those former Rutgers students among the veterans seemed determined to rebuild this dimension of the University. Student Council, led by men who had gained maturity during their years of military service, had never been more effective in promoting student welfare or—when occasion demanded—in contending against administrative myopia or inertia.

The area of student life that posed the greatest problems was that of the fraternities. Crippled by the loss of members during the war and generally lacking the resources to tide them over the crisis, the fraternities seemed to be on the verge of disaster. In September 1945, only six houses were in operation, as compared with nineteen a few years earlier. Four other chapters still owned houses, but they had turned them over to the University to be used for other purposes. The future looked bleak because it was generally believed that the veterans would not be interested in joining fraternities. Moreover, to the dismay of many fraternity alumni, the University authorities did not appear willing to extend much assistance and instead instituted stringent regulations that seemingly complicated the task of rehabilitation. Nevertheless, with some guidance from the Alumni Interfraternity Council and with extraordinary exertions by the individual chapters, the fraternities managed to reestablish themselves. By 1948 seventeen houses were in operation and two other chapters were active, and within the next few years other fraternities were to be established on the campus. As the fraternity system entered its second century at Rutgers, it appeared to have survived a formidable threat and demonstrated its strong hold on the interest of undergraduates.

Once reestablished, however, the fraternities were confronted with a new challenge. After months of investigation and study the Student Council, reflecting a concern that was being manifested on other campuses, adopted and sent to the Trustees in March 1949 a report that denounced discriminatory practices in fraternities and called for prompt action to eradicate "this perniciously destructive element in our University." Earlier, the Interfraternity Council had recognized that discriminatory clauses in fraternity constitutions represented an "unhealthy situation," and the member chapters agreed to work within their national organizations for the elimination of such restrictions. It was estimated at the time that half of the twenty-two fraternities had restrictions on their membership based upon factors of race or religion. The Trustees commended the actions taken by the Student Council and the Interfraternity Council and agreed that the fraternities should be free to choose their members without prejudice, whether self-imposed or dictated from without. But instead of promulgating any drastic edicts they agreed to permit the Rutgers chapters a reasonable time to work for the elimination of discriminatory regulations. Annually thereafter reports were made to the Trustees on the situation, and year by year the number of fraternities with discriminatory clauses decreased. It was observed, though, that even under the new dispensation most chapters continued to be predominantly of the same ethnic composition as before.

Behind the façade of confused activity some general characteristics distinguished student attitudes. Contrary to expectations, the veterans as a group did not experience difficulties in adjusting to college routines. Dean Silvers reported that they were "a stabilizing factor in undergraduate life; more mature in judgment than the average student, more philosophical in their approach to problems, more tolerant in attitude and better self-disciplined." Early in the period some ex-servicemen urged the formation of a veterans organization on the campus, but the majority sentiment was strongly opposed to such a move, on the grounds that it would merely prolong the "veteran feeling," which most wished to forget. In the classroom, because of their maturity and motivation, the veterans commanded the admiration of their instructors for the seriousness with which they pursued their studies. Somewhat surprisingly, the undergraduates, veterans and non-veterans alike, seemed to be little concerned with national politics or world affairs. "The undergraduate today finds himself, as do his contemporaries, in a confused era," observed an astute student reporter. "If there is clarity it should be found in the calmer reaches of campus and classroom. However, at Rutgers the undergraduate is too hot on the chase from lab to lecture hall to involve himself over deeply. He has little urge to reshape the world."

Perceptive though this appraisal was, it failed to give adequate recognition to the lively spirit of innovation that lent excitement to student affairs. The reforming zeal of Student Council, evidenced most conspicuously in its battle against discrimination, was all but unprecedented and—combined with the crusading fervor of *Targum*—gave a vigorous tone to campus politics. Unusual initiative was displayed by a determined group of students who, irate over the policies and prices that prevailed at the University-run bookstore, overcame many obstacles to start a cooperative store in 1949 that led an uncertain existence for several years. Others invested their energies in establishing a campus radio station, WRSU, an enterprise that soon became one of the most popular of student activities. Those with a theatrical flair produced a musical comedy, "Boys in Ivy," in 1950, which was so successful as to inspire subsequent annual efforts until declining enthusiasm and woeful financial difficulties terminated the series.

There were even attempts to revive class spirit. In 1948 an interclass athletic tournament was reestablished as an annual event, and a year later, with the overwhelming endorsement of a student referendum, non-compulsory regulations reinstituted the wearing of a distinctive hat, necktie, and button by Freshmen. In a similar vein, an "All University Outing" brought together students from all the colleges for a gay boatride on the Hudson in 1950 and for a few years thereafter. To show their support for the University's endeavors to secure lower tuition and other benefits from the state, the undergraduates organized a "Student Committee for a Greater State University," which through its own public relations projects sought to influence opinion. Contrary to some contemporary opinion, these were not years of apathy.

The period was also notable as a "golden age" of sports at Rutgers.

Fortified with large numbers of mature athletes whose years in the service had not dulled their zest for competition, the football teams of 1947 and 1948 scored successive victories over Princeton and lost only three games in two seasons. Baseball, too, experienced a revival of fortune, climaxed by the progress of the team to the semi-finals of the National Collegiate Athletic Association tournament in 1951. The crew, now equipped with a handsome boathouse, entered into major competition; wrestling enjoyed several winning seasons; and other sports, with the notable exception of basketball, posted commendable records. Not the least among the triumphs of these years was the successful campaign in 1949 to have the campus designated as the future site of the National Football Hall of Fame in recognition of the pioneering contribution of Rutgers to the game.

Cultural and intellectual enterprises also found favor. An especially notable development was the formation of the University Choir, which made an impressive debut in 1950 with the Rochester Philharmonic in a Bach festival. The Choir's annual performances with leading symphony orchestras won high critical acclaim. With the establishment in 1950 of a University department of drama, student productions staged at the Little Theatre at the College for Women attained new levels of excellence. Also symptomatic of the heightened emphasis on intellectual activity was the inauguration in 1948 of the "book-of-the-year" project, which sought to have all students and faculty read one book of special significance with a view to encouraging serious discourse. *Anthologist,* the literary magazine at the men's colleges, exhibited unusual vitality, although the publication of one article dealing with the subject of abortion drew forth such a storm of protest from sources outside the University that publication was suspended and a special committee of Trustees was appointed to investigate the matter, but in due course the magazine was permitted to continue. There was a remarkable revival of religious activities. Several denominations sponsored student religious groups in accordance with a general policy formulated by a faculty committee. At the same time, one of the oldest of the campus traditions came to an end when, in 1946, attendance at Sunday chapel was made voluntary.

Conditioning the attitude of students in ways too subtle to elucidate was the ever-threatening world situation. The crisis of the Cold War and the omnipresent threat of nuclear conflict could not be ignored. The abrupt outbreak of war in Korea in June 1950 was hardly anticipated, but by December the full impact of the national emergency was felt on the campus when it became known that 4,500,000 men were to be called into service. Already reports had been received of the first two casualties among the alumni. As the men students wondered what their fate would be, a special convocation was held in January 1951, when they were assured that they could probably expect to complete the year but that all who were eligible would be well advised to enroll in the advanced R.O.T.C. and Air Force R.O.T.C. programs. Although only small numbers were later drafted for military service, the aura of uncertainty hung over the campus for the next two years. Meanwhile, the rise of McCarthyism, with its implied threat to any who espoused beliefs that could be labelled "Un-American," added its own peculiar terror and served to inhibit the free expression of ideas. For whatever reasons —the passing of the veterans, the decline in enrollments, the sombreness of the Korean emergency, or the pall of McCarthyism—it seemed that a period of peculiar vitality had ended.

Preoccupied as the University was with equipping itself to cope with the sheer volume of students, it nevertheless found sufficient resources to strengthen and diversify its educational programs and even to launch important new ventures. The forces of innovation were especially apparent in the College of Arts and Sciences, largest of the colleges in the University. In part as a result of the enforcement of the general education requirements but also as a reflection of student interest, there occurred a considerable expansion of courses in the humanities. In particular, the departments of art, music, and philosophy experienced phenomenal growth. With the strong encouragement of Dean Harry G. Owen, several experimental interdepartmental courses were instituted in an attempt to break down what was deemed to be the overly rigid compartmentalization of knowledge. Drawing on wartime experience with similar programs, "area studies" were introduced, focusing initially on American civilization and Latin American civilization but later embracing the Russian area as well. Honors work continued to be a topic of interest, and in 1950 the Henry Rutgers program, which enabled selected Seniors to engage in independent study and write a thesis, was inaugurated. In general, the sharp increase in the number of students made possible the establishment of new departments, the augmentation of older departments, and a multiplication of course offerings in every field.

Elsewhere there were similar signs of ferment. The College of Engineering, struggling with the assistance of its makeshift facilities at University Heights to accommodate more than three times its prewar enrollment, introduced a new program in engineering administration and also added courses in city and regional planning. The College of Agriculture continued its notable achievements in research and extension services and added a curriculum in agricultural engineering. At the College for Women, less affected by the vicissitudes of war and reconversion than the men's colleges, the emphasis was on educational experimentation to meet the needs of an increasingly selective student body. University College opened a new division at Paterson in 1948, utilizing the facilities of the State Teacher's College there, and broadened its curricula far beyond its initial emphasis on business administration.

The colleges at Newark, fearful at first that they would be regarded as mere colonial outposts by the authorities in New Brunswick, shared in the general program of expansion and development. Within a few years after the merger, the growth in student enrollment necessitated the acquisition of new quarters for the Law School and the School of Business Administration in the vicinity of Washington Street and the rehabilitation of several former residences to serve as classrooms and offices for the College of Arts and Sciences. The School of Law steadily advanced its admission requirements while both the School of Business Administration and the College of Pharmacy initiated graduate programs. Hampered in many ways by having to utilize former residences, office buildings, and factories as substitutes for properly designed academic facilities, the Newark Colleges nevertheless fulfilled the promise of serving the educational needs of the urban area and earned a respected position within the University structure.

The scope and influence of the University was further extended by the establishment of two entirely new units. In 1947 the Institute of Management and Labor Relations—an outgrowth of the Labor Institute started in 1931—was brought into existence by legislative enactment. Offering a wide range of non-credit courses for both labor and management and conducting research in the areas of its special interest, the Institute served its intended purpose of improving mutual understanding between the two groups. In quite a different area the geographical dimensions of the University were extended when the College of South Jersey in Camden was absorbed in 1950. Founded in 1926 by Arthur E. Armitage as the South Jersey Law School—to which a junior college was added subsequently—the institution had produced 3,000 graduates, but faced extinction when the New Jersey Supreme Court in 1949 ruled that graduates of unaccredited law schools could not sit for the New Jersey bar exams. In response to strong political pressures and not without some misgiving, the Trustees agreed to take over the institution, and the necessary legislation was enacted in May 1950. Immediate plans were made to transform the junior college into a four-year school, and the law school was operated as a branch of the school in Newark. A full evening program conducted by the University College was also instituted. In due course the College of South Jersey, like the Newark Colleges, expanded and became a valued asset to the Camden area.

Quite apart from the achievements directly associated with the expansion of individual colleges, the most significant development within the University was the emphasis placed upon the role of research. Prior to the war the funds available to support research outside of the College of Agriculture were miniscule; as late as 1944–1945 they amounted to less than $200,000. But with the strong encouragement of the Research Council, under the imaginative direction of Dr. William H. Cole, and with the growing recognition that an able faculty could be sustained only in an environment where opportunities were provided for scholarly investigation, funds were secured in increasing amounts to support research in every field of inquiry. By 1951–52 these funds totaled $1,265,203, nearly half of which represented contracts with Federal military agencies. An approximately like amount was expended on agricultural research. Although the greatest support was concentrated in the areas of the biological sciences, ceramics, and physics, the social sciences and, to a lesser extent, the humanities also benefitted, chiefly through subsidies from the University Research Fund and through the increased availability of fellowships from the private foundations and the Fulbright program.

Unquestionably the magnificent achievement of Dr. Selman A. Waksman and his associates in 1945 in discovering streptomycin, the conqueror of tuberculosis, served to dramatize the importance of research to the University. The discovery, for which Dr. Waksman was honored with a Nobel Prize in 1952, represented the culmination of nearly thirty years of patient and brilliant investigation in the field of soil microbiology carried out in the laboratories of the College of Agriculture. When the economic potential of the drug was recognized, the Rutgers Research and Endowment Foundation was established in 1946 to receive income from patent rights and apply the proceeds to the furtherance of research. Three years later the Institute of Microbiology was created with funds supplied by the Foundation, which in 1954 erected a building at University Heights to house the Institute. The Institute immediately acquired international recognition as an outstanding center of research on antibiotics and reflected great credit both upon Dr. Waksman and the University.

Another major center of research was the Bureau of Biological Research. When it observed its fifteenth anniversary in 1951, it boasted a staff of twenty-seven senior scientists and eighteen research assistants and technicians under the direction of Dr. James B. Allison. Supported largely by grant funds, it was noted for its work in protein evaluation, cancer research, and metabolism studies. A new dimension of the Bureau was the Serological Museum, established in 1948 by Dr. Alan A. Boyden. Similar though less substantial bureaus conducted cooperative research in mineralogy and economics. In 1950, with the encouragement of the New Jersey State League of Municipalities, a bureau of government research was created not only to conduct research but to offer training programs for local governmental officials.

The heightened importance attached to productive scholarship was further evidenced by the rapid growth of the Rutgers University Press. Barely established before the war, the Press now came to prominence under the directorship of Earl S. Miers. It received national recognition in 1947 when one of its products—*The Lincoln Reader*—was selected by the Book-of-the-Month Club, and its prestige was further enhanced when it undertook the publication of the collected writings of Abraham Lincoln. The Press successfully stimulated members of the faculty to produce eligible manuscripts and, together with the Research Council, it was a major influence in fostering the scholarly life of the University.

Paralleling the expansion of research was a comparable growth in graduate studies. Prior to 1940 there had been strong graduate programs in the College of Agriculture and modest offerings in certain of the scientific departments. Between 1945 and 1950 the number of students in the Graduate School rose from little more than 100 to ten times that number. In June 1950, forty-eight doctorates were conferred, more than three times the number in any previous year. The sciences continued to attract the great majority of the candidates for advanced degrees, but there were now graduate offerings in forty fields, and the departments of history, political science, economics, and English were moving forward rapidly in the graduate area.

The "Era of the G.I.," then, was marked by extraordinary accomplishments and fundamental changes in the orientation of the University. In addition to more than doubling the size of its student population, Rutgers strengthened its faculty, enriched its educational offerings, created an environment favorable to research, and entered vigorously into graduate education. The transition, involving not only numbers and physical growth but objectives and functions as well, was so sudden as to leave many bewildered. Those who had known the institution in the relatively placid years before 1940 were often disturbed as they saw the changes that were being wrought. But those who could view the scene from a larger perspective recognized that Rutgers was in the process not only of finding its role as the State University of New Jersey but also as a major university, in the sense in which that term was best understood.

Impressive as were these evidences of growth and development, the picture had its ominous side as well. The very suddenness of the transition created stresses within the institution; so long as morale remained high and the pace of progress was maintained they could be minimized or ignored, but ultimately they would have to be reckoned with. Far more critical was the insecure foundation on which expansion had been based. With no permanent academic buildings constructed after 1927, the University resorted to the use of makeshift, temporary facilities to meet its needs and mortgaged its slender resources to pay for them. In some areas, most conspicuously in engineering, it jeopardized its academic standards by accepting more students than it could provide for. When faculty salaries fell behind the rapid increase in the cost of living and ceased to be competitive in the academic market place, a heavy exodus of the staff was a dire possibility. Finally, the students, who had experienced the discomforts of the Raritan Arsenal barracks and crowded classrooms and who felt that somehow they had been short-changed in their treatment at the State University, grew increasingly restive or—upon receiving their diplomas—severed all ties with Rutgers.

What had happened, in essence, was that the University had over-extended itself, expecting that the state would come to its aid, and the aid was not forthcoming. On an official level, the relationship between Rutgers and the state defined in the legislation of 1945 seemed to function smoothly. Governor Edge gave positive evidence of his interest. Relations with the State Board of Education, and particularly with Dr. John H. Bosshart, the Commissioner of Education, were entirely harmonious. The State Board, deeply involved with its own educational problems, did not interfere in University matters. On the initiative of Commissioner Bosshart, a plan was worked out whereby the University would cooperate with certain of the state teachers' colleges in offering programs in the liberal arts, but it was never implemented. The basic difficulty did not appear to be organizational; rather, it was financial. With its determinedly "no new taxes" philosophy, the state simply lacked the money to sustain adequate public services, including higher education. A contributing factor, no doubt, was the failure of Rutgers to establish itself in the public mind as the State University.

After 1945, although state appropriations for operating expenses mounted, they continued to be at the level of about one third of the budgeted expenses, a proportion that had obtained since the 1920's. Needless to say, this was well below what the University requested. By 1947 President Clothier was insisting that faculty salary scales were distressingly inadequate, that there were too few state scholarships, and that valid educational needs could not be met. Meanwhile students complained of the tuition rates, which were among the highest in the nation for a state university. But the most alarming deficiency was in buildings. The physical plant was hardly adequate for a student body of one third the size, and the situation grew more desperate year by year.

In projecting postwar plans, University authorities saw an immediate need for $40,000,000 in plant additions, including new buildings for chemistry, agricultural sciences, engineering, biological sciences, new libraries both at the men's colleges and at the College for Women, and several dormitories. Later, following the merger with the Newark Colleges, the capital program was extended. Annually, in preparing the University's asking budget, requests were included for amounts ranging from five million in 1946 up to ten million in 1948 to finance construction, but the response was discouraging. In 1946, $965,000 was appropriated for the first unit of a new chemistry building and a year later $1,000,000 was voted for an agricultural science building. Because of rising costs, it was necessary to seek supplementary appropriations, with the result that actual construction could not begin till 1948 and the facilities did not come into use until 1951.

When it became apparent that annual state appropriations would never be adequate to meet the University's capital requirements, other alternatives were explored. With the encouragement of Governor Alfred E. Driscoll a plan was concocted whereby the University would borrow as much as $25,000,000 to finance its building program, with the state assuming responsibility for servicing the loan. This scheme, however, had many inherent weaknesses, so a state-financed bond issue was considered. The legislature was confronted with huge requests for capital funds not only from the State University but also from the six teachers' colleges and the several welfare institutions, and a bond issue seemed to offer the only feasible method for meeting these demands. Early in 1947 representatives of the State University conferred with officials of the Department of Education and the Department of Institutions and Agencies about their mutual needs, and these conferences quickly produced a joint agreement to endeavor to obtain approval for a bond issue, the proceeds of which would be used for urgently needed capital construction in all three areas.

Leadership of the campaign was assumed by the New Jersey Committee for Adequate Welfare and Educational Buildings, made up of 700 distinguished citizens of the State under the chairmanship of Colonel Franklin D'Olier, former president of the Prudential Insurance Company. The committee launched its effort in the summer of 1947, but because there was to be a referendum that November on a new state constitution —drafted by a convention that met in the University Gymnasium—it was decided to defer the major effort until 1948. Then the campaign to meet what was termed "New Jersey's Gravest Problem" moved into high gear. From the outset the appeal encountered strong resistance, not so much because the needs were challenged but rather on the grounds that the taxpayers would be overburdened or, more ominously, that Rutgers should not be included in the program because it was not wholly a public institution.

When the proposal came before the legislature early in 1948, a major controversy ensued over whether the bond issue should be a "single package," including all three agencies, or whether the voters should be given the opportunity to vote on each issue separately. The D'Olier committee—supported by the Driscoll administration—contended for the single-package bond issue, and after a long struggle this scheme was adopted. As finally passed by the legislature in September, the bond issue, if approved in a popular referendum, would provide $50,000,000, which would subsequently be allocated among the three agencies by the legislature.

In this form the question was submitted to the electorate. By now opponents were concentrating their attack on the inclusion of Rutgers in the single package, contending that this arrangement would insure the defeat of the whole proposal. Prominent among the opposition were John J. Rafferty, the authorized spokesman of the Catholic Church on secular matters in New Jersey; the Bayley-Seton League, affiliated with Seton Hall University; and the Essex Division of the Catholic Youth Organization. Also extremely vocal was T. James Tumulty, flamboyant legislator from Hudson County, who charged that Rutgers was still a Dutch Reformed institution dedicated to the training of Protestant ministers and that its department of history was "blasphemous." The New Jersey Taxpayers Association, which at that time consistently opposed any spending programs, was another formidable antagonist. Although scores of organizations in the state endorsed the bond issue, many influential newspapers were lukewarm in their support and even Governor Driscoll was restrained in his advocacy of it. The University did its best to counter the attacks, mobilized its alumni and friends, and, through its public relations department, bore the brunt of the campaign in cooperation with the D'Olier committee. But the argument that Rutgers—still managed by what was predominantly a non-public Board of Trustees—was not a genuine state university was extremely effective.

In the November election the voters turned down the referendum by more than 80,000 votes out of a total of slightly more than 1,000,000. Only five counties gave majorities to the bond issue. Informed observers were nearly unanimous in concluding that antagonism to Rutgers was the basic cause of the defeat. This opinion was validated when the welfare institutions in 1949 and the teachers' colleges in 1951 were successful in obtaining approval for bond issues.

The defeat of the 1948 bond issue was a multiple catastrophe for the University. In immediate and practical terms, it seemingly ended any hopes that the urgent physical requirements of the institution could be met. In another context, it reopened the question of the status of Rutgers as a state university, a question that presumably had been settled by the legislation of 1945. Shortly after the election, Governor Driscoll let it be known that he believed that the position of the University should be further "clarified," possibly by having a majority of the Trustees appointed by the state, before any appropriations were made for capital improvements. Discussions in the legislature demonstrated that political support for Rutgers was at a low ebb. Within the ranks of the University, there was a general conviction that all of its policies must be reexamined in an effort to discover why it had failed to win popular confidence. But before the University had begun to recover from the shock of the defeat of the bond issue, an upheaval of unprecedented proportions, involving both faculty and students, produced a serious internal crisis.

Many factors combined to bring about an alarming deterioration of faculty morale early in 1949. The basic concerns were security and status. By 1948 the enrollment peak was obviously passing; thereafter the veterans would constitute a dwindling fraction of the student body, and recent high school graduates, given the low birth rates of the depression years, would not entirely fill their places. Forecasting this decline in enrollments, the University administration saw no alternative but to reduce the teaching staff proportionately. To make matters worse, the University faced a large financial deficit for the year, the first it had incurred in more than two decades. The prospect that many of them would be dropped from the staff induced a feeling akin to panic within the faculty. Only minor adjustments had been made in the 1945 salary scale, despite soaring living costs, and a survey conducted by the local chapter of the American Association of University Professors indicated that 65 per cent of the instructional staff had to borrow money, draw on savings, or seek extra employment in order to make ends meet. There was also general resentment over what the faculty conceived to be the minor role assigned to them in the formulation of policy and severe condemnation of the manner in which certain high University officials wielded their authority. Contributing to the atmosphere of insecurity were the increasingly frequent attacks on members of the faculty by religious and veterans organizations, which were viewed as assaults on academic freedom, and the enactment early in 1949 of a requirement that all state employees subscribe to an anti-subversive loyalty oath. So long as the hope could be sustained that the State University would realize the ambitions inspired by the act of 1945, these grievances were tolerable, but the defeat of the bond issue dashed that hope, and the pent-up frustrations exploded.

The crisis was precipitated early in March 1949, when certain instructors who had reason to believe that they would be retained were informed that they—together with a large number of others who had previously been told of their dismissals—would not be reappointed. Rumors enlarged the dimensions of the staff cut, and when a faculty committee sought from the administration assurances with respect to this and the other matters that were troubling them, they felt, as some of them expressed it, that they were "getting the run around." In April an extreme version of the faculty's complaints was deliberately "leaked" to the local newspaper, and for the next two weeks the New Jersey press aired the story of the difficulties at Rutgers, along with numerous demands from various quarters that a legislative investigation should be started. The administration at first chose to regard the fracas as merely the result of unfortunate misunderstandings, but when it became clear that the grievances were genuine and deep rooted, President Clothier convoked a meeting of the University Assembly, at which all the issues were bared, promised to appoint a new committee on personnel procedures to propose remedies, and soon took a series of actions on his own initiative to improve conditions.

There were comparable manifestations of dissatisfaction among the students. In December 1948, *Targum* published an open letter signed by all members of the Student Council that was intensely critical of the administration for its paternalistic attitude and for its devious manner of handling student complaints. The undergraduates had a long list of grievances—ranging from bad conditions in the Commons, high prices of rooms, board, and books, and inadequate parking facilities, to administrative hostility to their plans for a cooperative bookstore—but uppermost was their feeling that they were not being dealt with fairly or candidly. Following a second student outburst in February, President Clothier stated, "No responsibility for, or participation in the management of the University, rests upon the students, nor do they have the authority to investigate the actions of the administrative agents of the trustees." This edict, of course, produced another uproar, which subsided only after the president agreed to meet monthly with the Student Council and institute various administrative reforms.

From one perspective, the internal disturbances could be related not only to the defeat of the bond issue and the repercussions of declining enrollments but also to the intense pressures under which the University had been operating since 1945. Preoccupied with the problems of reconversion and expansion, and constantly hampered by inadequate funds, administrative officers had neither the resources nor the infinite wisdom required to meet every contingency. The fact that President Clothier was ill during much of this period and that many responsibilities were assumed by the comptroller and the dean of the University made the situation worse. Now that the explosion had occurred, however, prompt steps were taken to repair the damages and improve internal conditions.

President Clothier's action in appointing the Committee on Personnel Procedures served to direct the current of discontent into a constructive channel, and for the ensuing year the Committee, like its counterpart five years before, solicited suggestions from the faculties and prepared a lengthy report. Its recommendation that faculty members be given adequate advance notice of whether they were to be retained or dismissed was speedily implemented, as were other detailed proposals regarding the handling of appointments and promotions. But plans that the Committee advanced for strengthening the role of the faculty in the formulation of policy, specifically through the establishment of college executive committees and the creation of a faculty senate, became bogged down in discussions with the administration and ultimately came to naught. In 1953 the name of the University Council was changed to University Senate, but the body continued to be composed of both faculty and administrative personnel. The search that had been under way intermittently since 1925 to find an appropriate substitute for the old College Faculty, which had represented the authentic voice of the entire faculty, had met with another and perhaps a final failure.

Other innovations resulted from the crisis. The president brought into existence two new faculty committees, one to advise him generally about matters of concern to the faculty and another to consult with him on the formulation of the budget. As a means of encouraging faculty members to express their views and engage in discussion of University problems, an all-university educational conference was held in September 1949, at which the genuine interest of the faculty in University affairs was strongly manifested. The 100-page report summarizing the deliberations contained a host of proposals for advancing the welfare of the University. The conference plan was repeated in 1950, but lapsed soon thereafter. These measures were effective in rebuilding the morale of the faculty, which was strengthened as well by a new salary scale, effective July 1, 1949, that ranged from $3,000 for a beginning instructor to a maximum of $7,400 for a professor. Additional staff benefits within the next two years included a group hospitalization plan and a revised retirement program, which reduced the mandatory retirement age from seventy to sixty-five.

The faculty crisis was responsible also for precipitating a major overhaul of the University's administrative structure. In June 1949, the Trustees created the office of provost, and this official, under the president, was to have general charge of the administration of the University in all its branches. At the same time the duties of the comptroller and of the dean of the University were redefined to insure, among other considerations, that the preparation and administration of the academic budget would be the responsibility of the academic officers. Appointed to the newly created post was Dr. Mason W. Gross, who had joined the faculty in 1946 as a member of the Department of Philosophy and Assistant Dean of the College of Arts and Sciences. Possessing in an unusual degree the confidence of the faculty and the student body, Dr. Gross by his personal tact and his boundless energy infused a new spirit into the University administration. The presidency, as the *Rutgers Alumni Monthly* expressed it, had now become a two-man job, and Dr. Gross admirably complemented Dr. Clothier in discharging the duties of the burdensome office.

Beyond the problems immediately associated with the faculty unrest lay larger issues, for the University now had to readjust to new conditions created by the defeat of the bond issue, declining enrollments, and the nation's involvement in the Korean War. Because the vote on the bond issue referendum was generally interpreted as indicating a lack of popular acceptance of Rutgers as the State University, consideration had to be given to possible changes in the relationship of Rutgers to the state. At the same time, University authorities sought to devise means of holding on to the gains that had been made in the preceding few years despite the cutbacks necessitated by the departure of the veterans. Between 1948 and 1951 full-time undergraduate student enrollment dropped from 8,656 to 6,318, with the heaviest losses being felt in the College of Engineering and the College of Arts and Sciences. Because the veterans had paid tuition at the rate fixed for out-of-state students—roughly $100 more a year than the resident fee—the University's income fell off disproportionately, ushering in a period of budgetary austerity and continuing reductions in staff. With the outbreak of hostilities in Korea in June 1950 and the subsequent declaration of a state of national emergency, there was the prospect that the University would find itself confronted with conditions similar to those that had prevailed during World War II. It was in the face of these extremely uncertain circumstances that plans for the future had to be formulated.

There were conflicting views within the University both as to the reasons why Rutgers had failed to commend itself to the people of New Jersey as the State University and as to the course that should now be taken. One extremely influential Trustee maintained that, while accepting the substance of the 1945 act, the University had retained the appearance of a private university, even neglecting to describe itself as the State University of New Jersey in its own press releases. In a similar vein, a knowledgeable administrator, who was also an alumnus, observed, "There have been two Rutgers in the minds and hearts of the University's alumni for decades, and it is this concept of dualism which must be ended if the future is to be bright." An editorial in the *Rutgers Alumni Monthly* posed the question, "Are We Standing With Reluctant Feet Where the State and Ivy Meet?" It implied an affirmative answer and stirred up a host of letters pro and con. The Trustees gave brief consideration to altering the name of the institution, possibly to the "University of New Jersey," and to the suggestion that state appointees should be a majority of the Board, but neither proposal won support. There was also reluctance to adopt a plan put forward by Commissioner Bosshart that would have greatly extended the fiscal controls of the State Board of Education over the University. The conclusion arrived at after months of deliberation was that the partnership arrangement devised in 1945 was completely sound but that it was misunderstood by officials in Trenton and by the people of the state at large. The solution was for the University to intensify its public relations program in order that the extent and quality of its services as the State University might be fully appreciated.

Accordingly, a special Trustees' committee under Charles H. Brower, an experienced advertising executive, made a thorough study of the University's public relations, and in response to its recommendations the program was completely overhauled. The staff of the Department of Public Relations was expanded and the authority of the director to co-ordinate public relations activities throughout the entire University was strengthened. Henceforth the designation of Rutgers as the State University was to be emphasized. In order to reach the widest possible audience, the news service was increased, additional radio programs were scheduled, a handsomely illustrated annual report was issued, and a speakers bureau, drawing on the services of scores of faculty members, was organized. An attractive and informative newsletter, *Report from Rutgers,* was soon being sent to a huge mailing list of interested citizens, and the *Rutgers Alumni Voice* brought news of the University to every alumnus. Although hardly susceptible to measurement, the cumulative effect of these efforts no doubt made the University better known throughout the state.

While these steps were being taken to strengthen the popular image of Rutgers as the State University, a related campaign was launched to bring about a reduction in tuition. Faced with a budget deficit, the Trustees in July 1949 had been obliged to raise the tuition fee, along with dormitory rents and food prices, a trend that somehow had to be reversed. Known as "Operation Slash," this endeavor enlisted the support of alumni, faculty, and undergraduates, who broadcast the message that because Rutgers had the second highest tuition fees of any state university, many students from low-income families were subject to severe hardships. Specifically, the University sought an increase in the annual state appropriation sufficient to make possible the reduction of tuition from $385 to $175. Sentiment in Trenton was cool to the idea, for both fiscal and policy reasons, and nothing resulted.

The notion of partnership, as so frequently reiterated by President Clothier, implied only partial reliance on state support; the University recognized an obligation to seek from its friends and alumni resources to contribute to the joint enterprise. For many years the Trustees' committee on endowments had carried on desultory efforts to raise funds for special projects, with meagre returns, but in January 1949 it was decided to retain the firm of Marts and Lundy to conduct a study of fund-raising possibilities. The survey disclosed many adverse factors and produced the conclusion that although no vast amounts were in prospect, it would be feasible to attempt a modest campaign for at least one million dollars. Not without some misgivings, in view of past experiences, the Trustees in January 1950 approved an effort to raise that amount.

Even before this decision was reached, it had been determined that additional dormitory accommodations must be built at the men's colleges. No dormitories had been erected since 1931, and in the meantime Winants had been converted to other uses, with the result that there were accommodations for only 500 students. Fraternities, Raritan Arsenal, and rooming houses could take care of about 1,200, but this meant that 1,300—about one third of the men students—were obliged to commute. When the immediate postwar pressure to secure admission to colleges eased, many highly qualified students would not apply to Rutgers because they did not wish to endure the rigors of commuting or the sparse facilities of the Arsenal barracks. Thus it seemed to be essential, if both the quality and the quantity of the student population were to be sustained, to provide additional dormitories, especially for first-year students. The possibility of borrowing funds from an insurance company was explored, but ultimately it was agreed to include the major portion of the cost in the fund appeal. So urgent was the need that the Trustees resolved to proceed at once with plans for a 200-man dormitory to be erected on the Bishop Campus and to be named in honor of William H. S. Demarest.

When the plans for the fund campaign were announced in April with the formation of an all-university development committee under the chairmanship of Trustee Lansing P. Shield, the specified objectives included Demarest Dormitory, a student center at the College for Women, and a cafeteria and students' lounge at the Newark Colleges. During the course of the next year prospective donors were canvassed, and the final returns showed that 3,300 subscribers had pledged a total of $1,300,872. Although not all of this amount was available for the announced objectives of the campaign and some of the pledges were un-collectable, the effort had been worthwhile. Not only did it produce tangible results in the form of new student facilities at the men's colleges, the College for Women, and Newark, but it involved the alumni and friends of the University in a common endeavor at a time when a demonstration of loyalty and interest was especially important.

By 1951 the University had adjusted to the new conditions brought about by the reversal of the enrollment trend and by the defeat of the bond issue. Ahead lay a brief period of further retrenchment before another expansionist surge got under way. In the few short years since the ending of the war, Rutgers had undergone another transformation, taking on the identity of the State University, extending its operations to Newark, Camden, and Paterson, and broadening the scope of its objectives to give increased emphasis to research and graduate study. Simultaneously it had strained every resource to provide educational opportunities for the thousands of returning veterans. Intellectually strengthened by the augmentation of its faculty, which meant an infusion of new ideas as well as a proliferation of course offerings, and fortified, too, by new aspirations, the University had again demonstrated both its resilience and its capacity for achievement.

At this juncture Dr. Clothier decided to retire from the presidency. Now sixty-six years of age, he had held the office longer than any of his predecessors and by his tactful leadership had brought the University through the successive trials of the depression, the war, and the postwar era of reconversion. Ever a staunch defender of integrity of workmanship and of personal moral values, he lent the stamp of his own character to the institution and earned the respect of students and faculty. He submitted his resignation to the Trustees in January 1951, to become effective July 1.

In his final annual report, which he described as his "last official will and testament," President Clothier took the occasion to express his deeply held convictions about the future of the University. He voiced his confidence in the partnership relations with the state that had been given legal form in 1945. "But at no time and under no circumstances," he warned, "should the Trustees ever yield control of the University to the state as occasionally uninformed or misguided persons have suggested. Such a move would be a violation of the spirit of the partnership, a violation of the trust imposed on the Trustees by the original charter, and a disservice to the people of the state." This solemn admonition, which echoed the views he had expressed to the Trustees soon after assuming office in 1932, reflected the underlying philosophy of President Clothier's administration. It represented as well an almost desperate outcry against impending change.

Chapter Twelve

Rutgers, The State University

It was with an unusual air of expectancy and hope that the members of the Rutgers community received the announcement on September 7, 1951, that Dr. Lewis Webster Jones had been selected to head the University. Disturbed by the steady decline in enrollments, by the continuing uncertainty of support from the state, and by the slow pace of physical development, they looked to the new president for the leadership that would enable the University to resume the forward surge that had been interrupted after 1948. Dr. Jones viewed the Rutgers post as offering a tremendous challenge, for he envisioned the as yet unrealized potentialities of the University. Discarding the emphasis on "partnership" that had characterized the previous administration, he made it apparent that he regarded Rutgers as the State University, and it was within this context that he defined the role and functions of the institution.

Dr. Jones brought a rich educational experience to his task at Rutgers. A native of Nebraska, he was a graduate of Reed College and after receiving his doctorate at the Brookings Institution in the field of economics had undertaken postdoctoral studies abroad. When Bennington College was founded in 1932 he became a member of the original faculty and, together with his wife, shared the excitement of participating in what was widely hailed as a significant experiment in collegiate education. He served from 1941 to 1947 as president of Bennington, leaving there to assume the presidency of the University of Arkansas. At Arkansas he enjoyed remarkable success in winning the respect of legislators and influential citizens and enhanced his stature by serving as a member of the President's Commission on Higher Education. Broadly educated and with wide-ranging interests, his enthusiasms extended from football to the fine arts. It was characteristic that in his inaugural address he stressed the catholicity of the University, proclaiming that it should serve people of all classes, faiths, economic conditions, and age

291

groups who had the desire and ability to learn. Denying the existence of any conflict between quantity and quality, or between the ideals of service and high academic standards, he was equally opposed to both pedantry and cultural barbarism. He found especially desirable at Rutgers the peculiar combination of the Colonial-founded institution, the land-grant college, and the state university, for this admixture blended the distinctive elements of the best in American higher education.

As Dr. Jones entered upon his duties, he was immediately confronted by grave issues involving the management of the University. For some years prior to 1949 the Board of Trustees had played a relatively subdued role in initiating and directing University policies. Numbering over fifty members and ordinarily meeting only four times a year, the Board commonly ratified proposals that had been formulated by the president and the Executive Committee. Following the defeat of the 1948 bond issue and the subsequent internal difficulties, there was evident within the Board a disposition to exercise more authority and to place less reliance on the Executive Committee. At the same time, there was also the feeling that the entire administrative structure of the University should be studied with a view to increasing efficiency, reducing costs, and clarifying lines of responsibility. Accordingly, a professional management firm was engaged to survey administrative procedures. The study got under way in October 1951. It was not completed until almost a year later, but a preliminary report in January 1952 dealt with the reorganization of the Board of Trustees.

The management specialists recommended that the Executive Committee be replaced by an executive board that would meet twice a month and through which all other committees would report to the full Board of Trustees; that the Board be served by a well staffed secretariat; and that the chairman of the Board be someone other than the president. After considering these proposals, the Trustees adopted a radically different plan. The full Board of Trustees, instead of meeting quarterly, would convene seven times a year; the old Executive Committee would be restricted to exercising only "administrative powers" in intervals between Board meetings; and the president—as had become traditional—would be the chairman of the Board. Unfortunately, this new arrangement was not effective and was congenial neither to the president nor to the Board. Attendance averaged less than 60 per cent, the decision-making process was unduly cumbersome, and important matters were too frequently postponed or referred to committees for further study. "Actually," reported a special Trustees' committee in 1955, "the Board has no mechanism for assuming its responsibility or exerting its power."

With respect to internal administrative reorganization, the elaborate recommendations of the management firm were studied and discussed for a year, and then a framework was adopted that owed little to the firm's suggested blueprint. In an effort to free the president from operational concerns and improve the coordination of University-wide affairs, the authority of the provost was increased, notably with regard to budgetary matters, and both a president's cabinet, made up of the principal administrative officers, and a provost's cabinet, composed chiefly of college deans and directors, were constituted. This scheme did not commend itself to expert evaluators who studied the University in 1956, but it reflected local conditions and proved to be feasible because of the unusual abilities of the provost. The difficulties and delays attendant upon the consideration and implementation of reorganization plans were vexatious and impeded action on many other matters of urgent concern.

Also diverting the energies of the president, the Trustees, and indeed the entire University community from ordinary channels was a prolonged controversy over the highly charged issue of the policy that should be adopted toward members of the faculty who invoked the Fifth Amendment when questioned about possible Communist affiliations. National concern with "subversion" was an almost inevitable concomitant of the cold war, and following upon the sensational trial of Alger Hiss, the passage of the McCarran Act, and the fantastic charges made by Senator Joseph R. McCarthy, this concern assumed the proportions of hysteria. As early as 1948, writing in the *Rutgers Alumni Monthly*, Earl S. Miers had pointed with alarm to the menace to freedom that inhered in "red baiting," and by 1950—with the frustrations of the Korean War added to other tensions—there were signs that the campus was not immune to the fears that gripped the nation.

Prompted by certain incidents involving public statements by faculty members that aroused controversy, President Clothier in December 1950 had appointed a Trustee-faculty committee to recommend procedures that would, while safeguarding academic freedom, protect the University from public misunderstanding. The committee's proposals, as revised by the Trustees after extended deliberations, resulted in the adoption of new statutory provisions regarding academic freedom in October 1951. In essence, professors were assured of freedom from institutional discipline when discussing in the classroom subjects with which they were competent to deal as scholars. When speaking or writing outside the classroom context, however, they were to be aware of their "special obligations" to their profession and to the University and to conduct themselves appropriately. If a professor did not observe these cautions, or if his utterances were such "as to raise grave doubts concerning his fitness for his position," the matter was to be referred by the appropriate administrative officer to the committee of review of his college for hearing, consideration, and recommendation. Although these regulations were not deemed to be entirely satisfactory by many faculty members, they were substantially in accord with the procedure sanctioned by the American Association of University Professors. They were, however, hardly adequate to the problems that were soon to arise.

On September 24, 1952, an associate professor at the College of Pharmacy invoked both the First and the Fifth Amendments when refusing to answer questions put to him by the Senate Internal Security Subcommittee. Although he subsequently assured President Jones that he was not and had never been a member of the Communist Party, he declared that he regarded any inquiry into his beliefs as offensive. The professor's action provoked widespread newspaper comment. On September 26 Dr. Jones appointed a special committee of Trustees, faculty, and alumni to advise him on the course of action he should pursue in this matter. Subsequently, newspapers called attention to the fact, which was fully known to University authorities, that on March 28 an assistant professor at the Newark College of Arts and Sciences had invoked the Fifth Amendment when questioned about past Communist affiliations by the same Senate committee, whereupon his case was also referred to the special committee. The committee after intensive study concluded that the behavior of the two professors raised questions "as to their fitness to continue as teachers on the University faculty," and the president was advised to convene a faculty committee of review of five members to "hear and advise concerning the cases of the professors."

The issues involved were both grave and intricate. In the public mind, the refusal of the professors to answer the questions put to them implied that they must, indeed, be guilty of Communist ties or that, at best, they were unwilling to assist their government in routing out subversive elements. The subtle complexities of the Fifth Amendment, the Smith Act, and the McCarran Act, as well as the distinctions between heterodoxy and treason were little understood, whereas the menace of Communism was overwhelmingly evident. The fact that the men involved were teachers and were employed at a public institution seemed to be a cause for special concern. The situation was also a novel one. Although there had been major furores at the University of Washington in 1948 and at the University of California a year later that resulted in the dismissal or resignation of numerous professors, these incidents had grown out of state actions. The Rutgers cases were the first in the nation to raise the issue of the use of the Fifth Amendment by a professor before a Congressional committee. Consequently, the University had little in the way of precedent to rely on for guidance.

After an exhaustive study of the case, including a full consideration of the propriety of a professor invoking the constitutional privileges available to him, the faculty committee concluded that no further disciplinary action against the professors was called for. This report was presented to the Trustees on December 12, 1952. On the same day the Board rejected the findings of the faculty committee, insisting that the question at issue was not solely one of the legal rights of the professors as citizens but rather involved their "special obligations" as members of a learned profession and representatives of the University. Moreover, it was argued that their refusal to respond to inquiries addressed to them by a Senate committee impaired confidence in their fitness to teach and was incompatible with the standards required of them as members of a learned profession. This reasoning led to the adoption of a resolution:

> that this Board considers that it is cause for the immediate dismissal of any member of the faculty or staff of the University that he refuse, on the ground of the Fifth Amendment to the Constitution of the United States, to answer questions propounded by any duly constituted investigatory body, or in any judicial proceeding, relating to whether he is, or has been, a member of the Communist Party.

The two professors were thereupon directed to signify their willingness to appear again before the Senate Internal Security Subcommittee, failing which they would be dismissed as of December 31.

The Trustees' edict shocked the University community. It was heatedly criticized by the *Targum,* and at a hastily convened session of the University Assembly the faculty and staff voted their opposition in a series of resolutions. An emergency faculty committee drafted a lengthy plea asking that the cases be reconsidered, but the Trustees in January reaffirmed their previous position, and Dr. Jones issued a statement elaborating the reasoning that lay behind the "immediate dismissal" resolution:

> Under all the circumstances of our relations to world communism, a minimum responsibility would seem to be that members of the University state frankly where they stand on matters of such deep public concern, and of such relevance to academic integrity, as membership in the Communist party, even when by a straightforward statement they believe they might incur certain personal risks. . . . These risks must be balanced against the risk of damage to the entire University, and to the profession to which the two men belong, incurred by refusal to testify on the grounds of possible self-incrimination.

The stand taken by the president and the Trustees met with over-whelming popular approval, but it continued to be opposed by the majority of faculty and students. The issue was kept alive when an associate professor at the School of Law employed the Fifth Amendment before the House Committee on Un-American Activities in March 1953 and subsequently accepted the alternative of resigning rather than facing dismissal. A month later a part-time instructor in University College was suspended and not reappointed following a similar incident. Meanwhile other universities were being confronted with like problems, and although some of them pursued the same course as Rutgers, others—led by Harvard—took a different position and refused to regard the invoking of the Fifth Amendment as a sufficient cause for dismissal. The long-drawn-out controversy, which did not subside until 1957, was symptomatic of the tensions that affected the academic community in the McCarthy period, and its consequences were felt in all areas of University life. Teachers and students alike resentfully but prudently recognized the temper of the times and grew cautious about expressing opinions that might provoke the charge of "Un-American." It was a nightmarish period, one unlike any the University had ever experienced, and it raised enduring questions about the limits of freedom in America.

While grappling with the time-consuming matters of internal reorganization and the Fifth Amendment cases, President Jones was somewhat impatiently attempting to find solutions to critical problems facing the University. There could be little doubt that the most pressing need was for greatly expanded physical facilities, not only to make up for the deficiencies that had existed for a quarter of a century but also to prepare for the anticipated upswing in enrollments that would occur in the immediate future. Obviously, much would depend on the policy of the state, but it was understood that private benefactions and even borrowing would be required.

Initially there was heartening progress. In his budget message in January 1952 Governor Driscoll recommended an appropriation of $2,000,000 for a new University library, and when in due course the legislature made the sum available there were assurances that an additional $2,000,000 would be granted a year later to make possible the erection of a building that would be adequate for the foreseeable future. The old Voorhees Library had long since been outgrown, with the result that a substantial proportion of its collections had to be stored in warehouses and basements in various remote locations. The news of the library appropriation, ending a three-year moratorium on state funds for capital construction, was tremendously encouraging. Among other vital considerations, it sustained the hope that the growing graduate program, especially in the social sciences and the humanities, could develop on a sound foundation. The carefully planned building, designed to hold over 1,500,000 volumes and to seat 1,200 students, was formally dedicated in November 1956. The most imposing structure on the campus, it was to contribute in many ways, under its devoted head, Donald F. Cameron, to the intellectual enrichment of the University.

Unfortunately, the high anticipations aroused by the appropriation for the library were not realized. In 1953 the legislature provided the second installment for the cost of the library. A year later, as the result of intense pressures over a period of several years from the long-denied agricultural constituency, about $2,000,000 was appropriated to construct major facilities for the horticulture and poultry departments at the College of Agriculture, but in 1955 the capital appropriation declined to $1,000,000, to be used for a library at the College of South Jersey and to defray part of the cost of a proposed law center in Newark. At this modest rate, the University was falling ever further behind, and when no capital sums whatsoever were made available by the state in 1956 the prospect was little short of desperate. By its own most conservative estimate, prepared in 1954, the University required new buildings that would cost nearly $45,000,000, of which no more than one third could be obtained from other than state sources. But so long as New Jersey retained the lowest per capita state taxes in the nation, it clearly lacked the income to provide capital facilities on a pay-as-you-go basis. Only a bond issue, which would have to be approved in a referendum, could provide the needed funds, but there were as yet formidable obstacles standing in the way of that alternative.

Recognizing that at best the state could not meet all its urgent needs, the University authorities explored other possibilities. Aside from academic buildings, there was a critical shortage of dormitory accommodations. Even with the completion of Demarest Hall, there were rooms for only a quarter of the students in the men's colleges, and administrative officials were convinced that enlarged facilities would attract more students and better quality students to the University. There was no thought of seeking state funds for such a purpose and the University's own resources were already overcommitted, so the only recourse remaining was to borrow funds. After preliminary investigations disclosed that a Federal loan could not be obtained in an adequate amount, the decision was reached late in 1953 to borrow $3,500,000 from the National Life Insurance Company, to which the University was already indebted for about $2,000,000.

Boldly anticipating a sharp increase in the numbers of men students at a time when postwar enrollment had reached its lowest point, the Trustees agreed to more than double the existing accommodations by erecting three huge dormitories. Equally imaginative was the decision to erect the buildings on the narrow strip of land between George Street and the canal. The new dormitories were a radical innovation also, in that they were nine stories in height and contained on their lower levels twenty-four classrooms. Completed in 1956, the admirably sited structures housed over 900 undergraduates and brought the proportion of students resident on the campus in dormitories and fraternities from about half to nearly three quarters. In conjunction with the three dormitories, the first approximation of a student center, named "The Ledge," was erected; this provided the men undergraduates with a highly popular all-purpose meeting place. Much as the University Library had raised the morale of the faculty, the dormitory complex greatly improved the lot of the undergraduates and reestablished the residential character of the men's colleges. The entire project was significant, too, in that it exemplified the often-demonstrated willingness of the Trustees to strain every resource to extend educational opportunities to larger numbers of worthy students.

Encouraged by the obvious success of this venture in borrowing funds to erect self-liquidating facilities, the Trustees in 1956 took the further step of negotiating a loan through the Housing and Home Finance Agency to erect a splendidly equipped health center for the men's colleges and two dormitories at the College for Women. The latter buildings, which represented the first addition to the residential facilities for women in thirty years, were attractively designed and were constructed as the first units of what was to become the new Neilson Campus, adjacent to "Woodlawn." Completed by 1960, they housed 480 students and made possible a major expansion of the women's college.

As in the past, efforts to secure funds from private sources to construct academic buildings met with little success. A partial exception was the campaign to raise money to build a well conceived law center in Newark. Launched in 1952 with the cordial endorsement of the Trustees and of the Advisory Council of the Newark Colleges, it was hoped that this project would be the first step in a general program to provide the urban institution with proper facilities. After two years, over $500,000 had been obtained, but this sum was not deemed to be adequate, and in 1955 a matching grant was secured from the state to insure the eventual construction of the building. An enterprise especially cherished by President Jones envisioned the construction of a many-faceted arts center, but when a survey failed to disclose the likelihood of financial backing, the idea had to be abandoned. By 1956, when the prospects of timely state appropriations for critically needed facilities for the biological sciences and engineering seemed dim, various schemes were explored, but the results were all negative.

Although the gap between resources and requirements seemed

enormous in 1957, especially in view of the impending "tidal wave" of students, there had in fact been substantial accomplishments since 1951. The chemistry building—appropriately named the Ralph G. Wright Laboratories in honor of the former department head and Trustee—and the agricultural science building—named Lipman Hall in tribute to the first dean of the College of Agriculture—were now in use, along with the Institute of Microbiology, the University Library, Demarest Hall, and the three river-front dormitories, presently bearing the familiar names of Frelinghuysen, Hardenbergh, and Campbell. Nearing completion were the new buildings for horticulture and poultry, and the library at the College of South Jersey, while in the advanced planning stage were the health center and the two dormitories at the College for Women. Not since the period of the mid-1920's had the University witnessed such construction activities. Nevertheless, there was a general recognition that a crisis was impending and that extraordinary measures were called for if the State University was to meet its increasingly heavy responsibilities.

The years of Dr. Jones's administration were marked not only by a determined effort to improve the physical facilities of the University but also by searching inquiries into problems of educational philosophy and methods and ambitious ventures into new areas of service. The interval between the end of the postwar enrollment boom and the forecasted "tidal wave" that hit the University in the late 1950's provided an opportunity for stock-taking, self-examination, and curricular experimentation. And wherever the resources could be found there was constructive innovation as well.

The most interesting arena of intellectual ferment was the College of Arts and Sciences in New Brunswick. There a vigorous "self-study" committee, aided by a grant from the Ford Foundation, sought to grapple with basic issues of educational policy and curricular reform, as well as with such ancillary matters as relations with secondary schools, academic advising, and effective teaching. As the committee viewed it, the crucial problem confronting the College was how to balance the acknowledged need for specialized training in a discipline with a program of general education that would produce "commonly shared experiences" rather than a haphazard array of loosely related courses, as prescribed by the requirements adopted in 1945. In broad terms, the solution advanced was to introduce comprehensive "divisional" examinations in the humanities, the social sciences, and the sciences and to encourage departments within each of these fields to collaborate in offering integrated courses. The objective was to insure that graduates of the College would possess broad but integrated knowledge of each field as part of their common experience. The committee was groping for a means of retaining or strengthening the unity of the liberal arts college, which was seemingly endangered by the growing emphasis on departmentalization and specialization.

The committee's recommendations occasioned debates within the faculty, the echoes of which were to reverberate for many years, and although the central proposals were generally approved, many influences combined to defeat or delay their implementation. In spite of recurrent attacks on the evils of "compartmentalization" and strong official sanction for interdepartmental and interdisciplinary courses, the trend toward fragmentation and specialization was not reversed. On the contrary, specialism was intensified as faculty members became ever more strongly oriented toward graduate work and research. And as their numbers multiplied after 1956, courses proliferated, areas of competency narrowed, and the traditional ideal of the unity of the liberal arts college, though still cherished, was obviously imperiled.

Efforts to formulate a University-wide educational philosophy revealed a continuing dependence on traditional concepts, hardly anticipating the character that Rutgers would assume as a "multiversity" in the post-Sputnik era. A statement of educational philosophy, drafted by a faculty committee and made the subject of wide-ranging discussions at an all-university conference in September, 1955, held that Rutgers faced a twofold task. "This task requires that Rutgers provide the means whereby the intellectual and creative talents of the University community extend the frontiers of knowledge and enrich the cultural heritage, and that Rutgers provide educational opportunities for all qualified persons . . ." In a more practical vein, President Jones at the same conference directed attention to the problems that would be created by the impending vast increase in the numbers of students and outlined some possible solutions. Ways must be found to simplify the curriculum by halting the proliferation of courses. New methods must be devised—such as television and lectures to large classes—so that individual instructors could teach more students. The costs of higher education must be kept within bounds, in part by reducing the tendency toward "spoon feeding" and placing more responsibility on the student. No doubt these sober attempts at self-analysis and thoughtful projection were fruitful, but they could scarcely take into account the radically changed conditions that were soon to prevail and that would confront all American universities with bewildering challenges.

Without regard for explicit philosophical considerations or even for rigidly conceived blueprints, the several units of the University continued to develop, often following the paths of expediency. At the Newark Colleges, where physical needs were most acute, borrowed funds were used to purchase the former Marlin factory, the Y.W.C.A. building, and other smaller structures to take care of the most critical requirements. With a strengthened faculty, improved library and laboratory facilities, modest provisions for research, and even varied extracurricular programs for the students, the urban institution had made great progress since 1946. Among other developments, nursing education curricula were introduced in 1952, which led to the establishment in 1956 of a full-fledged college of nursing. At the College of South Jersey, which offered a full four-year program after 1951, expansion was carried forward through the acquisition of makeshift facilities, and somehow a remarkably strong morale sustained the faculty and student body under Dean W. Layton Hall. The College for Women, which exercised its female prerogative by changing its name from New Jersey College for Women to Douglass College on April 16—Founders Day—1955, appropriately entered upon a new stage of growth and vitality under Dean Mary I. Bunting, who succeeded Dean Corwin in July of that year. Still cherishing its unique autonomy and rightfully priding itself upon its attentive concern for the intellectual and social development of its selective student body, Douglass was to be drawn into closer association with the men's colleges through the increasing participation of its faculty in the work of the Graduate School. The ties between the two sides of town were also strengthened by the adoption in 1959 of a new class schedule that facilitated the movement of students between the two campuses.

Especially significant for the future course of development of the University was the establishment of new graduate and professional programs. The creation of a graduate school of social work had been authorized by the legislature in 1948, but not until 1954 were funds appropriated to finance the undertaking. Having as its major purpose the training of social workers, the school was established in 1954 with the appointment of H. Wayne Vasey as dean. Working in close collaboration with state and local welfare agencies to provide its students with practical experience, the school quickly demonstrated its ability to fill an important need. The Graduate School of Library Service, the establishment of which had been urged by a special committee appointed in 1951 by the State Commissioner of Education, offered its first classes in 1954. Under Dean Lowell A. Martin a faculty of unusual distinction was recruited, and almost from the beginning this unit secured a position among the leading library schools of the country. In recognition of the changes that had taken place in its actual functions, the School of Education in 1960 became the Graduate School of Education, thereafter concentrating its efforts on graduate-level programs of instruction and research.

Also reflecting the growing diversity of the University, and further differentiating its complex structure, was the trend toward the establishment of institutes or centers oriented toward very specific functions. A bequest of nearly $2,000,000 from the estate of Florence P. Eagleton, long-time Trustee, for the purpose of furthering "an intelligent interest in the cultivation of civic responsibility and leadership among American people in the field of practical politics" led to the establishment of the Eagleton Institute of Politics. Through a varied program of undergraduate forums, graduate courses, informal meetings for people active in public life, and research and publication projects, the Institute under the directorship of Donald G. Herzberg sought to give new dignity and meaning to the term "practical politics." In a related area, a five-year grant from the Ford Foundation in 1959 made possible the creation of the Urban Studies Center, where it was hoped that the plan of combining research and extension in the service of agriculture might be utilized with equal efficacy in dealing with the problems associated with urbanization. Meanwhile, in other fields there were being organized the Radiation Science Center, the Center for Information Processing, the Statistics Center, and many others. At the instructional level, institutes financed by the National Science Foundation offered advanced or experimental training for teachers of mathematics, physics, and biology in intensive summer programs. In effect, the conventional framework of colleges and schools no longer sufficed to contain the scope of the University's manifold activities and, frequently with some special source of financing to encourage them, the centers and institutes proliferated.

Closely paralleling and complementing these developments was the steady growth of graduate studies and research. In recognition of its enhanced status, the Graduate School acquired a dean—Dr. Walter C. Russell—in 1952. By 1957 it had nearly 1,000 students, and in June of that year it conferred 178 advanced degrees, including 64 doctorates, of which 60 were in scientific fields. Expenditures for research continued to mount, though not so precipitously as was the case after 1957. A significant milestone in the progress of these areas was passed early in 1960 when the governing body of the University adopted a major policy statement defining the obligations of the institution with respect to graduate studies and research. Because nearly half of New Jersey's college graduates planned to engage in advanced graduate or professional study, the State University, as the capstone of New Jersey's system of public education, had to provide programs of instruction and research at the highest level. Graduate work and research were "not to be regarded as incidental functions that have merely been added to the traditional function of educating undergraduates. Rather, Rutgers is redefining itself as a university, and in such a way that this concept should operate to influence every aspect of the institution's operations."

In odd contrast to the evidences of vigor and imagination within the realms of the administration and faculty, the undergraduate scene was strangely quiescent. Whether the cause was the feeling of uncertainty engendered by the troubled international situation, or the sense of caution instilled by McCarthyism, or more subtle factors associated with the background of this new generation was a frequent subject of inconclusive debate, but observers were aware that student attitudes and customs were changing. The words that were used most frequently in describing the undergraduate temper were "cool" and "apathetic."

The campaign against discrimination in fraternities, for example, which had engendered such heat a few years earlier, lost much of its fervor. In 1952, in fact, a referendum on a proposition that would have directed the Student Council to take action against fraternities having discriminatory clauses was defeated by a narrow margin. The issue remained alive, however, and in 1957 the University authorities took the decisive step of ordering the three fraternities that still retained restrictive clauses to get rid of them by September 1, 1959, or face suspension. One house that failed to comply with this deadline was suspended. In the meantime, new fraternity chapters were established— Zeta Beta Tau, Phi Sigma Delta, Gamma Sigma, Alpha Gamma Rho, and Alpha Epsilon Pi—bringing the number of houses to twenty-five and the proportion of students enrolled as members up to 50 per cent. As the fraternities grew in strength, the Scarlet Barbs declined, and in 1956, following a year in which no independent candidates had been elected to campus political office, the organization disbanded.

There was little interest shown in student elections, no vestige of political radicalism, even a decline in attendance at athletic contests. Formal dances, a feature of student social life for over seventy years, lost favor. By 1957 the phenomenon of the "danceless" Prom, featuring a jazz concert, a celebrated comedian, or a folk-singing group had come into vogue. "It is evident that the contemporary Rutgers man is not satisfied by the traditional forms of recreation," a student reporter concluded. "And his requirements must be satisfied by an evolution of social events." When early in 1959 the C.B.S. television network produced a two-hour "special" on undergraduate mores, based upon filmed discussions with Rutgers faculty and students, it labelled the show "Generation without a Cause." With due allowance for dramatic exaggeration, the production portrayed the students as cautious, security-minded conformists, whose motto was "play it safe." But the program also conveyed the impression that the students were trying extremely hard to be "mature" in their judgments, at the same time that they were groping for ways to achieve personal satisfactions as individuals, rather than as members of vast, impersonal aggregations.

No doubt student morale, like that of the alumni, was adversely affected by the dismal performance of the athletic teams in the early 1950's. Over the period from 1950 to 1954 the football, basketball, and baseball teams won less than half their games, and the other squads posted comparable records. By 1953 the *Rutgers Alumni Monthly* was asking editorially, "What's Wrong with Rutgers Sports?" and two years later the leading newspaper in the state devoted a series of four articles to the same vexing subject. Some blamed tightened eligibility rules, others declaimed on the need for more scholarships, and virtually all clamored for coaching changes. In 1956 John R. Stiegman was brought in to build a winning football team, and within two years he had more than accomplished that objective. Simultaneously, other teams improved their records, raising the sagging spirits of students and alumni. In broader terms, the situation improved when the expenses of intercollegiate athletics were made chargeable to the University budget, the number of alumni-sponsored scholarships was increased, and recruiting efforts directed at out-of-state students were intensified. Somehow, it continued to seem important that the University should be represented by successful athletic teams. In quite a different context, the most notable athletic achievement of the decade was registered by two unheralded students, Thomas S. Price and Charles P. Logg, Jr., who won the pairs-without-coxswain rowing event in the 1952 Olympics at Helsinki, the first time Americans had ever won this particular competition.

Not entirely by coincidence, the low state of athletic fortunes was paralleled by a corresponding slump in alumni interest. Whereas in 1952 there had been thirty-four active Rutgers Clubs, there were but seventeen by 1955. The situation was sufficiently critical so that the *Rutgers Alumni Monthly* published a series of articles on the general theme, "What's Wrong with Our Alumni?" and even commissioned a professor of sociology to make a survey of alumni attitudes. Not surprisingly, the study revealed a high correlation between alumni enthusiasm—as evidenced by annual contributions to the Alumni Fund—and prior participation as undergraduates in extracurricular activities. More significant was the discovery that 60 per cent of the alumni had graduated in the past fifteen years, making the alumni body as a whole a relatively young group. Important in strengthening the ties of the alumni to the University was the establishment in 1956 of an Alumni-Faculty Club in a renovated residence on upper College Avenue. Such an amenity had been sorely missed ever since the demolition of the old Alumni House, originally the President's House, and the new quarters provided a pleasant and convivial meeting place for both faculty members and former graduates.

By any criteria the University was struggling forward on many fronts despite the oft-cited deficiencies that hampered its effectiveness. It was gaining strength internally and adding to its academic reputation. Yet the question of its acceptability as the State University remained clouded by doubts, and once again those doubts came to the fore when the University became involved in another defeat in a public referendum. The question at issue was the establishment of a state medical college.

In response to the urgings of the Medical Society of New Jersey and other interested groups the legislature in May 1950 created the New Jersey Medical College Commission. After more than a year of study the Commission recommended that a medical and dental college should be established at New Brunswick in close proximity to the State University and that there should be a bond issue to provide the funds to defray the construction costs. New Jersey had no medical or dental school, and it was a simple matter to demonstrate the need for training more practitioners in both of those fields. The legislature seemingly was disposed to act on the Commission's recommendations, but the issue soon became snarled in local and partisan rivalries. Jersey City, which had a partly vacant Medical Center that operated at a deficit of more than $5,000,000 a year, launched a strong campaign to have the proposed medical school located there. Also entering the lists was Newark, which sought to have the school attached to its deficit-ridden City Hospital. Recognizing that this competition had explosive political overtones, the legislature remained prudently inactive.

The issue slumbered until early in 1954, although University authorities continued to make tentative plans for a medical center and to conduct discussions with other proponents of the measure. Then, in February, Governor Robert B. Meyner announced his support for a state-financed medical and dental college, and in the same month bills to implement the proposal were introduced in the legislature. Once again, Jersey City came forward and offered its Medical Center as a location for the school, and when it seemed unlikely that the state would accept the offer, the mayor of Jersey City publicly advertised the terms on which the Medical Center would be made available to any university that was desirous of establishing a medical school there. In August the city authorities announced that Seton Hall University had agreed to launch a medical school, using the facilities of the Medical Center, and although the lease was not actually signed until December 10, it was immediately announced that New Jersey now had a medical college.

Meanwhile, the legislature in June had provided for a public referendum on a $25,000,000 bond issue to build a state medical-dental school. Seeking to avoid the controversy over location, the legislation specified that the site of the school would be determined after the results of the election were known. Supporters of the bond issue, ranging from labor and agricultural groups to medical societies and the New Jersey Taxpayers Association, formed a committee that conducted a public campaign. The University also lent support to the effort, although it was in an exceedingly awkward position. It was not adverse to accepting responsibility for a medical school and even anticipated that if the bond issue was approved the school would be associated with the University. But because the question of location was so controversial and uncertain Rutgers could scarcely risk making a strong case in its own behalf.

The campaign was relatively sedate until October, when the political leaders of Hudson County declared their unalterable opposition to the bond issue. The mayor of Jersey City stumped the state, insisting that New Jersey already had a medical school and charging that a state-supported institution would cost far more than the projected $25,000,000 and would lead to the imposition of burdensome new state taxes. In the final week before the election, New Jersey dioceses of the Roman Catholic Church joined the attack. Hostile editorials appeared in the diocesan newspapers in Newark, Trenton, and Camden, and on the Sunday before the election priests urged their parishioners to vote "no" on the bond issue. The referendum produced a decisive vote in opposition to the question, with Hudson County piling up a 94,000 majority against it.

Rutgers, of course, suffered in the debacle. Even though it had not been specified that the medical school would be under its jurisdiction, such an eventuality had been widely assumed, and the overtones of the opposition campaign gave credibility to the assumption that antagonism to Rutgers was influential in bringing about the defeat of the referendum. In due course the Seton Hall College of Medicine and Dentistry began operations, but, somewhat ironically, after nearly a decade of difficulties with the Jersey City authorities over arrangements at the Medical Center and soaring indebtedness, Seton Hall gladly turned the institution over to the State of New Jersey in 1964.

Along with a series of other developments, the defeat of the medical-school bond issue compelled the Board of Trustees to consider drastic changes in the management of the University. It was obvious that under the state relationship that had been defined in 1945 Rutgers had failed to secure the degree of public acceptance and State financial support that was required to equip the State University to meet its manifold responsibilities. Governor Meyner made plain his belief that, unless the state were given a larger voice in the control of the University, there was little prospect that capital appropriations could be increased. So long as Rutgers operated under what was largely a private board of trustees, the citizens of the state could not be convinced that it was really a state university. The Trustees were also approaching the conclusion that the arrangements that had been made in 1952 to have the entire Board engage actively in the formulation of policy was too cumbersome to be effective. With these considerations in mind, a special committee, headed by Charles H. Brower was appointed in September 1954 to study the reorganization of the Board.

After extensive preliminary discussions, the Brower Committee decided to recommend a plan of reorganization put forward by President Jones. In essence, full management of the University would be vested in a board of governors appointed by the governor, with the consent of the Senate. The Board of Trustees, with some modifications in its composition, would continue in existence to serve in an advisory capacity, manage certain funds, and act as a "watchdog" on educational standards. In presenting its report to the Trustees, the committee emphasized its conviction "that Rutgers cannot longer hope to enjoy the support of the State that it has had in the past unless it becomes what the man in the street would call 'a real State University.'" This proposal was debated by the Board in January 1955, following which the president was authorized to appoint another committee to proceed further with the formulation of a plan of reorganization.

The new committee, headed by Lansing P. Shield, held numerous conferences with Governor Meyner, other state officials, and prominent citizens and, with the assistance of its special counsel, Waldron M. Ward, studied the intricate legal problems involved in transferring authority from the Trustees to a state-appointed board. Its report, which proposed that control over the University be vested in a board of governors, a majority of whom would be state appointees, was thoroughly discussed at a special meeting of the Trustees on November 11, 1955, and was adopted by a vote of 28 to 8 at an adjourned meeting on November 25. Understandably, many of the Trustees strongly opposed surrendering control of the institution to another agency. Others were uncertain as to whether they could, as Trustees, legally divest themselves of responsibility for managing the institution. Accordingly, it was provided that the transfer would not become effective until a court decree had been obtained declaring that the Board might take such action.

The next step was to obtain the enactment of the necessary legislation to implement the reorganization plan. A bill to this effect was introduced in the legislature, and when it was made the subject of a public hearing in May the only opposition was voiced by John J. Rafferty, spokesman for Roman Catholic interests. Meanwhile, the several alumni organizations of the University, the faculty, and the press of the state expressed approval of the measure. The bill passed both houses of the legislature with only one dissenting vote and was signed by the governor on June 1, 1956. Subsequently, on July 19, a judgment by Superior Court Justice Thomas A. Schettino held that the reorganization plan was legal, and on August 10 the Board of Trustees formally accepted the new order.

The legislation that gave effect to the reorganization plan made fundamental changes in the charter, corporate structure, and control of the University. Whereas since 1945 the facilities of the University had been fully under the management of the Trustees, although impressed with a public trust and subject to the general superintendence of the State Board of Education, now these facilities were to be directly managed by a publicly controlled board of governors. Even the name of the corporate body was changed from "The Trustees of Rutgers College in New Jersey" to "Rutgers, The State University."

The Board of Governors was to be composed of eleven voting members—six of whom were to be appointed by the governor and five by the Trustees from among their membership—together with the president of the University and the Commissioner of Education as ex officio members. The new board was to conduct the affairs of the University. Specifically, it was empowered to determine policy and study the educational and financial needs of the institution; prepare and present the annual budget; disburse all monies, including endowment income received from the Board of Trustees; borrow money, with the advice and consent of the Trustees; plan and construct buildings; appoint all officers and employees; and establish new departments and schools. There were certain limitations on its powers. It was obliged to present the annual budget jointly with the State Board of Education, and salary schedules and the establishment of new departments or schools were subject to the approval of that agency. The appointment of a president required the advice and consent of the Board of Trustees.

The Board of Trustees retained limited functions. It was to serve in an overall advisory capacity and control certain funds and properties that were, however, at the disposal of the Board of Governors. The Trustees reserved the right to withhold or withdraw the assets under their jurisdiction, valued at approximately $50,000,000, if, without their consent, the University ceased to be designated and maintained as the State University, or the name of the University was changed, or the essential autonomy of the institution was impaired, or the state failed to appropriate funds "adequate for the conduct of a State University with high educational standards and to meet the cost of increasing enrollment and the need for proper facilities." Thus the state and the Trustees were joined in a contractual relationship, which might be voided if the terms of the contract embodied in the legislation were not fulfilled. The composition of the Board was altered. In brief, the state officials who had previously served, ex officio, as members, were replaced by the state-appointed members of the Board of Governors; the size of the Board was reduced by decreasing the number of so-called charter Trustees from thirty to fifteen; and all Trustees were to serve for limited, rather than indefinite, terms.*

Ever since the early years of President Thomas' administration the question of the degree to which the state should participate in, or control, the management of Rutgers had been a lively one, requiring frequent consideration by the Board of Trustees and occasioning intermittent public controversy. Now, persuaded that such a move was in the best interests of public higher education in New Jersey and on the basis of certain guarantees, the Trustees took the momentous step of transferring the authority they had exercised for 190 years to a board of governors on which their representatives were in the minority. Not quite an agency of the state and with its autonomy seemingly insured, Rutgers was to become something more than an "instrumentality of the State" in its new role as Rutgers, The State University.

The complex task of implementing the reorganization plan was accomplished efficiently and harmoniously by the Trustees and Governors. At their first meeting on August 20, 1956, the Board of Governors chose as their chairman Howard A. Smith, an alumnus of the class of 1911 and a charter Trustee, who served with unusual dedication in that post until 1959. Dr. Jones was re-elected president of the University and of the corporation and members of a joint committee were appointed to cooperate with the Trustees in working out the details of the relationship between the two bodies. Under the arrangement that was ultimately adopted, the Board of Governors met twice monthly and operated with five standing committees, on all but one of which there were representatives of the Trustees. The Trustees adopted new by-laws, in accordance with which Lansing P. Shield was elected chairman. Meeting quarterly, the reconstituted Board had its own standing committees, was represented on the joint committees of the Trustees and Governors, and in addition appointed advisory committees for each of the schools and colleges, with a member of the Board of Governors serving as a liaison for each committee. Despite its apparent com-

* In 1962 the size of the Board of Trustees was increased to a maximum of 58, chiefly for the purpose of according representation to the alumni of the several colleges.

plexity, the new scheme proved to be feasible, and relations between the Trustees and the Governors were cordial and cooperative.

During the period of transition both bodies were involved in the adjustment of some long-standing issues. Almost from its earliest years, the Board of Trustees had assumed responsibility for administering certain funds, the purpose of which was to provide scholarships for students destined for the Dutch Reformed ministry. In an amicable agreement, sanctioned by a judicial opinion, the administration of these funds was turned over to the General Synod of the Reformed Church in America, thus ending the last vestige of any connection between the State University and the Church. An even more ancient tie was severed when the Rutgers Preparatory School assumed a completely separate status under its own board of trustees on June 30, 1957. It was anachronistic for the State University to continue to maintain a private preparatory department, and after many years of study, hesitation, and negotiation the school—whose origins were contemporaneous with those of Queen's College—became independent and established itself on a new campus.

Another matter of unfinished business that required the immediate attention of the Board of Governors was the reconsideration of the "immediate dismissal" rule that had been adopted by the Trustees on December 12, 1952. The issue came to a head when in April 1956 the University administration was formally censured by the American Association of University Professors. Later in the same year it was threatened with similar action by the Association of American Law Schools. At first the University authorities declined to retreat from the position that had been taken, but in October 1956 President Jones reviewed the problem for the new Board of Governors and stated that he would interpret the rule of December 12, 1952, liberally and would not regard the invocation of the Fifth Amendment as cause for *automatic* dismissal. At the same time, it was decided that, because the University was under new management, prior statutes were no longer binding, and a special committee, headed by John O. Bigelow, was appointed to formulate a new statement on academic freedom.

Working in consultation with the Trustees and faculty representatives, the Bigelow Committee recommended altered procedures, which were adopted by the Board of Governors in November 1957. The rule of December 12, 1952, was abandoned. Hereafter faculty members might be charged with incompetence or with conduct that was "reprehensible and detrimental to the University." Hearings would then be conducted by a five-member faculty panel chosen by lot from the University Senate, and the findings of this body were to be given "great weight" by the Board of Governors, with whom rested the final decision regarding dismissal. With this reversal of former policy, the censure that had been imposed on the University administration was removed. No action was taken, however, to reopen the cases of the men who had been dismissed or induced to resign.

The real test confronting the Board of Governors was, of course, their ability to secure adequate support for the State University while remaining free from unwholesome political interference. For a time the prospects were anything but heartening. Right at the outset a group of senators sought to block the appointment of John O. Bigelow to the Board of Governors. A distinguished jurist of impeccable character, Judge Bigelow, at the request of the Essex County Bar Association, had served as counsel for a Newark school-teacher who faced dismissal because he had invoked the Fifth Amendment. The incident touched off a storm of controversy, as bar associations, civil rights organizations, and leading citizens protested the treatment accorded Bigelow. Governor Meyner refused to yield, and after nearly two weeks of bitter wrangling, the appointment was confirmed. But the incident did not quiet the fears of those who anticipated that in its new status Rutgers would more than ever be subjected to political pressures.

There were unexpected difficulties, too, with the State Board of Education. When in 1956 the Board of Governors prepared budget requests for the ensuing fiscal year, they were subjected to minute scrutiny and general criticism by the State Board, which charged that the University lacked an overall educational plan and complained that specific items were not properly justified. The wide-ranging attack surprised and alarmed the University authorities, for the act of 1956 had in no way extended the powers of the State Board over the University's budget; if anything, the legislation had presumably strengthened Rutgers' autonomy. After numerous conferences, the differences were ostensibly reconciled and mutual pledges of cooperation were exchanged, but the animosities engendered by this controversy occasioned strained relations for the next several years.

Equally discouraging was the action taken by the legislature with respect to the budget. With a gubernatorial election in prospect, the Republican-controlled legislature determined to make an issue of economy and slashed the amount recommended by Governor Meyner, which was well below the University's request. Despite the urgent appeals of the Board of Governors, the final appropriation act contained no funds for capital construction and a disappointingly small increase in operating funds. So critical was the University's financial predicament that the Governors were obliged to resort to the undesirable expedient of raising both tuition fees and dormitory rates. The plight of the University stimulated the undergraduates to form a "Greater State University Committee," which published a pamplet, *Years of Crisis,* and, when another budgetary emergency threatened in May 1958, organized a mass march of students to Trenton. As they looked back upon their first hectic year, the Board of Governors had reason to be discouraged about the results of their efforts.

Fortunately, strong influences that were to affect profoundly the whole educational climate were becoming operative, and Rutgers, along with institutions of higher education generally, was to move abruptly into an extraordinary new era. The climactic event that shocked the nation into an intense awareness of its educational deficiencies was the spectacular achievement of the Soviet Union in placing Sputnik into orbit on October 4, 1957. The United States, accustomed to technical supremacy, suddenly found itself in second place, and almost frantically set about overhauling its educational system with a view to producing the scientists and technicians who would reestablish American leadership. Critics of elementary and secondary education, who had long complained of the lack of discipline and content in the progressive-oriented schools, now were hailed as prophets. Strongly influenced by the reports of James B. Conant and others, and urged along by foundation grants and Government subsidies for special programs, the schools moved away from "life adjustment" towards an emphasis on high academic achievement. Federal expenditures for research and for the training of personnel in critical fields multiplied tenfold between 1957 and 1964, and funds from the National Science Foundation, the National Institutes of Health, and the several defense agencies made up an ever increasing proportion of university budgets. In 1958 the National Defense Education Act laid the foundations for vastly broadened Federal aid to undergraduate and graduate students, especially those who were preparing for careers in teaching or in science, and in 1963 the Higher Education Facilities Act went far beyond the College Housing Loan Act of 1950 in making funds available to institutions of higher education for construction purposes.

Federal support for higher education had a long history, but now assistance was to be given on a truly massive scale and was to be justified on the basis of the defense needs of the nation. Although they had many qualms about the direction in which affairs were moving, the educators played upon the national concern to "catch up with the Russians." "The Sputnik and other evidences of Soviet scientific progress have emphasized the importance of scientific education and research in this country," Dr. Jones told the legislative appropriations committee early in 1958. "Our future national security will surely be determined by what goes on in the classrooms and laboratories of this nation." Such an appeal could scarcely be ignored.

Adding to the urgency of the problem was the certainty that the numbers of young men and women who would be seeking a college education would more than double in the decade ahead. In the simplest terms, because of the sharp rise in birth rates after the war there would be more young people. A report published by the State Department of Education in 1956 pointed out that the college-age population in New Jersey would swell from 239,000 in 1954 to 517,000 in 1973, and this was a conservative estimate. The magnitude of the challenge was enlarged by reason of the fact that increasing proportions of high school graduates would be seeking advanced education; it was calculated that the percentage might rise from 30 in 1954 to around 50 a decade later. However the estimates were formulated, it was evident that a "tidal wave" of students would soon engulf the colleges of New Jersey and that unless immediate and drastic steps were taken to double and even triple the available facilities, thousands of qualified candidates would be denied admission.

With so much attention focused on the field of education by official agencies, national fervor mounted and assumed what might be termed in the parlance of the times the dimensions of a "crusade." As public concern rose, politicians discovered that education was a popular cause and vied with one another to be its advocates. Both the "New Frontier" delineated by President John F. Kennedy and the "Great Society" envisioned by President Lyndon B. Johnson accorded high priority to education. Among other favoring circumstances, the national economy expanded at a rate that exceeded expectations, ushering in an age of affluence. In brief, a combination of circumstances created an environment unusually favorable to advances throughout the whole field of education, and Rutgers was to share in the forward movement.

Recognizing that a crisis lay ahead, the State Board of Education undertook the formulation of a comprehensive plan for expanding the facilities for higher education in New Jersey. As a first step, it prepared estimates of future enrollment trends to 1973 and projected the number of additional places that would have to be provided by the private and public colleges of the state to meet anticipated needs. These findings were published in July 1956 in a pamphlet, *The Closing Door to College,* that clearly outlined the dimensions of the problem. Next, in 1957, it sought to translate the needs it had defined into a building program. Enlisting the expert services of Dr. George D. Strayer, who had made comparable studies in several other states, the State Board called upon the State University, the Newark College of Engineering, and the six state teachers colleges to report what would be required to double their undergraduate enrollments by 1965 and then sought to coordinate and combine these requests into an integrated program of development.

The Rutgers Board of Governors, through its Committee on Planning and Policy, worked out a construction schedule that would have cost over $77,000,000, of which nearly $47,000,000 would be sought from the state. After prolonged conferences and negotiations with the State Board of Education, the latter figure was reluctantly scaled down to about $36,000,000. Similar reductions were made in the requests from the other state-supported institutions, for it was the judgment of the State Board of Education that it would be impolitic to seek too large a sum. The total figure ultimately arrived at was $76,550,000. In a widely distributed report, *College Opportunity in New Jersey,* published in December 1957, the State Board explained what use would be made of the funds and proposed that they should be raised by means of a bond issue.

The legislature that convened in 1958 was sympathetic to the program that had been shaped by the State Board of Education but priority was given to a bond issue that would provide for the development of additional water resources. However, as an evidence of its intention, the legislature appropriated the unprecedented sum of $10,000,000 for academic buildings, of which $3,700,000 was allocated to the State University. This sum, together with supplemental funds from other sources, made possible the construction of a spacious new biology building at University Heights and a 150,000-volume library at Douglass College, both of which facilities had been accorded high priority on the schedule embodied in the University's recommendations to the State Board of Education.

At this point, on August 15, 1958, Dr. Jones submitted his resignation as president of the University in order to accept the presidency of the National Conference of Christians and Jews. The abruptness of this announcement prompted widespread speculation in the press of the state as to the circumstances that lay behind his decision, and it was reported that friction between the president and the Board of Governors as well as between the University administration and the State Board of Education was involved. The president gave confirmation to these rumors when, in a final address to the student body in September 1958, he intimated strongly that other criteria than economy and efficiency must be considered in evaluating University policies and that the distinctive functions of a university of high quality were inadequately understood by those who exercised responsibility for public higher education in New Jersey. "Don't settle for mediocrity," he urged, "and for Heaven's sake don't plan for it." His administration had been a productive one, marked by notable progress in physical development, by the expansion of graduate and professional programs, and by the reorganization of the governing structure of the University. Contending against conditions that were often discouraging, he brought the University to the threshold of what was to be its most brilliant period of development.

The University community—faculty, students, and alumni—was virtually unanimous in urging the selection of Dr. Mason W. Gross to succeed Dr. Jones, and on February 27, 1959, he was elected to the presidency by both the Board of Governors and the Board of Trustees. During his long period of service as provost, he had acquired a close familiarity with every phase of the operations of the University, he was well known and held in high regard throughout the state, and he had consistently manifested the strength of his dedication to Rutgers. A philosopher by training, he had been educated at Cambridge University and at Harvard, had taught briefly at Columbia, and had served with the Air Force during World War II before coming to Rutgers in 1946. His eminent qualifications for educational leadership were to be abundantly demonstrated in the eventful years that lay immediately ahead.

While the transition from the administration of Dr. Jones to that of Dr. Gross was being effected, intensive preparations were being made for the anticipated program of capital expansion. Work was begun on a comprehensive master plan to relate the projected structures to existing facilities, and a supervising architect was retained to oversee the development of building plans. In order that space requirements might be calculated with the utmost precision, the firm of Robert Heller and Associates was engaged early in 1959 to make detailed studies and to prepare recommendations that were extremely influential in shaping the ultimate character of the building program. Preliminary negotiations were also conducted with officials at Newark and Camden looking toward the acquisition of large tracts of land suitable for redevelopment as centers for the University's operations in those cities.

Equally intensive efforts were under way to insure legislative approval of the bond issue proposal and public support for the referendum. Working in close cooperation, the State Department of Education, the New Jersey Education Association, the State University, and the other publicly supported institutions of higher education fostered the organization of "The Citizen's Committee for College Opportunities in New Jersey," which launched a determined and well financed campaign in July 1958. Although Governor Meyner continued to state his preference for a "pay-as-you-go" program of financing, the legislature in February 1959 unanimously enacted a measure providing for a referendum on a bond issue exactly in accordance with the recommendations of the State Department of Education. In the months that followed, an extremely effective publicity campaign, in which the alumni of the institutions concerned were especially active, made the people of New Jersey aware of the urgent need for doubling the facilities for higher education in public institutions. On election day, the voters responded by giving their overwhelming approval to the referendum; Hudson County alone registered its dissent.

Few events in the annals of Rutgers were as climactic in their significance as the approval of the bond issue. Not only did it promise the achievement of long-deferred hopes for adequate physical facilities, it meant also that Rutgers had at last gained public acceptance as New Jersey's State University—an acceptance that it fully reciprocated. It is at this juncture that the first volume of the history of the University should properly conclude, for what lay ahead, even in the ensuing few years, represented such a transformation of the institution in every dimension as to constitute the inauguration of an entirely new era. What follows, then, is partly postscript, partly prelude.

The immediate and tangible result of the passage of the bond issue was the initiation of a vast construction program. Of the total amount of $66,800,000 approved by the voters, $29,850,000 was allocated to the State University. Together with funds already in hand from the 1958 appropriation and others obtained from Federal loans and grants as well as generous gifts, there was $47,360,000 available at once for capital expenditures. In the course of the next few years every campus of the University was transformed.

Among the major structures erected on the old campus of the men's colleges were a general classroom building, Scott Hall, a building for the Graduate School of Education, a new dormitory complex with accommodations for 1,000 students, an immense new Commons, a graduate dormitory, and a substantial addition to the Gymnasium. Across the river, at University Heights, the long-projected science center took form with the erection of the Biology Building, the Physics Building, and—largest of all—the sprawling facilities for the College of Engineering. At Douglass College additional dormitories, a strikingly designed dining hall, and a new gymnasium as well as a handsome library and a classroom and office building constituted the first notable additions, with the exception of the Student Center, in thirty years. The Newark Colleges looked forward to the development of an entirely new campus occupying several blocks between Washington Street and High Street, in close proximity to the Newark College of Engineering, where the Law Center, two classroom and laboratory buildings, and a library offered a welcome contrast to the makeshift quarters which had been utilized for so many years. At Camden, large sites were cleared for the erection of a science building and a student center, giving an entirely new aspect to the College of South Jersey.

By 1964, when substantially all of the new facilities were in use, the

University had attained the goal envisioned in 1957 of doubling full-time undergraduate enrollments, which rose from 6,407 to 11,756. There was a comparable increase in the number of students enrolled in University College from 4,348 to 7,181. Looking ahead to 1970, by which time it was anticipated that the 1957 figures would be trebled, the voters of the state in 1964 gave their approval to a second major bond issue for higher education totalling $40,100,000, of which $19,069,000 was allotted to the State University. This amount, supplemented again by Federal grants, would provide additional classroom buildings at Newark and Camden, new quarters for the Graduate School of Library Service, and a library of science and medicine. Moreover, on land obtained from the Federal Government at Camp Kilmer there would be erected the first of three projected undergraduate coeducational colleges.

Impressive as the construction program was, it did not keep pace with the needs. The University authorities had advised the State Department of Education in 1957 that the program that was approved for Rutgers was a minimal one, even with respect to projected undergraduate demands, and that inadequate consideration had been given to the expansion of graduate schools and research. Consequently, enrollments had virtually to be frozen after 1964 because facilities were overtaxed, with the result that thousands of qualified candidates had to be turned away.

Although public attention was centered largely on providing expanded educational opportunities for undergraduates, the University was no less aware of its responsibilities in the areas of graduate and professional education and research. More than half of the college graduates in this period would pursue advanced studies; at the College of Arts and Sciences in New Brunswick the proportion was closer to 70 per cent. Between 1957 and 1964 the number of graduate and professional students rose from 2,736 to 5,586, a rate of increase even greater than that at the undergraduate level. Stimulating this remarkable growth were Federal grants for fellowships and facilities, the increasing employment of graduate students as teaching and research assistants, and the augmentation of the faculty. Within the Graduate School the most notable development was the phenomenal build-up of programs in the nonscientific fields, notably in history, English, economics, political science, and modern languages. In 1961 the establishment of a two-year Rutgers Medical School, which might ultimately be extended to offer a full four-year course, marked another major advance, and preparations were made to admit the first class in 1966.

Most spectacular of all was the burgeoning of research. Total expenditures for sponsored research—chiefly from Federal sources—soared from approximately $3,000,000 in 1955 to more than four times that amount a decade later. Every area of the University felt the impact of the new funds, but the sciences were especially affected. Representative of the greatly enhanced facilities for experimental investigation was the 15,000,000 electron volt tandem accelerator that was acquired for physics research with a combination of state funds, Federal grants, contributions from industry, and the proceeds of a substantial bequest. The trend toward the establishment of centers and institutes continued; among the most notable additions were the Institute for Animal Behavior in Newark, the Interdisciplinary Research Center, and the Center for Alcohol Studies. Quite obviously, an entirely new balance was being effected among the three broad areas of undergraduate teaching, graduate training, and research.

The quantitative dimensions of the changes that transformed the University after 1959 are readily describable; less susceptible to accurate appraisal are the subtle effects of the new environment on students and faculty. The post-Sputnik generations of undergraduates—products of reformed high school curricula that featured "enriched" courses, intensified training in science and mathematics, and a sobering emphasis on scholastic achievement—had been made aware of the necessity for getting good grades and high scores on batteries of examinations administered by the Educational Testing Service if they hoped to gain admittance to the college of their choice. Consequently, they arrived at Rutgers better prepared than ever before, and by all objective criteria they were also brighter than ever. Once in college, the majority who were looking ahead to the next hurdle, that of securing admittance to a graduate or professional school, continued their keen academic competition by applying themselves with remarkable seriousness to their courses of study. No longer a "generation without a cause," many of them gave their adherence to the civil rights movement, to the Goldwater cause, or to such "new left" groups as Students for a Democratic Society. Others gloried in the role of "beatniks," grew beards, and strove to emphasize their generalized revolt against traditional middle class values. Restlessly aware that they were getting less individual attention from the faculty and that their lives were being directed increasingly by I.B.M. machines, they sought new definitions of their group identity, protesting established social regulations, denouncing the doctrine of *loco parentis,* and claiming the privileges of self-reliant adults.

For the faculty, too, the new period was a time of reorientation. As enrollments swelled throughout the nation, the academic market place reflected the relative scarcity of trained personnel, with the result that between 1951 and 1961 faculty salaries at Rutgers doubled but then continued upward at a pace that was hardly rapid enough to overtake competing institutions. Together with other factors, the increasing prevalence of academic "raiding" encouraged a feeling of mobility within the faculty, with erosive effects on institutional loyalties. In fields where lavish financial support was obtainable from Federal agencies or foundations, those with particular promotional talents could distinguish themselves in the exciting and prestigious game of "grantsmanship." The new conditions fostered a reduction in the number of hours spent in classroom teaching to compensate for the additional time devoted to research or to the supervision of graduate students. Whether because the institution had become so bewilderingly complex or because the academicians had become discipline oriented, or whatever the cause, the old insistence that the faculty should be accorded a larger responsibility for shaping University policies seemed to subside. Concern with basic questions of educational philosophy and curricular reform was scarcely commensurate with the challenges posed by the drastically altered environment within the University; the roving intellect that could break through the farthest frontiers of knowledge with cyclotron, microscope, and computer rarely focused the same intense curiosity and disciplined thought on the problems of higher education. As had been the case for more than a century, external influences—among the most important of which were Federal largesse and overwhelming numbers of students—reshaped the academic pattern.

Those responsible for directing the destiny of the University in this period of explosive development, the Board of Governors, the president, and the principal administrative officers, wrestled with increasingly complex organizational problems, with expansion plans that only a decade before would have seemed visionary, and with manifold relationships to governmental agencies. In 1945 there had been only seven major educational units within the University; now there were twenty-seven colleges, schools, and autonomous centers or institutes. Between 1956 and 1966, more than $75,000,000 was committed to physical expansion, and plans had been formulated that contemplated the expenditure of several times that amount within the next decade. Whereas the state government had been looked to as the chief source of public funds, there was now increasing dependence on Federal grants and loans for ever widening purposes and from several different agencies. The whole framework of higher education in New Jersey was changing, with the rapid development of relatively new private institutions, the beginnings of a system of county colleges, the projected transformation of the teacher's colleges into state colleges, and movements towards a new organizational structure for public higher education. Meanwhile, there continued to be signs that New Jersey would move upward from its accustomed position near the bottom of the list of states in support for higher education; such, at least, were the hopes engendered by the enactment of a sales tax in 1966.

The prospect, if perplexing, was exciting and promising. With its position as the State University firmly established, with demands for its varied educational and research programs growing ever more pressing, and with a strong internal drive towards excellence, Rutgers, The State University, entered upon its third century with the assurance derived from a long and worthy record of accomplishment. Released from the conflict of a duality of identity that had often blurred its role in the past, it could now place the best of its traditions at the service of the people of New Jersey and the larger constituencies that extended beyond the borders of the state.

Index